D0821499

The Tyndale Old Testament Commentaries

General Editor:
PROFESSOR D. J. WISEMAN, O.B.E., M.A., D.Lit., F.B.A., F.S.A.

2 CHRONICLES

This work is dedicated to those churches where I have
learnt to love the Lord and his word:

Holy Trinity Parish Church, Wallington
Heath Evangelical Church, Cardiff
Stoneleigh Baptist Church, Epsom

2 CHRONICLES

A COMMENTARY

by

MARTIN J. SELMAN, B.A., M.A., Ph.D.
Director of Postgraduate Studies, Spurgeon's College, London

INTER-VARSITY PRESS
Leicester, England
Downers Grove, Illinois, U.S.A.

InterVarsity Press
P.O. Box 1400, Downers Grove, Illinois 60515, U.S.A.
38 De Montfort Street, Leicester LE1 7GP, England

©*Martin J. Selman 1994*

InterVarsity Press®, USA, is the book-publishing division of InterVarsity Christian Fellowship®, a student movement active on campus at hundreds of universities, colleges and schools of nursing in the United States of America, and a member movement of the International Fellowship of Evangelical Students. For information about local and regional activities, write Public Relations Dept., InterVarsity Christian Fellowship, 6400 Schroeder Rd., P.O. Box 7895, Madison, WI 53707-7895.

Inter-Varsity Press, England, is the publishing division of the Universities and Colleges Christian Fellowship (formerly the Inter-Varsity Fellowship), a student movement linking Christian Unions in universities and colleges throughout the United Kingdom and the Republic of Ireland, and a member movement of the International Fellowship of Evangelical Students. For information about local and national activities in Great Britain write to UCCF, 38 De Montfort Street, Leicester LE1 7GP.

UK ISBN 0-85111-848-8 (paperback)
USA ISBN 0-8308-1432-9 (hardback)
USA ISBN 0-87784-246-9 (paperback)
USA ISBN 0-87784-880-7 (set of Tyndale Old Testament Commentaries, hardback)
USA ISBN 0-87784-280-9 (set of Tyndale Old Testament Commentaries, paperback)

Text set in Great Britain
Printed in the United States of America ♾

Library of Congress Cataloging-in-Publication Data

Selman, Martin J., 1947-
    2 Chronicles: a commentary/by Martin J. Selman.
        p.   cm.
    Includes bibliographical references.
    ISBN 0-8308-1432-9 (U.S.).—ISBN 0-87784-246-9 (U.S.: pbk.)
    1. Bible.   O.T.   Chronicles, 2nd—Commentaries.   I. Title.
II. Title: Second Chronicles.
BS1345.3.S46   1994
222'.6407—dc20   *94-3579*
                                                           CIP

British Library Cataloguing in Publication Data
A catalogue record for this book is available from the British Library.

15	14	13	12	11	10	9	8	7	6	5	4	3	2	1
06	05	04	03	02	01	00	99	98	97	96	95	94		

CONTENTS

Note: The introduction to 1 and 2 Chronicles is to be found in
the companion volume, 1 Chronicles, p. 19.

CHIEF ABBREVIATIONS

AASOR	*Annual of the American Schools of Oriental Research.*
AB	Anchor Bible.
AHwb	W. von Soden, *Akkadisches Handwörterbuch*, 3 vols. (Wiesbaden: Harrassowitz, 1965ff.).
Albright	W. F. Albright, 'The chronology of the divided monarchy of Israel', *BASOR* 100, 1945, pp. 16–22.
ANET	J. B. Pritchard (ed.), *Ancient Near Eastern Texts Relating to the Old Testament* (Princeton: Princeton University Press, 1950).
AOAT	*Alten Orient und Alten Testament.*
Aram.	Aramaic.
Ass.	Assyrian.
BA	Biblical Archaeologist.
Barthélemy, *CTAT*	D. Barthélemy, *Critique Textuelle de l'Ancien Testament*, vol. 1, *Orbis Biblicus et Orientalis* 50/1 (Göttingen: Vandenhoeck & Ruprecht, 1982).
BASOR	*Bulletin of the American Schools of Oriental Research.*
BBET	*Beiträge zur biblischen Exegese und Theologie.*
Begrich	J. Begrich, *Die Chronologie der Könige von Israel und Juda* (Tübingen: Mohr, 1929).
Bib.	*Biblica.*
BTB	*Biblical Theology Bulletin.*
BZAW	*Beiheft zur Zeitschrift für die altestamentliche Wissenschaft.*
CAD	A. L. Oppenheim, *et al.*, *Chicago Assyrian Dictionary* (Chicago: Oriental Institute, 1956ff.).

CBC	Cambridge Bible Commentary.
CBOTS	*Coniectanea Biblica Old Testament Series.*
CBQ	*Catholic Biblical Quarterly.*
Childs	B. S. Childs, *Isaiah and the Assyrian Crisis* (London: SCM Press, 1967).
ET	English translation.
Exp.T.	*Expository Times.*
FOTL	Forms of Old Testament Literature.
GK	E. Kautzsch and A. E. Cowley (eds.), *Genesius' Hebrew Grammar* (Oxford: Clarendon Press, 1910).
HAT	*Handbuch zum Alten Testament.*
HTR	*Harvard Theological Review.*
Hughes, *Secrets*	J. Hughes, *Secrets of the Times, JSOTS* 66 (Sheffield: JSOT Press, 1990).
IBD	*The Illustrated Bible Dictionary* (Leicester: IVP, 1980).
ICC	International Critical Commentary.
IDB	*Interpreter's Dictionary of the Bible* (Nashville: Abingdon, vols. I–IV, 1962; Supplement, 1976).
IEJ	*Israel Exploration Journal.*
Japhet, *Ideology*	S. Japhet, *The Ideology of the Book of Chronicles* (Frankfurt: P. Lang, 1989).
JBL	*Journal of Biblical Literature.*
JETS	*Journal of the Evangelical Theological Society.*
JQR	*Jewish Quarterly Review.*
Johnstone, 'Guilt'	W. Johnstone, 'Guilt and Atonement: the theme of 1 and 2 Chronicles', in J. D. Martin and P. R. Davies (eds.), *A Word in Season*, JSOTS 42 (Sheffield: JSOT Press, 1986), pp. 113–138.
JSNTS	*Journal for the Study of the Testament, Supplement Series.*
JSOT	*Journal for the Study of the Old Testament.*
JSOTS	*Journal for the Study of the Old Testament, Supplement Series.*
JTS	*Journal of Theological Studies.*
KB	L. Koehler and W. Baumgartner (eds.), *Hebräisches und Aramäisches Lexikon* (Leiden: Brill, [3]1967ff.).

Keil   C. F. Keil, *The Books of the Kings* (Edinburgh: T. & T. Clark, ²1883).

Kleinig, *Song*   J. Kleinig, *The LORD's Song: The Basis, Function and Significance of Choral Music in Chronicles*, JSOTS 156 (Sheffield: JSOT Press, 1993).

McKenzie, *Use*   S. L. McKenzie, *The Chronicler's Use of the Deuteronomic History*, Harvard Semitic Monographs 33 (Atlanta: Scholars Press, 1985).

Mason, *Preaching*   R. A. Mason, *Preaching the Tradition* (Cambridge: Cambridge University Press, 1990).

Mosis, *UTCG*   R. Mosis, *Untersuchungen zur Theologie des chronistischen Geschichtswerkes*, Freiburger Theologische Studien 29 (Freiberg: Herder, 1973).

NCB   New Century Bible.

NIDNTT   C. Brown (ed.), *New International Dictionary of New Testament Theology*, 3 vols. (Exeter: Paternoster Press, 1975–78).

OTL   Old Testament Library.

OTS   *Oudtestamentische Studiën.*

PEQ   *Palestine Exploration Quarterly.*

Polzin, *Typology*   R. Polzin, *Late Biblical Hebrew: Toward an Historical Typology of Biblical Hebrew Prose*, HSM 12 (Missoula: Scholars Press, 1976).

SBB   *Stuttgarter Biblische Beiträge.*

SBLMS   *Society of Biblical Literature Monograph Series.*

SVT   *Supplements to Vetus Testamentum.*

TB   *Tyndale Bulletin.*

TC   R. Le Déaut and J. Robert, *Targum des Chroniques*, 2 vols. (Rome: Biblical Institute Press, 1971).

TDOT   G. Botterweck and H. Ringgren (eds.), *Theological Dictionary of the Old Testament* (Grand Rapids: Eerdmans, 1974ff.).

Thiele   E. R. Thiele, *The Mysterious Numbers of the Hebrew Kings* (Grand Rapids: Eerdmans, ³1983).

Throntveit, *Kings*	M. A. Throntveit, *When Kings Speak*, Society of Biblical Literature Dissertation Series 93 (Atlanta: Scholars Press, 1987).
TOTC	Tyndale Old Testament Commentary.
VE	*Vox Evangelica.*
von Rad, *GCW*	G. von Rad, *Das Geschichtsbild des chronistischen Werkes* (Stuttgart: Kohlhammer, 1930).
VT	*Vetus Testamentum.*
WBC	Word Biblical Commentary.
Willi, *CA*	T. Willi, *Die Chronik als Auslegung* (Göttingen: Vandenhoeck & Ruprecht, 1972).
Williamson, *IBC*	H. G. M. Williamson, *Israel in the Books of Chronicles* (Cambridge: Cambridge University Press, 1977).
WTJ	*Westminster Theological Journal.*
ZAW	*Zeitschrift für die alttestamentliche Wissenschaft.*

TEXTS AND VERSIONS

Ar	Old Arabic version of the Old Testament.
AV	Authorized (King James) Version, 1611.
EVV	English versions.
GNB	Good News Bible (Today's English Version), 1976.
JB	Jerusalem Bible, 1966.
LXX	Septuagint (pre-Christian Greek version of the Old Testament).
LXX (A)	Septuagint, Codex Alexandrinus.
LXX (L)	Septuagint, Lucian recension.
MT	Massoretic Text (the standard Hebrew text of the Old Testament).
NEB	New English Bible, 1970.
NIV	New International Version, 1984.
NRSV	New Revised Standard Version, 1989.
OL	Old Latin translation of the Bible.
P	Peshitta (the Syriac translation of the Bible).

REB	Revised English Bible, 1989.
RSV	Revised Standard Version, 1952.
RV	Revised Version, 1881.
Tg.	Targum.
VSS	Versions, *i.e.* the ancient translations of the Bible, especially Greek (LXX), Aramaic (Tg.), Syriac (P), Latin (Vulg.).
Vulg.	Vulgate (the main, late fourth-century, Latin translation of the Bible by Jerome).

COMMENTARIES

Commentaries on 1 and 2 Chronicles (introductory commentaries are marked with an *)

Ackroyd	P. R. Ackroyd, *I & II Chronicles, Ezra, Nehemiah*, Torch Commentary (London, SCM Press, 1973).
Allen	L. C. Allen, *1, 2 Chronicles*, The Communicator's Commentary (Waco: Word Books, 1987).*
Bertheau	E. Bertheau, *Commentary on the Books of Chronicles* (Edinburgh, T. & T. Clark, 1857).
Braun	R. L. Braun, *1 Chronicles*, WBC 14 (Waco: Word Books, 1986).
Coggins	R. J. Coggins, *The First and Second Books of Chronicles*, CBC (Cambridge: Cambridge University Press, 1976).*
Curtis and Madsen	E. L. Curtis and A. L. Madsen, *The Books of Chronicles*, ICC (Edinburgh: T. & T. Clark, 1910).
de Vries	S. J. de Vries, *1 and 2 Chronicles*, FOTL 11 (Grand Rapids: Eerdmans, 1989).
Dillard	R. B. Dillard, *2 Chronicles*, WBC 15 (Waco: Word Books, 1987).
Japhet	S. Japhet, *I & II Chronicles*, Old Testament Library (London: SCM Press, 1993).
McConville	J. G. McConville, *Chronicles*, Daily Study Bible (Edinburgh: St Andrew Press, 1984).*
Michaeli	F. Michaeli, *Les livres des Chroniques* (Neuchâtel: Delachaux & Niestlé, 1967).

Myers, *1 Chronicles*	J. M. Myers, *I Chronicles*, **AB** 12 (New York: Doubleday, 1965).
Myers, *2 Chronicles*	J. M. Myers, *II Chronicles*, **AB** 13 (New York: Doubleday, 1965).
Rudolph	W. Rudolph, *Die Chronikbücher*, *HAT* (Tübingen: Mohr, 1955).
Wilcock	M. Wilcock, *The Message of Chronicles*, The Bible Speaks Today (Leicester: IVP, 1987).*
Williamson	H. G. M. Williamson, *1 and 2 Chronicles*, NCB (London: Marshall, Morgan & Scott, 1982).

Commentaries on 1 and 2 Samuel and 1 and 2 Kings

Anderson	A. A. Anderson, *2 Samuel*, WBC (Waco: Word Books, 1989).
Cogan and Tadmor	M. Cogan and H. Tadmor, *II Kings*, **AB** (New York: Doubleday, 1988).
Gray	J. Gray, *I and II Kings*, OTL (London: SCM Press, ³1977).
Hertzberg	H. W. Hertzberg, *I and II Samuel*, OTL (London: SCM Press, 1964).
Hobbs	T. R. Hobbs, *2 Kings*, WBC (Waco: Word Books, 1985).
Jones	G. H. Jones, *I and II Kings*, NCB (London: Marshall, Morgan & Scott, 1984).
McCarter	P. K. McCarter, *II Samuel*, AB (New York: Doubleday, 1984).
Nelson	R. D. Nelson, *First and Second Kings*, Interpretation (Atlanta: John Knox Press, 1987).
Šanda	A. Šanda, *Die Bücher die Könige* (Munster: Aschendorffscher Verlag, 1911–12).
Wiseman	D. J. Wiseman, *1 and 2 Kings*, TOTC (Leicester: IVP, 1993).

ANALYSIS

ANALYSIS

F. Solomon prepares for the temple (2 Ch. 1:1 – 2:18)
    i. Solomon's splendour (1:1–17)
      a. Solomon's kingdom established (1:1)
      b. Solomon's worship (1:2–6)
      c. Solomon's wisdom (1:7–13)
      d. Solomon's wealth (1:14–17)
    ii. Solomon's preparations (2:1–18)
      a. Building instructions (2:1)
      b. Census of labourers (2:2)
      c. Solomon's letter to Hiram (2:3–10)
      d. Hiram's letter to Solomon (2:11–16)
      e. Census of non-Israelite labourers (2:17–18)
G. Solomon builds the temple (3:1 – 5:1)
    i. Beginning to build the temple (3:1–2)
    ii. The ground-plan and porch (3:3–4a)
    iii. The golden temple (3:4b–13)
    iv. The veil (3:14)
    v. The pillars (3:15–17)
    vi. The Temple equipment (4:1–22)
      a. The bronze altar (4:1)
      b. The Sea (4:2–6, 10)
      c. The ten gold lampstands and ten tables (4:7–8)
      d. The courtyards (4:9)
      e. Bronze work (4:11b–18)
      f. Gold objects (4:19–22)
    vii. Completion of the temple (5:1)
H. Solomon dedicates the temple (5:2 – 7:22)
    i. The ark and the cloud (5:2–14)
      a. Solomon assembles all Israel (5:2–3)
      b. The ark's final journey (5:4–6)
      c. The ark's final resting-place (5:7–10)
      d. God's glory and Israel's praise (5:11–14)
    ii. Solomon's praise and prayer (6:1–42)
      a. Solomon responds to God's glory (6:1–2)
      b. Solomon's testimony to God's promise (6:3–11)
      c. Solomon's dedicatory prayer (6:12–42)
    iii. God's answer to prayer (7:1–22)
      a. God's fire and glory (7:1–3)
      b. Israel's sacrifice and praise (7:4–10)
      c. God's promises (7:11–22)
I. Solomon completes the temple (8:1–16)
    i. Solomon's other building work (8:1–6)

COMMENTARY

F. Solomon prepares for the temple (2 Ch. 1:1 – 2:18)

Despite the break between 1 Chronicles and 2 Chronicles, the account of Solomon basically continues the story of David. The reigns of the two kings are really a single unit, as Solomon's involvement in David's temple preparations has illustrated (1 Ch. 22, 28–29). The sense of partnership continues here, particularly in several passages unique to Chronicles where David is linked with Solomon (*e.g.* 2:3, 7; 3:1; 6:42; 7:10; 8:14). Another sign of this co-operation is the way the Davidic covenant is developed (1 Ch. 17), with Solomon fulfilling the first stage of God's promises by ascending David's throne and building the temple (especially 2 Ch. 6:4–11; *cf.* also 1:8–9; 5:4–11; 6:14–17; 7:17–18). The covenant theme in fact underlies Chronicles' entire presentation of Solomon, which is much more concerned with Solomon's significance in the purposes of God than listing the major events of Solomon's life. It is for this reason that Chronicles has left out many important features found in the Kings account, such as Solomon's personal details. Included in the omissions are not only the negative aspects like his polygamy, his idolatry, and his military disasters (1 Ki. 11:1–40), but also his accession (1 Ki. 1–2), his famous wise ruling (1 Ki. 3:16–28), his administration and wisdom (1 Ki. 4:1–34), and even some of the details of the building of the temple (*e.g.* 1 Ki. 6:4–19; 7:27–37) and the royal palace (7:1–12).

By removing those elements deemed unnecessary to his purpose, Chronicles has produced a simplified but distinctive portrayal of this king. This is best demonstrated by setting out the total structure of Solomon's reign, which shows a basic chiastic formation:

1:1–17 Solomon's wisdom, wealth, and fame
  2:1–18 Solomon prepares for the temple

3:1 – 5:1 Construction of the temple
5:2 – 7:22 Dedication of the temple
8:1–16 Solomon completes the temple and other
building work
8:17 – 9:28 Solomon's wisdom, wealth, and fame

This layout immediately reveals a number of inner connections. Clearly the actual building and dedication of the temple form the centre of the account (chapters 3–7). However, an obvious link between chapters 1–2 and 8–9 is also evident, and further examination confirms that the temple theme extends even to these opening and closing chapters. This is most easily seen in Solomon's correspondence with Hiram (ch. 2) which is directly concerned with temple preparations, but it emerges too from the parallel passage (8:1–16) where the nationwide building work is understood as the extension and completion of the temple project. Additional confirmation comes from a series of editorial markers, several of which are wholly or in part the Chronicler's own contribution (*cf.* 2:1; 3:1; 5:1; 7:11; 8:16). Even the outer parts of the structure support the same theme. The description of Solomon worshipping at the Tent of Meeting (ch. 1) clearly anticipates his worship at the temple (*cf. e.g.* 1:6 with 5:6; 7:5–7), while the temple provides the chief evidence of Solomon's divinely given wisdom (1:12; *cf.* 9:4). In fact, Solomon's wealth and wisdom (1:1–17; 8:17 – 9:28) are best understood as a theme parallel to that of the temple, since they are all visible symptoms of the effectiveness of God's kingdom in human affairs (*cf.* 1 Ch. 28:5–6; 29:11; 2 Ch. 9:8). In comparison with Kings, therefore, where the temple is merely the central section in a varied narrative about Solomon (1 Ki. 5:1 – 9:9, *i.e.* four and a half chapters out of eleven), the Chronicler has given it such prominence that it completely dominates his account.

In addition to the basic chiastic structure, the Chronicler has used several other literary patterns. The central chapters have a consecutive arrangement, dealing with the construction of the building (ch. 3), its furnishing and equipping (ch. 4), the installation of the ark (ch. 5), the dedicatory prayer (ch. 6), and God's response (ch. 7). The effect is to make chapter 7 the climax of the entire temple account, and indeed of the entire work of the Chronicler. Comparison with Kings also reveals that Chronicles is more interested in the temple's

significance than in its architecture. Another literary scheme is
the request–response pattern, of which there are three major
examples. Explicit answers to Solomon's requests are given
not only by God (*cf.* 1:8–10 and 1:11–12; 6:14–42 and
7:12–21) but even by a pagan king (2:3–10, 11–16). The first
two examples show clearly that prayer works! A further pattern is that of fulfilment, which has both literary and theological features. Again, three different examples must suffice.
Firstly, God's promises of wisdom, wealth, and fame are
fulfilled in Solomon's own life (8:17 – 9:31). Secondly, Solomon testifies that God's covenant promises to David have
been fulfilled in specific ways (6:4–11). Finally, Solomon's
temple is repeatedly shown to fulfil the principles underlying
Moses' Tent or tabernacle. For instance, Solomon and the
temple architect Huram-abi follow in the tradition of Bezalel
and Oholiab who were responsible for the Tent's construction, Solomon like Moses carries out the divinely revealed
blueprint, and the shekinah glory which dominated the
opening ceremonies for the Tent has the same effect at the
temple dedication. All these examples provide ample evidence
of the Chronicler's creativity and flexibility as an author.[1]

Alongside the major themes of covenant and temple, a
number of other emphases are worth noting. Far from
exhibiting a ritualistic approach to religion, there is a strong
emphasis on God's sovereignty and presence. He is unique in
heaven as well as on earth, and exercises his freedom to
invade the temple and disrupt its services at his own con-
venience (*e.g.* 2:5–6; 5:13–14; 6:14, 18: 7:1–3). He is also a
God who reveals his will directly in a way that surpasses his
people's expectations (1:7–12; 7:12–21). Worship is another
major interest, where prayer and sacrifice form a regular
partnership. Prayers occur at key points, such as 1:8–10;
6:14–42, and these serve as encouragements to everyone,
whether Israelite or not (*cf.* 6:32–33), to seek God in prayer
for themselves (*cf.* 1:5; 7:14). Sacrifice frequently takes place
alongside prayer. God accepts the temple as a 'house of sacrifice' (*cf.* 7:12), and the regular pattern of sacrificial worship
(2:4; 8:12–15) is just as important as the special dedicatory

[1] For a different understanding of the chiastic nature of the Chronicler's
Solomon, *cf.* Dillard, pp. 1–7. It should be noted in particular that Dillard's
scheme has no room for 3:1 – 5:1, and fails to draw attention to the variety of
Chronicles' literary patterns.

offerings (5:6; 7:1, 5, 7). Worship, however, is acceptable only if it is offered in a wholehearted spirit (6:7–8, 14, 30; 7:10), providing further evidence of the Chronicler's concern for the heart as well as the form of worship. Despite the preoccupation with Solomon, Chronicles does not lose sight of Israel's role. In some passages (1:2, 3, 5; 9:8), Israel as a whole is given greater prominence than in Kings, as are the Levites in 5:11–13. Their contribution is also underlined in passages such as 5:2–3, 6; 6:3, 12–13, 22–39; 7:8–10. Solomon's wisdom, wealth, and fame (1:1–17; 8:17 – 9:31) as a sign of God's blessing is also shared by the people as reflected glory.

Finally, the Davidic-Solomonic era serves as a standard for Israel's future life. Covenant obedience, which includes the Mosaic as well as the Davidic versions, provides the measure against which all must be compared (*e.g.* 6:16–17; 7:17–22). However, Chronicles' real emphasis is to underline that God's forgiveness is constantly and unexpectedly available to anyone who comes to him in humble repentance. The prime motive for prayer in the temple is that there is always hope for sinners, as God affirms in his remarkable promises in 7:12–16. Such is the background against which the rest of Israel's history will unfold (chs. 10–36).

i. Solomon's splendour (1:1–17)

'God . . . said to him, "Ask for whatever you want me to give you"' (1:7).

1:2–13a – *cf.* 1 Kings 3:4–15
1:13b – *cf.* 1 Kings 4:1
1:14–17 – *cf.* 1 Kings 10:26–29

This chapter presents a rather different introduction to the reign of Solomon than do the books of Kings. Instead of the prolonged account of Solomon's accession (1 Ki. 1–2), which may have a possible allusion in verse 1, the reader is brought immediately to an account of Solomon's wisdom and wealth. It is almost a commentary on 1 Kings 10:23. Apart from a brief introduction underlining how the blessings of David's reign continued under Solomon, the main part of the chapter falls into two parts, both of which are based on separate passages from Kings: (a) Solomon's gift of wisdom (vv. 2–13); (b) Solomon's wealth (vv. 14–17).

Two threads connect these apparently independent subjects. The first is that both wisdom and wealth are gifts of God.

This is made abundantly clear by God's answer to Solomon's prayer (vv. 11–12), for which David's prayer (*cf.* 1 Ch. 29:10–16) was more than adequate preparation. The second is the temple, indicated by the fact that this chapter is followed immediately by the preparations for building the temple. The temple offers the primary example of Solomon's exercise of wisdom and the most significant use of his wealth.

All this arises from the picture of Solomon at worship. As one who offers sacrifices and especially as a man of prayer, Solomon shows himself to be suitably qualified to build a temple which will be a 'temple for sacrifices' (2 Ch. 7:12; *cf.* 2:6) and a 'house of prayer' (Is. 56:7; *cf.* 2 Ch. 6:40; 7:14, *etc.*). In fact, the portrayal of the worshipping Solomon is the main focus of the chapter, since his wisdom and wealth result from his praying. Chronicles again shows that prayer is a vital ingredient of successful kingship as well as of acceptable worship (*cf.* 1 Ch. 16:8–36; 17:16–27; 29:10–19; 2 Ch. 6:4–42; 20:6–12).

In all this, Solomon provides an excellent model for Christians. The task of building and developing God's church is not something that can be undertaken by human resources alone. Indeed, God has specifically given the gifts of his Holy Spirit for the building up of his church (1 Cor. 12:7; 14:12), and himself lives among his people for the same purpose (Eph. 2:22). The gift of wisdom is paramount in this undertaking. It is both a primary requirement of leadership, as Solomon demonstrates (vv. 10–11; *cf.* Paul's description of himself as a 'wise master builder', 1 Cor. 3:10, AV), and is available to all who ask for it in faith (Jas. 1:5–7).

Material wealth is not, of course, promised to the New Testament church in the same way as wisdom. This chapter demonstrates quite clearly, however, that from time to time it can be part of God's gifts, though the Old Testament as well as the New Testament would also add that riches are fundamentally 'uncertain' (*cf.* 1 Tim. 6:17; Lk. 12:13–21; Ps. 49). Although it is doubtful whether any of the New Testament churches could be described as rich in worldly terms, they did have a number of wealthy members (*e.g.* Mt. 27:57; Rom. 16:23). Even Paul had learned at times to be 'in plenty' (Phil. 4:10–13). But they would find greater value in aiming at contentment, and Paul was also confident that whatever the church's needs were, they would be met through God's 'glorious' riches in Christ Jesus' (Phil. 4:19).

a. Solomon's kingdom established (1:1). Every phrase in this verse illustrates that David's blessings continued under Solomon, as indicated by the addition of *son of David* to the original text (1 Ki. 2:46b). David also had been 'strengthened' (*cf.* REB, NEB) at the beginning of his reign (*cf.* 1 Ch. 11:10), *God was with him*, had made him great (1 Ch. 11:9), and *made him exceedingly great* (also 1 Ch. 29:25). This continuity is not just the result of instituting a dynasty, but of God keeping his promises about establishing David's house (*cf.* vv. 8–9; 2 Ch. 6:3, 10; 1 Ch. 17:23–27). David's prayers that God would be 'with you' (1 Ch. 22:11, 16, 18; 28:20) have also been instrumental in bringing this situation about. 'Strengthened his hold' (REB, NEB; *cf. established himself*, NIV, NRSV, RSV) occurs several times in the introduction to a king's reign (1 Ch. 11:10; 2 Ch. 12:1; 15:8; 17:1; 21:4; 25:3). Where details are supplied in other passages, some kind of conflict is always involved, almost certainly indicating that the phrase summarizes Solomon's difficulties in making his throne secure (*cf.* 1 Ki. 1–2).

b. Solomon's worship (1:2–6). The gathering at *Gibeon* is described quite differently from the record in 1 Kings 3:4ff. Whereas the earlier version speaks only of Solomon's personal relationship with God, here *all Israel* (*cf.* 1 Ch. 29:23, 24, 25) or *the whole assembly* (*cf.* v. 5) is involved with him. This is typical of the Chronicler, who constantly emphasizes the people's unity under their leader (*cf.* 1 Ch. 13:1–6; 15:25–29). The event has become a public enterprise, as if to encourage ordinary people of future generations that they too would receive a response from God when they sought him through his temple (*cf.* 2 Ch. 6:21–40; 7:13–16). Most of the officials listed in verse 2 also occur at 1 Chronicles 28:1, stressing continuity with David, and, though mention of *the judges* is slightly unexpected, they too had a continuing role in Israel (*cf.* 1 Ch. 26:29; 2 Ch. 19:8–11). 'Gave an order' (v. 2, GNB) is preferable to the usual but misleadingly mild *spoke to* (NIV, etc.).[1]

The incident has been deliberately modelled on Chronicles' account of David's plans to restore the ark to Jerusalem (1 Ch. 13:1–6). In addition to the parallel of *all Israel* and *the whole assembly* (vv. 2, 3, 5; *cf.* 1 Ch. 13:2, 4, 5, 6), the two passages are

---

[1] For this use of *wayyŏ'mer*, *cf.* 1 Ch. 14:12.

linked by references to the officials (v. 2, *cf.* 1 Ch. 13:1), the mention of the *ark* (v. 4), and especially the verb 'sought' (v. 5, RSV; *enquired of*, NIV; *cf.* 1 Ch. 13:3). As with verse 1, the element of continuity from David to Solomon is underlined, with Israel worshipping God by means of the Tent (v. 3) and the bronze altar (v. 5) in the same way as David worshipped before the ark.

Comparison with the parallel account in 1 Kings 3, by contrast, reveals several significant changes. Kings' distinctly apologetic approach to the *high place at Gibeon* (1 Ki. 3:2–3; 2 Ch. 1:3, 13; *cf.* also 1 Ch. 16:39–42; 21:29) is replaced by a strenuous effort to treat the Gibeonite sanctuary with the greatest possible respect. In Chronicles, it is the site of God's *Tent of Meeting* (*cf.* Dillard, 'tent for meeting God') and the *bronze altar* (v. 5), and is authenticated by *Moses* (v. 3) and *Bezalel* (v. 5), the chief architect of the Tent (*cf.* Ex. 31:2; 35:30; 36:1, 2; 37:1; 1 Ch. 2:20).[1] The changes may not be as drastic as they appear, however. The issue of the 'high places' was no longer as pressing in the Chronicler's day as it had been around the beginning of the exile when Kings was compiled, and Chronicles' much more extensive account of preparations for the temple made it very clear that Gibeon's days were numbered. David's experience had also indicated that the future lay with Jerusalem rather than Gibeon (1 Ch. 21:30 – 22:1). Further, the stress here on the separation of the Tent at Gibeon from the *ark* in its own *tent in Jerusalem* (v. 4; *cf.* 1 Ch. 16:1) was another clear mark of irregularity. Finally, despite Chronicles' obvious concern for the external purity of Israel's worship, such issues are still secondary to the reality of Solomon's actual meeting with God at Gibeon.

That experience is described in terms of the fact that Solomon 'sought' (v. 5, RSV; *enquired of*, NIV) God, both by sacrifice (v. 6) and prayer (vv. 7–12). Although it is not entirely clear whether he sought 'the LORD' (RSV, *cf.* NIV, GNB) or 'it', *i.e.* the altar (with LXX, Vulg.; so REB, NEB, NRSV, *cf.* JB; in favour of the former is that nowhere else in the Bible is an altar sought, and

---

[1] Continuity with the Mosaic era is not meant to be taken as far as implying that Solomon is a 'new Bezalel' (Dillard, p. 4). Rather, the link underlines the necessity of divine revelation and the spiritual gift of wisdom in designing God's house. If anything, Solomon is modelled on Moses as the divine mediator, and Bezalel's successor as architect is Huram-abi (2 Ch. 2:13–14).

Chronicles almost always has God as the object of this verb),[1] 'seeking God' is a standard by which Chronicles measures the faith of Israel's leaders (*cf.* 1 Ch. 10:14; 2 Ch. 22:9; 26:5). Its meaning here (it is not found in 1 Ki. 3) seems to be that at the beginning of his reign at least, Solomon worshipped and asked for God's guidance in obedience to his father's instructions (1 Ch. 22:19; 28:8–9). Despite 2 Chronicles 7:14, the word is not used of him again (though it is a key word for some of his successors, *e.g.* Jehoshaphat, 2 Ch. 17:4; 18:4, 6, 7; 19:3; 20:3; 22:9), and, according to 1 Kings 11, he became careless about religious matters in his latter years.[2]

c. Solomon's wisdom (1:7–13). Solomon's seeking leads to a remarkable conversation between himself and God. It took place *that night*, a typical time for revelations from God to be communicated (*cf.* 1 Ch. 17:3; 2 Ch. 7:12). There is no mention here that it came via a 'dream' (1 Ki. 3:5, 15), though this omission is as likely to be the result of Chronicles' abbreviation of the earlier account as for any more sinister reason (see Dillard, p. 12). The whole passage again underlines the importance of prayer for the exercise of leadership, notably, as here, in the political arena. Chronicles' account is an abbreviated version of 1 Kings 3:5–14, omitting material that can be found elsewhere in Chronicles in order to concentrate on the absolute necessity of wisdom to fulfil the purposes of God.

God initiates the conversation with an extraordinary invitation, 'Ask what you would like me to give you' (v, 7, JB). There is nothing quite like it anywhere in the Old Testament, though there are certain parallels in some of the royal psalms (Pss. 2:8; 20:4; 21:2, 4), and in Isaiah's provocation to Ahaz (Is. 7:11). Jesus, however, has not only confirmed God's invitation (*e.g.* Mt. 7:7–8; Lk. 11:9–10), but extended and clarified it. Every Christian is invited to 'ask whatever you wish, and it will be given you' (Jn. 15:7; *cf.* 14:13–14; 15:16; 16:23, 26), as long as the prayer is made by faith in Jesus' name (Jn. 15:23; 1 Jn.

[1] On the other hand, 'seeking the altar' is supported by LXX and Vulg., by the idea of 'seeking the ark' possibly found in 1 Ch. 13:3; 15:13, and by the use of various diverse direct objects for *dāraš* such as places (Dt. 12:5; Am. 5:5), God's words or commands (1 Ki. 22:5; 1 Ch. 28:8), or peace (Je. 29:7).

[2] *Cf.* R. Braun, 'Solomonic apologetic in Chronicles', *JBL* 92, 1973, pp. 503–516, especially pp. 505–506.

5:14–15). The problem for many Christians, then, is not whether they will receive anything when they ask, but whether they will ask at all (*cf.* Jas. 4:2; Is. 65:1). Solomon at least was willing to believe that God meant what he said. He was aware that although neither of his predecessors could claim the throne by dynastic succession as he could, in comparison with them he suffered from the apparently fatal disadvantage of having no obvious charismatic gift to qualify him for kingship (*cf.* 1 Sa. 9:1; 10:1–10, 19:24; 16:1–13; 18:5–8). He needed above all the people's recognition that God had given him the necessary gifts.

First, however, Solomon acknowledges that God made a covenant promise to David ('You have shown ['*āśîtā*] great [*gādôl*] and steadfast love', v. 8, NRSV; *cf.* 1 Ch. 17:19, NIV, 'You have done ['*āśîtā*] this great thing' [*hagg^edullâ*]) that was partly fulfilled in his own accession (*You . . . have made me king in his place*, v. 8; *cf.* 1 Ch. 29:23). At the same time, God has also kept his promises to the patriarchs that he would so multiply his people that they could not be counted ('a people as many as the dust of the earth', v. 9, RSV; *cf.* Gn. 13:16; 28:14; contrast David, 1 Ch. 21:1–30; 27:23).

Solomon asks God for two things, (a) that God would confirm his *promise* made to David (v. 9), and (b) that he might receive *wisdom and knowledge* (v. 10). The first request, which is just as important as the second, looks backwards to David's prayer (*cf.* Heb. *yē'āmēn*, 'be confirmed', in 1 Ch. 17:23, 24 and here) and forwards to the temple's completion (2 Ch. 6:17). God's promise will be fulfilled only when the second house of 1 Chronicles 17, *viz.* the temple, is completed.[1] The second request, for *wisdom and knowledge*, is briefer than in 1 Kings 3:9 (NRSV, RSV, 'an understanding mind . . . able to discern between good and evil'). The differences, however, are more superficial than substantial. The 'mind' (lit. 'heart') is the seat of the intellect, will, and conscience in Hebrew thought, while the Old Testament concept of wisdom is moral and spiritual as well as intellectual. 'Wisdom' and 'understanding' are frequently paralleled in the Old Testament (*e.g.* Pr. 2:2; 3:13, 19; 4:5), and, although the word for knowledge is mainly post-exilic, it is closely associated with wisdom as exemplified by Daniel and his friends (Dn. 1:4, 17). Israelite wisdom is also

---

[1] *Cf.* Mosis, *UTCG*, pp. 130–135.

practical, which is why Solomon asks that he might *lead* and *govern* his people by it (v. 10; *cf*. Pr. 8:15–16). The first expression, literally, 'to go out and go in before this people' (*cf*. RSV), is usually military in character (*cf*. 1 Ch. 11:2) but can be used of leadership generally (*cf*. Dt. 31:2), and the second, literally, 'to judge', is often used with the sense, 'to govern, rule', in the historical books, including Judges (= 'Leaders, Rulers').

11–12. God's reply is one of the clearest examples of answered prayer in the Bible. It is typical of the one 'who is able to do immeasurably more than all we ask or imagine' (Eph. 3:20), and illustrates the principle that God responds to the *desire* of the *heart* (*cf*. 1 Ch. 28:9; 29:19) by including an unexpected bonus (*cf*. 1 Ch. 13:13–14; Mal. 3:10–12; Mt. 6:33). Solomon had asked for wisdom, and received not only his request but in addition *wealth, riches, and honour* (*cf*. v. 11 and 1 Ch. 29:25). The importance of all this is underlined by the triple use of 'asked' (v. 11) in contrast to the double appearance of 'give' (v. 12).

Riches does not occur in 1 Kings 3:13, but is probably a post-exilic expansion of the previous word influenced by Aramaic usage.[1] Solomon's wealth made him unique among the kings of Israel (v. 12b; *cf*. 1 Ch. 29:25), and even though a comparison formula similar to that used of Solomon is also found with later kings (2 Ki. 18:5; 23:25), no-one approached him in wealth. Here as elsewhere the Old Testament affirms that material things have real value in God's sight, as long as they are not treated as an end in themselves. It has to be said, however, that Solomon's use of these gifts was marked by neither consistency nor wisdom, and the harsh burden of his financial policies led to the eventual division of his son's kingdom (*cf*. 2 Ch. 10:3–19).

13. Finally, Solomon returns to *Jerusalem*.[2] According to 1 Kings 3:15, he worshipped before the ark, but Chronicles seems to have been content not to detract from the life-changing encounter at Gibeon.

d. Solomon's wealth (1:14–17). This paragraph has greater significance than it appears. Though it has been taken over

---

[1] *Cf*. E. Vogt, *Lexicon Linguae Aramaicae* (Rome: Biblical Institute Press, 1971), p. 112.

[2] Modern EVV correctly follow LXX, Vulg., in reading 'from the high place' against MT's 'to the high place' (also AV).

almost unchanged from Kings, it has been moved to quite a different position (1 Ki. 10:26–29), and is repeated with amendments at 2 Chronicles 9:25–28. Its main purpose is to show that God has kept his word about Solomon's wealth (especially v. 15), but also to demonstrate that this wealth was being partly prepared for the temple (*cf.* 2:1).

Solomon's wealth is measured by the strength of his armaments (v. 14), and the wide availability of precious metals and luxury items such as *cedar*. Its primary source was trade, of which that in *horses* and *chariots* was a prime example. For Solomon's *chariot cities cf.* 1 Kings 9:17–19.[1] *Gold* has been added to 1 Kings 10:27, but with some justification (*cf.* 1 Ki. 10:10, 14–15, 23). The tree with which cedar is compared is the 'sycomore' (GNB; *cf.* REB, NEB), which is a common type of fig and not at all like the European sycamore.[2] For more precise details of the import and export trade, see the helpful summary in Dillard, pp. 13–14. In the case of the imports, the main alternatives are either that the horses originated from modern southern Turkey ('Musri and Cilicia', GNB, v. 16) and the chariots from *Egypt*, or, more probably, that Egypt supplied both commodities but that horses also came from *Kue* (NIV, *cf.* NRSV, RSV; = Roman Cilicia). Chariots and horses were re-exported to *the kings of the Hittites and of the Arameans, i.e.* modern northern Syria. 'For a price' (v. 16, RSV) adds nothing to the over-all sense, and really means, 'at the current rate', *i.e.* Solomon's state traders negotiated their purchases at an agreed rate.[3]

ii. Solomon's preparations (2:1–18)

'Solomon sent this message to Hiram king of Tyre, ". . . 'I am about to build a temple for the Name of the LORD my God'"' (2:3–4).

2:3–4 – *cf.* 1 Kings 5:2–5
2:8 – *cf.* 1 Kings 5:6
2:10 – *cf.* 1 Kings 5:11

---

[1] *He kept* (v. 14; 'stationed', NRSV, RSV) is greatly preferable to the equivalent verb in 1 Ki. 10:26 (lit. 'he led, guided').

[2] M. Zohary, *Plants of the Bible* (Cambridge: Cambridge University Press, 1982), pp. 68–69; F. N. Hepper, in *IBD*, p. 1592.

[3] Heb. *mᵉḥîr* corresponds to Old Babylonian *maḥīrat illaku*, 'at the going rate', *cf.* A. Goetze, *The laws of Eshnunna*, AASOR 31 (New Haven: American Schools of Oriental Research, 1956), pp. 111–112.

2:12 – *cf.* 1 Kings 5:7
2:13–14 – *cf.* 1 Kings 7:13–14
2:16 – *cf.* 1 Kings 5:9
2:2, 18 – *cf.* 1 Kings 5:15–16

Chronicles' record of Solomon's achievements moves straight away to the construction of the temple. Several important items in the account of his reign in Kings are left out as a result, such as his wisdom in action, administration, educational reforms, and some building activities (*e.g.* 1 Ki. 3:16 – 4:34; 7:1–12). These were not unimportant, but, for Chronicles, they were all subsidiary to the temple.

The temple is to be built for the worship of God, though temple worship involved a fundamental paradox. On the one hand, the place of God's earthly residence was where he could be encountered (*for the Name of the* LORD, vv. 1, 4), yet on the other, *even the highest heavens cannot contain him* (v. 6). In true temple worship people must be enabled to draw near to God in his mercy as well as to appreciate his eternal majesty. He is to be worshipped 'for ever' (v. 4, NRSV, RSV, *etc.*) because of his *love* in keeping his promise to *David* (v. 11, *cf.* v. 3), and because he is *greater than all other gods* (v. 5; *cf.* vv. 6, 9, 12). Every reference to God in this chapter also anticipates the more detailed description of the temple in chapters 6–7, stressing that the preparation of materials and personnel is worthless without a proper awareness of God.

These final stages (*cf.* 3:1) build on David's own preparations (*cf.* esp. 1 Ch. 22). Here the emphasis falls on foreign contributions, by *Hiram king of Tyre* (vv. 3–16) and the 'foreigners living in the land of Israel' (vv. 2, 17–18, GNB). In the structure of Chronicles' account of Solomon, further details are provided in the parallel passage in 8:1 – 9:12, where, in addition to Hiram and the foreigners, the Queen of Sheba and the daughter of the king of Egypt also play their part in the nations' praise of God. Some of the links in the two passages are quite specific, such as the building of palaces (2:1; 8:1, 11), slave labour by the 'foreigners in the land' (2:2, 17–18; 8:7–8), the focus of the temple in regular worship (2:4; 8:12–15), co-operation between Hiram's and Solomon's workers (2:8, 14; 8:18), and praise by a foreign ruler for God's gifts of love and wisdom to Solomon (2:11–12; 9:5–8). All this indicates both that Israel had finally achieved its desired 'rest' (*cf.* 1 Ch. 22:9–10; 28:2–3; 2 Ch. 6:41), and that other nations

not only recognized but actually contributed to God's blessings on Israel (*cf.* 1 Ch. 14:17; 2 Ch. 9:1–8). God's prophetic
promises that the Gentiles would bring their gifts to him in
future days (*cf.* Is. 60:13–14; Zp. 3:9–10) were already
beginning to be fulfilled (*cf.* Ex. 3:21–22; 12:35–36; Hg.
2:7–9).

The chapter has the pattern of a simple chiasm:

a. Census of labourers (v. 2);
  b. Solomon's letter to Hiram (vv. 3–10);
  b_1. Hiram's letter to Solomon (vv. 11–16);
a_1. Census of non-Israelite labourers (vv. 17–18).

Here the focus is not on a central sentence or theme, but
on the relationship between the letters in the central sections.
Hiram's reply indicates his support for God's purposes and
promises everything Solomon had asked for. As in chapter 1,
Solomon's requests are again answered in the unseen workings of providence. The Chronicler's primary source is 1
Kings 5, but he has omitted and added material quite freely
in comparison with the earlier account. The effect of the
changes is to heighten the request–response relationship
between the letters. It also results in an even greater concentration on the temple, reaffirming God's sovereign rule over
the nations as well as over the temple.

Such a view of the temple challenges all small-minded
views about its worship. Many of the Chronicler's contemporaries were doubtless tempted to succumb to fear of
outside threats (*e.g.* Ezr. 4:1–24; Est. 4:1–3), forgetting not
only Hiram's contributions but also those even of Persian
emperors for the rebuilding of the temple (Ezr. 1:1–4;
6:1–14). But God's authority could not be confined to the
land of Israel, any more than it is limited to the familiar
churches and denominations in which Christians worship
today. Also, Hiram's recognition of God is another step
towards God's wider purposes for the nations. It points not
only to the temple's role as 'a house of prayer for all nations'
(Is. 56:7; Mk. 11:17; *cf.* 2 Ch. 6:32–33), but beyond it to the
church, where in Christ all human barriers can be broken
down (Eph. 2:11–22). Such co-operation can become reality,
however, only when worship becomes the highest priority
and full account is taken of God's authority among the
powers of earth and heaven (vv. 6, 12).

a. Building instructions (2:1).[1] With gifts of wisdom and wealth provided (ch. 1), Solomon is enabled to build the *temple* and the *royal palace*. The temple is *for the Name of the LORD* (also v. 4), a phrase naturally associated with Deuteronomy. God's name represented his whole being, which would be present and resident at the temple (*cf.* Dt. 12:5, 11; 16:2, 11; 18:6–7). One could 'call on the name of the LORD' at any time (*e.g.* 1 Ki. 8:29, 41–44), in the confidence that prayers would be heard and answered. The Chronicler makes only passing mention of Solomon's palace (2:12; 7:11; 8:1; 9:11), clearly expecting his readers to know where fuller details were to be found (1 Ki. 7:1–12). The palace is always linked with the temple in Chronicles, presumably because together they represented the establishing of David's dynasty (*cf.* 1 Ch. 17:10–14; 28:2–7).

b. Census of labourers (2:2). Despite EVV, the first verb here ('counted') is identical to that in verse 17, so that a census is really being described. These were a slave labour force of non-Israelites living in Canaan, who had already been assembled by David (v. 17; 8:7–10; *cf.* 1 Ch. 22:2, 15–16). The number of *thirty-six hundred* foremen differs from 1 Kings 5:16 (3,300), but the LXX of Kings is quite insecure here, and Chronicles may preserve the better reading (see further Dillard, p. 22).

c. Solomon's letter to Hiram (2:3–10). This letter centres on two requests, marked by the repeated *send me*, for a skilled craftsman (v. 7) and more timber (vv. 8–10). By way of encouragement, Solomon simply asks Hiram to continue the kindness he had previously shown to David (v. 3), and reminds him that the project is for God's glory rather than Solomon's (vv. 4–6).

The relationship between Solomon and *Hiram* is probably based on a parity treaty between equals (*cf.* 1 Ki. 5:12), rather than one where Solomon was the superior party. While it is true that by omitting Hiram's initial greeting (1 Ki. 5:1) and with Hiram addressing Solomon as 'my lord' (v. 15), Solomon might seem to be taking the initiative, he certainly did not have things all his own way. His opening is distinctly tentative,

---

[1] Verse numbers in MT are smaller by one than in EVV, since v. 1 in EVV is 1:18 in Heb.

and he is not in full control of the financial arrangements (*cf.* vv. 15–16; 1 Ki. 5:9–11).[1] On the form of Hiram's name ('Huram' in Ch.), see on 1 Ch. 14:1.

Both Solomon and Hiram hark back repeatedly to *David* (vv. 3, 7, 12, 14). This is not just a reminder of Hiram's earlier treaty with him (*cf.* 1 Ch. 14:1; 22:4), but a hint that Solomon's plans will fulfil God's promise to David.[2] Further, several details of the Mosaic law are specifically fulfilled (vv. 4–5).

4–6. The place where God's *Name* dwells, the regular pattern of worship (based on Ex. 30:1–10; Lv. 24:1–9; Nu. 28–29), and the specific reminder of God's greatness (*cf.* Ex. 18:11; Dt. 4:7–8) all have direct associations with Moses. However, the pattern of worship, which was so important for Chronicles (*cf.* 1 Ch. 23:28–31; 2 Ch. 13:10–11; 31:2–3), *was a lasting ordinance* ('ordained for ever', NRSV). The temple therefore also looks forward, in two ways. It would be firstly a place to *burn sacrifices*, a central function in the pre-exilic temple but one that was especially emphasized after the exile (*cf.* 2 Ch. 7:12; Mal. 1:6–14; the same list recurs in 2 Ch. 31:3). What is meant here are the regular worship activities listed in verse 4, the daily *burnt offerings*, the weekly *Sabbath* offerings including the *consecrated bread* ('showbread', RSV), the monthly *New Moon* feasts and the annual festivals (*appointed feasts*). Christians are similarly called 'continually [to] offer to God a sacrifice of praise' (Heb. 13:5). Secondly, however, such sacrifices were to be offered to a God whom even the *highest heavens* cannot contain (*cf.* 2 Ch. 6:18). God's transcendence, another post-exilic emphasis, is as important as his presence, reminding Israel that even the completed temple by no means exhausted his plans for them.

7. Solomon's first request, for a leading craftsman, does not appear in the earlier form of this letter (1 Ki. 5:3–6; but *cf.* 1

---

[1] NIV's bold opening to the letter is quite misleading, which actually begins with an unfinished comparative clause ('As you did . . .', v. 3) followed by an explanatory parenthesis (vv. 4–6). No request is actually made in MT until v. 7. The best way in English to reflect Solomon's initial caution is to add a phrase at the end of v. 3 ('so deal with me', RSV) rather than at the beginning (with GNB, JB).

[2] It is unnecessary to include the expansionist addition of 'his son' after 'I' (v. 4), as in LXX, OL (against *e.g.* Dillard, Rudolph). The longer text is unsupported by 1 Ki. 5:5 (EVV; MT, v. 19), and is probably influenced by the mention of 'my father' there and in 1 Ki. 5:3 (EVV; MT, 5:17).

Ki. 7:13–14). It highlights the necessity of wisdom for building the temple (*skilled*, twice here, is lit. 'wise' in Heb.), and
strengthens the temple's link with Moses' Tent (or 'tabernacle'). The leading craftsmen for the Tent, Bezalel and his
assistant Oholiab, were both similarly skilled in a range of
abilities (*cf.* Ex. 31:1–6; 35:30 – 36:2). Kings and Chronicles,
however, differ in their description of the necessary skills, for
whereas in 1 Kings 7:13–47 Huram-Abi (there called Hiram)
is a worker in bronze, here he has many skills (vv. 7 and
13–14; *cf.* 2 Ch. 3:15 – 4:18). But even though verses 7 and 14
seem to have Bezalel and Oholiab consciously in mind, a range
of talents was required for the temple (*cf.* 2 Ch. 3:4–14,
especially v. 14), and it is certainly not impossible for Huram-
abi to have supplied them. The Chronicler's influence is also
traceable in a unique Aramaic form of the word for *purple* (the
usual Heb. form is in 2:13; 3:14), a probable Persian loanword
for *crimson*, and the common post-exilic phrase *Judah and
Jerusalem.*[1]

8–9. Solomon's second request is for timber. As with the
craftsmen (1 Ch. 22:15–16; 28:21), it is additional to that
provided by David (*cf.* 22:4, 14; 29:2), though skill in felling
and cutting was just as important to Solomon as the materials.
Algum wood ('juniper', GNB) is unknown, though it is probably
cognate with Akkadian *elamukku* and Ugaritic *almg* and grown
in northern Syria. One Ugaritic text even quotes it in a list of
trees exported from Lebanon, though according to 1 Ki.
10:11–12 ('almug'), it was an import from Ophir.[2] For most
Israelites, of course, all the timber was simply of foreign
origin, like the silver and gold (*cf.* 2 Ch. 1:16–17), so that
ultimately the temple would be *magnificent* (v. 9, NIV, GNB;
'wonderful', NRSV, RSV, REB, NEB) 'in the sight of all the nations'
(1 Ch. 22:5).

10. The payment details show several differences in comparison with 1 Kings 5:11. In the earlier passage, Hiram is
invited to name his price, *barley* and *wine* are not mentioned,
the *oil* is of special quality and different quantity, and annual
payment is made. Since textual variations underlie the
amount of oil in Kings, the differences between Kings and

---

[1] For this phrase, *cf. e.g.* 2 Ch. 20:18; Ezr. 1:2; 9:9 Mal. 3:4.
[2] *Cf.* J. C. Greenfield and M. Mayrhofer, 'The *'algummīm/'almuggīm* problem reexamined', *SVT* 16, 1967, pp. 83–89.

Chronicles may have a similar cause.[1] Alternatively, Chronicles may be describing Solomon's negotiating position, which Hiram subsequently amended considerably (*cf.* 1 Ki. 5:6, 9).

d. Hiram's letter to Solomon (2:11–16). Hiram's reply is considerably longer than 1 Kings 5:7–9. This is due partly to the Chronicler's fondness for using written sources such as this *letter* (v. 11; *cf.* 1 Ch. 28:19; 2 Ch. 21:12; 30:1; 35:4; 36:22), and partly because verses 13–14 are expanded from 1 Kings 7:13–14. Verses 11–12 (EVV; vv. 10–11, MT); seem to have a double beginning, though this is much clearer in Hebrew than in EVV, which smooth out the opening words of both verses, literally, 'And Hiram said'. While the problem is sometimes solved by reversing verses 11 and 12 (Ackroyd, Curtis and Madsen), it is more likely that verse 11 is based on 1 Kings 5:1 and verses 12ff. on 1 Kings 5:7ff. (Williamson).

The form of the reply follows Solomon's letter closely, *viz.*: (a) Theological and historical context (vv. 11–12; *cf.* vv. 3–6); (b) Huram-abi as chief craftsman (vv. 13–14; *cf.* v. 7); (c) Materials and payment (vv. 15–16; *cf.* vv. 8–10).

11–12. It is perhaps surprising that Hiram acknowledges so clearly and enthusiastically the temple project as the will of Israel's God. It could appear excessive even for a friendly Gentile ruler to affirm Solomon's accession as a consequence of Yahweh's covenant *love*, Yahweh as the creator of all things, and Solomon's wisdom, 'intelligence and understanding' (v. 12, NEB) as gifts from Yahweh.[2] But theological declarations of this kind are not unknown in the Old Testament (*cf.* Dn. 4:34–35; 6:26–27), and do not necessarily imply conversion to Yahwism. In Chronicles they occur at significant points (*cf.* 2 Ch. 9:5–8; 36:22–23), with this passage having a direct parallel in a speech by the Queen of Sheba (*cf.* Solomon's wisdom in 2:12 and 9:5–7; Yahweh's love in making Solomon king in 2:11 and 9:8; the blessing of Yahweh in 2:12 and 9:8). Both Hiram and the Queen of Sheba confirm Yahweh's supreme authority to *build the temple* (v. 12). The temple, then, did not

[1] It is not clear whether *ground* ('crushed', NRSV; perhaps even 'shredded wheat'!) is an error for 'as food' (*cf.* 1 Ki. 5:11 and REB, NEB, 'provisions') or whether it is also based on a variant text.

[2] For 'love' as typical covenant/treaty vocabulary, *cf.* W. Moran, 'The ancient Near Eastern background of the love of God in Deuteronomy', *CBQ* 25, 1963, pp. 77–87. *Cf.* also Dt. 7:9; 1 Sa. 18:1–4; 2 Sa. 7:15.

become a house of prayer for all nations by accident. The nations even played a part in its construction!

13–14. Hiram responds to Solomon's first request by sending *Huram-Abi* (NIV, NRSV, RSV, JB; called 'Hiram' in Ki.), who had the added advantage of Israelite parentage. Variations on a person's name are not unknown in the Old Testament (*cf.* Jehoiachin/Coniah/Jeconiah; Joshua is formerly called Hoshea), but modern scholars frequently understand the '–abi' suffix as meaning 'master' (lit. 'father'; *cf.* Gn. 45:8; Jdg. 17:10), and so prefer 'master Huram' (NEB, *cf.* GNB). This is possible, but it lacks clear analogies. Although the name of Bezalel's assistant Oholiab may well explain Chronicles' preference for the form Huram-Abi (*cf.* comment on v. 7 and Ex. 31:6; 35:34–35), it is doubtful whether Oholiab's name can be explained in this way. Another link between Huram-Abi and Oholiab is that their mothers both came from *Dan*. Although 1 Kings 7:14 states that Huram-Abi's mother is of the tribe of Naphtali, ancestry from more than one tribe cannot have been uncommon, either because of contrasting geographical and genealogical links or as a result of the lineage of earlier generations (*cf.* Samuel as Ephraimite and Levite). Huram-Abi's chief qualification, however, is that he is, literally, 'a wise man who knows understanding' (v. 13), who will work with 'your wise men' (v. 14), *i.e. your craftsmen*. In God's providence, the appropriate wisdom or skill has been supplied through a foreign architect as well as through God's chosen king.

15–16. Finally, Hiram promised to send the required *logs*, though, as a shrewd businessman, only after payment had been received. The present vocabulary of verse 16 seems to reflect the post-exilic era. The mention of *Joppa*, not specified in 1 Kings 5:9, is almost certainly influenced by the transportation of timber for the second temple which arrived at the same port (Ezr. 4:7). The words for *need* and *rafts*, which are unique in the Old Testament though the first has an Aramaic cognate, are probably from the author's own time.

e. Census of non-Israelite labourers (2:17–18).
This paragraph is the source of the information already given in verse 2 (*cf.* 1 Ki. 5:15–16). Here, however, these workers are clearly *aliens* ('foreigners', GNB) who were counted after David's *census*. While 1 Chronicles 22:2 may be in mind, that event is

not described as a census, and the ill-fated incident of 1 Chronicles 21 is probably meant. More interesting is Chronicles' attempt to clarify the rather confused identity of Solomon's workforce in 1 Kings 5:13–18. The earlier passage seems to include temporary gangs of 30,000 Israelites under Adoniram as well as 153,000 permanent but unidentified slaves. Here, however, only the latter group is mentioned and identified as non-Israelite. At the risk of oversimplifying a complex problem, they are probably the same group as in 1 Kings 9:20–21 (= 2 Ch. 8:7–8), while the embittered tribes who confronted Rehoboam (1 Ki. 12 = 2 Ch. 10) are more likely to have suffered under Adoniram (*cf*. 2 Ch. 10:18).[1] It was normal in the ancient world to enslave subject peoples, but for Israelites to fall into any form of slavery, especially at the hands of their own people, denied the very freedom for which they had been redeemed. While therefore, the Chronicler does not ignore the heavy price Israelites paid for Solomon's success, he concentrates here on the submission of the non-Israelites in Canaan as a sign of Israel's full occupation of the land and that preparations for the temple were now complete (*cf*. 3:1).

G. Solomon builds the temple (3:1 – 5:1)

Finally the point is reached where Solomon *began to build the temple* (v. 1). It is a little surprising, then, that after all the preparations (which really began as far back as 1 Ch. 17:1, 4, 12), Chronicles' account of the temple's construction is actually much briefer than in Kings. Seventy-seven verses in 1 Kings 6–7 (omitting the account of the royal palace, 7:1–12) have been condensed into forty verses in 2 Chronicles 3:1 – 5:1. Since the Chronicler then goes on to devote more space to the opening ceremonies (chs. 5–7) than to the building work, it is clear that his real concern is with the temple's meaning rather than its architectural details. In other words, the temple will be complete not when the last stone is in place but when God takes up residence.

Chapters 3–4 have a common structure as well as common content. Following an outline of the temple's basic plan (vv.

---

[1] *Cf.* Jones, I, pp. 157–158; R. Dillard, 'The Chronicler's Solomon', *WTJ* 43, 1980, pp. 289–300, especially pp. 294–296.

3–7), fourteen paragraphs in 3:8 – 4:11 all begin with the phrase *he made* (Heb. *wayya'aś*; 3:8, 10, 14, 15, 16a, 16b; 4:1, 2, 6, 7, 8a, 8b, 9, 11a). The purpose is to draw attention to an analogy with the construction of the Tent, where a longer version of the same pattern recurs (Ex. 36:1 – 39:32). Solomon, like Moses, is faithful to the plans revealed by God (*cf.* especially 1 Ch. 28:11–19 where most of the details of the building listed here are also mentioned). The association between Solomon's temple and Moses' Tent is featured several times in chapter 3 (see also vv. 9, 14). Since none of these links occurs in 1 Kings 6–7, they are Chronicles' way of underlining that the purpose of the Tent, a travelling sanctuary, was fulfilled in the 'rest' signified by the temple.

The chapter provides a simple tour through the building, beginning with the porch (v. 4), then the main sanctuary (vv. 5–7), and the Holy of Holies (vv. 8–13), with separate notes on the veil (v. 14) and the entrance pillars (vv. 15–17). The centre of attention is undoubtedly the *Most Holy Place* (or Holy of Holies), where the ark will soon find its permanent home (5:7–10). The repeated references to various types of *gold* (vv. 4–10) and to the *cherubim* (vv. 7, 10–14) are also striking, since both receive greater prominence than in Kings. Gold is generally a mark of royalty, so that its presence throughout the building probably demonstrates that the temple was a place fit for Israel's true king, the LORD. This view is also supported by the fact that the cherubim, often mentioned in the context of God's heavenly majesty (*e.g.* Ezk. 10:1, 20–22; Ps. 99:1), decorated the sanctuary and veil as well as the Most Holy Place.

Such an awareness of God's presence, however, must have produced conflicting responses in Israel. On the one hand, God's nearness was a reason for real joy (*e.g.* Ps. 27:4–6), and attendance in God's earthly temple gave access to his heavenly presence (*cf.* 2 Sa. 22:7; Jon. 2:7). But the very architecture of the building also emphasized the enormous difficulty of approaching God. One must remember that ordinary Israelites never saw what is described here, since only priests and Levites were allowed into the temple, and of course, only the high priest entered the Most Holy Place once annually on the Day of Atonement. To most Israelites, therefore, the temple was an unseen world. God had drawn near to them, but the way to him was hedged around with many restrictions.

Only when one grasps this sense of unapproachable majesty does the immensity of Jesus' achievement begin to dawn. For he not only tore through the veil obscuring God from human beings once and for all (Mt. 27:51), but even gives his people 'confidence to enter the Most Holy Place by the blood of Jesus, by a new and living way opened for us through the curtain' (Heb. 10:19–20). Whereas Solomon's sanctuary was only 'a copy and shadow of what is in heaven' (Heb. 8:5), Christ has opened the way to the Most Holy Place in heaven itself. Nonetheless, one should not underestimate the real satisfaction even in Israel of knowing God through his temple: 'In your presence there is fulness of joy' (Ps. 16:11, NRSV; *cf.* Pss. 73:16–17; 84:1–4, 10). The temple played a vital role in helping Israel to experience God's reality (*cf.* 2 Ch. 5:13; 7:12–16).

i. Beginning to build the temple (3:1–2)

'Then Solomon began to build the temple of the LORD' (3:1). Special note is made of the fact that *Solomon began to build* (the same verb begins both verses in Hebrew; *cf.* also Ezr. 3:8; 5:2). The site is doubly identified, as the place where *the LORD appeared* to both Abraham and David (*cf.* Gn. 22; 1 Ch. 21).[1] It is, in both cases, a place where God revealed himself and where special sacrifice was offered, themes especially associated with the temple. There is some uncertainty about the verb usually translated *appeared* (*cf.* EVV; 'was provided', referring to the place, is also possible; so Michaeli, Rudolph; *cf.* Gn. 22:8, 14), because it has no obvious subject. However, EVV rightly follow LXX in adding 'the LORD', and it can even be argued that the verb actually contains an abbreviated form of 'Yahweh'.[2] That God's appearing is meant is not contradicted by the fact that in both passages 'the angel of the LORD' is revealed (Gn. 22:11; 1 Ch. 21:16ff.), since God's angel was often regarded in the Old Testament as a form of God (*cf.* Ex. 3:2–6; Jdg. 13:2–23). *Moriah*, mentioned elsewhere only in Genesis 22:2, is the land where Abraham sought to sacrifice

[1] 'The site which David had prepared' (v. 1, REB, NEB; *cf.* NIV, NRSV, RSV, AV, *etc.*) involves a slight readjustment of MT, but is supported by the vss. It is preferable to the alternative translation, 'which [Solomon] had established on David's site'.

[2] *Cf.* G. R. Driver, *Textus* 4, 1964, p. 90; *cf.* L. C. Allen, *The Greek Chronicles*, 2, *SVT* 27 (Leiden: Brill, 1974), p. 83.

Isaac. Here it is called a *Mount*, by implication from Genesis 22:14. The several allusions to Genesis 22 here strongly suggest that the same place is meant in both passages.[1]

Kings' synchronization with the date of the exodus is omitted (*cf.* 1 Ki. 6:1), presumably in favour of the more theologically suggestive links of verse 1. A further link with the date when the second temple began to be built is also hinted at (*cf.* Ezr. 3:8). *On the second day* (NIV, JB) has probably been added in error to 1 Ki. 6:1 by dittography.

ii. The ground-plan and porch (3:3–4a)
Cf. 1 Kings 6:2–3

Verse 3 describes the ground plan (*foundations*, NIV, REB, NEB), rather than the measurements alone (NRSV, based on Tg.; *cf.* Rudolph, Myers), or the actual digging of foundations. By omitting almost all height measurements in Kings (*cf.* vv. 3, 4, 10 and 1 Ki. 6:2, 20, 23), the Chronicler shows his interest in the temple's basic layout rather than its over-all shape. It measured 60 × 20 cubits (or 26.67m × 8.89m) by the *cubit of the old standard*,[2] which by the Chronicler's time had been replaced by one that was longer by a handbreadth (Ezk. 40:5; 43:13). The temple therefore was not particularly large, and was smaller than many church buildings today.

The temple was entered through a porch or 'vestibule' (v. 4, NRSV, RSV, REB, NEB; *portico*, NIV; 'entrance room', GNB). The measurements given are additional to those for the main building, though the Hebrew text seems to be defective on three counts. Firstly, the relationship between the porch and the temple is unclear because MT has become corrupted. The simplest solution is to include 'house'/'temple' with LXX in the first phrase, so reading, 'The porch which was at the front of the temple ... was twenty cubits long' (*cf.* NIV, REB, NEB). Secondly, the lack of any width measurement in MT makes it impossible to be sure of the shape of the porch. It may well have been a square, 'twenty cubits long corresponding to the width of the temple' (*cf.* Rudolph), or possibly a rectangle twenty cubits long by ten cubits wide (*cf.* 1 Ki. 6:3), though some have understood its width to be twenty cubits and its

[1] See also H. G. M. Williamson, in W. Horbury (ed.), *Templum Amicitiae*, *JSNTS* 48 (Sheffield: Sheffield Academic Press, 1991), pp. 20–25.
[2] The 'generally accepted figure' for the cubit is 44.45 cms = 17.5 ins (D. J. Wiseman, *IBD*, pp. 1635–1636).

length unknown (*cf.* GNB). Thirdly, its height measurement should read *twenty cubits high* (NIV, REB, NEB), as against a literal translation of MT, 'and its height 120'.[1] The concept of a tower (GNB, NRSV, RSV, JB) may reflect the kind of design which was later used for Herod's temple, whose porch was 100 cubits high (*cf.* Josephus, *Jewish Wars* V. 207).[2]

iii. The golden temple (3:4b–13)

3:4b–5 – *cf.* 1 Kings 6:20b–21, 29
3:7 – *cf.* 1 Kings 6:22
3:8 – *cf.* 1 Kings 6:20a
3:10–12 – *cf.* 1 Kings 6:23–24, 27–28

Since 1 Kings 6:3 contains no hint that the porch was decorated with *gold*, the last phrase of verse 4, a skilful combination of parts of 1 Kings 6:20–21, probably introduces the golden theme of the following verses. *He overlaid* (v. 4) is a generalization for inlay as well as overlay.

In addition to *gold* (vv. 5, 6, 7), the *main hall* (vv. 5–7; 'nave', NRSV, RSV; 'main room', GNB) was decorated with *cypress, palms and chains* (v. 5), *precious stones* (v. 6; *cf.* 1 Ch. 29:2), and *carved cherubim* (v. 7). Over-all, it was to be a place of beauty (v. 6, JB) and majesty, fit for the presence of the King of kings. The palms (= the tree of life?) and the cherubim may symbolize that through the temple lay the way back to the ideal conditions of the Garden of Eden (*cf.* Gn. 3:22, 24; Ezk. 31:2–9).[3] *Parvaim* (v. 6) is unknown, though, according to a tenth-century AD Arab historian, it was a gold-mine in north-east Arabia called *el-farwain*. Alternatively, it may be one of several terms in this context for high-quality gold ('pure gold', v. 4; 'good gold', vv. 5, 8; '*sāgûr* [red?] gold', 4:20, 22; 'solid gold', 4:21).

The *Most Holy Place* or 'Holy of Holies' (vv. 8–13) was a secret room, largely hidden from human view, where Israel's

---

[1] The Chronicler's measurements in this section are always expressed by the plural form of 'cubits' before the relevant number. In view of Chronicles' omission of all other references to height in this context, one should take seriously the proposal to read here 'ten cubits wide' (*cf.* 1 Ki. 6:3 and Williamson, p. 206).

[2] On the changes in temple design in ancient Israel, *cf.* C. L. Meyers, 'The elusive temple', *BA* 45, 1982, pp. 33–41.

[3] *Cf.* J. Strange, 'The idea of afterlife in ancient Israel: some remarks on the iconography of Solomon's temple', *PEQ* 117, 1985, pp. 35–40; H. Gese in H. Gese and H. P. Rüger (eds.), *Wort und Geschichte*, *AOAT* 18, 1973, p. 82.

sins were forgiven on the basis of the covenant symbolized by the ark (cf. 2 Ch. 5:7–10). It was actually a complete cube (cf. 1 Ki. 6:20), symbolizing the perfection of its design as well as its purpose. It glittered with *six hundred talents* of gold (v. 8) and a further *fifty shekels* for *nails* (v. 9), as well as the golden *cherubim* (vv. 10–13). Neither the 600 talents nor the nails occur in 1 Kings 6, and both are probably included for symbolic reasons. The former was the price of the temple site (1 Ch. 21:25). It was probably regarded as David's contribution towards the provision of atonement for others, even though he could not atone for his own sins (cf. 1 Ch. 21:25; 28:11). The nails recall the hooks on which hung the Tent's veil (Ex. 26:32, 37). The small amount of gold, about twenty ounces, was probably used for gold leaf.[1] 'Upper chambers' (v. 9, NRSV, RSV, REB, NEB) are not mentioned directly elsewhere, though, as the height of the Most Holy Place was only twenty cubits as against thirty cubits for the building, it is often thought that there may have been a room above and/or below. Less plausibly, the associated side rooms may be meant (cf. 1 Ki. 6:5–6, 8–10).

The *cherubim* (vv. 10–13) receive special attention, although the information is much abbreviated from 1 Kings 6:23–28. They represent angelic beings who live in God's own presence (cf. Ezk. 10:2ff.), and their wings reaching from one wall to another symbolized how completely they protected the ark (cf. 1 Ch. 28:18; 2 Ch. 5:7–8).

iv. The veil (3:14)

Only here does the Old Testament mention the temple 'veil' (RSV, REB, NEB, JB) or *curtain* (NIV, GNB, NRSV). The Tent of course had a veil (Ex. 26:31–35; 36:35–36; cf. this verse with Ex. 26:31; 36:35), but 1 Kings 6:31–32 speaks only of doors carved like the rest of the main hall. The existence of a veil in Solomon's temple, however, may be supported by the presence of one in Herod's temple (Mt. 27:51 = Mk. 15:38 = Lk. 23:45).[2] Two further factors lead in the same direction. Firstly, Hebrew *pārōket* actually means 'divider, barrier' (a separate word is used for 'curtains'), and cognate words in

---

[1] RSV's 'The weight of the nails was one shekel to fifty shekels of gold' is an emendation based on LXX, but assumes unjustifiably that the nails were solid gold.

[2] For possible textual support in 1 Ki. 6:21, cf. Rudolph, pp. 204–205; Jones, I, pp. 169–170.

related languages are used in association with various types of obstacle.[1] Secondly, the Chronicler clearly believed that Solomon's temple had both veil and doors (*cf.* 2 Ch. 4:22), as was also the case in Herod's temple (Josephus, *Jewish War* 5.5). The Chronicler was interested in the veil because of its continuity with the Tent, but for Christians the tearing of the veil when Jesus died (Mt. 27:51, *etc.*) supersedes all other associations.

v. The pillars (3:15–17)

3:15–17 – *cf.* 1 Kings 7:15–17, 20–21

According to 1 Kings 7:13ff., the *two pillars* in front of the temple head the list of bronze objects made by Huram-abi (= Hiram, 1 Ki. 7:13; *cf.* 2 Ch. 2:13). Confirmation of this is found in the Chronicler's inclusion of the decorated pillars in his summary of the architect's work (2 Ch. 4:11–13). The full list of bronze work occurs in 3:15 – 4:18.

Evidence from other sanctuaries suggests the pillars were probably free-standing, but there is no certainty about their origin or function. Their names (v. 17) *Jakin* (= 'he establishes'?) and *Boaz* (= 'strength is in him'?) suggest the theme of confirming. This might be linked with the idea that Yahweh's covenant was confirmed through the temple, or with Solomon's efforts in setting up the temple. Either is a more probable explanation than reading these as names from David's ancestry (*cf.* Nu. 26:12; 1 Ch. 24:17; Ru. 4:13–22) or as hangovers from Canaanite religion.[2]

Their height is given here as *thirty-five cubits* (v. 15), as against only eighteen cubits (= 8 m) in 1 Ki. 7:15 (also 2 Ki. 25:17; Je. 52:21). The most likely explanation is that this is a combined figure for both pillars (the reverse seems to have happened with the *pomegranate decorations, cf.* v. 16 and 1 Ki. 7:20). Less probable is that figures for the height, circumference, and capital have been erroneously combined (18 + 12 + 5). It has been suggested that the unique word usually translated *capital* (v. 15) may mean 'gold-plating'.[3] The *chains* (v. 16) may have been *interwoven* (GNB, NIV) or had a 'necklace' pattern (RSV, REB

---

[1] *Cf.* J. Hoftijzer, *Dictionnaire des inscriptions semitiques de l'ouest* (Leiden: Brill, 1960–62), p. 235; J. C. L. Gibson, *Textbook of Syrian Semitic Inscriptions* (Oxford: Clarendon Press, 1982), pp. 124–127; W. von Soden, *AHwb*, p. 828.

[2] For further details, see D. J. Wiseman and C. J. Davey, *IBD* 2, pp. 726–727 (including diagram); Jones, I, pp. 181–183.

[3] W. G. E. Watson, 'Archaic elements in the language of Chronicles', *Bib.* 53, 1972, p. 196.

NEB), on the basis of a commonly accepted emendation, though the Hebrew actually reads, 'he made chains in the Most Holy Place'. The presence of chains on the pillars as well as in the Holy of Holies and the main hall (v. 5) would conform with the use of gold and cherubim in different parts of the building, and would further underline the unity and complementarity of the temple's design.

vi. The temple equipment (4:1–22)

4:2–5 – *cf.* 1 Kings 7:23–26
4:6a – *cf.* 1 Kings 7:38–39a
4:10–22 – *cf.* 1 Kings 7:39b–50

There is no real break between chapter 3 and chapter 4, and the pattern of short paragraphs beginning with 'he made', begun at 3:8, continues here to verse 11a. The one main difference is that whereas chapter 3 focused on the structure of the building, chapter 4 concentrates on its furnishings and equipment.

As before, an opportunity is taken to underline the connection between Moses' Tent and Solomon's temple (*cf.* vv. 1, 6b–9), though, conversely, the temple of the Chronicler's time seems to have had little influence on this passage (*cf. e.g.* Ezr. 3:1–13; 6:13–18). Since Solomon's temple is larger and more lavishly equipped than the Tent, it was clearly not a slavish imitation in more permanent form. The reader's attention is therefore drawn to the principles underlying the temple's design rather than the details of its furnishings. It is also significant that those same principles on which the Tent was based illustrate the heavenly sanctuary opened to us in Christ (Heb. 8:1 – 10:25).

Three of those principles are emphasized through this chapter. Firstly, the temple's structure and equipment signify in various ways what it means to be in God's presence. The need to be washed, the symbolism of the lampstands and the bread, the doors of the Most Holy Place, and even things like sprinkling bowls and censers, speak of God's grace in drawing near to humankind as well as of his glorious holiness. Secondly, the emphasis on the temple vessels, as well as the association between Tent and temple, underlines the continuity represented by the temple. The return of the temple vessels to the second temple was one of the chief signs that post-exilic Israel remained a worshipping community of covenant people (*cf.*

Ezr. 1:7–11; 6:5; 8:24–34).[1] The ongoing significance of this equipment is underlined by reference to various kings restoring and repairing it for use in worship (*cf.* 2 Ch. 13:11; 23:18–19; 29:18–19; 33:16). Thirdly, the detail shows that Solomon was careful to follow God's written instructions, with almost every item listed in 1 Chronicles 28:11–19 repeated here. The pattern of Moses' obedience in constructing the Tent (*cf.* Ex. 25–31 and 35–40) is therefore continued, in both cases culminating in God's house being filled with his glory (5:13–14; *cf.* Ex. 40:34–38).

The temple's interior also helps Christians understand what it means to worship God in his heavenly sanctuary. Although the way was not fully disclosed in Old Testament times (Heb. 9:8), as a result of Jesus' death the way to heaven is now available to Gentiles as well as Jews. Its earthly point of entry is the cross 'outside the camp' (Heb. 13:11–14). There Jesus died for sins once and for all (*cf.* Jn. 19:30), rendering any further earthly temple and altar quite superfluous (*cf.* Heb. 8:13). This Most Holy Place in heaven is to be a place of continuing worship as well as completed atonement. Here every believer may enter as a priest (1 Pet. 2:5, 9), confident of never being turned away from the presence of Jesus, the Bread of life and the Light of the world (*cf.* Jn. 6:35; 8:12; 9:5). Christians are therefore encouraged to 'draw near to God with a sincere heart in full assurance of faith' (Heb. 10:22).

The structure of the chapter is very simple:

4:1–11a Temple equipment (continued from 3:8)
4:11b–18 Summary of Huram-Abi's bronze work
4:19–22 Summary of gold objects
5:1 Completion of the entire work

Although the Chronicler has derived most of his material from Kings, ultimately it probably comes from as many as three different temple records. This is the most likely explanation of the lack of consistency between the summaries and the main report, which Chronicles seems to have made no attempt to harmonize in all details. Some items are described twice but in different ways (*cf.* v. 13 and 3:16), while others, such as the stands (v. 14), the golden altar (v. 19) and the doors (v. 22), are

---

[1] *Cf.* P. R. Ackroyd, 'The temple vessels – a continuity theme', *SVT* 23, 1972, pp. 166–181.

included for the first time in the summaries. Since the Chronicler concentrates on the over-all impression created by the gold and bronze as symbols of God's presence among his people, he omits detailed description of the stands (1 Ki. 7:27–37), but adds features which speak both of God's presence and of a place for his people (vv. 6b–9).

This section lists eight different items of temple equipment, each sub-section beginning with *he made* (vv. 1, 2, 6, 7, 8a, 8b, 9, 11a; Heb. *wayya'as*). The most important are as follows:

a. The bronze altar (4:1). Although this verse does not appear in 1 Kings 7 (but *cf.* 1 Ki. 8:64; 9:25; 2 Ki. 16:14), the style and vocabulary are in fact more typical of Kings than Chronicles, and it was probably omitted from the earlier text by accident (see Rudolph, Dillard). This was the large stepped altar (8.89 × 8.89 × 4.445 m) which stood outside in the courtyard in front of the temple entrance (*cf.* 6:12; Ex. 40:6; Ezk. 43:13–17).[1] Apparently it simply replaced the much smaller version (*cf.* Ex. 27:1) at Gibeon where Solomon worshipped (1:5–6). Even such an important object as an altar appears not to have been sacrosanct when something greater could take its place.

b. The Sea (4:2–6, 10). This strangely named object was actually a large water 'tank' (GNB), placed just inside the *south-east corner* (v. 10) of the temple. Its nearest equivalent in the Tent was the basin (or laver) which stood between the bronze altar and the Tent entrance (Ex. 30:18–21). Both were to be *used by the priests for washing* (2 Ch. 4:6; *cf.* Ex. 30:19–21). Since only the Chronicler specifies a use for the Sea, it is frequently assumed that he is consciously avoiding earlier mythological associations. Such an assumption, however, is not clearly supported in any description of this object, and it is most natural to interpret its name on the basis of its size and its function. Priests who did not wash to make themselves clean would die (Ex. 30:20), and a spiritual washing is equally essential for Christians (*cf.* Jn. 13:10; 15:3; Heb. 10:22). The *basins* (v. 6; 'lavers', RSV) were also used for washing, but for those 'parts of the animals' given as a burnt offering (GNB; *cf.* Ex. 29:17; Lv. 1:9, 13; Ezk. 40:38) rather than for utensils (*cf.* NRSV, RSV).

[1] For the standard cubit as 44.45 cm, see *IBD*, pp. 1635–1636.

The Sea stood on *twelve* bulls (v. 4), and was decorated with, literally, 'something like bulls' (v. 3), which REB, NEB, RSV translate as a rare word for 'gourds' (from 1 Ki. 7:24). Either the Chronicler did not understand the earlier text (Willi) or he felt that the decoration matched the supporting structure. The symbolism of flora and fauna in the temple may either indicate God's sovereignty over the created order or be another allusion to the harmony of all created things in God's presence as in the Garden of Eden (*cf.* 3:5). The capacity of *three thousand baths* (v. 5) is apparently based on a cylindrical shape, as against the 'two thousand baths' of 1 Kings 7:26 which assumes a hemisphere.

c. The ten gold lampstands and ten tables (4:7–8). Solomon's temple was also better equipped than the Tent in the case of the light and bread. Whereas the Tent had a single seven-branched candlestick and one table for the 'showbread' (*cf.* Ex. 25:23–40), the temple had ten of each, though the lamps were possibly of a different shape. Although the purpose of the tables is not given here, the regular practice of referring to tables for the bread in the same context as the lampstands suggests that these were for the 'Bread of the Presence' rather than to support the lamps (*cf.* 1 Ch. 9:32; 28:16; 2 Ch. 4:19–20; 13:11; also Ex. 25:23–40; 40:4, 22–25). This conclusion is valid even though Chronicles sometimes refers to only one table (2 Ch. 13:11; 29:18). While one table may indeed have been used at other times, the mention of 'each table' in 1 Chronicles 28:16 seems decisive for the period of David and Solomon.[1]

The light and the bread both speak of God's continuing presence with his people, a special emphasis in Chronicles (vv. 7–8 are not in Ki.).[2] Even in times of darkness and poverty, God remained the source of light and food for his people (*cf.* Dt. 8:3; Ps. 36:8–9; Jn. 6:35; 8:12).

d. The courtyards (4:9). It may seem strange for these to be included, but a courtyard is part of the pattern of the Tent (*cf.* Ex. 27:9–19) and of the instructions in 1 Chronicles 28:12. The verse anticipates 6:13, confirming that the temple was for all Israel, not just the priests and Levites. The division into the two courts is already mentioned briefly in 1 Kings 6:36; 7:9, 12,

[1] *Cf.* M. Haran, *Temples and Temple Service* (Oxford: Clarendon Press, 1978), p. 189.
[2] *Cf.* J. I. Durham, *Exodus*, WBC (Waco: Word Books, 1987), pp. 360–365.

though the rare word for the large *court* (NIV, NRSV, RSV; 'precinct', REB, NEB; *cf.* also 2 Ch. 6:13; 20:5) is found only in post-exilic passages. A priests' court, *i.e.* an inner court, is found in *e.g.* Ezekiel 40:44–47; 44:17–19, 27.

e. Bronze work (4:11b–18). Two summaries of temple equipment are included, one for the *bronze* (or 'copper', NEB) work (vv. 11b–18) and one for the *gold* (vv. 19–22). Together they emphasize the temple's lavish decoration, including the 'great quantities' of bronze (v. 18, NRSV, RSV, *cf.* REB, NEB), but the differences in the metals are also significant. They illustrate the principle of gradation, whereby the costlier metal represents a greater degree of holiness. Thus, the bronze objects are all associated with the temple entrance, but the gold is reserved for the interior.

In the first list, the *pillars* and their decorations (vv. 12–13) partially repeat 3:15–17, the *Sea* and the smaller articles (vv. 15–16) resume 4:10–11, while the *stands* (NIV, NRSV, RSV; 'trolleys', REB, NEB; 'carts', GNB) for the basins (v. 14) are described in 1 Kings 7:27–37.[1] The bronze was *Huram-Abi's* work (v. 16; *cf.* v. 11 and 2:13–14), which was carried out in 'earthen foundries' (v. 17, Myers, *cf.* REB, NEB; *clay moulds*, NIV, *cf.* NRSV, RSV) in the Jordan valley. The actual location of Solomon's copper mines is less certain, though the traditional site at Timna in the far south is not entirely excluded.[2]

f. Gold objects (4:19–22). The *gold doors* (v. 22) are mentioned for the first time (*cf.* note on 3:14), while reference is made to the *golden* incense *altar* (v. 19a) and the *tables* and *lampstands* (vv. 19b–20) at 1 Chronicles 28:18 and 2 Chronicles 4:7–8 respectively. The actual phrase *bread of the Presence* (v. 19) occurs only here in Chronicles (other expressions are found in 1 Ch. 9:23; 23:29; 2 Ch. 2:4; 13:11; 29:18). It is particularly associated with the Tent (Ex. 25:30; 35:13; 39:36; *cf.* 1 Sa. 21:7), and is especially meaningful in a passage anticipating the reality of God's glorious presence (5:13–14).

---

[1] REB, NEB, GNB, JB correctly read 'ten (stands)' in v. 14 with 1 Ki. 7:43 instead of MT's 'he made', which is out of place here.

[2] *Cf.* the contrasting views of J. J. Bimson, 'King Solomon's mines? A reassessment of finds in the Arabah', *TB* 32, 1981, pp. 123–149, and F. Singer, 'From these hills . . .', *Biblical Archaeology Review* 4, 1978, pp. 11–25.

vii. Completion of the temple (5:1)

'All the work Solomon had done for the temple of the LORD
was finished' (5:1).

5:1 – *cf.* 1 Kings 7:51

The two summary lists lead naturally into this final statement,
which confirms that the temple was a joint enterprise between
David and *Solomon*. David had several times *dedicated* material
for the temple (*cf.* 1 Ch. 17:8, 11; 26:26–27), following the
practice of Joshua (*cf.* Jos. 6:24). He had also prepared for the
treasuries, both in terms of their Levitical personnel (1 Ch.
26:20–28; *cf.* 9:26) and their construction as upper and side
rooms of the temple (*cf.* 1 Ki. 6:5ff.; 2 Ch. 3:9; 1 Ch. 9:26). So
the great achievement was *finished* (contrast 'began', 3:1, 2),
ready for the very special opening ceremonies (chs. 5–7).

H. Solomon dedicates the temple (5:2 – 7:22)

i. The ark and the cloud (5:2–14)

'The priests then brought the ark of the LORD's covenant to its
place in the inner sanctuary of the temple, the Most Holy
Place' (5:7).

5:2–11a – *cf.* 1 Kings 8:1–10a

5:13b – *cf.* Psalm 136:1, *etc.*

5:13c–14 – *cf.* 1 Kings 8:10b–11

With the temple preparations which David began as far back
as 1 Chronicles 22:2 now completed (5:1), the story of the
building of the temple reaches its climax. The account
occupies three chapters, 5:2 – 7:22, and is in three phases: (a)
the ark and the cloud of God's presence occupy the temple
(5:2–14); (b) Solomon gives praise to God and prays to him
(6:1–42); (c) God responds with fire and a message of hope
(7:1–22).

The Chronicler has made a number of brief but important
additions to the comparable material in Kings (*e.g.* 5:11b–13a;
7:12b–15). This expansion contrasts with his treatment of the
building work (chs. 3–4) where the earlier account was
reduced by almost 50%, confirming that the Chronicler's real
interest is in what the temple signifies. These chapters therefore are not so much about the temple of God as the God to
whom the temple belongs. There is no better illustration of
this than 5:13c–14, where the priests are unable to carry out
their expected duties because of the overwhelming effect of

God's glorious presence. In other words, as soon as the temple is opened for business, all the carefully planned ceremonies and services have to be suspended because God takes over the entire building for himself. The temple is to be for God's glory, not for that of human beings (*cf.* comment on 1 Ch. 17), as part of his purpose to forgive, heal, and restore his people (7:14).

Chapter 5 sets the scene by concentrating on the final act of furnishing the temple, *i.e.*, the *ark*'s installation in the Most Holy Place (vv. 4–10). Like the *cloud* which subsequently fills the temple (vv. 13c–14), the ark symbolizes God's presence, so that the chapter describes God taking up residence at the centre of his people's life. The ark also speaks of the *covenant* God made with Israel at the exodus (vv. 7–10) – in fact, 'ark of the covenant' is a specially favoured phrase in Chronicles.[1] In this context, it refers particularly to God's commitment to Israel, an emphasis which would have been especially appreciated by Chronicles' original readers. Even though, in their time, the ark had long since disappeared and their own temple was but a shadow of Solomon's glory, this was a reminder that the God represented by these symbols had certainly not abandoned them. Indeed, they could be equally aware of his presence by engaging in praise and worship led by the Levites' musical ministry (vv. 11–14).

The Old Testament sense of divine glory merely prepares the way for its full revelation through the earthly and the exalted Christ (Jn. 1:14). It is particularly associated with certain special moments of Jesus' life, including his birth (Lk. 2:9), his transfiguration (Lk. 9:32), his cross (Jn. 12:23; 13:31–32; 17:1ff.), his ascension (Acts 1:9–11), and the coming of his kingdom (Mt. 24:30; 25:31). God's glory, however, is not confined to the Son of God, but is also granted to believers through the work of the Spirit (2 Cor. 3:18). The New Testament also maintains a strong link between worship and the experience of divine glory, sometimes in the context of Old Testament symbolism such as the ark (*cf.* Heb. 10:19–22; Rev. 11:19). As at the temple dedication, such experiences of God's glory can continue to be quite overwhelming, such as the revelation of the risen Christ given to John (Rev. 1:12–18).

Although most of this chapter is very similar to 1 Kings

[1] 1 Ch. 15:25, 26, 28, 29; 16:6, 37; 17:1; 22:19; 28:2, 18; 2 Ch. 5:2, 7.

8:1–11, the Chronicler's own emphases emerge in two familiar ways. Firstly, a series of mainly minor additions and a substantial addition in verses 11b–13a underline the role of all Israel, especially the Levites. Secondly, the actual wording is influenced by several analogies derived from two earlier Old Testament passages. The chapter as a whole reflects the story of David's transportation of the ark to Jerusalem (though without his difficulties! *Cf.* 1 Ch. 13–16), while verses 13c–14 have strong echoes of the revelation of God's glory at the Tent's dedication ceremony (*cf.* Ex. 40:34–35). These links illustrate the way in which the Chronicler saw God's purposes continuing across the centuries, in this case showing how Solomon's achievements developed the work of both Moses and David. Comparison between Solomon and these earlier leaders does reveal at least one substantial difference, however. Whereas the Tent was a temporary structure and David could only deposit the ark in a temporary home, Solomon's provision for God's earthly residence has a clear sense of finality.

a. Solomon assembles all Israel (5:2–3). When Solomon assembled (vv. 2, 3; *summoned* and *came together* are both from the same Heb. root) the leaders, his action typified the 'good' kings in Chronicles, particularly in connection with temple gatherings (*e.g.* David, 1 Ch. 13:2, 4, 5; 22:2; 23:2; 28:1; 29:1; Solomon, 2 Ch. 1:3, 5; Jehoshaphat, 2 Ch. 20:5, 14, 26; Hezekiah, 2 Ch. 30:13, 23, 25). Several factors hint at a change of emphasis away from Solomon and towards the theme of 1 Chronicles 13 that, as with David, transporting the ark was an act of the people rather than of the king. Emphasis is given to *all the men of Israel* (v. 3), the *elders* (vv. 2, 4) and family heads (v. 2) who represented all the tribes (*cf.* 1 Ch. 2–9), while references to Solomon in 1 Kings 8:1–2 are omitted in verses 2–3.[1]

The event took place at *the festival in the seventh month* (v. 3; *cf.* 7:8–10), *i.e.* Tabernacles (made explicit in Tg. and GNB).

---

[1] The following phrases also occur in 1 Ch. 13–16: 'to assemble/assembly' (vv. 2, 3; *cf.* 1 Ch. 13:2, 4–5; 15:3); 'elders' (vv. 2, 4; *cf.* 1 Ch. 15:25) and other leaders (v. 2; *cf.* 1 Ch. 13:1); 'to bring up the ark' (v. 2; *cf.* 1 Ch. 15:3, 12, 25, *etc.*); 'the ark of the LORD's covenant' (v. 2; *cf.* 1 Ch. 15:25, 26, 28); 'city of David' (v. 2; *cf.* 1 Ch. 15:29); 'all (the men of) Israel' (v. 3; *cf.* 1 Ch. 13:5; 15:3, 28; 16:3).

Since the temple was completed in the eighth month, almost certainly in the previous year (*cf.* 1 Ki. 6:38), an extensive period leading up to the opening ceremony is implied in addition to all the other preparations. Why no reference is made to the Day of Atonement, which should have taken place five days before (*cf.* Lv. 23:27, 34), is not clear, especially given the circumstances which gave rise to the temple (1 Ch. 21) and the emphasis on forgiveness in chapters 6–7. Probably it was either not properly observed throughout the pre-exilic period, or hardly observed at all. Those who first returned from exile celebrated the dedication of the altar at Tabernacles as well (Ezr. 3:4), presumably to underline their continuity with Solomon's temple.

b. The ark's final journey (5:4–6). The functions of the *Levites* (v. 4) and the *priests* (v. 5; *cf.* v. 7) are differentiated in contrast to 1 Kings 8:3–4. Since it was the Levites' special responsibility to carry the ark (*cf.* Nu. 4:15; 1 Ch. 15:14–15), their final action in doing so is specifically mentioned before they take up their temple-based ministries (vv. 12–13). That the 'levitical priests' (JB, *cf.* NIV) assisted them in bringing the *Tent of Meeting* and all its *sacred furnishings* (v. 5) is not surprising if this is the Tent from Gibeon (*cf.* 1 Ch. 16:39; 2 Ch. 1:3). The priests had been based there, while the ark in Jerusalem had been cared for only by Levites (1 Ch. 16:37–42).[1]

Several features indicate that this was Moses' Tent rather than David's (for the latter, *cf.* 1 Ch. 16:1). 'Tent of Meeting' is not used in Kings and Chronicles for any other tent, mention of the holy vessels or furnishings stresses the continuity between Tent and temple (see above, p. 48n.), and the united presence of Asaph, Heman, and Jeduthun (v. 12) alongside the priests confirms the merging of personnel from Gibeon and Jerusalem. Though it may seem surprising that the end of such an important item as Moses' Tent is mentioned only in passing, in reality it was now redundant and unlikely to be in a first-class state of repair. The ark, by contrast, had an ongoing

---

[1] It is unnecessary to restore 'priests and Levites' in v. 5, with the vss and 1 Ki. 8:24, as in most EVV. 'Levitical priests' is a deliberate phrase in Ch. (*cf.* 2 Ch. 23:18; 30:27) based on Dt. 17:9; 18:1, *etc.* If this verse is understood as identifying the main tasks of each group rather than a comprehensive comment on all who were involved, the need for emendation is avoided.

role, even though it was only a symbol of something greater.

The last act of the people ('the whole congregation', REB, NEB), before the ark disappeared for ever from their view was to offer sacrifice (v. 6). While this may have been a thank-offering that the journey had taken place without mishap (*cf.* 1 Ch. 13:9–13; 15:26), it was also an appropriate act of devotion to God for all that the ark represented. The extravagance of the offering was typical of Solomon (*cf.* 7:4; 7), far exceeding the size of David's comparable sacrifice (1 Ch. 15:26).[1]

c. The ark's final resting-place (5:7–10). The *priests* (v. 7) take over from the Levites in bringing the ark into the Holy of Holies, since only the former were allowed there. The tempo of this section slows right down. The only action is contained in the initial verb *brought*, the rest being a description of the ark's surroundings. Four features are mentioned: (a) the ark is located in the *Most Holy Place* (v. 7), also called the *inner sanctuary* (*cf.* 3:8–14); (b) it is completely covered by the *cherubim* (vv. 7b–8; *cf.* 3:10–13); (c) the ends of its carrying *poles* were visible outside the veil, though not outside the temple (v. 9) – this rather quaint note was only for the benefit of priests and Levites, since only they could enter the temple; and (d) it contained the *two tablets* of the *covenant, i.e.* the ten commandments, symbolizing God's permanent commitment to Israel (v. 10).[2] This is a rare mention in Chronicles of the Sinai covenant, but it is clear nevertheless that the exodus from Egypt forms the foundation of God's promises about the temple and Davidic kingship (*cf.* 1 Ch. 17:5, 21). That same divine grace joined not only Solomon's and the Chronicler's generations to God's past promises, but in the same way links today's reader to Christ through the new covenant.[3]

d. God's glory and Israel's praise (5:11–14). With only minor disruption to the syntax, the Chronicler has inserted a

[1] Parallels with 1 Ch. 13–16 in this paragraph include: 'carry (Heb. *nāśā'*) the ark' (v. 4; *cf.* 1 Ch. 15:15, 26, 27); 'Levites' and 'priests' (vv. 4, 5, 7; *cf.* 1 Ch. 15:2ff., 11ff.); sacrifice on the journey (v. 6; *cf.* 1 Ch. 15:26).

[2] For an explanation of how *extending from the ark* (NIV) could have arisen instead of 'from the Holy Place' (NRSV, RSV, *etc.*, with 1 Ki. 8:8), see L. C. Allen, *The Greek Chronicles*, 2, *SVT* 27 (Leiden: Brill, 1974), p. 145.

[3] Compare with 1 Ch. 13–16: a 'place' for the ark (v. 7; *cf.* 1 Ch. 15:1, 3); 'poles' (vv. 8, 9; *cf.* 1 Ch. 15:15); 'Moses' (v. 10; *cf.* 1 Ch. 15:15).

long parenthesis into a simple sentence in 1 Kings 8:10, 'When the priests withdrew from the Holy Place [v. 11a here], the cloud filled the temple of the LORD [v. 13c here]'. The addition gives two further reasons why the cloud of glory filled the temple. The *priests, en masse* and apparently with some enthusiasm (*regardless of their divisions*), had *consecrated themselves* (v. 11b; *cf.* 1 Ch. 15:12, 14; 2 Ch. 23:6; 26:18; 29:5ff.). Then a united orchestra and chorus of *Levites* from Gibeon (*Heman* and *Jeduthun*) and Jerusalem (*Asaph*), together with *120 priests sounding trumpets*, joined in a song taken from the Psalms to praise God for his goodness and love (*e.g.* Pss. 107:1; 118:1; 136:1; *cf.* 2 Ch. 7:3; Ezr. 3:11). Priests and Levites were indicating through their unity, commitment, and praise their desire to worship God, and the Chronicler clearly intends this to be seen as an example to be followed. When God's people set themselves apart for him to express heartfelt worship and praise, God will surely respond with some sign of his presence.

For the priests' *divisions* (v. 11), see comment on 1 Chronicles 24. While blowing *trumpets* (v. 13) was the only musical activity in which the priests engaged (*cf.* 1 Ch. 15:24, 28), the Levites' musical service was their major function once the ark was installed (*cf.* 1 Ch. 6:31–32; 23:30–31; 25:1–31). In this way, they verbalized Israel's praise in God's very presence. Their position *east . . . of the altar* (v. 12), *i.e.* between the great bronze altar in the courtyard and the temple door, demonstrated their unity with the people and their closeness to God. *Fine linen* seems to have been their special clothing, since it is mentioned in connection with the Levites only here and in 1 Chronicles 15:27. Their unity is underlined by a double expression, *in unison* and *as with one voice* (v. 13a).

The quotation from the Psalms (v. 13b) encapsulates in a sentence what the entire temple project was about, that over the years since God's first promise to David (1 Ch. 17:12), God's faithful *love* (Heb. *ḥeseḏ*) had ensured the project's success. Underlying the temple was the person of God: *He* is good.[1] That is why he responds to Israel's worship with what later Jews called the shekinah glory (vv. 13c–14). Both in the case of the *cloud* and the *glory* filling the temple, the associations with Moses are very close (especially Ex. 40:34–35).

---

[1] *It* is good' (REB, NEB) is surely wrong. This well-known phrase never has this impersonal sense elsewhere, and in any case the quotation really begins with 'the LORD' (*cf.* Ps. 107:1; 118:1; 136:1).

Clouds are a particularly rich biblical symbol of God's presence (*e.g.* Ex. 13:31–32; Dn. 7:13; Acts 1:9), emphasizing his mystery and majesty. The temple could never belong to humankind, not even to priests who, though they had sanctified themselves, now found it quite impossible to carry out any of their prescribed tasks.[1]

ii. Solomon's praise and prayer (6:1–42)

'Hear from heaven, your dwelling-place; and when you hear, forgive' (6:21).

6:1–12 – *cf.* 1 Kings 8:12–22
6:14–39 – *cf.* 1 Kings 8:23–50a
6:41–42 – *cf.* Psalm 132:8–10, 1

Now that God has taken up residence in his house, Solomon responds in praise and prayer. His words fall into three parts: (a) prayer of response to the cloud of God's glory (vv. 1–2); (b) testimony about God's faithfulness to David's house (vv. 3–11); (c) dedicatory prayer for the temple (vv. 12–42).

The first two sections look backward, praising God for keeping two promises – to dwell with his people (vv. 1–2; *cf. e.g.* Ex. 25:8; 29:44–46) and to establish Solomon on David's throne (vv. 3–11; *cf.* 1 Ch. 17:10–14; 22:6–13; 28:2–10). The third looks forward to the prayers to be offered in and towards the temple, examples of which are found in 2 Chronicles 10–36 (*cf. e.g.* vv. 24–25 with 2 Ch. 20:1–30 or vv. 36–39 with 2 Ch. 33:10–13). The theme of the temple as a house of thanksgiving and of intercession clearly occupies a central place within Chronicles.

This chapter forms a vital link between Chronicles' two major words from God. Its foundation is God's covenant promise to build David a house (1 Ch. 17:10–14), and its development occurs in God's promise about the temple (2 Ch. 7:12–22). It therefore shows how prayer plays a key role in the unfolding of God's will for humankind.

---

[1] The links in this paragraph with 1 Ch. 13–16 are particularly extensive, because it contains Chr.'s major contribution to the ch.: 'consecrated themselves' (v. 11; *cf.* 1 Ch. 15:12, 14); 'musicians' (vv. 12–13; *cf.* 1 Ch. 15:16, 19, 27); 'Asaph, Heman, Jeduthun' (v. 12; *cf.* 1 Ch. 15:17, 19; 16:37, 41, 42); 'fine linen' (v. 12; *cf.* Ch. 15:27); 'cymbals, harps, lyres' (v. 12; *cf.* 1 Ch. 15:16, 19–21, 28; 16:5); priests blowing 'trumpets' (v. 12; *cf.* 1 Ch. 15:24; 16:6); 'to give praise and thanks' (v. 13; *cf.* 1 Ch. 16:4, 7, 36); 'to raise the voice' (v. 13; *cf.* 1 Ch. 15:16); quotation from psalms (v. 13; *cf.* 1 Ch. 16:8–36); 'He is good, his love endures for ever' (v. 13; *cf.* 1 Ch. 16:34).

The chapter keeps remarkably close to the Chronicler's main source (1 Ki. 8:12–50). A few changes are worth noting, however, including two points where Chronicles seems to have preserved a text superior to Kings (vv. 5b–6a, 13; for details, see Rudolph, Dillard). From what appear to be Chronicles' special contributions, two emphases may be discerned. Firstly, there are signs of a more contemporary application. For example, some aspects of the Kings text relating to specific historical incidents are omitted, such as details of the exodus (*cf.* v. 11 with 1 Ki. 8:21; also 1 Ki. 8:50b–53) and the word 'today' in 1 Kings 8:28 (*cf.* v. 19 here), while adding *to them* in verse 25 (*cf.* 1 Ki. 8:34) applies the gift of the land to every generation of pray-ers. Similarly, the use of *according to my law* (v. 16) for 'before me' (1 Ki. 8:25) probably reflects the interest of the post-exilic community in the guiding principles established by Ezra and Nehemiah (Ezr. 7–10; Ne. 7–13). Secondly, a reduced emphasis on the exodus is replaced by a new focus on the covenant with David. This is apparent not only in the importance of verses 5–11, 14–17, but above all from the use of a paraphrase of parts of Psalm 132 as a new ending in place of 1 Kings 8:50b–53. Although the Mosaic covenant and the exodus clearly remain the foundation of the Davidic promises (*cf.* vv. 5, 11, 32), the prominence of the Davidic covenant is unmistakable.

The most likely reason for these changes is that they affirm the central significance of the temple for post-exilic Israel. Chronicles brings out two features of this. Firstly, the temple was a symbol of God's sovereign rule promised to David's family. By preserving Solomon's request for God to go on keeping his promise to David (vv. 16–17), the Chronicler was giving a clear signal that even in his day, David's kingdom still had a future. Secondly, the temple was a reminder to the scattered post-exilic community, whether they were near to or far from Jerusalem (*cf.* v. 36), that it was God's earthly dwelling-place and constituted a permanent invitation to confident prayer. The joining of these elements together amounts to a permanent invitation to pray for the visible coming of God's kingdom. 'Your kingdom come' would have been a highly appropriate motto for the temple.

Of course, by Jesus' time, the earthly temple had almost outlived its usefulness, and Jesus gives different reasons for encouraging his people to pray. But despite the differences,

Jesus' teaching about prayer, especially in John 14–17, has several emphases remarkably similar to this chapter. For example, there is a close connection between praying in Jesus' name (*e.g.* Jn. 14:13–14; 16:23–24) and praying towards the temple that bears God's name (*e.g.* vv. 5, 6, 7, and fourteen times in all in this chapter). The name of God has always been the signature over which God's people bring their requests to him. Another link is between the presence of the Holy Spirit with each Christian (*e.g.* Jn. 14:16–18; Rom. 8:26–27) and God's continual presence with Israel in the temple. The presence of God, by whatever means, is a real stimulus and encouragement to prayer. Though we now approach God in his dwelling-place in heaven (v. 18; *cf.* Eph. 4:10; Heb. 10:19–22), our praying still needs his help here on earth just as vitally as in Old Testament times. Indeed, without the Spirit's presence and the authority of Jesus' name, we cannot pray at all.

a. Solomon responds to God's glory (6:1–2). This brief statement, which is part testimony and part prayer, evokes a sense of wonder that the same God whose glory fills the temple (5:13–14) also dwells in 'thick darkness' (v. 1, NRSV, RSV, REB, NEB). This latter phrase is associated with the cloud of God's mysterious presence at Mount Sinai (Ex. 20:21; Dt. 5:22) and with his appearing on the Day of the Lord (Joel 2:2; Zp. 1:15). Solomon is amazed that this intangible, sovereign deity whose mystery is symbolized by the darkness of the windowless Holy of Holies now promises to *dwell* in this temple (v. 2). The theme of God's dual residence cascades through the chapter, without ever being logically resolved. It is enough to know that God lives on earth as well as in heaven. Even though the temple is 'exalted' (NRSV, RSV, KB; *cf.* REB, NEB), it cannot physically contain God any more than he can be confined by human philosophy. And yet anyone can approach him in prayer (vv. 18–40).

b. Solomon's testimony to God's promise (6:3–11). Solomon now addresses the *whole assembly* (vv. 3, 12, 13). This phrase is taken over from 1 Kings, but it fits in with Chronicles' theme that the temple is for the people, not just the king (*cf.* 2 Ch. 5:2–3; also 1 Ch. 13:2ff.; 15:3). Even when Solomon *blessed* the people in his priestly role (v. 3; *cf.* 1 Ch. 16:2), he acted as the people's representative rather than one completely set apart for religious duties. He prayed as a sinner, as one of the people (*cf.* v. 36). This was supposed to be the people's temple (*cf.* Lk. 18:9–14), even though it sometimes became little more than a royal sanctuary (*cf.* 2 Ki. 18:10–18; 21:4–7).

Solomon gives thanks for the way God has made the recent sequence of events possible. He mentions three things: (a) that he *succeeded* David as king (v. 10), (b) that he has been enabled to build the temple (v. 10), and (c) that the *ark* has been placed in its proper home (v. 11). All this is in fulfilment of what God had said to *David* (vv. 4, 10) and of the covenant made in the exodus (vv. 5, 11).

The important notion of fulfilment is expressed through a series of anthropomorphisms. God has fulfilled with his *hands* (v. 4, *cf.* v. 15) what he promised with his *mouth* (vv. 4, 10; *cf.* v. 15). These phrases are typical of chapters 6–7, where various physical terms are attributed to God. As well as hands and mouth, his eyes (vv. 20, 40; *cf.* 7:15–16), his ears (v. 40; *cf.* 7:15), and even his heart (7:16) are said to be present in the temple. Though only Jesus is God incarnate, the temple was a clear sign that God in all his being was committed to living among his people. The mention of God's hands (lit. 'fulfilled with his hands') really means that God's actions have confirmed his words – it is as if God's unseen hands were active in all the human hands who contributed to the construction work (*cf.* 1 Ch. 29:16).[1]

God fulfils (vv. 4, 10–11) what appear to be two prophecies (vv. 5–6, 8–9) given to David. In reality, these 'prophecies' are an amalgam of three earlier versions of the Davidic covenant (for Chronicles' tendency to condense various divine messages into a single unit, *cf.* 1 Ch. 10:13; 11:3). *Since the day I brought my people out of Egypt* (v. 5) is based on 1 Chronicles 17:5, and the rest of verses 5–6 follow 1 Chronicles 28:4–6 closely. Verse 7 is based on 1 Chronicles 22:7; 28:3, the phrase *you are not the one to build the temple* (v. 9) has close parallels in 1 Chronicles 17:4; 22:8; 28:3, and 'your son who shall be born to you shall build the house for my name' (v. 9, NRSV) should be compared with 1 Chronicles 17:11–12; 22:9–10; 28:6. Even the *throne of Israel* (v. 10; *cf.* 1 Ch. 28:5) and the *ark* (v. 11; *cf.* 1 Ch. 22:19;

---

[1] For an identical expression, *cf.* Je. 44:25.

28:3) have echoes in all three passages, so that this entire speech is shot through with the conviction that God's words have been fulfilled in every detail.

Four emphases stand out in the speech. Firstly, the focus on God's choice in verses 5–6 is emphatic and unusual (it is paralleled in Ch. only in 1 Ch. 28:4–6). Here God's original choice of *David* and *Jerusalem* is in mind, rather than of Solomon as in 1 Chronicles 28. This specific link of chosen king and chosen city is rare in the Old Testament, being found mainly in the Psalms (*e.g.* Pss. 2:6–7; 78:67–72). The second emphasis is the rather surprising commendation for David's heartfelt desire to build the temple, in contrast to his previous disqualification because of his wars (v. 8; *cf.* 1 Ch. 22:8–9; 28:3). In fact, this is a complementary rather than contradictory statement. It confirms that David's disqualification was not due to sin, but because the concept of God's rest must be regarded as the unique and final stage in building the temple (*cf.* v. 41). David's motives actually set a pattern for others to follow, for a right attitude of heart is essential for any worship (vv. 14, 30; *cf.* 1 Ch. 29:17–19; Mk. 7:6). Thirdly, the temple was especially associated with God's *Name* (vv. 5, 6, 7, 8, 9, 10). This typically Deuteronomic idea fits in well with the chapter's over-all sense of God's presence in earth and heaven, though here it extends to the idea of God's choice (see also on vv. 18–21). Finally, there are more frequent reminders than usual in Chronicles that the Sinai covenant underlies all that God is doing. As well as specific mentions in verses 5 and 11, references to the 'thick darkness' (v. 1, NRSV, RSV; *dark cloud*, NIV; *cf.* Ex. 20:21; Dt. 5:22), 'covenant of love' (v. 41; *cf.* Dt. 7:9), or God's 'mighty hand and outstretched arm' (v. 32; *cf.* Dt. 5:15) indicate that all who worship in the temple are indebted to God's mighty love and power demonstrated in the exodus. Unusually, the *covenant* (v. 11) is identified with the tablets of the ten commandments.

c. Solomon's dedicatory prayer (6:12–42). Solomon turned towards the *altar* (v. 12), *knelt down* (v. 13), and *spread out his hands* (vv. 12–13). These various postures for prayer and worship are attested throughout the Bible (for standing, Ne. 9:2; Rev. 7:9; for kneeling, Ps. 95:6; Eph. 3:14; for lifting hands, Ps. 28:2; 1 Tim. 2:8). The altar as the place of sacrifice has an important if often overlooked role in the dedication ceremony (vv. 12, 23; 7:7, 9, 12; *cf.* 4:1):. Verbal prayer is not necessarily superior to sacrifice, despite the comments of some (*e.g.* Williamson, Ackroyd, McConville). Biblical worship includes the offering of physical gifts as well as prayer and praise (*e.g.* Phil. 4:18; Heb. 13:15–16).

The exact nature of the structure on which Solomon stood (v. 13) is unclear, but was most probably a temporary *platform* or dais made specially for the occasion (*cf.* Ne. 8:4). The fact that its dimensions are identical to those of the Tent's bronze altar (*cf.* Ex. 27:1; 38:1) is probably coincidental.[1] Also, the suggestion (Wellhausen, Mosis) that it is included as a means of diminishing Solomon's priestly role in the light of Uzziah's error (2 Ch. 26:16–20) seems unnecessary. The *altar* where Uzziah transgressed was the inner altar, whereas this was the altar of burnt offering outside where laymen could offer sacrifices (*e.g.* Lv. 4:22–24, 27–29). Further, the word for *court* (v. 13) is a rare term used in 2 Chronicles 4:9 for the outer court, and, with the Levites positioned between the altar and the temple (5:12), there is no way in which Solomon's action could be regarded as parallel with Uzziah's.

The prayer itself is in four main sections: (i) request for continuing fulfilment of the Davidic covenant (vv. 14–17); (ii) basic principles of intercession (vv. 18–21); (iii) Situations in which prayer might be offered (vv. 22–40); (iv) request for God's continuing presence and power (vv. 41–42).

i. Request for continuing fulfilment of the Davidic covenant (6:14–17). As with so many prayers in Scripture, Solomon begins with praise (vv. 14–15) before making any requests (vv. 16–17). The praise concentrates on two aspects of God's nature, that he is unique (*there is no God like you in heaven or on earth*, v. 14a), and that he is faithful to his *covenant of love* with his obedient people (vv. 14b–15). Mention of the Davidic covenant seems to inspire repeated praise about God's incomparability (1 Ch. 17:20; *cf.* 1 Ch. 16:25–26; 2 Ch. 2:5). Such praise arises from hearts committed to God (*wholeheartedly*, JB, NIV, v. 14), a repeated emphasis in this chapter (vv. 7, 8, 30; *cf.* 1 Ch. 29:17–19). *Now* (v. 16) introduces Solomon's request, that God's *promises* to David's line should continue to 'be confirmed' (v. 17, REB, NEB, NRSV, RSV; *come true*, NIV, GNB). David

[1] Against Mosis, *UTCG*, pp. 145–146.

had made an identical petition (1 Ch. 17:23–24), and both prayers indicate that God often looks for people to work with him in prayer rather than him fulfilling his purposes automatically (*cf*. 'Your will be done on earth as it is in heaven').

ii. Basic principles of intercession (6:18–21). Understanding what prayer is means understanding who and where God is. Solomon therefore precedes his main requests by acknowledging that even heavenly superlatives cannot limit God (*even the highest heavens cannot contain you*, v. 18). This does not mean, however, that God is far away or that prayer is an exercise in remote control. Solomon reaffirms that God also dwells *on earth with men* (v. 18; *cf.* vv. 1–2). The temple's function is to locate God, not to limit him, to bring human beings into direct contact with the one whose *dwelling-place* is in *heaven* (v. 21; *cf.* vv. 30, 33, 39).

A basic pattern for intercessory prayer follows in verses 19–21. Five essential elements of intercession are mentioned, and several phrases are repeated throughout the chapter.

(a) The words for *prayer* are characterized by sincerity and urgency ('supplication', vv. 19, 21, 24, 35, 37, which is really a *plea for mercy*, as NIV in v. 19; *cry*, v. 19; call, v. 33, RSV).

(b) God is called upon to have his *eyes* open (vv. 20, 40) and especially to *hear* (vv. 19, 20, 21, 23, 25, 27, 30, 33, 35, 39, 40). This seems to be the central issue. If God hears, Solomon is content that prayer requests will be properly dealt with (*cf.* 2 Ch. 7:12–16).

(c) The prayers to be offered in or towards *this house/place* (vv. 18, 20, 21, 22, 24, 26, 29, 32, 33, 34, 38, 40) come before God (v. 19) in his heavenly dwelling (vv. 21, 30, 33, 39). This is because God's *Name* is on this temple (vv. 20, 34, 38; *cf.* vv. 5, 6, 7, 8, 9, 10, 24, 26, 32, 33). To pray in or towards this temple is to pray to or in the name of the God to whom it belongs, which is the Old Testament equivalent of prayer in the name of Jesus (*cf. e.g.* Jn. 14:13; Acts 2:21). The name here is a symbol of God's presence and authority, and is a kind of seal upon the covenant promises signified by the temple.

(d) Prayers may be offered by individuals (vv. 19, 22), by *your people Israel* (vv. 21, 24, 25, 26, 29, 34, 39) or even by *foreigners* (vv. 32–33). God is accessible to anyone who acknowledges Yahweh as *my God* (vv. 19, 40), as *God of Israel* (v. 14), or as having a *great name* (v. 32).

(e) To *forgive* sins is the purpose of most of these prayers (vv. 21, 25, 27, 30, 39). This is not to diminish the importance of other types of prayers, such as for guidance, meditation, or adoration, but to draw attention to humanity's basic need before God. Three observations may be made on this point. Firstly, the promise of forgiveness addresses the real need for setting up the temple, both in the case of David (1 Ch. 21) and of all Israel (*e.g.* 1 Ch. 5:25; 9:1; 2 Ch. 36:14). Secondly, every prayer of intercession is necessarily offered by sinners. Every petition must therefore be made on the basis of a sin-offering, which for Christians is the sacrifice of Jesus, the Lamb of God. Thirdly, the fact that forgiveness is available in and through the temple shows that atonement is available through prayer and sacrifice together. Christ's sin-offering on the cross affirms the fact of forgiveness, but it becomes accessible only as we pray.

iii. Situations in which prayer might be offered (6:22–40). The temple was to be a permanent invitation and inspiration to come and pray, and no-one was to be excluded, not even despised tax collectors (Lk. 18:9–14). In national defeat, in affliction, as a foreigner, even when under God's deserved punishment, the temple on earth and in heaven (Heb. 9:23–24; Rev. 21:22) was the God-assured route to forgiveness and restoration.

Seven different scenarios, each depicting a situation where many might regard prayer as useless, illustrate the extent of the invitation. Some are related to covenant curses (Dt. 28:15–68; *cf.* Lv. 26:14–45), indicating that even divinely deserved punishment can be reversed through repentance and prayer (see details below and *cf.* Gal. 3:10–14). Each paragraph follows the same pattern: (a) a situation of need, usually involving sin; (b) temple-based prayer and confession; (c) request for God to hear; (d) restoration and forgiveness.

The situations are as follows:

(a) The taking of oaths (vv. 22–23). An unproven accusation can be settled only by taking an oath before the Lord (*cf.* Ex. 22:7–12; Nu. 5:11–28). Where no human being can justly decide, Solomon asks God to be the effective and righteous Judge (*cf.* Gn. 18:25; Heb. 12:23).

(b) National defeat (vv. 24–25; *cf.* Dt. 28:25; Lv. 26:17). Even corporate *sin* can be forgiven through repentance, when

328

people *confess your name* (also v. 26). Exile is apparently assumed (v. 25), though since prayer in the temple is expected, it seems to be more limited than that envisaged in verses 36–39.

(c) Drought (vv. 26–27; *cf.* Dt. 28:23–24; Lv. 26:19). *Rain* was regarded as one of God's special gifts (Dt. 28:12; Je. 5:24), and its prolonged absence was often seen as a sign of God's anger (*cf.* 2 Ch. 7:13). Restoration involved obeying God's *teach*ing (v. 27) as well as confession (v. 26). The word for 'teach' (*tôrê* from *yrh*) may be intended to recall the word for the law (*tôrâ*; *cf.* v. 16), since the law was given for God's people to live by (Dt. 8:3; Rom. 10:5).

(d) Disasters and diseases (vv. 28:31; *cf.* Dt. 28:21–22). Several different types of affliction are mentioned, including epidemics, plant diseases, insect invasions, enemies, or individual illness. Though the request to *forgive* (v. 30) again assumes sin as the underlying cause, these troubles have to be seen in the light of Deuteronomy 28:21–22, to which this section corresponds quite closely. The real problem is covenant disobedience arising from wickedness in the human *heart* (v. 30; *cf.* vv. 7, 8, 14; 1 Ch. 29:17–19; Mk. 7:14–23), for which the solution is to *walk*, *i.e.* live, in God's *ways* (v. 31).

(e) Foreigners (vv. 32–33). This is the most fascinating paragraph in the prayer, and is adopted with minimal changes from 1 Kings. It envisages immigrants, resident aliens, or pilgrims worshipping in the temple because of what they have heard about the exodus (*cf.* Jos. 2:8–13), a situation without parallel in Chronicles. However, the idea that other nations will *fear*, *i.e.* worship, Yahweh (v. 33) is typical of Chronicles, so that the paragraph is certainly not out of place (*cf.* 1 Ch. 14:17; 2 Ch. 20:29). What is especially notable is that foreigners could know and fear God 'like your people Israel' (v. 33, REB). This hope of equality in worship was rarely expressed in the Old Testament (*e.g.* Gn. 12:3; Is. 19:24–25; Zc. 8:20–22), and even Jesus' closest disciples found its fulfilment hard to take (Acts 10:1 – 11:18).

(f) War (vv. 34–35). This is the only section where Israel is pictured on the offensive rather than the defensive, though the conflict is qualified by the phrase *wherever you send them* (v. 34; *cf. e.g.* 2 Ch. 13:4–13; 14:11). The prayer is not for forgiveness, but for God to *uphold their cause* (v. 35; *cf.* v. 39; Ps. 20).

(g) Exile (vv. 36–39). This final section brings together many themes in the prayer to describe the worst possible scenario for any Israelite, which was to be removed from the Promised Land and from God's presence in the temple. The same principles still apply, however, though a deeper intensity is noticeable. Confession for sin (v. 37) is in triplicate, repentance is *with all their heart and soul* (v. 38), and prayer is directed towards the *land* and *city* as well as the temple (v. 39). The sense that sin is all-pervading dominates, epitomized in one of the clearest biblical statements about sin's universality (*there is no-one who does not sin*, v. 36). No greater indication of the need for a place of atonement and forgiveness could be given.

Solomon concludes by asking God to have his *eyes* and *ears open* to all such prayers (v. 40). The secret of prayer is again concerned with the presence of God (*cf.* v. 20), and the request will soon be answered (7:15).

iv. Request for God's continuing presence and power (6:41–42). The most extensive changes from the original prayer occur right at the end (the same thing happened in 1 Ch. 16:8–36), suggesting that verses 41–42 were especially important for the Chronicler. A special feature is that whereas the rest of the chapter corresponds closely to its source in 1 Kings 8, these verses are a free adaptation from a quite different passage (Ps. 132). Another variation is that this final prayer is based on God's covenant with David whereas 1 Kings 8:50b–53 is based on the Sinai covenant.

Solomon finally asks God to *arise . . . and come to your resting place* (v. 41). Since these verses are almost certainly the Chronicler's own adaptation of the original psalm, this is a prayer asking God to do for his own generation what he had done for Solomon and those who worshipped in the first temple. He wants the God who appeared in cloud and glory (5:13–14; 7:1–3) to continue to reveal himself in 'power' (JB, GNB) or *might* (NIV, NRSV, RSV). Since the ark signified God's permanent rest in Israel (*your resting place, cf.* 1 Ch. 28:2), it was an appropriate symbol of that power, and even though the ark no longer existed in the Chronicler's day, it recalled a God who had promised never to forsake his people.

The request for God's presence leads to four further requests: (a) that the *priests* should be *clothed with salvation* (v. 41), *i.e.* that they should be fully committed to their God-given ministry of bringing salvation to Israel (*cf.* Is. 61:10); (b) that the *saints rejoice* in his *goodness* (v. 41). The 'saints' in the Old Testament are always God's people (Pss. 85:9; 148:14), who here are filled with joy (*cf.* Ps. 16:11); (c) that God's anointed ones (some Heb. MSS; *anointed one* EVV)[1] are not *rejected* (v. 42; the plural probably refers to the Davidic kings as a group parallel to the priests (v. 41), though it might include kings and priests together); (d) that God should *remember* the *love* of/for *David* (v. 42). It is difficult to be sure of the precise translation, but the objective genitive (NIV, JB, GNB, NRSV, RSV) is preferable for the following reasons: it is supported by the general context of the prayer, especially verses 11, 14–17; this appears to be the meaning in the phrase's only other occurrence in Isaiah 55:3; this is the sense of Psalm 132:11–12; and Chronicles usually refers to David in terms of God's promises to him. The subjective meaning (REB, NEB) cannot be supported from 2 Chronicles 32:32; 35:26, since these verses do not have the precise phrase *ḥasᵉḏê Dāwîḏ*, while the fact that verse 42b is loosely based on Psalm 132:1 does not mean that both verses have to say the same.

iii. God's answer to prayer (7:1–22)

'If my people, who are called by my name, will humble themselves and pray . . ., then I will hear from heaven and forgive their sin and will heal their land' (7:14).

7:1a – *cf.* 1 Kings 8:54a
7:4–5 – *cf.* 1 Kings 8:62–63
7:7–8 – *cf.* 1 Kings 8:64–65
7:10–12a – *cf.* 1 Kings 8:66 – 9:3a
7:16–22 – *cf.* 1 Kings 9:3b – 9

Chapter 7 is not only central to the message of Chronicles, but it is also one of the most important chapters in the Old Testament. It offers hope to any who call on the name of the

---

[1] Though 'anointed one' occurs in both LXX and Ps. 132:10 and is favoured by most commentators, the plural reading must be given serious consideration (*cf.* Dillard, Myers). Not only is it less easy to explain how an original singular might have become corrupted, but the plural is consistent with the priests and the saints as the two preceding objects of Solomon's prayer. In its favour too is the Chronicler's use of the only other instance of 'anointed ones' in the OT (1 Ch. 16:22; and parallel Ps. 105:15), and his interest in the Davidic dynasty and David and Solomon's joint kingship rather than in individual kings (*cf.* the preference for David and Solomon for an earlier singular form in 1 Ch. 18:8 (*cf.* 2 Sa. 8:8) and 2 Ch. 7:10 (*cf.* 1 Ki. 8:66); *cf.* also *e.g.* 2 Ch. 11:17; 30:26).

Lord, even if they have incurred God's wrath, because God's desire is for full reconciliation. The over-all theme is encapsulated in a passage most of which is unique to Chronicles (vv. 12–16), and which contains one of the best-known verses in Chronicles (v. 14).

The chapter is in two parallel sections, both of which are about answered prayer. The genuineness of God's promise about forgiveness and healing (vv. 11–22) is confirmed and preceded by a very public and dramatic reply to Solomon's prayer (vv. 1–10; *cf.* 6:14–42). The wider context is also important, however. Verses 12b–22 are in the form of a direct message from God which must be read alongside God's earlier promise about David's dynasty and the temple (1 Ch. 17:3–15). Together, they form the foundation for the Chronicler's entire work, with the earlier passage providing a secure basis for God's invitation here. The account of the Divided Monarchy which follows (chapters 10–36) then demonstrates by actual examples how God answered prayer on the principles of verses 12–16 (*e.g.* 2 Ch. 20:1–30; 33:10–23).

The significance of such a message would have been easily understood in post-exilic Israel. By presenting the temple as a place where right sacrifice and prayer could be accepted, an opening was being provided to exchange Israel's present bleak circumstances for a more positive future. It offered an opportunity to change the course of Israel's history. Sadly, the story of the post-exilic and intertestamental periods shows that this opportunity was largely ignored, despite the few who continued to look for the consolation of Israel (Lk. 2:25).

Perhaps surprisingly, the New Testament makes no direct reference to this chapter, though it does develop several of its themes. The theme of answered prayer, for example, is central to the teaching of Jesus, and Christians are assured that God hears and answers prayers offered in Jesus' name (Jn. 14:13–14). Even when the prayer is one of repentance for sin, God's kindness (Rom. 2:4) will certainly lead to renewal of salvation (2 Cor. 7:9–11) and fellowship with God (Rev. 3:18–22). Christians are invited too to pray towards God's heavenly temple, where his throne of grace promises mercy and grace in needy times (Heb. 4:16). The availability of such a direct route to God's heavenly sanctuary offers even greater encouragement to draw near to God than Solomon had in his experience of God's glory (2 Ch. 7:1–3, 15–16).

A greater number of significant changes from Chronicles' source text have taken place than in chapters 5–6. The most notable are the addition of verses 1b–3 and 12b–16a, both of which deal with the theme of God's purposes in answering prayer. Some freedom has also been exercised in verses 17–22 (*cf.* 1 Ki. 9:4–9), though it mainly simplifies the original and is of little theological significance. The major additions, however, have achieved a marked change of emphasis as compared with 1 Kings 8:54 – 9:9. In place of a repeated challenge to obedience, God invites both obedient and disobedient people to experience God's healing and joy. Israel's need in this context is to find their way back to him. It is therefore inadequate to characterize verses 11–22, as most commentators do, as illustrating the principle of immediate retribution. Even though retribution is sometimes given a positive connotation, this is a technical usage which is not paralleled by the general meaning of the word. This restoration, furthermore, is given not because it is deserved in any sense but because of God's undeserving favour. The repentant were still sinners who needed to be forgiven, and for that they were totally dependent on God's kindness. Those who deserved retribution were really the unrepentant, but even their punishment was not necessarily immediate. The retribution which led to the temple's destruction (vv. 20–22) resulted from persistent rather than short-term disobedience. Above all, the temple remained 'the lasting symbol of God's will to forgive'.[1]

a. God's fire and glory (7:1–3). 'As' (v. 1, REB) Solomon was finishing his prayer (6:14–42; rather than *when* he had finished as implied by most EVV), God responded by sending *fire from heaven* (vv. 1, 3). The fire was a traditional if unexpected sign of God's direct response to prayer (*cf.* 1 Ch. 21:26; 1 Ki. 18:38; Lv. 9:24), whose chief New Testament analogy is the tongues of fire on the day of Pentecost in response to the prayers of the early church (*cf.* Acts 1:14; 2:1–4). Here, however, it signifies the provision of atonement through the temple. This theme is in fact one of several associations with the story of David's sin in 1 Chronicles 21 (1 Ch. 21:26). Other links include the necessity of forgiveness (v.

[1] De Vries, p. 266.

14; *cf.* 1 Ch. 21:8, 17), plague as a punishment for sin (v. 13; *cf.* 1 Ch. 21:12, 14), the provision of an altar as a means of atonement (v. 12; *cf.* 1 Ch. 21:18), the necessity of humble prayer (v. 14; *cf.* 1 Ch. 21:16), and the bringing of sacrificial offerings (v. 7; *cf.* 1 Ch. 21:26). In both instances, fire consumed *burnt offerings* and *fellowship offerings* (*cf.* v. 7; 1 Ch. 21:26) laid on an *altar* God ordered to be built (*cf.* 21:18, 26).[1] The altar itself was a reminder both of God's gracious forgiveness (1 Ch. 21:8, 17; *cf.* 2 Ch. 6:26, 38) and of any plague sent to punish sin (1 Ch. 21:12, 14, 22; *cf.* 2 Ch. 6:28). The house of prayer and of sacrifice was therefore God's decisive answer to Satan's incitements (*cf.* 1 Ch. 21:1).

While the fire descended, God's *glory* seems to have continued both to fill the temple (vv. 1–3; *cf.* 5:13–14) and to overflow it. It was seen *above the temple* as well as inside it, and was visible to *all the Israelites* (v. 3). The description of the scene includes some fairly obvious allusions to several Pentateuchal passages, such as Exodus 40:34–35 (glory), Leviticus 9:23–24 (fire), and Exodus 20:18; 24:10 (the people watching).[2] Here as elsewhere in Chronicles, Moses' generation provided a model for the Chronicler. The paragraph also reflects other parts of the Old Testament, such as prophetic descriptions of temple glory (Is. 6:1–4; Ezk. 43:1–5), and the Psalms' repeated praise for God's eternal love (vv. 3, 6; *cf.* Pss. 106:1; 107:1ff.; 118:1, 29; 136:1; *cf.* Je. 33:11). God's glory is regularly revealed throughout biblical times, though it is most clearly visible in Jesus (Jn. 1:14–17).

b. Israel's sacrifice and praise (7:4–10).
This experience of God's presence led directly to great joy in worship, and Chronicles' record of the occasion is illustrated by several typical themes. For example, mention of *the king and all the people* (vv. 4–5; *cf.* 1 Ch. 15:28; 2 Ch. 1:3) shows the people as a whole joining in worship. Secondly, *priests* and *Levites* took particular care of the musical side of worship (v. 6) as well as the *sacrifices* (vv. 4, 5, 7), notably through the priests' use of *trumpets* (v. 6 is additional to the original: *cf.* 1 Ch. 15:24; 2 Ch. 5:12; 29:26). The intention was perhaps to encourage Chronicles' readers to make more use of music in worship. The

---

[1] The term *sacrifices* (v. 1) means the same type of offering as that described as 'fellowship offering' (NIV) or 'peace offering' (RSV; *cf.* 1 Ch. 21:26; 2 Ch. 7:7).
[2] See Japhet, *Ideology*, pp. 72–74; Mosis, *UTCG*, pp. 148–152.

'help' of the Levites in offering 'praise' is also noteworthy (REB, *cf*. NRSV, RSV; for 'help', *cf*. 1 Ch. 12:17–22; 22:17; 2 Ch. 14:11). Thirdly, *David* and *Solomon*'s joint involvement in the temple project is indicated by a background comment on the *musical instruments* (v. 6; *cf*. the addition of 'and Solomon' in v. 10 and *e.g.* 2 Ch. 1:4; 11:17). David's provision of musical instruments is mentioned in 1 Chronicles 23:5 (*cf*. 2 Ch. 29:26–27). Finally, the ceremony demonstrates further continuity between the principles of worship in the Tent and the temple. The offering of large numbers of *sacrifices* (v. 4; *cf*. Nu. 7:87–88) and making the *dedication of the altar* a central feature of the ceremony (v. 9; *cf*. Ex. 29:44; Nu. 7:84, 88) are reflections of the Mosaic system of worship.

It is impossible to assess whether the enormous numbers of sacrifices (v. 5) are to be taken literally or not. Apparently, 142,000 animals would have meant an offering every three seconds for ten hours a day for twelve days.[1] The most that can safely be said is that the numbers were unusually large even for Solomon's time, requiring a special consecration of the *courtyard* (v. 7) and presumably simultaneous offerings.

The *dedication of the altar* (v. 9) and of the temple (v. 5) link this occasion with other religious ceremonies of dedication (*e.g.* Nu. 7:10–11; Ezr. 6:16–17; Ne. 12:27). The concept of dedication was not just about holding a special opening service, however. Since the underlying idea involved initiating something or someone into its, his or her proper role (*cf*. Dt. 20:5; Pr. 22:6, where 'train a child' is the verb 'to dedicate'), the ceremony would establish a distinctive pattern of sacrificial worship in which God and human beings could have fellowship with each other (*cf*. also vv. 12–16).

The chronological details (vv. 8–10) are explained more clearly than in 1 Kings 8:65–66. The week-long dedication directly preceded the Feast of Tabernacles, which was normally held from the 15th to the 22nd of the *seventh month* (*cf*. Lv. 23:34–36, 39–43). The expected Day of Atonement rituals on the tenth day are notable only for Chronicles' complete silence about them. The *eighth day* (v. 9) was that of Tabernacles, and so came at the end of the celebrations on the 22nd. The 'solemn assembly' (NRSV, RSV) was held on that day (*cf*. Lv.

---

[1] J. Wenham, 'Large numbers in the Old Testament', *TB* 18, 1967, pp. 19–53, *cf*. p. 49.

23:36, 39; Nu. 29:35), allowing the people to be dismissed on the 23rd (v. 9). The exact nature of such assemblies is never clarified in the Old Testament. This paragraph is also part of Chronicles' 'Festival schema', which is used to describe a number of major celebrations, most of which are not mentioned in earlier sources. The schema regularly incorporates details of date, participants, ceremonies, and joyful worship (*cf.* 2 Ch. 15:9–15; 30:13–27; 35:1–19).[1] The temple dedication therefore became a model for regular large-scale occasions of celebration.

The key point, however, was that all Israel had participated, their *hearts* full of *joy* and *gladness* for all God's *goodness* (v. 10). The word for *assembly* in verse 8 (another word is used in v. 9) usually refers in Chronicles to a united gathering of Israel as God's people (*cf. e.g.* 1 Ch. 13:4; 29:1, 10; 2 Ch. 20:14). Their unity is expressed in geographical terms as well as by a unity of spirit – *Lebo Hamath to the Wadi of Egypt* (v. 8) indicates the widest possible extent of Israel's occupation of the Promised Land. This phrase recalls 1 Chronicles 13:5, and shows that the process of establishing a central place of worship had been a commitment of the whole people from beginning to end. For *Lebo Hamath*, see notes on 1 Chronicles 13:5; the relationship between the *Wadi of Egypt* and the River Shihor (1 Ch. 13:5) is uncertain, though both seem to mark the Egyptian border.

c. God's promises (7:11–22). An introductory comment (vv. 11–12a) leads into a speech from God (vv. 12b–22) which sets the standard for temple worship during the Divided Monarchy (2 Ch. 10–36). It appears that God spoke to Solomon after the *royal palace* as well as the temple was completed (v. 11), that is, thirteen years after the temple's dedication (*cf.* 1 Ki. 6:38 – 7:1; 9:10). The time gap is not important either here or in 1 Kings 9:1–9; both see this passage as an answer to Solomon's prayer (2 Ch. 6:14–42; *cf.* also the answer in 7:1–2). That God spoke to Solomon *at night* (v. 12) recalls a similar occasion at the previous sanctuary (2 Ch. 1:17). Combining the two passages demonstrates that God stimulates and answers prayers associated with the temple.

God's message falls into four parts, with a chiastic pattern

---

[1] De Vries, pp. 264–265.

underlying the first two sections (vv. 12–16).[1] The central part
of the chiasm highlights repentant prayer as God's chief provision for reversing Israel's fortunes (v. 14a). The outer parts
of the pattern contrast God's actions in earth and heaven. He
either restores or punishes his land and his people by opening
or closing his heavenly house (vv. 13–14b) according to the
prayers offered in the earthly temple (vv. 12, 15–16).

i. God accepts Solomon's prayer and the temple building (7:12b).
This indicates his acceptance of the principles in Solomon's
prayer (6:14–42) as a basis for hearing the prayers of others.
God has *chosen this place*, a phrase otherwise found only in
Deuteronomy (12:18; 14:25; *etc.*), and a rare mention of the
idea that God specifically chose the temple (elsewhere only in
v. 16 and 33:7). It is to be a house of prayer and a (lit.) 'house
of sacrifice', the latter phrase reflecting post-exilic rather than
pre-exilic usage (it is added to 1 Ki. 9:3; *cf.* Ezr. 6:3). This
combination of the temple's functions is striking, and is one of
several indications in 2 Chronicles 5–7 that prayer and sacrifice are to be understood as 'two sides of the same coin'.[2]
Worship needs an outer form as well as an inner heart, and
for prayer to be accepted it has to be accompanied by a visible
sacrifice for sin. Christians can pray precisely because Jesus
has offered one final and complete sacrifice for their sins
(Heb. 10:12, 19–22).

ii. God will hear his people and heal their land (7:13–16). This
paragraph reveals the heart of the books of Chronicles, and is
actually Chronicles' summary of the essential message of the
Old Testament. It invites people to take advantage of the
enormous and unexpected benefits God gives through prayer.
Most of this great promise is unparalleled in 1 Kings 9, though
closer examination reveals that verses 12b–16a have been
inserted into 1 Kings 9:3 with a view to bringing out the
emphasis of the earlier text much more clearly. This has been
done by incorporating key words and phrases from elsewhere
in Scripture. Some of the wording is closely based on Solomon's dedicatory prayer, such as the various circumstances
in which prayer might be offered (v. 13; *cf.* 2 Ch. 26, 28),

---

[1] B. Kelly, 'Retribution and eschatology in Chronicles', unpubl. Ph.D. thesis,
University of Bristol, 1993, ch. 3.
[2] Japhet, *Ideology*, p. 80.

turning as the appropriate mode of repentance (v. 14; *cf.* 2 Ch. 6:24, 26, 37) and God's promise to hear and forgive (vv. 14–15; *cf.* 2 Ch. 6:25, 27, 30, 39, 40). Other phrases, however, are derived from elsewhere in the Old Testament, making God's invitation securely founded in the law and the prophets. God's promise to restore Israel to their land (v. 14), for example, is based partly on Leviticus 26:41 where it is addressed to those who humble themselves, and partly on, for example, Jeremiah 30:17; 33:6–7 where it is described as God's healing. Leviticus 26:40–45 and Jeremiah 33:1–11 seem in fact to have been particularly significant for Chronicles, since they are also quoted in other passages dealing with restoration (*cf.* Je. 33:11 in 1 Ch. 16:34–36, and Lv. 26:34–35, 43 in 2 Ch. 36:21). These promises, therefore, are a natural fulfilment of God's purposes throughout the Old Testament as well as a specific answer to Solomon's prayer.

God's promise is in three parts: (a) a summary of the disasters mentioned in Solomon's prayer (v. 13); (b) God's declared purpose to forgive and heal (v. 14); (c) God's assurance of his attentiveness and nearness (vv. 15–16).

(a) The description of the situations in which people might pray (v. 13) recognizes that such disasters can be sent by God. But it is also a clear indication that even when God is angry, the only effective way out is to turn to the same God for forgiveness (*cf.* 1 Ch. 21:13).

(b) Although God's invitation is initially given to *my people* (v. 14), 6:32–33 has made clear that anyone who acknowledges God's name and authority may pray with the same confidence of a hearing. This passage is therefore consistent with others where the invitation is explicitly extended to 'all who call on the name of the LORD ...' (Joel 2:32; Acts 2:21; Rom. 10:13; Zp. 3:9; 1 Cor. 1:2). The different uses of God's name here are worth noting: 'to be called by the name' indicates ownership, 'to call on the name' speaks of prayer in the name of Jesus or Yahweh, and 'the house that ... bears your Name' (6:33; *cf.* 6:5–8, 10, 20) refers to God's presence. In every case, to know God's name is to have hope.

There then follow four expressions summing up the right approach to be adopted in prayer. These expressions are best understood as four facets of one attitude, that sinners should seek God himself in humble repentance, rather than as four separate steps on a long road to forgiveness. Interestingly, from this point on in Chronicles, these expressions are often linked with repentance, a meaning which they did not generally have in previous chapters. Repentance has a new prominence from now on in Chronicles. This was not because Israel was becoming more sinful, but because the new temple represented a fresh basis for restoration and forgiveness.

The principles of restoration and the means by which it could be received are illustrated from now on through certain individuals, on the basis of verse 14. *Humble themselves*, for example, is the key motif in the accounts of Rehoboam (2 Ch. 12:6, 7, 12), Hezekiah (30:11; 32:26), and Manasseh (2 Ch. 33:12, 19, 23); *pray* is used of a plea for repentance in 2 Chronicles 6:19ff.; 30:18; 32:20; 33:13 (*cf.* also 1 Ch. 4:10; 5:20; 21:26, where different verbs are found); *seek (my face)* occurs in contexts either of repentance or of general distress (2 Ch. 11:16; 15:4; 20:3–4), though elsewhere it can refer to a general attitude towards God (1 Ch. 16:10, 11; 2 Ch. 22:9; 26:5); and *turn*, one of the Old Testament's main words for 'repent', is associated with the above phrases in 2 Chronicles 15:4; 30:6, 9; *cf.* also 36:13).

Humble repentance is a necessary stage in God's ultimate aim to *forgive* and *heal*. Another essential element in the process is God's promise to *hear* prayer. This is so important that an emphatic 'I' occurs in MT before *I will hear*, *i.e.* 'I will indeed hear'. It is clearly a direct answer to Solomon's own requests (*cf.* 6:19, 20, 21, 25, *etc.*), but the promise will also be explicitly fulfilled in 2 Chronicles 20:9; 30:20, 27; 33:13; 34:27. *Forgive* is the only one of these terms that does not occur later on, though it does not appear in Chronicles outside 2 Chronicles 6–7 either. The idea of forgiveness is expressed in other ways, however, such as God's wrath not being poured out (2 Ch. 12:7; *cf.* 30:8), being found by God (2 Ch. 15:2, 4, 15), God receiving an entreaty (2 Ch. 33:13, 19), and especially God's atoning or pardoning (2 Ch. 30:18). This last passage is particularly interesting, since it also contains the only other reference in Chronicles to God's healing (2 Ch. 30:20). Both 2 Chronicles 7:14 and 30:18, 20 indicate that forgiveness and healing are part of the same work of God. This conclusion is confirmed by a careful examination of 2 Chronicles 30:18–20 and of the way the verb 'to heal' is used throughout the Old Testament. Firstly, 'healed the people' in 2 Chronicles 30:20 is God's answer to a prayer for pardon by those who set their hearts to seek God. Secondly, the promise to *heal their land* (v. 14) seems to be fulfilled in 2 Chronicles 30:20 by the phrase 'healed the people' (it is probably also an answer to 6:25, 27, 31, 38). Thirdly, healing throughout the Old Testament has a mixture of spiritual and physical applications. Sometimes healing is specifically equated with forgiveness (*e.g.* Ho. 14:4; Is. 53:5; 57:18–19; Ps. 41:5); at other times it relates to physical healing (*e.g.* Gn. 20:17; Nu. 13:20; 2 Ki. 20:5, 8). When it is applied to the land, as here, it can refer to bringing the exiles back to the Promised Land (Je. 30:17; 33:6–7) or restoring the land and its people to peace and security (Je. 33:6; Is. 57:19). 'Heal their land' may justly be described therefore as a comprehensive phrase for the restoration of all God's purposes for the people of Israel and for the Promised Land.

How this promise may be applied in the modern world has been a matter of considerable debate, though restrictions of space must make the following brief comments suffice. Firstly, the prominence of the spiritual and moral aspects of healing make the Old Testament promises of healing consistent with the New Testament gospel. Both of them contain God's offer to forgive sins (*cf.* Acts 5:31; Eph. 1:7), in both instances making this promise available on a universal basis. Secondly, the fact that spiritual restoration is offered to one nation also makes it available in principle to any other nation. Although no other nation enjoys precisely the same relationship with God as did ancient Israel, the spiritual health of each nation is something in which God has a direct interest. How far the corporate life of one's own nation shows evidence of spiritual decline or progress depends to a significant extent on the prayers of Christian people. Thirdly, one must take note of the comprehensive nature of the biblical gospel. It has a strong corporate emphasis, in contrast to the individualism of much Western Christianity, and is just as concerned with the physical aspects of life as the spiritual. It is illuminating, for example, to read how much Jesus saw his ministry of physical healing as part of his message of the forgiveness of sins (*cf. e.g.* Mt. 8:1 – 9:8, especially 9:5–6). Though Christians today may find it hard to understand exactly how these various dimensions of God's purposes relate to each other, the Chronicler agrees with other biblical authors that God himself has joined them together.

(c) The promise of restoration is backed up by a remarkable

statement about God's presence in the temple. As God again answers a specific request of Solomon's (*cf.* v. 15 with 6:20, 40), he affirms that not only his *ears* and *eyes*, but also his *Name* and even his *heart* are in some undefined way present in the temple. The idea of God having a heart is extremely rare in the Bible, and the only other explicit reference speaks of God suffering heart pains because of the evil of humanity (Gn. 6:6; *cf.* also Gn. 8:21; 1 Sa. 13:14; Acts 13:22). Since the heart expresses the innermost parts of a person or thing, God here offers to humankind his deepest inner being, and reveals a wounded heart. The glory of the mysterious cloud (vv. 1–3) becomes also the glory of what is in effect God's preparation for Jesus' incarnation. It is hard to think of a more intimate way to indicate God's nearness, or a greater encouragement to prayer.

iii. God confirms Solomon's royal throne (7:17–18). God now reminds Solomon of the temple's significance as a symbol of God's commitment to the Davidic covenant. Prayer offered in the temple came before the God who had set David on his throne, and was in effect an appeal to God's own kingdom (*cf. e.g.* 1 Ch. 17:14; 28:5; 29:23; 2 Ch. 9:8). This particular promise was a direct answer to Solomon's prayer in 6:16–17. Note the closeness of the wording – the promise, 'You shall never fail to have a man ... on the throne of Israel' (6:16) is here confirmed as *You shall never fail to have a man to rule over Israel* (7:18). Two small changes in verse 18 (*cf.* 1 Ki. 9:5) underline God's commitment to the dynasty. 'As I promised' has become *As I covenanted* (for specific reference to the Davidic covenant, *cf.* 2 Ch. 13:5; 21:7), while *a man to rule over Israel* is a deliberate echo of the messianic promise of Micah 5:2. The point is not that Solomon should be viewed as a messianic figure, for verse 17 draws attention to his humanity and need of obedience. Rather, it was God, not man, who guaranteed the future of David's line, and only he had the authority to answer Israel's prayers.

iv. God may reject this temple (7:19–22). If the temple encouraged fresh hope of national restoration and the continuation of David's line, it must also symbolize Israel's commitment to God's written will. It must be a house of obedience as well as a house of prayer and of sacrifice, as the people are now reminded (the *you* of v. 19 is plural), following the pattern of earlier speeches directed partly to the king (or his son) and partly to the people (*cf.* 1 Ch. 22:6–16, 17–19 and 28:2–8, 9–10). The privileges associated with the temple were not granted automatically. If Israel decided to *forsake* God (v. 19) instead of showing humble repentance (v. 14), God could remind them of the temple's secondary importance by removing it altogether. Such judgment would actually reverse God's earlier promises – to be 'cast out of my sight' (v. 19, NRSV, RSV) is the opposite of the assurance that God's eyes are watching for one's prayers (vv. 15–16).

Interestingly, the situation in which such a disaster might arise is no different in kind from that described in verse 13 which might result in restoration. The distinction between the salvation of verse 14 and the judgment of verse 20 is not that the people in the former case were any better, but that they repented. While judgment can be earned, restoration is an undeserved gift. Repentance and restoration, however, were God's expected norm, whereas the destruction of such an 'exalted' (JB, NRSV, RSV; *imposing*, NIV) edifice would be so unusual as to excite the interest even of neutral bystanders (vv. 21–22).[1] The phrase 'laid hold on' (RSV; *embraced*, NIV) *other gods* offers a good example of this surprise element. The Hebrew verb means basically 'to hold strongly to', and to adopt such an attitude to gods other than Yahweh was a denial of the very pattern of faith previously envisaged (*e.g.* 1 Ch. 19:13; 22:13; 28: 7, 10, 20). To abandon the Lord in this way would be to reject all that he had done for them, in particular in the exodus, with the result that God would himself reject them in line with Deuteronomy 29:24–28 (v. 22). If Israel forsook the covenantal and historical foundation of their faith, the *temple* and the *land* would become meaningless.

I. Solomon completes the temple (8:1–16)

The final section of Solomon's reign (chs. 8–9) concentrates on the theme of praise for all that God has done for Solomon (see especially 9:8). This unit is clearly connected with the opening section about Solomon (2 Ch. 1–2), both of which

---

[1] REB, NEB's 'will become a ruin' (v. 21) is to be rejected as an easier reading based on the vss but unsupported in the Heb.

deal with Solomon's achievements and reputation. The chief difference is that whereas the earlier chapters describe Solomon's preparations in response to God's revelation at Gibeon, now that work is fulfilled. The real subject of chapters 8–9, therefore, is what God achieved through Solomon, rather than Solomon's own achievements.

The details of chapter 8 concern people and buildings in Israel, while chapter 9 is about Solomon's external reputation. Chapter 8 falls into three main categories:

vv. 1–6   Solomon's building work
vv. 7–11   Role of foreigners in Solomon's kingdom
vv. 12–15   Temple ceremonies and personnel
v. 16   Summary of Solomon's work

It may seem surprising that parts of the chapter return to the temple theme, since its construction was completed in chapter 7. Two features about this chapter, however, indicate that this arrangement is quite deliberate. Firstly, statements about the temple (vv. 1, 12–16) enclose details about Solomon's achievements throughout the land, apparently indicating that the latter are divine blessings resulting from Israel's faithfulness over the temple. This supports the principle that various blessings follow when worship is made a priority.

Secondly, the subjects listed here occur in the same order as in the parallel passage dealing with preparations for the temple (ch. 2). Mention of the temple and royal palace (v. 1 and 2:1) is followed by Solomon's relationship with Hiram king of Tyre (v. 2 and 2:3–16), and by the contribution made by foreigners (vv. 7–10 and 2:17–18). Chapter 8 therefore shows that Solomon has obeyed the order to build the temple (2:1) and has completed the work (8:1, *cf.* v. 16) with the aid of a Gentile king and Gentile conscripts. Comparison of chapter 8 with 1:1–13 also demonstrates that these results are not ultimately attributable to Solomon's own efforts. It was God himself, who had begun the work by making unexpected promises to Solomon (1:7–12), who had seen it through to completion (*cf.* Phil. 1:6).

The principles of God's faithfulness and the priority of worship are of course found extensively in the Bible, though their application to national prosperity is an Old Testament rather than a New Testament concern. Jesus' teaching contains a good summary of the basic concept: 'Seek first his kingdom and his righteousness, and all these things will be given to you as well' (Mt. 6:33; *cf.* Lk. 12:31). Christians are to give priority to Christ and to heavenly values (*cf.* Phil. 3:10–21), and to trust that whatever is needed for this life will be generously provided (Phil. 4:18–19). The Old Testament applies the same principle to national life, for God is the true source of wealth and prosperity (*cf.* Dt. 8:10–18; Pr. 8:15–18). Solomon could build the nation of Israel (vv. 1–6) because God is a builder and grower (*cf.* 1 Cor. 3:6–9), and he exercised authority over the Gentiles because God makes his enemies serve his own purposes (vv. 7–10; *cf.* Is. 14:2; 60:10; Phil. 2:10).

How much Solomon himself actually contributed to this prosperity is a matter of some dispute. It has often been said that the Chronicler has not allowed Solomon's glory to be obscured by any shadow, and had altered or omitted anything in 1 Kings 9:10–25 that could detract from such a presentation (*e.g.* Michaeli, Curtis and Madsen). Others, however, accept that the Chronicler has followed his source quite closely (*e.g.* Coggins, Dillard). The details of this issue will be examined below, but two general points are worth noting. First, the Chronicler clearly assumes that his readers are aware of his main source, the books of Kings. This is evident from the way he has kept largely to the order and wording of 1 Kings 9, despite significant differences at a few points (*e.g.* vv. 1–2, 3–4, 11). Secondly, some things, such as his rebuilding of Hazor and Megiddo (1 Ki. 9:15) and his gift of peace offerings (1 Ki. 9:25), have been strangely omitted if the author's main aim is to magnify Solomon. In fact, the Chronicler's purpose seems to be not to gloss over Solomon's weaknesses (especially 1 Ki. 11:1–40), but to emphasize that God blessed him and his people in spite of them.

i. Solomon's other building work (8:1–6)

8:1 – *cf.* 1 Kings 9:10
8:4a – *cf.* 1 Kings 9:18b
8:5b – *cf.* 1 Kings 9:17b
8:6a – *cf.* 1 Kings 9:18a, 19

Solomon's empire is described briefly, in similar vein to David's imperial achievements (1 Ch. 18:1–13). Emphasis falls on his building work, the verb 'to build' (often translated as *rebuilt*), occurring six times (vv. 1, 2, 4, 4, 5, 6). The whole land is included (v. 6b; *cf.* 7:8), particularly the north-west border with Tyre (v. 2), the north-east area adjoining Syria (vv. 3–4), and the south-east (vv. 5–6a). The note that this activity took place after the *temple* and *palace* were finished (v. 1) repeats 7:11 and is to be taken in parallel with it. God's promises to restore the land (7:12–18) and Solomon's building work are blessings that both follow from the temple's completion. These achievements seem to exemplify God's intention to 'heal their land' (7:14).

Though the general meaning is clear, however, several important details are not. For example, the *villages* that 'Huram' (*Hiram*, NIV; *cf.* 2 Ch. 2:3ff.; 4:11; *etc.*) had given to Solomon were, according to 1 Kings 9:11–14, given by Solomon to Huram! Several explanations of this apparent contradiction are possible, though to imagine that the Chronicler reversed the meaning of 1 Kings because he thought the latter too damaging to Solomon is unsupported and too naïve. If the idea of Solomon having to give away part of the Promised Land was so objectionable, it would have been simpler just to omit the section, as with others in 1 Kings 9. The Chronicler's aim in any case is not to explain how the villages came to be in Solomon's possession, only that he rebuilt them. While textual disturbance is possible (Willi, Williamson), it seems more probable that they had been returned to Solomon, either because they were unacceptable (1 Ki. 9:12–13) or because they had been collateral for a loan (1 Ki. 9:14).

A second problem concerns the unparalleled reference to Solomon's conquests and construction work in the north-east (vv. 3–4). There are three difficulties: that Solomon wins a military victory against *Hamath Zobah* in an area where he had previously been unsuccessful (*cf.* 1 Ki. 11:23–25), to identify Zobah's location and status, and whether to prefer the reading *Tadmor* (v. 4) with the vocalized text of 1 Kings 9:18, or 'Tamar', as in the consonantal text of 1 Kings 9:18.

Zobah (*cf.* 1 Ch. 18:3–10; 19:16–19) was situated in the area which stretched 120 miles north from Damascus to Hamath. The compound term *Hamath Zobah* reflects a change from David's time when Hamath and Zobah were distinct entities with separate policies towards Israel (*cf.* 1 Ch. 18:3–8, 9–10) to a period when they had come together, probably administered from Hamath. Zobah was known as *Subate* in eighth-century Assyrian inscriptions and as *Sbh* in Aramaic brick inscriptions found in Hamath dating from the tenth to eighth centuries BC.[1] Solomon's presence in this area is confirmed by the inclusion in Israel of Lebo Hamath (7:8; *cf.* 1 Ch. 13:5), a town in the province of Subate which the Assyrians called Laba'u, and by references to his kingdom extending, like David's, to the Euphrates (1 Ki. 4:21, 24; *cf.* 2 Sa. 8:3; 1 Ch. 18:3). Solomon's success, though, was probably less permanent than David's in view of his difficulties with Damascus (1 Ki. 11:24–25), and he probably received regular tribute rather than imposing direct rule (*cf.* 1 Ch. 18:6). However, his building of *store cities* in Hamath shows that his authority was real, a factor underlined by the Chronicle's use of *captured*, one of his favourite words (v. 3; 'took', RSV; Heb. *ḥāzaq*, 'to be strong'; *cf.* esp. 1 Ch. 19:13).[2]

Tadmor (Ass. Tadmar), is about 125 miles north-east of Damascus, and later become the important caravan city of Palmyra. Solomonic influence in Tadmor is consistent with that in Hamath, since as key places on major trade routes both would be appropriate to Solomon's known interests (*cf.* ch. 9). One reading of the parallel text, however, is 'Tamar' (1 Ki. 9:18, *Ketib*), usually located south-west of the southern end of the Dead Sea (*cf.* Ezk. 47:18–19; 48:28). It is interesting, though, that the place is in 'in the desert' (1 Ki. 9:18), an ascription that marks it out from its associated southern cities and which could apply to Tadmor. A northern interpretation is therefore possible in Kings, as well as being the best-attested reading in Chronicles. Alternatively, Kings and Chronicles could refer to different places, though this view is less satisfactory.[3]

Upper and *Lower Beth Horon*, together with *Baalath* (vv. 5–6a), were also on trade routes, linking Jerusalem with the

---

[1] *Cf.* A. Malamat, 'The kingdom of David and Solomon in its contact with Egypt and Aram Naharaim', *BA* 21, 1958, p. 101, n. 22; *idem*, in D. J. Wiseman (ed.), *Peoples from Old Testament Times* (Oxford: Clarendon Press, 1973), pp. 142–143; Y. Ikeda, in T. Ishida (ed.), *Studies in the Period of David and Solomon* (Tokyo: Yamakawa-Shuppansha, 1982), p. 237.

[2] It may be that these store cities played a significant role in Solomon's import of Anatolian horses, as well as being storage centres for grain (*cf.* Y. Ikeda, *op. cit.*, pp. 234–238).

[3] See *e.g.* Z. Kallai, *Historical Geography of the Bible* (Jerusalem: Magnes Press, 1986), pp. 73–74; F. C. Fensham, *IBD*, pp. 1513–1514.

coast. Baalath is probably that mentioned in Joshua 19:44, rather than in Joshua 19:8, though Baalah, an alternative name for Kiriath Jearim (*cf*. 1 Ch. 13:6), is also a possibility. Such routes would have required strong defences.[1]

The Chronicler's interest in royal building work here ties in with a special emphasis in chapters 10–36. Three phrases illustrate this, *viz. captured* (*ḥāzaq 'al*, v. 3; *cf*. 2 Ch. 27:5), *fortified cities* (*'ārê māṣṣôr*, v. 5; *cf*. 2 Ch. 11:5), and *walls ... gates and bars* (v. 5; *cf*. 2 Ch. 14:6). Like David's building work in Jerusalem (1 Ch. 11:8–9), they are signs of God's blessing and of God's commitment to build David's house (1 Ch. 17:10). God was building not just a dynasty, but a kingdom or 'dominion' (v. 6, NRSV, RSV, REB). Its extent is exemplified by the *store cities* (vv. 4, 6) and the *cities for his chariots* (v. 6; *i.e.* Hazor, Megiddo, Gezer, and *Jerusalem*), both situated in the north and the south.

ii. Foreigners in Solomon's kingdom (8:7–11)

8:7–11a – *cf*. 1 Kings 9:20–24a

Three groups are mentioned. The first is the slave labour force taken from the *descendants* of the pre-Israelite inhabitants of Canaan (vv. 7–8). It was common practice to impose conditions of this kind on former enemies, and this was one way to bring the Canaanites under formal Israelite authority. A distinction is made between Solomon's treatment of these Gentiles and of the *Israelites* (v. 9a), though 1 Kings 5:13–18, which Chronicles does not mention, has often been thought to contradict the more favourable attitude toward the Israelites. It is possible, however, that there were two different policies. A distinction is evident between the simpler term *mas* ('forced levy'; *cf*. 1 Ki. 5:13–14) and the phrase *mas 'ôbēḏ* ('state slaves', Mendelsohn, *BA* 85, 1942, pp. 16–17; *slave labour force*, NIV). The latter occurs in 1 Kings 9:21 and is probably to be read in verse 8 here (it is implied by *slaves* in v. 9). Also, the Israelites worked only on the temple for one month in three, whereas the Canaanites were subjected to a permanent arrangement for Solomon's nationwide construction projects (note the reference to *chariots* and horsemen (v. 9), implying work on the chariot cities).[2]

[1] See Z. Kallai, *op. cit*., pp. 73, 369; J. M. Miller and J. H. Hayes, *History of Ancient Israel and Judah* (London: SCM Press, 1986), pp. 209–210.

[2] See also Jones, I, pp. 157–158.

The *Israelites*, who took command in military (v. 9) and construction (v. 10) work, form the second group (vv. 9–10). 'His captains *and* lieutenants' (v. 9, with REB, NEB) is preferable to *commanders* of *his captains* (NIV).[1] The word for 'lieutenants' (REB; *captains*, NIV; Heb. *šālîš*) could refer to a 'third man' in the chariot, to an officer of the third rank, or to a member of a special three-man squad.[2] The figure of *two hundred and fifty* supervisors (v. 10) is at variance with the '550' of 1 Kings 9:23. Though simple scribal error could be a factor, it may be better to link these figures with the 3,600 supervisors in 2 Chronicles 2:18 and 3,300 in the parallel verse 1 Kings 5:16, since both Kings and Chronicles total 3,850.[3]

The third reference is to Solomon's unnamed Egyptian wife, *Pharaoh's daughter* (v. 11). The fact of this unique marriage (1 Ki. 9:16; 11:1) and the separate *palace* built for her (1 Ki. 3:1; 7:8; 9:24) are both taken from Kings, but mention of the *ark*'s holiness as the explanation for her move (v. 11b) has no parallel. It is widely assumed that this has to do with her sex, but, since the context is about foreigners, her paganism is the more likely reason (*cf.* Ezk. 44:7–9). If the former were true, one would also expect separate accommodation for Solomon's Israelite wives, but mention is made only of new buildings in connection with his foreign wives (*cf.* 1 Ki. 11:7–8). In fact, building a palace for her was probably part of a policy of separate shrines for foreign wives. *The palace of David* is assumed to be part of the temple complex (*cf.* Ezk. 43:7–9), and is probably the one built by Solomon but linked with David because of the ark.

iii. Temple ceremonies and personnel (8:12–15)

8:12 – *cf.* 1 Kings 9:25a

Regular observance of temple worship, with its proper sacri-

---

[1] The word *weśārê* should be read as *weśārāw*, as in 1 Ki. 9:22. The form in Chronicles has been influenced by another *weśārê* two words later, losing its final *waw* by haplography.

[2] *Cf.* N. Na'aman, 'The list of David's officers (*šālîšîm*)', *VT* 38, 1988, pp. 71–79; D. G. Schley, 'The *šālîšîm* (*sic!*): officers or special three-man squads', *VT* 40, 1990, pp. 321–326.

[3] See further, J. Wenham, 'Large numbers in the Old Testament', *TB* 18, 1967, p. 49; D. Gooding, *Relics of Ancient Exegesis* (Cambridge: Cambridge University Press, 1976), pp. 53–55. It is incorrect to argue that Gentile supervisors are mentioned in 2 Ch. 2:18, since no statement is made about their nationality (*cf.* Williamson).

fices (vv. 12–13) and personnel (vv. 14–15), is the basis of any continuing national prosperity (*cf.* vv. 2–11). This regularity is indicated by the pattern of daily, weekly, monthly, and annual ceremonies. The basic daily requirement for sacrifice (Nu. 28:1–8) was the *burnt offerings*, together with incense. The former symbolized lives wholly offered to God (*cf.* Ps. 103:1) and the gift of atonement (*cf.* 1 Ch. 21:26; Jb. 1:5), while the latter is often associated with prayer (*cf.* Ps. 141:2; Rev. 5:8; 8:3). Although 'peace offerings' and 'incense' are omitted from the parallel verse (1 Ki. 9:25), Chronicles is more comprehensive in covering every type of occasion when sacrifice was offered. The appointment of *priests* and *Levites* includes most of the Levitical functions previously mentioned, such as leading *praise*, *assisting* the priests, and acting as *gatekeepers* and as treasurers (*cf. e.g.* 1 Ch. 23:2–5, 28–31; 26:1–28).

In all this, Solomon is faithful to the commands of both *Moses* (v. 13) and *David* (vv. 14–15). The link with Moses is indicated by incorporating information from Deuteronomy 16:1–16 about the annual feasts.[1] David is confirmed as a second Moses (*cf.* 1 Ch. 15:15; 22:13; 2 Ch. 23:18), as Solomon carries out the instructions God revealed to David (*cf.* especially 1 Ch. 28:11–19; also 1 Ch. 23:31; 2 Ch. 2:3–4). The focus of the temple's regular ceremonies was the altar of burnt offerings (v. 12), where Israel daily offered praise and received forgiveness (*cf.* 1 Ch. 22:1; 2 Ch. 7:9).

iv. The temple completed (8:16)

'All Solomon's work was carried out' (8:16).

8:16b – *cf.* 1 Kings 9:25b

The final stage of the temple narrative is carefully unfolded, like each of the intervening ones (1 Ch. 29:6–9; 2 Ch. 2:1; 5:1; 7:8–10; *cf.* also 2 Ch. 29:35). Solomon's work was summed up in the temple, and the following blessings (8:17–28) represent God's bonuses given in answer to his opening prayer (2 Ch. 1:7–12). As with David, God shows his readiness to pour blessings on his people (*cf.* 1 Ch. 14–16).[2]

---

[1] *Cf.* J. R. Shaver, *Torah and the Chronicler's History Work* (Atlanta: Scholars Press, 1989), pp. 94–96.

[2] EVV are surely correct to read '*from* the day of the foundation' (with the majority of vss) rather than 'until the day . . .' (as MT). The latter seems to have been influenced by the following 'until'.

J. Solomon's splendour (8:17 – 9:31)

This section concludes the record of Solomon's achievements (chs. 8–9) by concentrating on Solomon's international relationships, in contrast to the Israelite setting of the previous one. Two striking examples of Solomon's dealings with foreign rulers, one from the north and the other from the south, introduce a more general account of Solomon's reputation among *the kings of the earth* (*cf.* v. 23). The material falls into three main sections:

8:17 – 9:12 Solomon and the rulers of Tyre and Sheba
9:13–28 Solomon's wisdom, fame, and fortune
9:29–31 Concluding formula for Solomon's reign

The text follows 1 Kings closely, with the one significant exception that it omits the extensive criticisms of Solomon in 1 Kings 11:1–40. The reason for this important change is not because the Chronicler saw Solomon as a paragon of unparalleled virtue and success, for it has been repeatedly shown that Chronicles' readers were expected to be familiar with the basic story in Kings (see also Coggins). Mention of Ahijah (v. 29; *cf.* 1 Ki. 11:29–39) and Solomon's unfortunate legacy (2 Ch. 10:1–15) clearly show that in the Chronicler's view his glory was not untarnished.

A wider survey of the Chronicler's use of Kings shows that substantial positive aspects of Solomon's reign have also been left out, including details of his wisdom and wealth that would have been directly relevant here (*cf.* 1 Ki. 3:16–28; 4:1–34). As in the case of David, the Chronicler has excluded most of his private life and several secular concerns. The effect of these changes is a sharper focus on the relationship between this chapter and Solomon's encounter with God at Gibeon (2 Ch. 1).

God had promised on that occasion to give Solomon not only the wisdom he asked for (1:11–12a) but wealth and fame for which he had not asked (1:12b). 2 Chronicles 9 shows that that promise was kept most faithfully. God himself is twice acknowledged as the source of Solomon's gifts, on both occasions through the impartial testimony of foreigners (vv. 8, 23). Though Solomon was obedient to God over the building of the temple, praise is really due to God for his faithfulness and love (v. 8).

All three of God's gifts are dealt with in some detail, and an emphasis on God's generosity is repeatedly evident. Solomon's *wisdom* is recognized and tested by the Queen of Sheba (vv. 2, 3, 6, 7, 8) and sought by many rulers (vv. 22, 23). The king was also far more generously endowed with this gift than the queen anticipated: *you have far exceeded the report I heard* (v. 6). The gift of wealth is not only acknowledged, but increased by Hiram of Tyre (8:18; 9:10–11), the Queen of Sheba (vv. 3–4, 9, 12), and by many merchants and kings (vv. 13–28). The third gift of 'honour' (2 Ch. 1:12), though not so frequently recognized, is equally prominent. The *report* of Solomon's *fame* (vv. 1, 5) is international in scope (especially vv. 22–24), and leads to expressions of Solomon's supremacy and uniqueness. He shows his supremacy in answering all the queen's questions (vv. 1–2), in giving her more than she had brought to him (v. 12), and in exercising sovereignty over many rulers (v. 26). His uniqueness is underlined in a series of phrases such as, *Nothing like it had ever been made for any other kingdom* (v. 19; *cf.* vv. 9, 11). This incomparability had also been promised by God (2 Ch. 1:12; *cf.* 1 Ch. 29:25), and confirms that even Solomon's glory (*cf.* Mt. 6:29) was dependent on and far outweighed by God's own glory (*cf.* 2 Ch. 7:1–3).

Most of the changes to Kings are fairly minor, but one stands out. In place of God putting Solomon on 'the throne of Israel', verse 8 states that God *has … placed you on his throne as king to rule for the LORD your God.* Mention of the kingdom of God alongside Solomon's unparalleled greatness has suggested to some that this section foreshadows the end times (Mosis, Dillard, Allen). This view is probably over-enthusiastic, since other Old Testament passages develop these themes in a much clearer eschatological fashion (*cf.* Ps. 72:10; Is. 60:6). What is in view here is the present reality of God's kingdom rather than its expectation in the future. God was still enthroned even in the Chronicler's day, despite the absence of any visible version of God's kingdom. Also his *love for Israel* had not changed, as is confirmed by an additional phrase not found in Kings: 'establish' (NRSV, RSV; *uphold*, NIV) *them for ever* (v. 8; *cf.* 1 Ki. 10:9).

In the New Testament, Solomon's glory and the Queen of Sheba's visit point to the greater reality of Christ (Mt. 12:42; Lk. 11:31). Wise men from the East, following in the queen's footsteps, brought traditional gifts from Sheba of frank-incense and myrrh to Solomon's descendant (*cf.* Mt. 2:1–12). Jesus himself commended the queen for recognizing the hand of God in Solomon's life, though he warned too that Sol-omon's splendour was limited and not to be envied (Mt. 6:28–29). His wealth and wisdom were special gifts sym-bolizing God's blessing on the newly established Davidic covenant and dynasty, whereas Christians are encouraged to value things in heavenly rather than earthly terms (Mt. 6:19–21) and to exercise wisdom by putting faith in Christ (1 Cor. 1:18–25). God's goodness to Solomon is not intended as a temptation to materialism, but as an invitation to seek God's kingdom first in the confidence that 'all these things will be given to you as well' (Mt. 6:33).

i. Solomon's international relationships (8:17 – 9:12)

'Blessed be the LORD your God, who has delighted in you and set you on his throne as king for the LORD your God' (9:8, NRSV, RSV).

8:17–18 – *cf.* 1 Kings 9:26–28
9:1–12 – *cf.* 1 Kings 10:1–13

Solomon's dealings with two important rulers of his day illus-trate his international reputation and extend God's praise. The famous incident involving the Queen of Sheba (9:1–9, 12) is sandwiched between two short paragraphs concerning Israel's maritime partnership with Tyre (8:17–18; 9:10–11, *cf.* 9:21).

a. Solomon and the king of Tyre (8:17–18; 9:10–11). There are some minor differences with the text of Kings in both paragraphs, which are often interpreted as the Chronicler misreading his source (see also v. 21). For example, Hiram sent ships in 2 Chronicles 8:18, whereas 1 Kings 9:26–27 says that Hiram sent sailors and that Solomon built the ships. However, the fact that in 1 Kings 9:27 Hiram's sailors were sent with the fleet confirms that even in the earlier version, the sailors did not travel unaccompanied. It is most likely that the materials were imported from Tyre and assembled by the Red Sea.

17–18. The Israelite port of *Ezion Geber* is probably to be located at Jezirat Fara'un, an island south of Eilat, rather than the traditional site of Tell el-Kheleifeh west of Aqaba. It preserves evidence of a maritime installation of substantial size and complexity, and the pattern of small harbours on offshore islands is repeated at Sidon, Tyre, and Arwad in the Phoenician homeland.[1] *Ophir* is much less certainly located, and could be in south-west Arabia, the horn of Africa, or even India. It is, however, linked with Sheba in Genesis 10:28–29 (= 1 Ch. 1:22–23), which makes the last proposal least likely.

9:10–11. The second paragraph is linked with the queen's visit as a second source of *precious stones* and of exotic imports. The identification of *algum* (better, almug; *cf.* 1 Ki. 10:11–12) wood remains unknown (see on 2 Ch. 2:8), as is the use to which it was put in the temple and palace (v. 11). The Hebrew word for the latter usually means 'highway', but that is hardly suitable here. 'Gateways',[2] *steps* (NIV, NRSV, RSV; *cf.* GNB), 'stands' (REB, NEB), or 'floorboards' (JB) have all been proposed, though, in the light of the following phrase, it may even be a term for another musical instrument!

b. Solomon and the queen of Sheba (9:1–9, 12). The name and identity of *the queen* remain tantalizing unknown. Her kingdom of *Sheba* or Saba corresponds roughly to modern Yemen and was well known in ancient times for its wealth, based on trade in frankincense and myrrh (*cf.* Ezk. 27:22–23). It is most likely that the context of the visit was a trade mission, though whether this was an attempt to protect Saba's overland routes to counter competition from Solomon and Hiram's sea-trade or to pay trade tariffs for the privilege of using the routes to the Mediterranean (*cf.* v. 14) remains uncertain.

The story, which closely follows that in Kings, has undergone considerable expansion and embellishment in later versions, in comparison with which the Old Testament accounts are 'the briefest and most concise'.[3] It is the legendary additions that speak of a union between the king and queen, based on a sexual understanding of the verb *came* (v. 2) and the

---

[1] A. Flinder, *Secrets of the Bible Seas: An Underwater Archaeologist in the Holy Land* (London: Severn House, 1985), pp. 42–82; *idem*, 'Is this Solomon's seaport?' *Biblical Archaeology Review* 15/4, 1989, pp. 30–43.

[2] This proposal is based on Assyrian analogies, *cf.* D. Dorsey, 'Another peculiar term in the Book of Chronicles: מְסִלָּה, "Highway"?' *Jewish Quarterly Review* 75, 1984–5, pp. 385–391, based on Assyrian analogies.

[3] E. Ullendorff, *Ethiopia and the Bible* (London: Oxford University Press, 1968), p. 132.

phrase *all she desired* (v. 12). According to Jewish and Ethiopian traditions respectively, either Nebuchadnezzar or Menelik I, the founder of the Ethiopian dynasty, were born from their union. The existence of a Sabean queen in Solomon's day, however, is perfectly reasonable, given references in eighth-century BC Assyrian texts to North Arabian queens, and to Sabean rulers from *c.* 800 BC.[1]

After the queen's arrival (v. 1), the biblical story concentrates on what the queen saw and heard (vv. 2–4), what she said (vv. 5–8), and what she did (v. 9). Her aim was to *test* Solomon with *hard questions* (v. 1). The latter is sometimes translated 'riddles', and includes not only popular riddles (*cf.* Jdg. 14:12–18), but the difficult issues of Old Testament wisdom such as the meaning of life and death (Ps. 49:4) or God's unfathomable wonders (Ps. 78:2; 'hidden things', NIV). The equivalent Greek word (*ainigma*) in the Septuagint occurs only once in the New Testament in 1 Corinthians 13:12, where it is usually translated 'darkly, dimly', typifying the way things are understood in this life. Solomon's supernatural gift of wisdom (*cf.* 1 Cor. 12:8), however, enabled him to respond to all the queen's probings (v. 2). In addition to its intellectual and problem-solving qualities, this wisdom was also practical and religious. Its evidence could be seen in 'the house' (NEB, NRSV, RSV; *palace*, NIV, REB, GNB) that *he had built* (v. 3), and in his administration (v. 4). The house almost certainly refers to the temple, since the royal palace is always separately identified as such (*cf.* 2:1; 7:11; 8:1), whereas 'the house' on its own signifies the temple (*e.g.* 2:4, 9; 6:2, 9). Among the list of items illustrating Solomon's wisdom the reading *burnt offerings* (v. 4, NIV, NRSV, RSV, *cf.* GNB) is based only on the vss and 1 Kings 10:5 (*cf.* 2 Ch. 5:6; 7:4–5, 7). MT reads 'upper chamber,' though most commentators prefer 'stairs, ascent', involving a small emendation (*cf.* NIV fn).

What the queen saw took her breath away (v. 4; 'left her breathless', JB; *she was overwhelmed*, NIV), literally, 'there was no more breath/spirit in her'. Apart from 1 Kings 10:5, the phrase occurs only in Joshua 2:11; 5:1, and on each occasion it is used of non-Israelite amazement at what God has done. When she did speak, it was to acknowledge that she now *believed* what she *saw* (v. 6), and so gave *praise* to God (v. 8).

[1] For fuller details, see *ibid.*, pp. 131–145.

The Hebrew words for *true* (v. 5) and *believe* (v. 6) are closely related, and provide an important theme in the story, though whether this faith simply acknowledged Yahweh's greatness (*cf. e.g.* Dn. 4:1–3, 34–37) or was of a more deep-seated character is not specified. It is, however, an interesting example of the adage 'seeing is believing', despite the principle of 2 Corinthians 5:7. Faith sometimes involves believing the evidence in front of one's eyes, as in the case of Jesus' resurrection (*cf. e.g.* Jn. 19:35; 20:8, 27–29).[1]

The queen's praise (v. 8) is important, since it summarizes in Chronicles' typical style the cause of Solomon's greatness. God's *throne* is in fact an important allusion to the kingdom of God, a distinctive concept in Chronicles, but one which is rare in the Old Testament and has no parallel in Kings (*cf.* 1 Ch. 17: 14; 28:5; 29:11, 23; 2 Ch. 13:8). The link between divine and human kingdoms highlights the origin and the purpose of Solomon's kingship. Because of God's *love for Israel*, Solomon reigns for them as well as over them. As in Deuteronomy, love expresses the idea of election (*cf.* Dt. 4:37; 7:7–8; 10:15), and the Chronicler combines here his special interest in Solomon's election (*cf.* 1 Ch. 28:4–10) with a rare mention of God's loving choice of Israel. With a parallel statement in 2:11, this latter concept forms a theological bracket around the Chronicler's account of Solomon. The purpose of Solomon's rule was to demonstrate *justice and righteousness.* This common pair of terms expresses God's covenant principles (*cf.* 1 Ch. 18:14) and the divine gift of wisdom (*cf.* 1 Ki. 3:28).

Though the translation of verse 12 is a little uncertain, the queen certainly returned home with *more than she had brought* (NIV, NRSV, RSV), possibly as a result of a mutual exchange of gifts (REB, GNB; *cf.* v. 9).

ii. Solomon's wisdom, fame and fortune (9:13–28)

9:13–25 – *cf.* 1 Kings 10:14–26
9:25a – *cf.* 1 Kings 4:26 (EVV) = 5:6 (MT)
9:26 – *cf.* 1 Kings 4:21a (EVV) = 5:1a (MT)
9:27–28 – *cf.* 1 Kings 10:27–29

[1] In v. 7, the reading 'your wives' (RSV, REB, NEB) is based on the vss, but is inferior to 'your men' (NIV, based on MT and 1 Ki. 10:8; *cf.* NRSV, GNB). It is not tautolgous with 'your servants/officials', since the former is more general and the latter more specific.

This is a more general summary of Solomon's wisdom, wealth, and fame, in which his wisdom at least is directly attributed to God (v. 23). His *gold* (vv. 13–21) and his supremacy among *all the kings of the earth* (vv. 22–28) receive special mention. His varied wealth also included *silver* (vv. 14, 20, 21, 24, 27), *ivory* (vv. 17, 21), *apes* and 'monkeys' (v. 21, GNB, REB, NEB; the latter may be *baboons*, NIV, or 'peacocks', NRSV, RSV following vss), *spices* (v. 24; *cf.* vv. 1, 9), 'myrrh' (v. 24, RSV; possibly 'perfumes', REB, NEB, or *weapons*, NIV, GNB, JB), *mules* (v. 24), *horses* and *chariots* (vv. 24, 25, 28), and *cedar* (v. 27).

a. Solomon's gold (9:13–21). Solomon's annual revenue of *gold* (vv. 13–14) seems extraordinary by modern standards, but, in the context of the ancient world, it was not out of place.[1]

The total amount is not given, though the *666 talents* (= approx. 22 tons) received annually probably derived from tribute and some trade.[2] Special mention is made of the use of gold for large and small decorated *shields* (vv. 15–16; *cf.* 2 Ch. 12:9), an ivory *throne* (vv. 17–19), and various vessels (v. 20). The shields were deposited in the armoury, that is, the *Palace of the Forest of Lebanon* (*cf.* Is. 22:8).[3] The measure of gold used for the shields is not specified in MT, which normally means that shekels are implied (so most EVV). NIV, though, has *bekas* or half-shekels, which attempts to harmonize with 'three minas' in 1 Kings 10:17. Since it is not always clear whether the mina was worth fifty or 100 shekels, however, caution is preferable. The unique *throne*, which was probably made of wood inlaid with *ivory*, had a golden *footstool* (v. 18), though 1 Kings 10:19 (MT) has 'a rounded top' or possibly 'a calf's head' (LXX). The simplest solution to these discrepancies is to accept that Kings and Chronicles were drawing attention to different features of this special throne.[4] *Kingdom* (v. 19) should probably be understood as 'king', the abstract term being used for

[1] A. R. Millard, 'Solomon in all his glory', *Vox Evangelica* 12, 1981, pp. 5–18.

[2] 'Revenues' (NIV) or 'tolls' (REB, NEB) or 'taxes' (GNB) involves a slight but necessary change from MT ('men').

[3] Various types of shield of the period are illustrated, mainly in Assyrian examples, in Y. Yadin, *The Art of Warfare in Biblical Lands* (London: Weidenfeld & Nicolson, 1963), pp. 13–15, 295, 360ff.

[4] For the translation 'footstool', *cf.* W. G. E. Watson, 'Archaic elements in the language of Chronicles', *Bib.* 53, 1972, p. 194.

the concrete, as in 2 Chronicles 12:8.[1] *Nothing was made of silver* (v. 20) is an additional phrase not in MT, and should be deleted. *Trading ships* (v. 21; *cf.* GNB) is a preferable translation to the more literal 'the ships that went to Tarshish' (JB; *cf.* NRSV, RSV, REB, NEB). By Tarshish, probably Tartessus in Spain, was simply meant a far-off place, just like 'the Indies' in the early days of European exploration (*cf.* 2 Ch. 20:37).

b. Solomon's international supremacy (9:22–28). The paragraph begins with *all the kings of the earth* (vv. 22, 23), is centred on *all the kings* (v. 26), and concludes with *all countries* (v. 28). It summarizes various elements, with verses 25–28 partially repeating 2 Chronicles 1:14–17 and verses 25–26 including scattered statements from 1 Kings 4:21, 26. Such extensive fame was no accident, and was certainly regarded as one of God's covenant blessings for David's dynasty (*cf.* 1 Ch. 17:8). It was also enjoyed by other kings who remained faithful to the Lord (*e.g.* 1 Ch. 14:17; 2 Ch. 20:29; 26:8, 15).

Horses were as much a symbol of wealth in the ancient Near East as gold and ivory, and had been introduced into Israel only by Solomon's father. Comparison between the numbers of *stalls*, *horses*, and *chariots* in verse 25 with those in the parallel passages (1 Ki. 4:26; 10:26; 2 Ch. 1:14) reveals some confusion in textual transmission. Though certainty is impossible, a reasonable solution is to think of 1,400 chariots (1 Ki. 10:26; 2 Ch. 1:14) and *twelve thousand horses* (NIV, REB, NEB; rather than 'horsemen', RSV), on the analogy of the Ugaritic practice of three horses to a chariot, and allowing for breeding and training. In this context, *four thousand stalls* is preferable to the 'forty thousand' of 1 Kings 4:26 (MT, 5:6). There are two further examples in verses 25–26 where Chronicles has preserved a text superior to Kings. *Kept* (v. 25; 'stationed', NRSV, RSV), is universally preferred to the equivalent defective verb in 1 Kings 10:26, while the word *to* before *the land of the Philistines* is omitted in 1 Kings 4:21. On the 'sycomore' (v. 27, GNB, *cf.* REB, NEB)], see on 1:15, and on 1:16–17 for further explanation of the trade in horses.

iii. Concluding formula for Solomon (9:29–31)
9:29–31 – *cf.* 1 Kings 11:41–43

[1] *Ibid.*, p. 204.

This paragraph follows the normal pattern of concluding formulae for royal reigns in Kings and Chronicles (for David, *cf*. 1 Ch. 29:26–30). It contains statements concerning the length of the king's reign (v. 30), his burial place, the name of his successor (v. 31), and the source of further information (v. 29). Only the last of these shows any significant deviation from 1 Kings 11:41–43. *From beginning to end* ('from first to last', JB, NRSV, RSV, REB, NEB) is a typical Chronicles expression not found in Kings (*cf*. 1 Ch. 29:29; 2 Ch. 12:15; 35:27). The prophetic sources (v. 29; *cf*. 1 Ch. 29:29) most likely refer to Kings, or possibly to prophetic collections within Kings. *Nathan*'s contribution comes from 1 Kings 1:1–53, *Ahijah*'s from 1 Kings 11:29–39, and *Iddo* is traditionally regarded as the anonymous prophet in 1 Kings 13:1–10 (*cf*. 2 Ch. 12:15; 13:22). The Chronicler maintains his strong interest in the prophets, confirming that his account of Solomon is based on the words of God's spokesmen (*cf*. 2 Pet. 1:21).

III. THE KINGDOM OF JUDAH (2 Ch. 10:1 – 36:23)

A. Rehoboam (10:1 – 12:16)

i. Israel separates from Judah (10:1–19)
'So Israel has been in rebellion against the house of David to this day' (10:19).
10:1–19 – *cf*. 1 Kings 12:1–19
The three stages of *Rehoboam's* reign correspond exactly to the chapter divisions (2 Ch. 10–12). The first (ch. 10) follows Kings very closely, though the second and third (chs. 11–12) diverge substantially from the earlier work, giving Chronicles' over-all view of Rehoboam quite a different feel from Kings. While accepting Rehoboam's very real failings as a leader, Chronicles is keen to demonstrate the value of repentance and the extent of God's mercy.

This chapter deals with the reasons for Israel's division after Solomon's death (*cf*. v. 19), setting the scene not only for the rest of Rehoboam's reign but for the rest of 2 Chronicles. The key phrase *turn of events* (v. 15; 'turn of affairs', NRSV, RSV; 'to bring about', GNB) translates a rare word in Hebrew which is to be interpreted alongside the related verb 'turn' in 1 Chronicles 10:14 (*cf*. 12:23). These two verses describe two great 'turning-points', pivotal events which usher in new eras concerning the setting up and downfall of David's dynasty. The first era opens with the transfer of Saul's kingdom to David (1 Ch. 10:14) and results in the dynasty of David and Solomon (1 Ch. 10 – 2 Ch. 9). This incident introduces a much sadder story, beginning with the division of Solomon's kingdom and culminating in the collapse of Israel and its monarchy (2 Ch. 10–36).

Why is there such a sudden change between chapters 9 and 10, giving the impression of a sharp decline after the golden age of Solomon (*cf.* 2 Ch. 4:7–8, 19–22; 9:13–21)? It is in fact most unlikely that the Chronicler intends to present the changeover as unconnected with Solomon, for as well as carefully preserving 1 Kings 12:1–19 (vv. 1–19), there are hints that he expects the reader to know about other aspects of Solomon, particularly Solomon's weaknesses (1 Ki. 11:1–25; *cf.* vv. 4, 9–11, 14), Ahijah's prophecy, and Jeroboam's flight to Egypt (1 Ki. 11:26–39; *cf.* 2, 15). According to this earlier material, the division was a more complex affair, but then the Chronicler's aim is not primarily historical. He concentrates not only on the reasons for the disaster but on the principles by which restoration might take place.

When Kings and Chronicles are read alongside each other, it is clear that Solomon, Rehoboam, and Jeroboam must all take a share of the blame. Both writers insist that Solomon imposed a *heavy yoke* on the people (vv. 4, 9–11, 14), that Jeroboam rebelled (v. 19; *cf.* 2 Ch. 13:6–7; 1 Ki. 11:26–40), and that Rehoboam rejected the elders' wise *advice* (vv. 6–8, 13). Though this chapter gives greater prominence to Rehoboam's folly while 2 Chronicles 13:6–7 highlights Jeroboam's rebelliousness, no individual is singled out. The common denominator is that all were disobedient to God's word given through the law and the prophets. Oppression, folly, and idolatry (*cf.* 1 Ki. 12:25–33; 2 Ch. 13:8–9) all show how these kings fell short of the standard of obedience which was required of David's line (*cf.* 1 Ch. 22:13; 2 Ch. 6:16; 7:17–18).

The matter is complicated, however, by the fact that on other occasions, all three received clear signs of God's favour. Solomon obeyed God's call to build the temple, Jeroboam was God's chosen king (1 Ki. 11:29–39), and Rehoboam repented when he heard God's word (2 Ch. 11:4; 12:6–7, 12). Clearly they were not uniformly bad. Nor does verse 15 imply that

God acted unfairly. It recognizes rather that certain behaviour is unacceptable in God's kingdom, but that God remains in over-all control. The kingdom's survival was a greater surprise, and verse 15 testifies to God's preserving grace (*cf.* 1 Ch. 17:13; 2 Ch. 21:7) as well as his righteous judgment.

One must also insist that the division was neither inevitable nor irreversible. Rehoboam had a definite opportunity to reverse at least the most serious effects of the situation, if not to avoid it altogether. The same point is made with Jeroboam (1 Ki. 12:25–33) and in Rehoboam's later life when presumably he was a little wiser (2 Ch. 12:6–12), and also in the lives of David (1 Ch. 21:13, 17–18) and Hezekiah (2 Ch. 32:24–26). It is important to recognize that Rehoboam had a choice, a point of special relevance to Chronicles' first readers. Though, in their day, the Davidic monarchy had not just divided but had long since disappeared, even their situation must not be regarded as hopeless. They too had opportunities to follow God's wisdom (*cf.* vv. 6–7), to repent (*cf.* 2 Ch. 7:14; 12:6), and to look for God's next 'turning-point' (*cf.* v. 15).

God's final turning-point came when Jesus inherited the kingdom. He came at the 'right time' (*cf.* Gal. 4:4) to inaugurate the new era of the 'last days' (Acts 2:17; Heb. 1:2). On that occasion too, God fulfilled his own plans through human beings who thought they were merely carrying out their own purposes. Neither the wicked men who nailed Jesus to the cross nor Solomon, Rehoboam, and Jeroboam in their selfish ambitions were aware that they were participating in a decisive act of God (Acts 2:23). The workings of divine sovereignty through human disaster, however, are a regular theme in Scripture, from the sufferings of Joseph (Gn. 50:20) to the persecution of the church (Rom. 8:28, 35–39), encouraging every reader to find hope below the surface of events.

a. Rehoboam's abortive coronation plans (10:1–5).

This paragraph sets the scene. *Rehoboam* is met by a tribal delegation intent on negotiating the terms of his kingship rather than celebrating the fact of it (vv. 3–4), as he expected (v. 1). He therefore suggests a delay of *three days* (v. 5). That he is surprised shows him to be out of touch with the real feelings of *all Israel* (vv. 1, 3). All twelve tribes are probably meant, since for Chronicles the ten northern tribes are just as much the covenant people (see also vv. 16–19).

Shechem (modern Nablus) was a traditional centre where the tribes had once renewed their covenant (Jos. 24:1–27), though David had been recognized as king at Hebron (1 Ch. 11:1–3). It seems to have become the first capital of the north (1 Ki. 12:25). The ceremony testifies to the vitality of Israel's democratic ideal of kingship, though, in comparison with David's and Solomon's coronations (*cf.* 1 Ki. 1:17, 29–30, 48), God is conspicuous by his absence.

The reference to *Jeroboam* raises some textual problems. The main reason is that the Greek text of 1 Kings 12:24 has a much longer account of Jeroboam's activities, though Chronicles' omission of Jeroboam's assumption of kingship in 1 Kings 12:20 is a complicating factor. However, the latter is left out because Chronicles is not concerned with the separate history of the northern kingdom. It is often alleged that 1 Kings 12:20 refers to Jeroboam's initial return from Egypt, and that reference to him in 1 Kings 12:2–3a, 12 is a later insertion based on Chronicles (see *e.g.* Rudolph, Jones, de Vries). If, however, 1 Kings 12:20 is seen as referring to Jeroboam's coronation rather than his initial return from Egypt, then the problem is greatly reduced. In that case, Jeroboam was indeed the leader of the northern tribes in the negotiations with Rehoboam (note 'they sent and summoned him', v. 3, JB). As a 'man of rank' (JB) who had been in charge of Solomon's forced labour gangs from Israel (1 Ki. 11:26–28), and as recipient of a prophecy in his favour (1 Ki. 11:29–39), he was well placed for this role.[1]

The tribes' accusations against Solomon were serious. The phrases *harsh labour* (*cf.* Ex. 5:9; 6:9) and *heavy yoke* (*cf.* Ex. 6:6–7; Lv. 26:13) charge him with oppressing Israel as Pharaoh had done (contrast Mt. 11:29–30; Gal. 5:1). In no sense, therefore, can Chronicles be said to exonerate Solomon as blameless (*contra* Dillard), especially as a further analogy between Zedekiah and the Pharaoh of the exodus is given as one of the reasons for the exile (*cf.* 2 Ch. 36:13). The specific complaints concerned taxation, forced labour, and a centralization policy which reduced the tribes' influence and authority. Nevertheless, the people still expected to make Rehoboam king – verse 4 is literally '*so that* we may serve you'.

---

[1] 'He returned' (v. 2) is a superior reading to 'he lived, dwelt' (1 Ki. 12:2). For fuller details of the textual issues, see *e.g.* Dillard, Williamson.

b. Advice for Rehoboam (10:6–15). Rehoboam consults first with the elders (vv. 6–8a) and then with his own younger advisers (vv. 8b–11) before giving the assembly his decision (vv. 12–15). Seeking and following wise advice are seen as essential requirements of leadership. The same point is illustrated by David (1 Ch. 13:1–4), Jehoshaphat (2 Ch. 20:21), and Hezekiah (2 Ch. 30:2; 32:3), though Rehoboam's folly was matched by Amaziah (2 Ch. 25:16–17). Two contrasting pieces of advice are sought (vv. 6, 8a; both begin with 'took counsel', RSV, *consulted*, NIV *etc.*), resulting in Solomon's *heavy yoke* (vv. 4, 9, 10, 11, 14) being replaced by more painful *scorpions* (vv. 11, 14, NIV, NRSV, RSV). The repetition clarifies the central issue, and also increases the feeling of oppression. Rehoboam's problem was not simply his youth, as illustrated by Solomon and others (1 Ch. 22:5; 29:1; Ecc. 4:13; Dn. 1:17–20), or the unavailability of advice. It was rather that he *rejected* (v. 8) the good advice and favoured the bad, failing to seek the source of true wisdom (*cf.* 1 Ch. 1:10; Pr. 2:6; Jas. 1:5).

The *elders* (vv. 6, 8, 13; 'old men', RSV, *cf.* GNB) held official positions in Solomon's court ('stood before', v. 6, RSV). They are probably not the tribal leaders, since there is no evidence that the Davidic monarchy had amalgamated this traditional structure into the court. Rather, they and the *young men* (vv. 8, 10, 14; really 'lads') were the older and younger royal counsellors, who are likely to have been the king's personal appointment (*cf.* the repetition of 'stood before', v. 8).[1] The younger men may well have been members of the royal family, perhaps Rehoboam's half-brothers (*cf.* 2 Ki. 10:1–6; Dn. 1:3–4).

The elders advised Rehoboam to do more than simply *be kind* (v. 7, NRSV, RSV, NIV, *etc.*) to the people. The Hebrew means literally 'good', which, together with 'good words' (NRSV, RSV), probably has a more formal meaning. The former often means 'be in alliance, concord with', and the latter 'make an agreement' ('considerate answer', GNB; *favourable answer*, NIV; *cf.* 1 Sa. 20:23; Is. 8:10). The same idea may also be present in 1 Kings 12:7, which speaks of king and people as servants of each other. Alternatively, Chronicles' language may simply be softer than Kings'. Presumably, though, these

---

[1] *Cf.* H. Reviv, *The Elders in Ancient Israel* (Jerusalem: Magnes Press, 1989), pp. 100–101.

elders had supported Solomon's harsh policies, which makes their advice all the more ironic and that of the youngsters even more oppressive.

The young men's threat is recorded carefully and with much repetition (vv. 8b–11), as if to show that it was a considered and not a casual policy. The *three days* delay (vv. 5, 12) and the phrase *we answer* (v. 9; GNB, REB, NEB wrongly have the singular) confirm this impression. A double metaphor strengthens the decision to increase Israel's burden. Firstly, Rehoboam's 'little thing' (a rare word usually translated *little finger* but possibly 'penis', *cf.* KB 1022) is thicker than Solomon's *waist*, paraphrased by Tg. as 'my weakness is stronger than my father's might' (*cf.* ironically 1 Cor. 1:25). Secondly, Rehoboam's *whips* will be more fearsome than any used by Solomon – the *scorpion* has been known since Ephraem Syrus in the fourth century AD as something with the reputation of a 'cat o' nine tails' ('horsewhip', GNB; 'loaded scourges', JB).[1] *Scourged* (v. 11; 'chastised', RSV) is often used of disciplining children, giving the impression that Rehoboam treated the people as wayward offspring.

Rehoboam's answer is conveyed to the people (vv. 12–14), who actually play a quite minor role in the whole event. It is possible that verse 14 increases the threat still further; the Hebrew has '*I* am making your yoke heavy, and will do so increasingly', though EVV read *My father*, as in verse 11. On the significance of verse 15, see above. Knowledge of the prophetic *word* in 1 Ki. 11:29–39 is assumed, though *Ahijah* has been mentioned in passing in 2 Chronicles 9:29. As frequently in Chronicles, the crucial moments in Israel's history fulfil what God has spoken by his prophets (*e.g.* 1 Ch. 11:2; 17:3–15; 2 Ch. 36:22–23).

c. Division of Israel and Judah (10:16–19). The moment of division is summarized in a remarkably bland way, *So all the Israelites went home* (v. 16, NIV, REB, NEB; 'to their tents', NRSV, RSV, JB; GNB's 'rebelled' is unwarranted). Only a poetic fragment (v. 16b) gives any hint of the people's view that Rehoboam was unsympathetic to their burdens, and so was unfit to rule.[2]

---

[1] *Cf.* Gray, p. 306.
[2] Though 'saw' is missing in MT, it is correctly supplied by EVV from 1 Kings 12:16. The reference to 'all Israel', repeated several times with variations in vv. 16–19, marks this off as the beginning of a paragraph, making it very unlikely that the sentence continues from v. 15 (see Williamson, Dillard).

A series of small changes brings out the full extent of Israel's divisions. Firstly, the would-be king was divided from the whole nation, who are called 'all Israel' (v. 16c, NRSV, RSV, *etc.*). The second occurrence of this phrase in verse 16 is adapted from 1 Kings 12:16 ('Israel') to correspond with verses 1, 3, 16a. Secondly, the people's unity is preserved by using the phrase *the Israelites* to describe both the inhabitants of the southern kingdom of *Judah* (v. 17; *cf.* also 11:3) and of the northern kingdom (v. 18; 'people of Israel', NRSV, RSV; 'all Israel' in 1 Ki. 12:18). Thirdly, the real division is *between Israel* and *the house of David* (vv. 16, 19; note the repetition of [house of] David). Fourthly, Israel's former unity is destroyed. The northern tribes' traditional rallying call (v. 16; *cf.* 2 Sa. 20:1) is deliberately contrasted with the support all Israel had once given to David (*cf.* the parallel between *David* and *Jesse's son* here and in 1 Ch. 12:18). Fifthly, the addition of 'each (of you)' before 'to your tents' (v. 16, NRSV, RSV, *cf.* JB) invites every individual in the north to separate from David's dynasty. A similar thought occurs in the phrase, 'share in David' (v. 16, NRSV, JB), implying that the northerners actually disinherited themselves from David's family.

18. Rehoboam makes one pathetic effort to restore unity, perfectly illustrating the poverty of his policy. Knowing that the people's tolerance had been exhausted by their experience of the *forced labour* system, it seems inconceivable that the sending of 'Hadoram' (also known as Adoram, 1 Ki. 12:18; *cf.* JB; *Adoniram*, 1 Ki. 4:6; 5:14; *cf.* NIV, GNB), one of Jeroboam's successors, could end in anything but disaster. In the end, Rehoboam himself only just managed to *escape*, in ironic contrast to Jeroboam's flight from Solomon (v. 2).

19. Israel's *rebellion* is probably a neutral term describing the separation, but may possibly anticipate Jeroboam's later idolatry and rebellion against Yahweh (1 Ki. 12:25–33). *To this day*, which is really based on the meaning in Kings, is one of the few instances which also applies to Chronicles' time (also 1 Ch. 5:26, in contrast to *e.g.* 1 Ch. 17:5; 2 Ch. 8:8; 21:10).

ii. Rehoboam's strength (11:1–23)
'They strengthened the kingdom of Judah' (11:17).
11:1–4 – *cf.* 1 Kings 12:21–24
The account of *Rehoboam's* reign over the southern kingdom

of Judah has been altered considerably from Kings. Chronicles' record is much longer (2 Ch. 11–12 as against 1 Ki. 12:1–4; 14:21–31), and has a different emphasis. In contrast to the presentation of Rehoboam as a man who 'did evil in the eyes of the LORD' (1 Ki. 14:22), his obedience and repentance feature prominently in Chronicles. This sounds like a contradiction, perhaps deriving from Chronicles' greater interest in theology than in history (so Coggins), but that would be to misrepresent the Chronicler's distinctive approach.

The extra length testifies to Rehoboam's greater importance in Chronicles. This arises from two factors. The first concerns Rehoboam's relationship with the northern kingdom, which, as has already been noted in passing, is virtually excluded in Chronicles (see comment on 2 Ch. 10:1–5). Whereas, in Kings, Rehoboam's reign is no more than a supplement to Jeroboam and is one of a collection of kings whose reigns are briefly summarized (1 Ki. 14:21 – 16:34; *cf.* Nelson, Jones), here Rehoboam is considered in his own right. The second factor is that as the first king of Judah, Rehoboam is an example of God's dealings with David's whole dynasty. Several typical themes in Chronicles occur in chapters 11–12, mostly without parallel in Kings, including obedience to the prophetic word (11:1–4), strengthening of the kingdom through building work (11:5–12), the activities of priests, Levites, and God-seekers (11:13–17), an expanding family (11:18–21), and humble repentance (12:5–12).

The reason for these changes seems to be to demonstrate that a way back to God exists even for the wicked. While the Chronicler confirms the judgment of Kings on Rehoboam (2 Ch. 12:1–2, 14), his primary purpose is to illustrate how the principles of forgiveness and restoration described in 2 Chronicles 7:13–14 work in practice. God responds directly to Rehoboam's repentance (12:12), without minimizing his weaknesses. Rehoboam's repentance, for example, seems to have been temporary rather than permanent, since he is summarized as one who *did evil* (12:14; *cf.* 1 Ki. 14:22). What is more, most of the 'good' that he did (*cf.* 2 Ch. 12:12) was due to the people rather than their king. It was *they* who *obeyed the words of the LORD* (11:4) and who 'set their hearts to seek the LORD' (11:16, NRSV, RSV), while Rehoboam did exactly the opposite (*cf.* 10:15, 16, where *listen*, NIV or 'hearken', RSV, is the same Heb. word as *obeyed*, 11:4 and 12:14).

Chapters 11–12, therefore, clearly affirm the reality and effectiveness of the gospel according to Chronicles. If God could show favour to a man such as Rehoboam, who typified the attitude which resulted in Judah's eventual collapse, there was always hope for those who humbled themselves before God. Indeed, the interest in the people was surely a direct encouragement to the Chronicler's contemporaries to seek God for themselves. The New Testament of course extends the same invitation, for repentance is both the way to God (*cf.* Mk. 1:4, 15; Acts 11:18) and part of the way of life of God's people (2 Cor. 7:9–10; Rev. 2:5, 16; 3:3, 19). The principle that God 'does not treat us as our sins deserve' (Ps. 103:10; *cf.* Ezr. 9:13) is by no means unique to Chronicles

In the light of these observations, it seems impossible to see in this section a doctrine of immediate retribution (*e.g.* Dillard) or divine retribution based on the principle of 'measure for measure'.[1] Although in Chronicles blessing regularly follows obedience and divine punishment succeeds rebellion, in every case God is more generous than ought to be expected. The blessings of Rehoboam's fortification work (vv. 5–12) and his family's prosperity (vv. 18–23) must have spilled over beyond the first three years of his reign (*cf.* v. 17), and he never felt the full force of God's anger for his wicked ways (10:13–14; 12:14). God preserved him from the results of his folly at the start of his reign (11:2–4), and ensured the dynasty would continue after his death (13:5).

Most of this chapter has no other biblical parallel. Only verses 1–4 follow 1 Kings, while the rest seems to depend on official sources of information (vv. 5–12, 18–23), probably including priestly as well as prophetic records (vv. 13–17; 12:15). Whatever these unknown sources were, verses 5–23 contain several passing references to the account of Jeroboam I in 1 Kings, especially concerning his priestly appointments (v. 15; *cf.* 1 Ki. 12:31; 13:33). The inclusion of this material should not be thought surprising, since the effects of setting up new national sanctuaries in the north were bound to be felt throughout Judah, especially as Bethel was only twelve miles north of Jerusalem.

In addition to the theme of God's forgiving grace, chapter 11 focuses on God's specific blessings for Rehoboam. The

---

[1] Japhet, *Ideology*, pp. 157, 170, following Loewenstamm.

characteristic term is 'strength' (*cf.* vv. 11, 12, 17), which is illustrated by building activity (vv. 5–12), an extensive family (vv. 18–21), and wise administration (vv. 22–23). The inward disposition of those who gave themselves first to the Lord also strengthened Rehoboam's kingdom (vv. 13–17). Several kings exhibited similar strength at the beginning of their reigns, but, as with Rehoboam, a good start was not always maintained (*cf.* 2 Ch. 1:1; 17:1; 21:4; 25:3, 11; 26:8–16).

a. Peace between Israel and Judah (11:1–4). This paragraph exemplifies Proverbs 16:9: 'In his heart a man plans his course, but the LORD determines his steps.' Rehoboam's response to the north's secession shows more heavy-handedness (v. 1), but this time the prophet *Shemaiah* (*cf.* 2 Ch. 12:5, 7, 15) makes sure he does not have his own way (vv. 2–4). Where Rehoboam aimed to *regain* (v. 1; 'win back', JB) the kingdom for himself, God had to remind him whose kingdom it really was (*this is my doing*, v. 4; *cf.* 10:15). David's plan to build a temple and the disciples' hope for Israel are further examples where a restricted view of God's *kingdom* had to be corrected (1 Ch. 17:1–15; Acts 1:6–8). God's will was peace, even in a divided kingdom, whereas the natural human inclination was to 'fight' (NRSV, RSV, REB, NEB) to preserve the old order. This is actually the only instance where Rehoboam responds positively to God. Elsewhere he either acts under duress (12:5–6) or depends on the people's spirituality (*cf. they obeyed . . . turned back*; also v. 16).

'The focus is on the word and its effect' (Nelson; *cf.* vv. 2–4). The climax is in verse 4, where one should note the close link between three imperatives, literally, 'Do not go up, do not fight, go back home', and the following verbs, 'they obeyed . . . and went back' (JB). The same Hebrew verb as in went back (JB; 'returned', RSV; 'did not go', GNB) recurs in *go home* (JB, NIV, GNB; 'return', RSV) and also in 'win back' (v. 1, JB; 'restore', NRSV, RSV, GNB; 'recover', REB, NEB), illustrating how Judah accepted God's will rather than Rehoboam's.

A dominant feature of this paragraph is the way in which the true Israel continues in both south and north (*cf.* 10:17–18). 'Assembled' (v. 1, NRSV, RSV; *mustered*, JB, REB, NEB, NIV) is given a heightened meaning in comparison with 1 Kings 12:21. It is a special verb in Chronicles, used when the united people of God were gathered (*cf.* 1 Ch. 13:5; 15:3; 28:1; 2 Ch.

5:2, 3; 20:26). 'All Israel', which has been added to verse 3 (NRSV, RSV; *all the Israelites*, other EVV; *cf.* 1 Ki. 12:23), is associated with both south and north (*cf.* 10:16). *Brothers* (v. 4) has the same connotation, and is to be compared with 2 Chronicles 28:8–15, where God's wrath is felt to rest on those who do not discern the true Israel (*cf.* also 2 Sa. 2:24–28). Finally, *every one of you* (v. 4; *cf.* RSV, JB) emphasizes the personal response of individual southerners to God's will (the same expression is applied to the north in 10:16). *A hundred and eighty thousand* (v. 1) could refer to eighteen military units (*cf.* Myers and on 1 Ch. 23:3), though whether or not it is taken literally, it is smaller than other Judean armies in 2 Ch. (*cf.* 13:3; 14:7; 17:14–19).

b. Judah fortified (11:5–12). This list of Rehoboam's building is comparable with an analogous statement about Rehoboam in 1 Kings 12:25. In Chronicles such passages are a sign of divine blessing and support (*cf. e.g.* 1 Ch. 11:8–9; 2 Ch. 8:1–6; 14:7; 26:9–10), though here it probably reveals defensive entrenchment rather than positive *strength* (*cf.* vv. 11, 12). These fifteen *fortified cities* (vv. 6–10) did not defend the northern border with Israel, but the eastern, southern and western approaches. They are therefore associated with Shishak's invasion from Egypt (12:2–11), and some at least must have been built in anticipation of that event (*cf.* 12:4). The fact that Shishak captured these towns and that they included only the Judean hills and the lowlands known as the Shephelah, a much smaller area than the Davidic-Solomonic empire, is one of several indications in this chapter that even Rehoboam's blessings had serious problems. His restricted kingdom is called *Judah and Benjamin* (vv. 10, 12; *cf.* vv. 1, 3, 23), reflecting post-exilic terminology with its ancient tribal associations rather than the pre-exilic political name (*cf.* 1 Ch. 9:3–9; 2 Ch. 15:2–9; 34:9).

The only place over which some doubt exists is *Gath* (v. 8), which is more likely to be Moresheth-Gath in Judah rather than the well-known Philistine city.[1]

---

[1] For fuller details of these sites, and the form and date of the list, see *e.g.* Williamson, Dillard, and the discussion between N. Na'aman ('Hezekiah's fortified cities and the *lmlk* stamps', *BASOR* 261, 1986, pp. 5–21; 'The date of 2 Chronicles 11:5–10 – a reply to Y. Garfinkel', *BASOR* 271, 1988, pp. 74–77)

c. True worship maintained (11:13–17). *Jeroboam's* religious reform, really based on Canaanite ideology with a superficial overlay of Yahwistic traditions, had serious consequences in the south as well as the north. The statement concerning the *priests and Levites* (vv. 13–15) goes beyond the earlier reference (1 Ki. 12:31; 13:33) by mentioning the Levites' rejection and migration (v. 14), and the *goat idols* (v. 15) or 'satyrs' (RSV, REB mg., NEB mg; 'demons'; REB, NEB, GNB). An important comment is also added about people *from every tribe of Israel* (v. 16) who came to Jerusalem to offer sacrificial worship.

This section is significant for several reasons. It adds firstly an important historical note to what is known from Kings concerning Jeroboam's reign. Though some Levites moved south at considerable personal sacrifice (on the Levites' property, *cf.* 1 Ch. 6:54–80; 13:2; 2 Ch. 31:19), others simply *sided with* Rehoboam (v. 13) or travelled to worship at *Jerusalem* (v. 16). Secondly, it highlights the leadership provided by the *priests* and especially the *Levites* (note that the laymen *followed* the Levites to Jerusalem, v. 16). This was probably intended to encourage the rather more diffident Levites of the Chronicler's day to offer spiritual leadership themselves. Thirdly, it stresses again the people's unity, with every tribe being represented. The Chronicler never lost sight of the ideal of Israelite unity, from the time when David was made king (*cf.* 1 Ch. 12:23–40), to other occasions when northerners rejoined their southern neighbours for worship at the Jerusalem temple (*cf.* 2 Ch. 15:9; 30:11). Fourthly, the phrase *set their hearts on seeking the LORD* (v. 16) underlines the inward aspect of biblical religion. 'The true kingdom is a gathered community' (Ackroyd) of those whose way of life is to seek God, that is, they continually seek his will for their lives (*cf. e.g.* 1 Ch. 13:3; 28:9; 2 Ch. 7:14; 15:4, 15). Such an attitude derives from a heart set towards God. This is a distinctive expression in Chronicles, with both positive (1 Ch. 29:18; 2 Ch. 19:3; 30:19) and negative (2 Ch. 20:33) examples. Ironically, Rehoboam must be counted in the latter category (2 Ch. 12:14). A right attitude in worship is not sufficient, however, but must be expressed through physical sacrifice and in a

and Y. Garfinkel ('2 Chr 11:5–10: Fortified cities list and the *lmlk* stamps – reply to Nadab Na'aman', *BASOR* 271, 1988, pp. 69–73). For a map, see J. M. Miller and J. H. Hayes, *A History of Ancient Israel and Judah* (London: SCM Press, 1986), p. 239.

particular place. Though New Testament worship removes all geographical restrictions (*cf.* Jn. 4:19–24) and the nature of sacrificial gifts is altered (*cf.* Phil. 4:18; Heb. 13:15–16), acceptable Christian worship continues to include a physical as well as a spiritual dimension (*cf.* Rom. 12:1).

The problem, however, was that this glimpse of good things (*cf.* 2 Ch. 12:12) was sustained for only *three years* (v. 17). The pattern set by the united kingdom of *David and Solomon* (*cf.* 2 Ch. 7:10; 33:7) was soon abandoned (12:1–2). To 'walk in the way of' (NRSV, RSV; 'follow the example of', REB, NEB, JB) seems to mean to keep the requirements of God's law (*cf.* 12:1) and worship God in his temple. This implies maintaining a loving attitude towards God (*cf.* Dt. 10:12; 11:22; 19:9; 30:16) rather than living a perfect life, and is applied primarily to the people.[1]

d. The royal family extended (11:18–23). Rehoboam's growing family is the final symbol of blessing (*cf.* 1 Ch. 26:5; *cf.* 25:5) and of strength (2 Ch. 13:21). Again, however, there are signs that this was not an unmixed blessing. While Rehoboam's father's wives had led him astray (1 Ki. 11:3), his own preference for a later wife, *Maacah* (vv. 20–21; note 'After her', v. 20, NRSV, RSV, JB; *Then*, NIV), and the promotion of her son *Abijah* as his successor (v. 22), directly contravened the Deuteronomic law (Dt. 21:15–17).

Both the named wives (vv. 18, 20) demonstrate the extent of Rehoboam's descent from David, assuming that *Absalom* (vv. 20–21) was the same as David's son. Absalom had only one daughter, Tamar (2 Sa. 14:27), so it is usually assumed that Maacah was Absalom's granddaughter through Tamar. However, since the names of this family apparently have different spellings (*e.g.* Abishalom, 1 Ki. 15:2, 10; Micaiah, 2 Ch. 13:2) and Maacah was a popular name in the family (2 Sa. 3:3), it is unwise to be emphatic about exact identities.[2]

The paragraph concludes with a note about *Abijah* (v. 22). The fact that he is called *chief prince* ('head of the family', JB) suggests a co-regency on the pattern of David and Solomon (1

---

[1] Though LXX has 'he walked', the plural of MT is to be preferred, in view of the two preceding verbs and the content of vv. 13–16.
[2] 'Abihail' (v. 18) should certainly be regarded as Mahalath's mother (with vss) rather than another of Rehoboam's wives (so apparently MT).

Ch. 23:1).[1] It also shows that the normal rules of primogeniture were overruled (*cf.* vv. 20–21). Possible opposition from other royal sons was partially countered by scattering them throughout the country (v. 23), though the policy was only made effective through the special favours of *abundant provisions* and *many wives*. The translation of verse 23 is difficult, but *he acted wisely* is preferable to 'he built' (JB), and *he took many wives* (NIV, *cf.* NRSV, RSV, REB, NEB) is superior to 'he consulted the many gods of his wives' (JB; though 'took' is an emendation for 'sought').

iii. Rehoboam's repentance (12:1–12)

'Because Rehoboam humbled himself, the LORD's anger
turned from him, and he was not totally destroyed' (12:12).

12:2 – *cf.* 1 Kings 14:25
12:9–11 – *cf.* 1 Kings 14:25–28

This third and final stage of *Rehoboam's* reign (*cf.* chs. 10–11) represents a considerable expansion of 1 Kings 14:21–31. Chronicles' account is more nuanced than Kings' assessment of Rehoboam's leadership, 'Judah did evil in the eyes of the LORD' (1 Ki. 14:22). While supporting Kings' basic conclusion, Chronicles shows how a national act of repentance turned aside God's anger (vv. 5–12).

It is often said that Chronicles is kinder to Rehoboam than Kings in mentioning *good* things (*cf.* v. 12) which are not in the earlier account. However, the opposite conclusion may be more accurate, since Rehoboam remains condemned despite his repentance (v. 14). The most serious judgments in the Bible are directed against those who continue to sin after receiving God's grace, and there comes a time when there is no further opportunity for repentance or of any atoning sacrifice (*cf.* Heb. 6:4–8; 10:26–29; 12:16–17). According to the New Testament, it is like crucifying the Son of God all over again (Heb. 6:6), and though the Old Testament expresses the matter differently (Je. 7:16; 11:11; Ezk. 8:18), it is no less emphatic. God's people went into exile because they repeatedly hardened their hearts against his temple and his word (2 Ch. 36:13–16), and it was this course on which Rehoboam had embarked.

---

[1] NRSV, RSV are probably correct to follow LXX, Vulg. in adding 'he intended' ('planning', REB, NEB), as required by the syntax of MT.

The main point, however, is to illustrate the effectiveness of Rehoboam's repentance, particularly in the verses which are the Chronicler's own contribution (vv. 5–8, 12). Some of Chronicles' most typical vocabulary can be found here, especially the contrast between *abandon* (vv. 1, 5) and *humbled* (vv. 6, 7, 12). These and other favourite terms such as *law of the LORD* (v. 1), *unfaithful* (v. 2), God's *wrath* (vv. 7, 12), *set his heart* and *seek the LORD* (v. 14), all confirm that Rehoboam is to be interpreted as a paradigm who presents the reader with a choice. One may go one's own way, recognizing that such attitudes divided a kingdom (ch. 10) and led to exile (ch. 36). Alternatively, the way of humility and repentance is always available, with the temple (*cf.* v. 14) and the word of the prophets (vv. 5, 7–8) as constant reminders of God's offer of restoration. The key feature, then, is God's grace rather than Judah's repentance. His desire is for people to set their minds on him (*cf.* 11:16; 12:4) rather than be subject to human rulers (v. 8).

a. Attack by Shishak of Egypt (12:1–4).

Kings commonly open their reigns in Chronicles by strengthening their position, but the language here, *was established* and *had become strong*, is doubly emphatic (v. 1). The first verb normally refers in Chronicles to God's establishing of Israel's kingdom, and God's unique absence here is probably deliberate (*cf.* 1 Ch. 14:2; 17:11; 28:7; 2 Ch. 17:5).[1] The second is more neutral, and is positive (*e.g.* 2 Ch. 1:1; 17:1; 27:6) or negative in meaning (*e.g.* 2 Ch. 21:4; 25:3) according to context. Here one should distinguish between the fact of Rehoboam's strength, which is taken as a good sign (*cf.* 11:11, 12, 17), and the effect of it, which led to a turning away from God. Rehoboam had failed to heed Deuteronomy 8:10–18, allowing his success (ch. 11) to degenerate into pride and self-reliance.

Rehoboam's failure is described by two of Chronicles' typical phrases: he *abandoned the law of the LORD* (v. 1) and *was unfaithful to the LORD* (v. 2). Verse 1 probably summarizes 1 Ki. 14:22–24, especially as it is the only section of Kings' record of Rehoboam not directly mentioned in Chronicles. The parallel between abandoning the law and *abandoned me* (v. 5) stresses

---

[1] 'Was established' (NIV, NRSV, RSV, *cf.* REB) represents a slight but acceptable change from MT, with Rehoboam as the probable agent.

God's personal link with the law (*cf.* 6:16, where to follow the law is to walk before God; for the law's written form, *cf.* 2 Ch. 17:9; 25:4; 34:14–15).[1] To abandon or forsake God, which is the opposite of seeking him (*cf.* v. 14; 1 Ch. 28:9; 2 Ch. 15:2), meant to reject the temple and worship other gods (*e.g.* 2 Ch. 7:19, 22; 2 Ch. 24:18; 34:25). The dangers of forsaking God's laws were potentially extremely serious, and verses 2–4 illustrate the effectiveness of the principles of 2 Chronicles 7:19–22, though the judgment of exile is held back because of God's mercy.

To be *unfaithful* (Heb. *mā'al*) to God is one of Chronicles' key terms (it never occurs in Samuel or Kings), and its regular occurrence shows Israel's constant estrangement from God. It appears at the turning-points of his work, such as the beginning and end of the genealogies (1 Ch. 2:5; 9:1), the beginning and end of the monarchy (1 Ch. 10:13; 2 Ch. 36:14), as well as being a typical feature of the Divided Monarchy (*e.g.* 2 Ch. 26:16, 18; 28:19, 22; 29:6, 19). It involves denying God the worship due to him, usually on a national scale, and is the primary reason given in Chronicles for the exile.

Rehoboam's unfaithfulness has two interesting analogies elsewhere in Chronicles. Firstly, the combination of his unfaithfulness (v. 2) with a failure to obey God's word (v. 1) or to seek God's will (v. 14), effectively makes him a second Saul (*cf.* 1 Ch. 10:13–14). Secondly, his pride in his own strength anticipates Uzziah's downfall (2 Ch. 26:16). Both parallels strengthen the typical nature of Rehoboam's sins.

The campaign of Pharaoh *Shishak*, or Shoshenq I (*c.* 945–924 BC), the first king of the twenty-second (Libyan) dynasty (vv. 2–4) seems to have been aimed primarily at Sheshonq's old ally Jeroboam (*cf.* 1 Ki. 11:40), and the biblical accounts are supported by a triumphal relief in the Amun temple at Karnak and a small stele fragment from Megiddo.[2] The impression of an isolated show of strength in which Jerusalem was not captured is also reflected in the extrabiblical sources. The *Libyans* and *Sukkites* were from the western side of Egypt while the *Cushites* (NIV, REB, NEB; 'Ethiopians', NRSV, RSV, JB; 'Sudanese', GNB) were from the south. How many of the

---

[1] *Cf.* T. Willi, 'Thora in den biblischen Chronikbüchern', *Judaica* 36, 1980, pp. 102–105.
[2] *Cf.* K. A. Kitchen, 'Where did Solomon's gold go?' *Biblical Archaeology Review* 15/3, 1989, pp. 32–33.

fortified cities in 11:5–10 were captured is unknown (v. 4), though Aijalon is listed in 11:10 and at Karnak.

Chronicles makes explicit what is implicit in Kings, that Shishak's invasion was a divine punishment (*because they had been unfaithful*, v. 2, has been added to 1 Ki. 14:25). This is typical of the frequent link in Chronicles between Israel's sin and national disaster (*e.g.* 2 Ch. 6:24–39; 21:10; 24:24), as well as between obedience and blessing (*e.g.* 1 Ch. 11:7–9; 2 Ch. 12:6–8), though it should not be assumed that Chronicles saw suffering as the automatic result of sin. Some attacks, for example, were clearly unprovoked (*e.g.* 2 Ch. 14:9–15; 16:1–7; 20:1–30), while blessings could never be earned, for no-one was without sin (2 Ch. 6:36). The Chronicler's concern is to show that sin, or unfaithfulness and forsaking God as he calls it, always leads to God's displeasure, but that God always mixes mercy with judgment. In contrast with the rest of the Old Testament, the strength of the connection is perhaps emphasized more sharply in Chronicles. The New Testament maintains the link, but has a greater emphasis on the afterlife than on the present, and on individual and church issues as against national ones. So whereas the immediacy of Rehoboam's punishment is paralleled by Herod Agrippa I (Acts 12:21–23), Ananias and Sapphira (Acts 5:1–11), or by disease and death among church members in Corinth (1 Cor. 11:29–32), Jesus' teaching concentrated on judgment to come (*e.g.* Mt. 13:40–42; Lk. 16:19–31). Similarly, while Christians may sometimes receive material benefits (*e.g.* Mt. 6:33b; Phil. 4:18), Jesus encouraged his followers to expect spiritual blessings both now and in the future (Mt. 19:28–30; Eph. 1:3–10).

b. Judah's humble repentance (12:5–12). Into this crisis, the prophet *Shemaiah* (*cf.* 11:2) brings messages of judgment (v. 5) and of mercy (vv. 7–8). Each receives a response, and, as in 11:1–4, the relationship between prophecy and fulfilment is critical. Although the response to the second prophecy is predictable, that is not so with the first. The principle (v. 5) that God abandons those who abandon him seems clear and simple enough. It is also basic to Chronicles' theology, being repeated almost verbatim in 1 Chronicles 28:9, 20; 2 Chronicles 15:2; 24:20, and expanded in 2 Chronicles 7:19–22 (*cf.* 'turn away, forsake' in vv. 19, 22). But as elsewhere in the Old Testament (*cf.* Jon. 3:4–10; 2 Ki. 20:1–6; 2 Ch. 24:20), a

pronouncement of unconditional judgment can be understood as a further opportunity to repent, as Israel's (=
Judah's, *cf.* v. 1) leaders *humbled themselves* (v. 6). Rather than
resign themselves to the judgments of 7:19–22, they clung to
the offer of forgiveness in 7:13–14. Humbling oneself in
repentance is Chronicles' recognized way back to God, as is
especially affirmed in 2 Chronicles 30–36 (*cf.* 30:11; 32:26;
33:12; 34:27). It is also the key term in this section (vv. 6, 7,
12), for it turns disaster into deliverance. Following David's
example (1 Ch. 21:13), it seemed preferable to trust in God's
'righteousness' (v. 6, RSV; *just*, NIV, *etc.*) than submit to Pharaoh's army (the end of v. 5 is lit. 'by the agency of, through
Shishak', *cf.* v. 7).

As a result of Judah's repentance, God promises 'a little'
('some', REB, NRSV, RSV) *deliverance* (v. 7, NIV, *etc.*; 'relief', REB),
or possibly, 'in a little while' (JB, *cf.* NIV). The language seems
to be influenced by Ezra 9:8–9 (*cf.* the reference to 'servants /
service', v. 8). This analogy would have given real encouragement to the Chronicler's contemporaries, as would also God's
promise to remove his 'anger' (GNB; *wrath*, NRSV, RSV, NIV, *etc.*),
which seemed to hang over post-exilic Israel (*cf.* 2 Ch. 34:25;
36:16; Ezr. 9:14; 10:14). The partial deliverance was so that
Israel could *learn* afresh what it meant to *serve* God (v. 8). This
involved not only keeping his law (*cf.* v. 1), but was also the
best hope of freedom from the tyranny of earthly *kings* (*cf.*
'whose service is perfect freedom').[1]

The beginning of verse 9 partially repeats verse 2, to show
that 1 Kings 14:25 is being resumed. Shishak is bought off
with a single payment of tribute (v. 10), which meant replacing
gold shields (*cf.* 2 Ch. 9:16) by *bronze* ones and installing a new
security system (v. 11). In addition to the *guards*, the shields
were kept in a special *room* – the Hebrew word is unique but
has the sense of 'inner room'.[2]

Verse 12 is best seen as a summary of the whole of
Rehoboam's reign, with the first sentence referring to verses
5–11, and the (lit.) 'good things' looking back to chapter 11.
The latter phrase is difficult to translate and interpret. NIV's
some good is as good an attempt as any, and though the phrase

---

[1] On 'kings' (v. 8; *cf.* REB, NEB) rather than 'kingdoms' (JB, NRSV, RSV), *cf.* 9:19
and W. G. E. Watson, 'Archaic elements in the language of Chronicles', *Bib.* 53,
1972, p. 204.
[2] *Cf.* Akk. *ṭā'um* (*AHwb*, p. 1340).

refers in 2 Chronicles 19:3 to reformation and renewal of worship, the context here suggests a wider meaning (for a similar comment in the NT, *cf.* Rev. 3:4).

iv. Concluding formulae (12:13–16)

> 12:13b–14 – *cf.* 1 Kings 14:21–22
> 12:15–16 – *cf.* 1 Kings 14:29–31

This paragraph combines the opening and concluding formulae in 1 Kings 14:21–22, 29–31. The dates of his *seventeen*-year reign are variously given as 937–921 (Hughes), 931/30–913 (Thiele) and 922–915 BC (Albright), depending on textual decisions. *Established himself firmly* (v. 13; lit. 'made himself strong') combines the first two verbs in verse 1, and probably refers to the over-all length of his reign. This view is based on MT's 'because', which occurs before the statements about his age and length of reign, though it is omitted in EVV. This is preferable to 'increased his power' (REB, NEB, GNB), which relates it to the aftermath of Shishak's invasion.

13–14. The statement that God *had chosen* Jerusalem (*cf.* 1 Ki. 14:21), and mention of God's *Name* are linked by the temple (*cf.* 2 Ch. 6:5–6, 34, 38; 7:12, 16; 33:7). They may also provide a backcloth to Rehoboam's humility, for the temple existed to encourage humble repentance (*cf.* 2 Ch. 7:14). In contrast, the final comment on Rehoboam heightens Kings' negative assessment. Where 1 Kings 14:22 has 'Judah did evil', Chronicles makes him personally responsible, and adds, 'he did not set his heart to seek the LORD' (NRSV, RSV). 'Seeking God' in Chronicles describes one's over-all attitude, and contrasts Rehoboam with Asa (2 Ch. 14:4, 7, *etc.*), Jehoshaphat (2 Ch. 20:3–4), Uzziah (2 Ch. 26:4–5), Hezekiah (2 Ch. 30:19; 31:21), and Josiah (2 Ch. 34:3), though Amaziah is a fellow unbeliever (2 Ch. 25:15, 20).

15–16. The concluding formula follows 1 Kings more closely, though with several small changes. It emphasizes the prophetic character of the Chronicler's sources (instead of 'the annals of the kings of Judah', 1 Ki. 14:29), on which the Chronicler may well have drawn directly, as least for information about *Shemaiah* (2 Ch. 11:2–4; 12:5, 7–8; for *Iddo*, *cf.* 2 Ch. 9:29). Another addition, though omitted in many EVV, is a reference to some kind of genealogical record (*cf.* NIV). While this may have something to do with the Levites (*cf.* JB, Ackroyd), it seems more likely to refer to the content of the prophetic sources. Though the Chronicler leaves out a second statement about Rehoboam's Ammonite mother (1 Ki. 14:31; *cf.* v. 13) presumably for stylistic reasons, his omission of Rehoboam's burial 'with his fathers' (1 Ki. 14:31) may reflect a negative judgment.

B. Abijah and Asa (13:1 – 16:14)

i. Abijah (13:1 – 14:1)

'Men of Israel, do not fight against the LORD, the God of your
fathers, for you will not succeed' (13:12, NIV).

13:1–2 – *cf.* 1 Kings 15:1–2, 6
13:22 – 14: 1 – *cf.* 1 Kings 15: 7–8

This account of *Abijah* is strikingly different from that in 1 Kings, where this king is known as Abijam. Chronicles' version is three times as long, but more importantly, seems to contradict Kings' assessment. Where the latter concludes that 'he committed all the sins his father had done before him' (1 Ki. 15:3), to the Chronicler he is a faithful ruler to whom God grants a miraculous victory. Why the discrepancy?

The differences are actually the result of the Chronicler's distinctive purpose and methods, and are not irreconcilable. The Chronicler's primary interest is in the development of God's plans rather than the personal life or spiritual orientation of individual kings. Abijah is less important for his own sake than for what God did through him, which is why chapter 13 concentrates almost entirely on a single incident concerning *the kingdom of the LORD* (*cf.* v. 8). It is clear that the Chronicler is not unaware of Abijah's failings, though as with Solomon, the details emerge in the record of his successor rather than in his own reign (2 Ch. 14:3–5; 15:8, 16–17).[1] These failings, however, did not disqualify Israel from experiencing God's deliverance, and as with Rehoboam (chs. 11–12), God responded to sinners who trusted in God (*cf.* v. 18). The crucial point concerns God's purposes for the Davidic kingship and Aaronic priesthood, in contrast to Jeroboam's kingdom which made no pretence to be orthodox. The Chronicler was therefore not rewriting history, but showing that imperfect people who expressed faith (13:15, 18) towards God

---

[1] *Cf.* D. G. Deboys, 'History and theology in the Chronicler's portrayal of Abijah', *Bib.* 71, 1990, pp. 48–62, especially pp. 51–52.

could have hope. The significance of this would not be lost on the Chronicler's contemporaries who needed every encouragement to exercise faith, which for them was a rare commodity (*e.g.* Ezr. 8:22–23, 31; Ne. 1:11; 2:20; 6:15–16).

Careful comparison of King's and Chronicles also reveals that far from treating Kings in a cavalier fashion, this version of Abijah is based on the earlier one, in addition to the probable use of an unknown source for the battle against Jeroboam (*cf.* Noth, Rudolph). Four elements of 1 Kings 15:1–7 are visible in this chapter. Firstly, the double mention in Kings of war between Judah and Israel indicates its importance there (1 Ki. 15:6, 7; *cf.* 2 Ch. 13:2). Secondly, the main thrust in Kings that God was preserving Jerusalem and David's dynasty as a small light amid the darkness is repeated in verses 5–12 (*cf.* 1 Ki. 15:4). Thirdly, the rather ambivalent assessment of 1 Kings 15:3 suggests that Abijah was not viewed entirely negatively in Kings. Fourthly, the Chronicler has structured his account around Kings' opening and closing formulae.

Abijah has a much higher profile in Chronicles because, like Rehoboam, his reign highlights several special emphases of chapters 10–36. Abijah's speech (vv. 4–12) is parallel in style and content to one by Hezekiah (2 Ch. 29:5–11; *cf.* 30:6–9). The latter, for example, confirms that the standard of faithfulness set by Abijah was continued in the latter years of Judah's kingship. Both speeches also have a stabilizing effect, Abijah's following the catastrophe of the division, Hezekiah's after the fall of Samaria and the disastrous reign of Ahaz (ch. 28).[1] Both crises also involve civil war, with defeats here for Israel and in the eighth century for Judah. Both nations in their turn fail God, and both speeches point to God-centred worship at the sole ground of future hope.

Chapters 13–16 form a distinct section around the theme of trust or reliance on the Lord. The key verb, 'rely' (Heb. *šāʿan*), occurs five times in these chapters with positive (13:18; 14:11; 16:8) and negative examples (16:7), and nowhere else in Chronicles. The theme is developed by a contrast between 'forsaking' (13:10–11) and 'seeking' God (14:4, 7; 15:2, 4, 12, 15; 16:12). Abijah and Jeroboam illustrate the alternatives, as also does Asa (chs. 14–15, 16).

[1] *Cf.* M. A. Throntveit, *Kings*, pp. 109–120.

These literary structures offer a message of hope for the undeserving. If chapter 12 highlighted the importance of repentance, here it is faith and trust. This is also a familiar New Testament theme. Analogies may be found in passages which speak of faithfulness in the face of apostasy or persecution (*e.g.* Heb. 10:32–39; Rev. 2:12–13) or that spiritual strength can be a reality in human weakness and inferiority (*e.g.* 1 Cor. 1:26–31; 2 Cor. 12:9–10). Even previous failure is no obstacle, for 'at each point there is the chance of a fresh start' (Wilcock).

a. Introductory formula (13:1–2a). This is the first introductory formula in Chronicles that actually occurs at the beginning of a king's reign (*cf.* 1 Ch. 29:22–24; 2 Ch. 12:13–14). It is also the only one in Chronicles to include a synchronization with Israel, presumably because the main event in this chapter concerns both kingdoms. Abijah's mother's details vary from 1 Kings 15:2. Her name is probably a scribal variant ('Micaiah' for *Maacah*), and *Uriel* may be a son of Absalom ('Abishalom', 1 Ki. 15:2), making Micaiah/Maacah the latter's granddaughter, though certainty is impossible.[1] Abijah's reign was short, datable to 921–916 (Hughes; *cf.* LXX), 913–910 (Thiele) or 915–913 BC (Albright). The lack of a theological evaluation is notable, perhaps indicating that his reign as a whole lacked clear direction, despite the positive example here (*cf.* 1 Ki. 15:3).

b. Civil war between Judah and Israel (13:2b–19). The only event in Abijah's reign which Chronicles records is the war with Jeroboam (*cf.* v. 2b). The latter was probably the aggressor, judging by Abijah's rather defensive speech (*cf.* v. 8) and by Jeroboam's attack (vv. 13–14). If this view is correct, this is Jeroboam's attempt to reunite the kingdoms. However, since both he and Rehoboam before him are rebuffed by God (*cf.* 11:1–4), it is clearly not yet God's time for reunification. The location at *Zemaraim* in Ephraim (v. 4) is usually linked with a Benjaminite place of the same name near Mount Ephraim (Jos. 18:22), probably Ras et-Tahuneh on the mountain's

---

[1] See also 2 Ch. 11:20–21 and Myers, *2 Chronicles*, pp. 79–80.

southern side.[1] The troop numbers (v. 3) are not to be understood literally and show Judah outnumbered two to one.

i. Abijah's speech (13:4–12). Abijah's 'sermon on the mount' (Rudolph) dominates this section. Though unexpected in terms of military strategy, it is typical of the speeches and prayers which occur at key points in Chronicles. The present form reflects the Chronicler's language and interests, though hints of Abijah's own outlook also appear (vv. 7, 10–11). It is addressed primarily to the people of Israel (vv. 4, 12; Jeroboam is referred to in the third person, vv. 6, 8), though they seem to be fully identified with their king. There are three sections.

(a) 13:5–8a. Kingship. Abijah makes two charges against Israel, that they have rejected God's gifts of David's dynasty and the temple. He, on the other hand, has been faithful. He acknowledges that the dynasty is given *for ever* (1 Ch. 17:12, 14) as a *covenant of salt* (v. 5), a metaphor for permanence based on Numbers 18:19.[2] It is also associated with the *kingdom of the LORD* (v. 8), an idea also reflected in verse 5, literally, '. . . gave *the* kingdom/kingship to David over Israel . . .'. This is a familiar theme in Chronicles (*e.g.* 1 Ch. 17:14; 28:5; 29:23; 2 Ch. 9:8), though surprising here in view of Abijah's idolatry (1 Ki. 15:3). A distinction is made between the two kingdoms, however, for God's kingdom was still under his authority, and was in the *hands* of David's family rather than those of an individual.[3]

Jeroboam, however, has *rebelled* against *his master*, *i.e.* Solomon (v. 6; the idea is taken from 1 Ki. 11:26–27), against *Rehoboam* (v. 7; *cf.* 2 Ch. 10), and intends to do the same with Abijah (v. 8). Abijah's defence of his father Rehoboam (v. 7) seems somewhat exaggerated in view of chapter 10, though the political device of presenting the facts in the best possible light is familiar enough! Though Rehoboam was indeed inexperienced and weak-willed ('young and irresolute', NRSV, RSV), at forty-one he was fully responsible for his folly (*cf.*

---

[1] Z. Kallai, *Historical Geography of the Bible* (Jerusalem: Magnes Press, 1986), p. 401. The more usual identification of Ras 'ez-Zemariah is rejected for archaeological reasons.

[2] *Cf.* Japhet, *Ideology*, p. 465; Rudolph.

[3] See further, M. J. Selman, 'The kingdom of God in the Old Testament', *TB* 40, 1989, pp. 161–183, especially pp. 163–171.

12:13). An ironic wordplay sums up Jeroboam – though Rehoboam could not *resist* him (v. 7), he can *resist* God (v. 8; *cf.* NIV, JB, GNB; 'withstand', NRSV, RSV).

(b) 13:8b–12a. Worship. The second charge concerns God's purposes for the temple, and focuses on the nature of God, priesthood and sacrifice. Firstly, Israel's gods are *not gods* (v. 9), an allusion to the *golden calves* of Hosea 8:6. As in ancient Near Eastern custom, these were apparently carried with the army as a protective charm (v. 8b). Secondly, Israel's *priests* are unqualified and the Aaronite priests and Levites have been dismissed (vv. 9–10; *cf.* 11:15). Thirdly, only the pattern of worship at Jerusalem is acceptable to the Lord, for Israel's fertility cults were polytheistic and idolatrous (v. 11; *cf.* 1 Ki. 12:26–33). These regular sacrifices, celebrated daily apart from the weekly replacement of *bread*, are a typical emphasis in Chronicles. They are the 'charge' (v. 11, NRSV, RSV, REB, NEB; *requirements*, NIV; but not 'ritual', JB) of the Lord, a sum-marizing word for cultic duties (1 Ch. 9:27; 23:32; 2 Ch. 35:2), and show that the temple was being put to proper use (*cf.* 1 Ch. 23:29–31; 2 Ch. 2:4; 4:7; 8:12–15).

Abijah's defence, expressed in a somewhat self-satisfied manner, is simple: *we have not forsaken him, … but you have forsaken him* (vv. 10–11). This was extremely serious, for God would forsake those who forsook him (1 Ch. 28:9; 2 Ch. 15:2; 24:20; *cf.* 2 Ch. 12:1, 5), whereas Judah could say, *God is with us* (v. 12). Though the division remained God's will (10:15; 11:4), Jeroboam's failure to acknowledge the legitimacy of Abijah's kingship and of the Jerusalem cultus meant that his kingdom was no longer approved by God. It was funda-mentally flawed, and offered no hope for any future Israel.

(c) 13:12b. Appeal. Abijah concludes with an appeal, *Do not fight against the LORD … for you will not succeed*. It is the focal point of Abijah's argument, and resembles a sermon text, as in other speeches where the text often comes at the end.[1] It contains two important themes, both of which are developed in 2 Chronicles 20:1–30, the centrepiece of the Divided Mon-archy. The first, which has its origin in the exodus, is that it is futile to oppose God, for he fights his own battles (*cf.* 1 Ch. 5:22; 2 Ch. 11:4; 20:17; 32:8; *cf.* Ex. 14:14; Dt. 20:4; Acts

---

[1] G. von Rad, 'The levitical sermon in 1 and 2 Chronicles', in *The Problem of the Hexateuch* (Edinburgh: Oliver & Boyd, 1966), pp. 267–280, especially p. 278.

5:39). The second is that one can *succeed* only with God's help, as illustrated positively (*e.g.* 1 Ch. 29:23; 2 Ch. 14:6; 20:20; 26:5) and negatively (*e.g.* 2 Ch. 24:20).

ii. Battle report (13:13–19). The account of the actual battle moves through four stages: (a) Jeroboam's ambush (vv. 13–14a); (b) Judah's prayers (vv. 14b–15a); (c) God's gift of victory to Judah (vv. 15b–16); and (d) the results (vv. 17–19). The whole paragraph reflects Israel's victories in earlier days, showing that overwhelming odds presented no problem when Israel *relied* (v. 18) on God. Israel had been opposed by an *ambush* in Judges 9:25, by an army at both *front and rear* in 2 Samuel 10:9 (= 1 Ch. 19:10), even by a *vast army* (v. 8) in 1 Kings 20:13, 28 (*cf.* 2 Ch. 14:9; 20:2, 12, 15, 24; 32:7). The sounding of a *battle cry* (vv. 12, 15) to the accompaniment of *trumpets* blown by *priests* recalls the memorable capture of Jericho (Jos. 6:1–20; *cf.* Nu. 10:9; 31:6). The account seems to draw particularly on Deuteronomy 20:1–4, 10–15, demonstrating Judah's faithfulness to the principles of covenant law. The emphasis on trust in God despite an enemy's superior strength, the affirmation that God is with his armies, and the offer of peace before the battle are especially noteworthy (v. 12). This pattern is often called a holy war, though, as applied to the Old Testament, the term is rather misleading.[1] Israel could never assume the right to go to war on God's behalf, for she could find herself at times opposed by God. A better term is 'Yahweh's war', which was sometimes appropriate for Israel's wars because she was Yahweh's nation, but is applicable to the church only when understood as spiritual warfare (*cf.* 2 Cor. 10:3–6; Eph. 6:10–20).'[2]

The central theme is reliance on God (v. 18). Judah 'cried to the LORD (v. 14, NRSV, RSV, *etc.*) and raised the *battle cry* (v. 15; *cf.* 2 Ch. 20:19–22), in contrast to Israel's forsaking God (v. 11). The victory belonged to God, who *routed* Israel (v. 15; *cf.* REB, NEB; lit. 'struck') and *delivered* (v. 16) her into Judah's hands. The term for Israel's defeat, *were subdued* (v. 18), is, literally, 'were humbled' (JB), *i.e.* exactly the opposite of that

---

[1] Especially G. von Rad, *Holy War in Ancient Israel* (Grand Rapids: Eerdmans, 1991) (ET of *Die heilige Krieg im alten Israel*, rev. ed., Göttingen: Vandenhoeck & Ruprecht, 1951).

[2] See *e.g.* A. Ruffing, *Jahwekrieg als Weltmetapher*, SBB 24 (Stuttgart: Katholisches Bibelwerk, 1992).

2CHRONICLES 13:1 – 16:14

which God desired (*cf.* 2 Ch. 7:14; 12:6, 12). The result was a 'great slaughter' (v. 17, NRSV, RSV; 'crushing defeat', GNB, JB), the Hebrew version of which normally referred to Israel's enemies (*e.g.* Jos. 10:10; 1 Sa. 19:8; 23:5), though it could be applied to rebellious Israelites (Nu. 11:33).

Despite Abijah's conquests in southern Israel, border conflicts continued for many years (v. 19, *cf.* 2 Ch. 15:8; 16:6; 17:2). *Bethel's* capture is an ironic comment on the golden calves' inability to defend their own sanctuary (*cf.* 1 Ki. 12:28–33).

c. Abijah's strength (13:20–21). Jeroboam's failure to *regain power* (v. 20) is a deliberate contrast to the fact that Abijah *grew in strength* (v. 21). Though Jeroboam outlived Abijah (1 Ki. 15:9), the former's death is understood as a sign of divine judgment (*struck down*, v. 20, is the same Heb. verb as *routed*, v. 15). For a large family as a sign of blessing and strength (v. 21), *cf.* 1 Chronicles 26:5; 2 Chronicles 11:18–21.

d. Concluding formula (13:22 – 14:1). A couple of changes to 1 Kings 15:6–7 are worth noting. Though 'story' (v. 22, NRSV, RSV, NEB; *annotations*, NIV) is literally 'midrash' (JB), it is probably another term for Iddo's writings (*cf.* 2 Ch. 9:29; 12:15) rather than an early use of a term for a type of rabbinic exegesis (also 24:27). The ten-year period of *peace* (14:1) refers to Asa's reign (*cf.* 14:5–7; 15:15, 19), since Abijah reigned for only three years (13:2).

ii. Asa (14:2 – 16:14)
'He commanded Judah to seek the LORD' (14:4).
'They entered into a covenant to seek the LORD their God with all their heart and soul' (15:12).
'He did not seek the LORD' (16:12, NRSV).

14:2 – *cf.* 1 Kings 15:11
15:16–18 – *cf.* 1 Kings 15:13–15
16:1–6 – *cf.* 1 Kings 15:17–22
16:11–14 – *cf.* 1 Kings 15:23–24

Asa is the third king in a row to whom Chronicles has given considerably more attention than Kings (2 Ch. 14–16; *cf.* 1 Ki. 15:9–24). In contrast to Rehoboam and Abijah, however, Chronicles' version is rather less complimentary. This is not because the Chronicler makes arbitrary judgments, but, as was noticed previously, to draw attention to certain over-all theological features rather than details about individuals. Two themes provide the framework for Asa's reign. The first is 'relying' on God, indicated by the occurrence of the Hebrew verb *šā'an* five times in chapters 13–16 but nowhere else in Chronicles. Both Abijah and Asa offer examples for others to imitate (13:18; 14:11; 16:8), though unfortunately Asa did not end as he began (16:7). The second theme, that of seeking God, is central to Asa's reign (the verb 'to seek' occurs nine times). King and people both live out the principle of 15:2 (14:4, 7; 15:4), committing themselves to God by a covenant (15:12, 15). Again, however, Asa falls away from his previous good practice (16:12), potentially putting himself under the curse of his own covenant (15:13).

A variety of other themes also bind the reign of Asa together. One of the most persistent is *war* and *peace* (or *rest*). Where humankind seems bent on making war (14:9–10; 15:5–6; 16:1, 4), God gives deliverance and peace (14:1, 5–7, 12–15; 15:15, 19) to those who put their trust in him, though he may send war as a punishment to those who look elsewhere for help (16:9). A related theme is that of strengthening the kingdom, both through fortifications (14:6–7; 16:6) and through inner strength (15:7–8; 16:9). Trust in God is also expressed through faithfulness to Yahwism, especially in a concern for the temple (15:8, 18) and an intolerance of the paraphernalia of Canaanite religion (14:2–5; 15:8, 16–18). A key feature is respect for the authority of the prophetic word. Two prophecies are prominent, one to which Asa responds with enthusiasm (15:1–8) and one which causes him great anger (16:7–10). The centrepiece of Asa's faithfulness, however, is undoubtedly the *covenant* made at a special assembly (15:10–15). This high point of Judah's national life so far is entered into by the whole people with heart and soul, and was accompanied by much sacrificial worship and rejoicing. There is, though, a reverse side to this in a covenant or treaty made between Asa and Ben-Hadad of Syria (16:2–3), whose unhappy consequences (16:7–12) replaced the blessings of the first covenant.

One very interesting aspect of this thematic approach is the extent to which Asa's reign parallels that of Hezekiah. Though Asa is not of the same stature, many features of his reign point directly to the great reformer. Both *prospered*

(14:7; 31:21) through doing what was *good and right* in God's sight (14:2; 31:20), *seeking* God (15:4, *etc.*; 31:21), serving him from the *heart* (15:17; 31:21), and duly obeying his *law and commandment* (14:4; 31:21). They removed the symbols of idolatry (14:3–5; 31:1), convened an *assembly* (15:9, 10; 30:13ff.) and renewed the people's *covenant* (15:12–15; 29:10). A particularly striking feature is that both kings welcomed Israelites from the north to worship at Jerusalem (15:9; 30:11). Both of them also suffered the misfortune of military invasion after very public expressions of loyalty to God, and both responded to these threats with a declaration that faith in God was superior to reliance on a vast army (14:9–10; 32:7–8). Even the final periods of their lives have poignant analogies. They both suffered illnesses attributable to a lack of trust in God, though it is not recorded that Asa repented as Hezekiah did (16:12; 32:24–26), and finally, they received special honour at their funeral services (16:14; 32:33). These parallels are not accidental, and point to a pattern of life which in the main the Chronicler commends to his readers.

The ups and downs of Asa's life are presented in a stylized form. Two patterns are employed, both of which are familiar elsewhere in Chronicles. One is the periodization of Asa's reign, which is most obvious from a series of dates without parallel in Kings (14:1, 9; 15:10, 19; 16:1, 12, 13). The effect of this arrangement is to characterize the majority of his reign as one of peace, interrupted only by an invasion (14:9–15) and occasional hostilities with Israel (15:8; 16:1–6). The second pattern is a chiastic-type structure centred round the covenant renewal ceremony (15:9–18), and can be presented as follows:

a. 14:2–7 Prosperity through seeking God
  b. 14:8–15 Victory through trust in God
    c. 15:1–8 Obedience to prophetic word
      d. 15:9–18 Covenant with God
      d_1. 16:1–6 Covenant with man (and temporary victory)
    c_1. 16:7–10 Rejection of prophetic word (and lack of
              trust)
a_1. 16:11–12 Incurable disease through not seeking God

Most of the connections between the paragraphs are quite plain, apart from 14:8–15 which is really paralleled both in 16:1–6 and 16:7–10. Asa's first battle plan (14:8–15) contrasts

sharply with his second (16:1–6), as illustrated by the specific
reference to the Cushites in 16:8 (*cf.* 14:9–13) and to those on
whom Asa relied (*cf.* 14:11; 16:7–8). 16:1–10, therefore, is an
'anti-covenant' (*cf.* 15:9–18) which combines military defeat
and disobedience to the prophetic word, and the whole structure shows how Asa's last years represented a complete *volte-
face* from his previous achievements.

Chronicles' account of Asa follows the basic framework of
Kings. For example, 14:3 – 15:15 fills out 1 Kings 15:11–15,
which shows how 'Asa did what was right in the eyes of the
LORD', and chapter 16 offers more details of Asa's Israelite
war, his final illness and death (*cf.* 1 Ki. 15:17–24). A more
complex issue is the relationship between the good and bad
periods of his reign, both of which are already present in
Kings. Though the Chronicler is often charged with imposing
his own artificial interpretation on Asa, a less hasty judgment
is more appropriate. The following points should be particularly borne in mind. Firstly, the chronological framework
does not support a rigid theology of reward and punishment,
since the attacks of 14:9; 15:1 occur after periods of faithfulness. Secondly, an explicitly theological approach does not
automatically undermine confidence in Chronicles' historical
value. Thirdly, there is evidence of dependence on various
sources (*cf.* Williamson). This is particularly true of the prophetic material, which plays a key role (15:1–8; 16:7–10) here
and throughout Chronicles. Fourthly, the apparent contradictions (see especially on 15:17, 19) may be due to several
possible causes. Only the question of the dates in 15:19 and
16:1 remains unresolvable for the present, though this must
also be seen as part of a wider problem of the chronology of
the monarchy. The issues of Asa's blamelessness (14:2; 15:17;
16:7–12) and his removal of the high places (14:3, 5; 15:17)
may result either from faithful but unharmonized quotation
of source material or from the inclusion of exceptions alongside summarizing statements.

Chapter 14 introduces the main themes of Asa's reign,
combining the emphases of seeking God (vv. 4, 7) and relying
on him (v. 11). In reality, these are different sides of the same
coin, namely, an attitude of faith and trust, though the former
is more general and the latter more specific. This trust is
worked out practically, through a religious reformation (vv.
3–5), a strengthening of fortifications (vv. 6–7), and a victory

over a superior invading army (vv. 8–15). Such a practical emphasis is a good illustration of the inner relationship between faith and works (*cf.* Jas. 2:14–26; Rev. 3:1–6). It also underlines that faith is most effective in a time of crisis when it arises out of a more general attitude towards God, a theme that occurs regularly in the Old Testament (*e.g.* Dn. 1–6; Gn. 12–22) as well as the New Testament (*e.g.* Heb. 10:32 – 12:3; Rev. 3:7–13).

a. Asa seeks God and is prosperous (14:2–7).[1] The first part of Asa's reign exemplifies faithfulness, expansion, and security. In the evaluation, *good* has been added to *right* (v. 2; *cf.* 1 Ki. 15:11), apparently as a parallel with Hezekiah (the phrase recurs only in 2 Ch. 31:20). The reform has three main features: worship (vv. 3–5), buildings and fortifications (vv. 6–7), and the army (v. 8).

The religious reforms (vv. 3–5), which are supplemented in 15:16–18 (= 1 Ki. 15:13–15), differ in detail from 1 Kings 15:12, though Chronicles is totally dependent on Kings for the origin of the idolatrous practices (vv. 3–5; they are attributed to Solomon, Rehoboam, and Abijah, 1 Ki. 11:3–13; 14:22–24; 15:3). However, three of the four elements of Canaanite religion mentioned in verse 3 do recur in Deuteronomy 7:5 (*cf.* Ex. 34:13; Dt. 12:3), underlining Asa's faithfulness to the Mosaic law. A strong link with Hezekiah also emerges, since all four elements of verse 3 are mentioned in 2 Chronicles 31:1, and the expression 'cut down the Asherah poles' occurs elsewhere only in Deuteronomy 7:5 and 2 Chronicles 31:1. The *sacred stones* (v. 3; 'pillars', NRSV, RSV, *etc.*; Heb. *maṣṣēḇôṯ*, v. 2, MT) were memorial standing stones usually dedicated to individual deities, and the *Asherah poles* (v. 3; 'sacred poles', REB, NEB, JB) were wooden objects representing the fertility goddess Asherah. The word for *incense altar* (v. 5) is uncertain, and might mean a small religious building, though the translation 'sun-pillar' is now rejected.

The 'law' and 'commandment' (v. 4, NRSV, RSV; *cf.* 2 Ch. 31:21) is variously described in Chronicles, indicating that the meaning of individual terms for the law was fluid rather than rigidly technical.[2] Law remained a living rather than a

---

[1] Verse numbers in Heb. are one lower than in EVV throughout the ch.
[2] *Cf.* Japhet, *Ideology*, pp. 235–236.

legalistic concept, and, since obedience is equated with seeking God, the law is viewed as a means of maintaining fellowship with God (*cf.* 6:16; 12:1, 5).

Building activities (vv. 6–7) are typically ascribed to faithful kings in Chronicles (*e.g.* 2 Ch. 11:5–2; 17:12; 26:6, 9–10; 32:29–30), though equipping the army is associated with kings of various reputations (*cf.* 17:14–19; 25:5; 26:11–15). These achievements are indications of God's gift of *peace*, *rest* (vv. 5–7; *cf.* v. 1) and *prosperity* (v. 7) because Asa's people *sought* God (v. 7). Rest symbolized Israel's occupation of the Promised Land (1 Ch. 22:9, 18; *cf.* Dt. 12:8–10), but it had to be maintained with vigilance and trust in God. Even faithful kings could suffer attack (contrast 2 Ch. 12:2, 5). Other kings who *prospered* (v. 7; Heb. *hiṣlîaḥ*, v. 6, MT) because of their faith included David (1 Ch. 22:11, 13), Solomon (1 Ch. 29:23), Jehoshaphat (2 Ch. 18:11, 14; 20:4, 20), and Uzziah (2 Ch. 26:5; contrast 2 Ch. 12:12; 24:20).

Asa's brief speech (v. 7), which shows the king taking the people into his confidence (*let* us *build*), ties in with the Chronicler's emphasis on the need for kings to consult (*cf.* 1 Ch. 13:1–5; contrast 2 Ch. 10:1–16). His invitation and the phrase 'while *the land is still ours*' (or 'while we are in control of the land', *cf.* Rudolph, GNB) would have constituted a special incentive to the people of the Chronicler's day to do what they could to rebuild the land. The repetition of *we sought* has seemed unnecessary to some, who prefer to read 'as we have sought the LORD . . ., he has sought us' (so REB, NEB, GNB, with LXX, P, Vulg.). MT is preferable, however, since although the proposed change reflects the principle found in 1 Chronicles 28:9; 2 Chronicles 15:2, God's seeking is confined to contexts dealing with judgment (1 Ch. 28:9; 2 Ch. 24:22).

b. Asa trusts God and is victorious (14:8–15). Since *Zerah the Cushite* is unknown outside Chronicles, his identity and even his existence is debated. Normally in the Bible Cush is the area south of Egypt, *i.e.* Sudan (*cf.* GNB; rather than modern Ethiopia, *cf.* NRSV, RSV). Mention of *Gerar* (vv. 13–14), however, just across the Judean-Philistine border, may indicate a more local bedouin conflict, perhaps supported by the parallel between 'Cushan' and Midian (Hab. 3:7; *cf.* Curtis and Madsen, Williamson, de Vries, *etc.*). The African interpretation is more likely, however, for the following reasons.

The Cushites are associated with the Libyans (2 Ch. 16:8, *cf.* 12:3), local bedouin tribes are unlikely to have owned 300 chariots when Judah had none (v. 9), and precise geographical conclusions should not be drawn on the basis of a single example of prophetic poetry, especially as Gerar is west of Judah and Midian is to the south. Zerah himself is most likely to have been a Nubian (= Sudanese) general in the army of Pharaoh Osorkon I (*c.* 924–884 BC), Shoshenq I's son and successor (*cf.* 12:2ff.). The war is dated in Asa's fifteenth year (*cf.* 15:10–11), approximately 897 BC, and took place on Judah's south-western border at *Mareshah* (vv. 9, 10; *cf.* 11:8). The *Valley of Zephathah* (v. 10) is otherwise unknown.[1]

Zerah's army (v. 9) is best understood as comprising 1,000 units, which would be more likely alongside *three hundred chariots* than 'a million' soldiers (GNB, *etc.*). However the figures are understood, the invading army was nearly twice the size of the Judean forces (v. 8), so that Asa was fully justified in calling for God's help against a 'multitude' (v. 11, NRSV, RSV; 'huge army', GNB, *cf.* NIV).

The theme of the battle report is that of 'Yahweh's war' (*cf.* 13:13–18). It centres on Asa's prayer (v. 11), which is to be understood as a plea in the *name* of Yahweh directed towards the temple (*cf.* 6:34–35). It also anticipates Jehoshaphat's classic prayer (20:5–31; *cf.* 13:4–12). It exhibits several emphases typical of Chronicles, such as God's *help* (*cf.* 1 Ch. 5:20; 15:26; 2 Ch. 18:31; 32:8), his concern for the *powerless* (*cf.* 2 Ch. 20:12), that he is Israel's God (*cf.* 2 Ch. 13:12; 32:8) on whom they rely (*cf.* 13:18; 16:8), and against whom neither this 'multitude' (NRSV, RSV; *vast army*, NIV; *cf.* 2 Ch. 20:12, 15; 32:7) nor 'mortal' man (REB) can prevail.[2] Victory is attributed to the Lord (vv. 12–13; 'defeated', v. 12, NRSV, RSV, JB, is the same verb as in 13:15, 20), as the opposition *fled* (v. 12; *cf.* 2 Ch. 13:16; 25:22) and were paralysed by *the terror of the LORD* (v. 14; *cf.* 1 Ch. 14:17; 2 Ch. 17:10; 20:29). This whole theme may be summed up, 'The battle is not yours, but God's' (2 Ch. 20:15; *cf.* Eph. 6:12; Col. 2:15; Rev. 5:5). Despite Israel's faithfulness and preparations (vv. 2–8), it was God who

---

[1] LXX's 'north of', based on a similar word, is an easier reading and probably secondary.

[2] It is a testimony to the power of this prayer that (in the AV version) it inspired E. G. Cherry's famous hymn, 'We rest on thee, our shield and our defender'.

proved the difference between destruction and victory.

Some details of the aftermath are provided (vv. 13–15). The Cushites were so (lit.) 'broken' (v. 13, NRSV, RSV) that there was 'no recovery' (*cf.* NIV, GNB, JB). The Hebrew for the latter is 'reviving' rather than 'life' (*cf.* Gn. 45:5; Ezr. 9:8–9), making RSV's 'none remained alive' (*cf.* REB, NEB) seem excessive. The people around Gerar (v. 14) and the *herdsmen* (v. 15) were presumably Zerah's allies, though the latter were probably *attacked* (NIV, NRSV, RSV, *etc.*) rather than 'killed' (REB, NEB). Interest in the spoil (vv. 13–15) is explained by its use in sacrifice (15:11).

c. Asa obeys a prophet's word (15:1–8). The account of Asa's reformation and restructuring (*cf.* 14:2–8) now moves in chapter 15 to its two main features, a prophecy by Azariah (15:1–8), and a covenant ceremony (15:9–15). Both events are unique to Chronicles, but they are supplemented by further details from Kings (vv. 16–18; *cf.* 1 Ki. 15:13–15).

Despite the inclusion of a couple of dates, the over-all chiastic arrangement in chapters 14–15 does not allow the order of events to be reconstructed with much confidence. The only reasonably definite conclusion is that the covenant ceremony (15:9–15) in Asa's fifteenth year (15:3) followed the Cushite war (14:13–15; 15:11) and was one of the consequences of Azariah's prophecy (*cf.* v. 9). This testifies to the importance of the prophetic word (15:1–8), even though it may not have provided the impetus for the reformation as a whole. It also marks out the covenant ceremony as the main event, probably as its climax (this may have implications for our understanding of the role of other reformations in the Old Testament, especially Josiah's, *cf.* 2 Ki. 22–23; 2 Ch. 34–35). The other events of the reform (14:2–5; 15:8, 16–18) were part of a wider process which could have taken place over a shorter or a longer period. What is more important is that it touched the entire nation, including the queen mother (15:16), all Judah (14:5), and even the north (15:8–9).

The theme of seeking God continues from chapter 14, occupying a central role in both the prophecy (v. 2, 4) and the covenant (vv. 12–13, 15). Two elements are stressed, that the purpose of seeking God is to be found by him (vv. 2, 4, 15), and that this is an attitude affecting the whole of life. Seeking is not an end in itself, but a God-given means to be restored to a relationship with him. That relationship is seen to encompass internal and external worlds, attitudes as well as actions. Neither pietism nor restructuring is adequate by itself, and any authentic movement of spiritual renewal should show evidence of both.

Though the New Testament encourages people to make a priority of seeking God, it emphasizes that God seeks us much more than we seek him. There is a sense in which no-one truly seeks God (*cf*. Rom. 3:11), even though God invites everyone to seek him (Acts 15:17; 17:27). Ultimately, people find God because Jesus came 'to seek and save what was lost' (Lk. 19:10), and was prepared to search for one lost sheep out of a hundred or for a wayward child (Lk. 15). Seeking God is nonetheless very necessary, and the New Testament renews the Old Testament's invitation, 'seek and you will find' (Mt. 7:7, *etc*.), and affirms that God rewards those who go on seeking him in faith (Heb. 11:6).

Otherwise unknown prophets such as *Azariah* are frequently referred to in the period of the Divided Monarchy (v. 1; *cf*. *e.g*. 16:7–10; 24:20–22; 28:9–11). They bring God's word directly to the people or to their leaders, sometimes for warning or judgment, less often as here to encourage them to a particular course of action (*cf*. 20:14–17). The coming of the *Spirit of God* (v. 1) on an individual often leads to the exercise of prophecy (*e.g*. 1 Sa. 10:10; Is. 42:1; 61:1; Ezk. 11:5), though it is notable that all the other instances of such language in Chronicles attribute this gift to people who are not actually called prophets (1 Ch. 12:18; 2 Ch. 20:14: 24:20). Neither in fact is Azariah called a prophet, and in view of his knowledge of the Scriptures it may be that he was either a priest (*cf*. v. 3; 2 Ch. 24:20) or a Levite (*cf*. 2 Ch. 20:14).

This prophecy is unusual in that it is an exposition of earlier parts of the Old Testament though as an example of the speeches in Chronicles it is not untypical. Its style is sermonic, but its prophetic character comes through in the immediacy of the final imperative (v. 7) and in its authoritative teaching (*cf*. Mt. 7:29). The sermon has three sections, a text (v. 2b), an exposition (vv. 3–6), and an appeal (v. 7).

The text is based on Deuteronomy 4:29; Jeremiah 29:13–14; Isaiah 55:6 (*cf*. also 1 Ch. 28:9). While elsewhere in the Old Testament the principle in this text constitutes an invitation to restore those who are scattered, here it includes a warning not to *forsake* God. However, a further promise is also added to maintain the positive thrust, *viz.* that *the LORD is with you when you are with him* (this translation is preferable to '. . . as/so long as . . .', GNB, JB). It is worth noting that the text summarizes God's message about the purpose of the temple (2 Ch. 7:13–22).

The main part the sermon illustrates from Israel's history God's intention to be found by his people. It shows that Israel suffered when they turned their backs on God (vv. 3, 5–6) and that they were restored as soon as they sought him in repentance (v. 4). Sometimes God sent *distress* (v. 6, *cf.* v. 4), characterized by religious anarchy (v. 3) and by general *turmoil* (v. 5; 'trouble', REB, NEB; 'disturbances', NRSV, RSV) among the nations (vv. 5–6), probably a reference to the judges period. Certainly there was then a lack of recognized *law* or *priest*hood (*e.g.* Jdg. 17:5; 21:25), though it was also an uncomfortably accurate description of recent events in the north (2 Ch. 11:5; 13:9). The priests' teaching role was vital to the moral and spiritual quality of national life (*cf. e.g.* Lv. 10:11; Dt. 33:10; Mal. 2:7; 2 Ch. 17:7–9), but when it was neglected, the truth about God was denied (v. 3) and the fabric of covenant society was undermined (*cf.* v. 3; Ho. 4:1–9; Mal. 2:8). The description of the *turmoil* (Heb. *mᵉhûmâ*) is influenced by various Old Testament passages. It seems to be based on Deuteronomy 7:23, though it transfers to Israel that which God intended for the nations. The picture of insecurity is very similar to Judges 5:6; 6:2, while Israelite unbelief as a cause of trouble in other nations occurs in 1 Samuel 5:9 (EVV, 'panic') and various prophetic passages (*e.g.* Is. 22:5; Am. 3:9; Zc. 8:10; 14:13). Restoration was always possible, however, when Israel repented (v. 4; *turned to the LORD*). *Sought* (v. 4) also expresses the idea of repentance,. and is really a synonym for 'humble themselves' (7:14; 12:5, 12).

Azariah appeals for Asa to seek God afresh (v. 7). Again the language is influenced by the prophetic literature. Though the temptation to *give up* (lit., 'let one's hands drop', *cf.* NRSV, RSV, JB) was strong (*cf. e.g.* Je. 6:24; Ezk. 7:17), it had to be resisted in the light of Zephaniah 3:16; Isaiah 35:3 and the promise of reward for their *work* in Jeremiah 31:16.

The allusions to the prophets reflects not only the Chronicler's literary style but also the needs of his readers. They too had been tempted to let their hands become weak (*cf.* Ne. 6:9;

cf. Heb. 12:12–13), but had responded to God's word and among other things *repaired* the temple *altar* (v. 8; *cf.* Ezr. 3:3).They would also have been encouraged by Asa's obedience – 'take courage' (v. 7, NRSV, RSV, JB; *be strong*, NIV, GNB, REB, NEB) is from the same verb in Hebrew as *took courage* (v. 8, NRSV, NIV; 'encouraged', GNB; 'emboldened', JB). Whether Asa responded just to Azariah's words (v. 8, NRSV, GNB) or to a further prophecy by Azariah's father *Oded* (so MT) is not entirely clear. Another problem is deciding when Asa *captured* (v. 8) *towns* in *Ephraim*, though this and 16:1 imply that military successes in the north by either Abijah (13:19) or Asa were short-lived in any case.

d. Asa's covenant with God (15:9–19).

(i) *A new covenant (15:9–15)*. The covenant ceremony was part of an assembly (vv. 9–10; *cf.* NIV, REB, NEB). Such assemblies are typical of a number of kings in Chronicles, including David (1 Ch. 13:2–5; 15:3; 28:8; 29:1ff.), Solomon (2 Ch. 1:3; 5:6), Jehoshaphat (2 Ch. 20:5; *etc.*), and especially Hezekiah (*e.g.* 2 Ch. 29:23; 28; 30:2, 25). This no doubt reflects the importance of the assembly in the period from Ezra and Nehemiah onwards (*e.g.* Ezr. 3:1; 10:12; Ne. 8:1ff; 13:1), and witnesses to the significant role played by the people, as in this covenant ceremony (*cf.* v. 13). The key features on this occasion were that God was *with him*, *i.e.* Asa (v. 9), and that *large numbers* of northerners were present (v. 9). Chronicles constantly highlights the opportunities for reunification (*cf.* 11:13–17; 30:11; 34:6), which always arose in the context of worship rather than as a result of military force (*cf.* 11:1–4; 13:8, 13–14). Unity was possible only when God was worshipped in the way that he had ordained. The reason for *Simeon's* presence is not entirely clear, since, though this tribe seems to have been included among the ten tribes of the north (1 Ki. 11:31), their territory was originally to the south of Judah (*cf.* Jos. 19:1–9; 1 Ch. 4:28–33). The date of the *third month* (v. 10) indicates that this assembly was probably part of the Feast of Weeks or Pentecost (*cf.* Ex. 23:16; 34:22; *etc.*)

The people's *covenant* (v. 12) forms the climax of the reform. It is the first of four such covenants listed in Chronicles as against only two in Kings (*cf.* 2 Ch. 23:16; 29:10; 34:31–32; 2 Ki. 11:17; 23:3), testifying to their greater significance for Chronicles.[1] All these covenants enabled the people to renew their commitment to God, though each had distinctive characteristics. This covenant, for example, committed the people to *seek* God (vv. 12, 13, 15), that is, to express total obedience to him. This is a special meaning of 'to seek'. Whereas elsewhere it referred either to a specific occasion (*e.g.* v. 4; 20:4) or to a general attitude of following God's way (1 Ch. 28:9; 2 Ch. 7:14; 34:3), here it is equivalent to total commitment to God. This is combined with a variety of covenant expressions associated primarily with Deuteronomy. The phrase *with all their heart and soul* (v. 12; *cf.* v. 15, 'with all their heart', NRSV, RSV, *etc.*) is found in *e.g.* Deuteronomy 6:5; 10:12; 11:13; a penalty of *death* for non-compliance (v. 13) follows Deuteronomy 13:6–10; 17:2–7; and a covenant confirmed by an *oath* (vv. 14–15) is mentioned in Deuteronomy 29:12, 14 (*cf.* Ne. 10:29).

These links indicate that this covenant is based on the tradition of the Sinai covenant. As with most covenant ceremonies, that tradition was being applied to new circumstances. The new situation had been created by the division of the monarchy twenty-five years earlier, so that this ceremony is really the installation of Judah's religious constitution, recognizing the continuation of God's covenant purposes based on the Davidic lines and the Jerusalem temple. That is why many northerners took part (v. 9), and were required to forsake (*cf.* v. 2) the idol worship of the north (*cf.* vv. 8, 16–18) as well as to care for the *altar* in *the* LORD'S *temple* (v. 8). The importance of the occasion probably also explains the reminders of the time of David and Solomon. The *acclamation* and rejoicing (vv. 14–15) are linked with David (1 Ch. 15:25, 28) and *rest on every side* with Solomon (1 Ch. 22:9, 18; 28:2). Uniquely in the Old Testament, Israel is said to be *found* by God (v. 15; *cf.* v. 2).

(ii) *Further reforms (15:16–19).* The additional details of Asa's reforms (vv. 16–18) are based on 1 Kings 15:13–15, though Chronicles' faithfulness to the earlier text has resulted in two apparent contradictions in verse 17, that Asa *did not remove the high places* (against 14:3, 5) and that his *heart was fully committed*

---

[1] One must distinguish between political and religious covenants, since Ch. repeats all three of the former type mentioned in Sa.–Ki. (1 Ch. 11:3 = 2 Sa. 5:3; 2 Ch. 16:3 = 1 Ki. 15:19; 2 Ch. 23:1 = 2 Ki. 11:4).

to the LORD *all his life* (against ch. 16). The Chronicler, however, did not always harmonize every detail when quoting from different sources. In this case, Asa's over-all blamelessness was not negated by the contrasting decline of his last few years. The same kind of explanation may also apply to the high places, so that 14:3, 5 would refer to Asa's general policy while verse 17 would indicate the fact that it was not carried out thoroughly. More probably, however, the addition of *from Israel* (*cf.* 1 Ki. 15:14; *cf.* v. 8) suggests that the Chronicler distinguished between the high places in Judah (14:3, 5) and those in Israel (15:17).[1]

The *queen mother*'s role (v. 16) was an important one, especially when as in Asa's case he was a minor on his accession and *Maacah* was probably in over-all control for the opening years of his reign. By calling her Asa's *grandmother*, NIV, REB, NEB, and GNB assume she is the same person mentioned in 13:2; 1 Kings 15:2, 10, but it is unwise to be so dogmatic. That she had a personal object of worship continues a tradition of royal wives going back to Solomon (*cf.* 1 Ki. 11:1–5; 16:31; 17:19). Her 'Asherah image' (*pole*, NIV) seems to have been particularly *repulsive* ('obscene', GNB, REB, NEB), a Hebrew word which occurs only here and in 1 Kings 15:13. The *Kidron Valley* was a well-known dump for unwanted religious objects (*cf.* 2 Ch. 29:16; 30:14; 2 Ki. 23:4, 6, 12).

The dedicating of articles of precious metal (v. 18) was a practice initiated by David (1 Ch. 18:11; 22:3; 29:1–2; 2 Ch. 5:1), though nothing is otherwise known of such acts of piety by Abijah or Asa.

Verse 19 seems to indicate that Judah and Israel were at peace between Asa's fifteenth and thirty-fifth years (*cf.* v. 10), confirming verse 15. This is just about reconcilable with the statement in 1 Kings 15:16 that a state of war existed between Baasha of Israel (*cf.* 16:1) and Asa throughout their reigns, allowing for hostilities some time between Asa's tenth (14:1) and fifteenth years (15:10) and also in his thirty-sixth year (16:1). What is not apparently reconcilable is that Baasha moved against Judah in Asa's thirty-sixth year, since Baasha died in Asa's twenty-sixth year (1 Ki. 15:33; 16:8). Israel's king in Asa's thirty-sixth year was Omri, Baasha's third successor!

[1] See further, especially Dillard, pp. 117–118.

Since Kings and Chronicles agree that Asa reigned for forty-one years (1 Ki. 15:10; 2 Ch. 16:13; *i.e.* either *c.* 910–869 BC [Thiele] or *c.* 913–873 BC [Albright]), it seems at first sight either that Chronicles is following a different scheme for the Israelite monarchy here (but only here!) or that some scribal error has occurred. Two other alternatives are possible, however. The more ingenious is to follow Thiele by seeing this and 16:1 as referring to the thirty-fifth and thirty-sixth years after the division, which would conveniently equate them with Asa's fifteenth and sixteenth years and fit perfectly with the date for the covenant. Such a formula would be unique in the Old Testament, however. Otherwise, the discrepancy may be attributed to the Chronicler's theological purposes, enabling Asa's piety to be followed by peace and his unbelief by affliction. This, however, is equally unsatisfactory, not least because Baasha's attack (16:1) cannot easily be fitted into such a scheme of reward and punishment. No solution, therefore, commends itself with any confidence.

e. Asa's covenant with Ben-Hadad (16:1–6). Asa's last five years, recounted in chapter 16, completely reverse the pattern of the rest of his life, a decline that is all the more unexpected in that it seems to have started from an act of unprovoked hostility (v. 1). From that point on, however, Asa seemed determined to go his own way, and he followed his initial rejection of God's help (vv. 2–3) by persecuting a prophet (v. 10), oppressing his people (v. 10), and neglecting God (v. 12). A pattern therefore developed, which, though it may have begun by accident, became a series of conscious decisions.

This is clearly brought out by a literary structure which shows how completely and deliberately Asa turned his back on his earlier attitudes and achievements (chs. 14–15). Each section of chapter 16 has a negative counterpart with earlier periods in Asa's life:

16:1–6   A covenant with Ben-Hadad of Syria
16:7–10   A prophecy by Hanani
16:11–14 Asa's death and burial

The covenant with Ben-Hadad (vv. 1–6) compares unfavourably with the covenant of 15:9–15, Hanani's prophetic warning (vv. 7–10) must be set against Azariah's encouragement (15:1–8), the conflict with Israel (vv. 1–10) reverses

Asa's experience of faith and victory in the Cushite war (14:8–15), and he no longer seeks God when he falls ill (vv. 11–12; *cf.* 14:4, 7; 15:2, 12, 15). Incidental phrases reveal other contrasts, such as *silver and gold* (v. 2; *cf.* 5:1; 14:13–15), that the Syrians or Arameans *escaped* though the Cushites had fled (v. 7; *cf.* 14:12), that Israel was now oppressed instead of her enemies being broken (v. 9; *cf.* 14:13), and concerning those whose *hearts* were *committed* to God (v. 9; *cf.* 15:17).

Chapter 16 is based on 1 Kings 15, but, though the changes are less extensive than in chapters 14–15, they lead to a significantly different interpretation. Whereas 1 Kings 15:16–24 is a matter-of-fact report of Asa's Israelite war and his illness, here Asa is criticized for lack of faith in a way that has no explicit analogy in Kings. Another element without parallel in Kings is the dating scheme used throughout the chapter. What sources the Chronicler may have used in presenting his material in this way cannot be discovered, though one source is named (v. 11) and the prophecy is doubtless connected with the Chronicler's frequent citation of prophetic authorities (*e.g.* 2 Ch. 9:29; 12:15).

The theme of the chapter is a negative version of chapters 14–15, turning from faith and trust to unbelief. Asa *relied* on human beings rather than God (vv. 6–7; *cf.* 14:11), and failed to *seek* God as he had done previously (v. 12). This contrast reveals three important aspects of faith. Firstly, the validity or even the existence of faith cannot be justified by the success or otherwise of an activity. Though Asa's defensive war against Israel was in a just cause and achieved its aims (vv. 4–6), that did not in itself constitute evidence of trust in God. True faith is about a right attitude toward God, and is basically a matter of spiritual discernment (*cf.* 1 Cor. 2:1–16), even though it may be exercised in the context of 'worldly' matters such as politics and war. Secondly, faith is often a matter of right priorities and timing (Gk. *kairos*, 'right time', rather than *chronos*, 'actual time') rather than of inflexible rules. Asa's unbelief was not related to a general disapproval of political alliances (vv. 2–3) or of the medical profession (v. 12). As it happens, both of these are commended elsewhere in the Bible. Although in matters of basic biblical teaching certain beliefs are right and others are wrong (*e.g.* Ex. 20:3–6; 1 Jn. 5:11–12), when and how to exercise faith on other issues will depend partly on one's circumstances. This can even result in what appear to be contradictions, such as the prophets' view of the defence of Jerusalem (Is. 37:33–35; Je. 19:1–15), or Jesus' willingness to be handed over to his opponents (Lk. 4:28–30; Jn. 18:1–9). Taking a wide view of Scripture produces much safer guidance for Christian living than isolating a single incident.

The third and probably most important issue is whether Asa's earlier faith was made invalid by this unbelief. The Bible takes several possible stances on this issue. It consistently recognizes that believers' lives are imperfect, requiring regular confession and forgiveness (*cf.* Ps. 51; Jn. 13:10; 1 Jn. 2:1–2), and that painful discipline is sometimes necessary (*cf.* 2 Sa. 7:14; 1 Cor. 3:15; Heb. 12:7–13). Conversely, those who persistently reject God after tasting his grace are more harshly dealt with (*cf.* Ezk. 18:24; Jn. 15:6; Heb. 10:26–31). However, in individual cases, it is better to trust in God's mercy for oneself rather than make superficial judgments about other people (*cf.* Mt. 7:1–5; Heb. 10:19–25, 32–39). This also seems to be the Chronicler's approach, though he does give a positive hint that Asa's experience of the grace of God was merely dented rather than destroyed (v. 14; *cf.* 14:2).

Baasha's aim in fortifying *Ramah* was probably to prevent access to Jerusalem for religious or trade reasons (v. 1; *cf.* 11:13–17; 15:9). Ramah is usually identified with er-Ram, on the main road just five miles north of Jerusalem.

Asa responded by buying a *treaty* (v. 3; 'alliance', JB, REB, NEB, NRSV; 'league', RSV) with *Ben-Hadad* of *Aram* (v. 2; 'Syria', RSV, GNB). A king Ben-hadad (Aram. Bar- or Bir-hadad) based in Damascus is well-known, but this is probably Ben-hadad I, to be distinguished from Ben-hadad II, who opposed Ahab and Joram (1 Ki. 20 – 2 Ki. 8).[1] This treaty is one of three mentioned in Chronicles (the Heb. word *bᵉrît* is the same as for 'covenant' (*cf.* 15:12), though only this one is international (*cf.* 1 Ch. 11:13; 2 Ch. 23:1). David was probably also involved in friendship treaties, however, with Hamath (2 Sa. 8:9–10; 1 Ch. 18:9–10) and Tyre (*cf.* 2 Sa. 5:11; 1 Ch. 14:1; 1 Ki. 5:1).

---

[1] *Cf.* F. M. Cross, 'The stele dedicated to Melcarth by Ben-hadad of Damascus', *BASOR* 205, 1972, pp. 36–42; K. A. Kitchen, *IBD*, p. 184. For the alternative view that two Benhadads should not be distinguished, see J. C. L. Gibson, *Textbook of Syrian Semitic Inscriptions*, 2 (Oxford: Clarendon Press, 1975), pp. 1–4.

Asa alludes to two further treaties, between Abijah and Ben-hadad's father and between Baasha and Ben-hadad, neither of which is known elsewhere (though *cf.* 13:20). Baasha may have sought protection against the expanding power of Damascus, but Ben-hadad was more casual. If the price was right, one treaty was as good as another. That price was *silver and gold* (1 Ki. 15:18 has 'all the . . .') from the palace and the temple (v. 2). It is probably the special nature of this wealth that made Hanani so critical of Asa (v. 7), since it represented the results of God's victories for Israel and the sacrificial gifts of his people (2 Sa. 8:6; 1 Ch. 18:11; 29:3–9; *cf.* 2 Ch. 12:9).

Initially, things went favourably for Asa, with Baasha losing territory on his northern and southern borders (vv. 4–6). *Ijon, Dan,* and *Abel Maim* (= Abel Beth Maacah, 1 Ki. 15:20) were all within *Naphtali* on or near the Rift Valley road (v. 4).[1] *Store cities* is 'Kineroth' in 1 Kings 15:20, which became Genneseret in the post-exilic period (Josephus, *Jewish Wars,* 2.573). The Chronicler's text here may have differed slightly from the MT of Kings, since 'store cities' could represent either the plural form of Kineroth or 'the whole land of Naphtali'. The location of *Geba* ('hill') and *Mizpah* ('look-out post') are disputed, partly because they could apply to several places. Most probably, however, they represent Jeba and Tell en-Nasbeh, about six and eight miles respectively north of Jerusalem, so pushing the border a few miles back into Israel. Geba became the recognized limit of Judah (2 Ki. 23:8), probably the first stable border post since the division, though it is unknown whether Asa's defensive building work belonged to this stage of the conflict (Je. 41:9).

f. Asa rejects a prophet's word (16:7–10). The limits of the prophecy are marked by *at that time* in verses 7 and 10 (Heb. has the same phrase, EVV have *at the same time* in v. 10). *Hanani* is probably to be identified with the father of the prophet Jehu, who was active in the reign of Asa's son (1 Ki. 16:1, 7; 2 Ch. 19:2; 20:34). *Seer* (Heb. *rō'eh*) is an old word usually associated with the period of Samuel (*e.g.* 1 Sa. 9:9, 19; 1 Ch. 9:22; 26:28; though *cf.* Is. 30:10). Its appearance here may

---

[1] *Cf.* D. Baly, *Geography of the Bible* (Guildford: Lutterworth, [2]1974), pp. 98, 192–193.

hint at the antiquity of the Chronicler's source for this prophecy.

The message of the prophecy is sharply opposed to Azariah's encouraging tone (15:1–7). Asa had done a *foolish thing* (v. 9) by not trusting in God (v. 7), and his treaty (v. 3) had negated his earlier covenant (15:9–15). He had also rejected the 'Yahweh war' principle (*cf.* 14:9–15). Where previously Asa had *relied* on God who had *delivered* him from a *mighty army* (v. 8; *cf.* 14:11), now he *relied* on human resources alone (v. 7). The enemy had therefore *escaped from your hand* instead of being *delivered into your hand* (vv. 7–8). Asa's reaction was matched only by acts of folly by Saul and David and by Ahaz' unbelief. By 'acting foolishly' (v. 9, REB, NEB), Saul lost a kingdom (1 Sa. 13:13) and David very nearly so (1 Ch. 21:8; the only other use of this verb in Ch.), while Ahaz' appeal to foreign military help left him in great trouble (2 Ch. 28:16–21).

Like Azariah, Hanani also finds support in the prophetic literature. Ahaz' unwillingness to believe in God when threatened by Israel (Is. 7:9) is reflected in Asa's non-reliance (*cf.* v. 7; 'to rely' also occurs in Is. 10:20; 31:1), while Zechariah 4:10 (*the eyes of the LORD range throughout the earth*), which is quoted directly in verse 9, is used to encourage those whose faith is committed to God.

Hanani mentions two surprising consequences of Asa's unbelief, that it was the Syrian rather than the Israelite (*cf.* LXX (L)) army that escaped (v. 7), and that Asa will experience future wars (v. 9). In fact, *Syria* was an increasing threat to Asa's successors, which Hanani implies could have been cut off at source (*cf.* 18:30; 22:5). Victory over Syria would also have extended Asa's earlier success, so that his unbelief should not be measured by victory over Israel (v. 6), but by a lost opportunity (*cf.* 1 Ki. 20:31–34; 2 Ki. 13:14–19). The second problem is that no further *wars* of Asa are mentioned, perhaps because the punishment was delayed until Jehoshaphat's reign (chapter 18). This is one occasion at least where retribution was not immediate.

Asa's *angry* response led to the first known case of prophetic persecution and to oppression of his own people (v. 10). The precise form of Hanani's punishment is unknown, though he was probably detained in some kind of jail (lit., 'house of stocks'; *cf.* NIV, *prison*; the word for 'prison' in 18:26 is different).

g. Asa fails to seek God (16:11–12). Three significant additions to 1 Kings 15:23–24 stand out in the account of Asa's death and burial in verses 11–14, all of which are paralleled by additions in the account of Hezekiah. The first is the addition of 'and Israel' in the first occurrence in Chronicles of *the book of the kings of Judah and Israel* (v. 11; *cf.* 2 Ch. 25:26; 28:26; 32:32). The title of this source, which is different from the biblical books of Kings, confirms that the kingdom of Judah is still the people of Israel (*cf.* 11:3; 12:1).

Secondly, extra details are given about Asa's illness (v. 12), which could be gout, dropsy, or 'gangrene' (NEB). The disease may be divine judgment (*cf.* vv. 7–10), but the more serious criticism is that Asa sought the 'doctors' (GNB, JB) rather than *the LORD* while he was ill. Since 'this is the only time in the Bible that consulting physicians is considered a sin', this cannot be an attack on the medical profession (for positive views, *cf.* Gn. 50:2; Je. 8:22; Is. 38:21; Col. 4:14).[1] Rather, Asa fails to recognize the Lord as the true source of healing (*cf.* Ex. 15:26; Ps. 103:3).The idea of seeking the Lord for healing may show influence from the Psalms (*e.g.* 34:4; 77:2) and from two ironic instances in Kings in which an Israelite king sought Baalzebub and died (2 Ki. 1:2, 6, 16) and an Aramean king was restored after seeking the Lord (2 Ki. 8:8). Since prophets were involved in both the incidents in Kings (*cf.* also 2 Ki. 20:5), it may be that Asa was expected to find help through a prophet, especially as 'doctors' might imply 'ancestors' or 'mediums'.[2] In all this, Asa turned his back on his own standard (14:4, 7; 15:12, 15), though strangely the pattern was also followed by Hezekiah, who, in spite of the fact that he was healed, 'did not respond to the kindness shown him' (2 Ch. 32:25).

h. Concluding formula (16:13–14). The third change provides fuller details of Asa's funeral (v. 14). Burials are important in Chronicles (information is added to Ki. in *e.g.* 21:20; 24:25), and the special *honour* accorded to Asa (*cf.* also Hezekiah, 2 Ch. 32:33) is probably a sign that despite his failings, the over-all assessment remained valid (*cf.* 14:2). The unusual nature of the tribute is indicated by the personal 'rock

---

[1] Japhet, *Ideology*, p. 256, n. 186.
[2] *Cf. e.g.* de Vries, p. 304; G. C. Heider, *The Cult of Molek*, JSOTS 43 (Sheffield: JSOT Press, 1985), pp. 399–400.

tomb' (GNB) that he had 'dug' (JB), the special variety of *spices*, and the fact that the fire was 'very great' (NRSV, RSV). Such fires were customary for royal funerals (*cf*. Je. 34:5), and were not for cremating the body but a sign of honour (*cf*. 2 Ch. 21:19).

C. Jehoshaphat (17:1 – 21:1)

i. Overture (17:1–19).

> 'The LORD was with Jehoshaphat' (17:3).

17:1a – *cf*. 1 Kings 15:24b

Jehoshaphat occupies the next four chapters (17–20), and, as with all his predecessors in the Divided Monarchy, the Chronicler's version differs significantly from Kings. Again Chronicles is much longer and has a more varied assessment, though the most striking difference is the new over-all importance attached to Jehoshaphat. Whereas in Kings he is mainly an adjunct of the northern kingdom (1 Ki. 22:1–38; 2 Ki. 3:4–27; *cf*. 1 Ki. 22:41–50), he takes centre stage in Chronicles' account of the Divided Monarchy (chapters 10–28), exemplifying many of Chronicles' key themes. He is a man of prayer and faith who removes idolatrous symbols, gives God's law new priority, and has a special concern for the Levites. In typical Chronicles fashion, he is blessed with a strong army, new buildings, wealth, and international recognition. On the other hand, his willingness for compromise with the northern kingdom is a notable weakness, and neither he nor his people are fully committed to God.

His reign, therefore, as with all the best kings of Judah, is mixed, and, far from brushing the negative features under the carpet, Chronicles adds two prophecies directly critical of Jehoshaphat (19:1–3; 20:37). The over-all effect, however, is to underline God's crucial role in preserving his people, as can be seen in a key passage epitomizing both Jehoshaphat's reign and the Divided Monarchy (20:14–22). A Levitical prophet and the king himself appeal to the people to *stand firm and see the deliverance the LORD will give you*, because they are assured that *the LORD will be with you* (20:17).

Chapter 17 is a kind of overture to chapters 18–20, briefly introducing many subjects that are dealt with more fully later on. This is particularly true of the opening section (vv. 1–6), but also applies to the subjects of teaching God's law and the fear of the LORD (vv. 7–11; *cf.* 19:1–11; 20:29–30) and to the armed forces (vv. 12–19; *cf.* chs. 18 and 20).

The main theme occurs in verses 1–6, where God's activity on Judah's behalf is balanced alongside Jehoshaphat's practical faith. God is mentioned four times, twice describing what he had done for Jehoshaphat (vv. 3, 5) and twice concerning Jehoshaphat's attitude to him (vv. 4, 6). God's being with the king and his people is especially important in chapters 17–20 (*cf.* v. 3; 19:6, 11; 20:17). It is another of Chronicles' favourite emphases, with examples stretching from Jabez (1 Ch. 4:10) to the exiles (2 Ch. 36:23), though it also comes to the fore in Asa's reign (2 Ch. 15:2, 9). It speaks of God's presence and of his help, as in the statement that God established Jehoshaphat's kingdom (v. 5). On the other hand, Jehoshaphat's part in seeking God (v. 4) and his pride in serving God (v. 6, *cf.* GNB, REB, NEB) is equally vital. His very real failings should not detract from the reality of his trust in God. His was no quietist faith, for on it the very survival of his nation depended. A similar balance appears in Paul's call for Christians to work out their salvation because God works in them (Phil. 2:12–13), and in his own experience of striving with all God's energy (Col. 1:29).

a. Jehoshaphat strengthens his kingdom (17:1–6) Jehoshaphat's various activities anticipate the rest of his reign. The following phrases all recur: the *troops* (v. 2; *cf.* 17:13b–19; chs. 18, 20) and the *fortified cities* (v. 2; *cf.* 17:12, 19; 19:5), his activity in *Ephraim* (v. 2; *cf.* 19:4), his receiving of *gifts* (v. 5; *cf.* 17:11), his possession of *great wealth and honour* (v. 5; *cf.* 18:1), that *the LORD* was, is or will be *with you* (v. 3; *cf.* 19:6, 11; 20:17), that he *sought* God (v. 4; *cf.* 18:4, 6, 7; 19:3; 20:3, 4; 22:9) and *walked in the ways* of *his father* (v. 3; *cf.* 20:32), and removed the *Asherahs* or sacred *poles* (v. 6; *cf.* 19:3). On the *high places*, which are the subject of contradictory statements in verse 6 and 20:33, see below.

The section is in two parts, the first concentrating on Jehoshaphat's military work (vv. 1–2) and the second on his religious activity (vv. 3–6). He *strengthened himself* (v. 1) is a familiar idea in Chronicles (*cf.* 2 Ch. 1:1; 12:1; 26:8, 15; 27:5). Its meaning is not primarily military, despite the immediate context of verse 2, but in the light of similar passages refers to the various topics mentioned in verses 1–6. Whether this strengthening took place in Judah or Israel is less certain. Most EVV read *against Israel*, assuming that Jehoshaphat was confirming Asa's extension of the Israelite border (*cf.* 16:6; 17:2), but 'over Israel' is preferable, understanding Israel in its religious sense. This view is supported by the facts that Chronicles only ever uses the expression 'to strengthen oneself' of a ruler's own kingdom, that Jehoshaphat was not hostile to the north (ch. 18; 20:35–37; 2 Ki. 3:4–27), and that the activities of verse 2 include Judah. Judah's *fortified cities* (v. 2) are presumably those built up by Rehoboam (11:5–12), and *the towns in Ephraim that his father Asa had captured* (v. 2) refer to the places in 15:8 (the Heb. phrase is almost identical, suggesting Mount Ephraim rather than the northern kingdom) rather than those in 13:19; 16:6, which were primarily Benjaminite.

Jehoshaphat's religious activities (vv. 3–6) are reflected in two interrelated patterns. Firstly, there is a chiastic arrangement involving various phrases about 'walking in the ways of' (vv. 3, 4, 6) and the verb 'to *seek*' (vv. 3, 4). The chiasm's outer part is formed by *walked in the ways* of *his father* (v. 3a) and *the ways of the LORD* (v. 6), and the inner part (vv. 3b, 4) by the contrasting phrases about the God whom Jehoshaphat *sought* (v. 3; *consult* and *sought* both translate the same Heb. verb). 'He walked in his commands' (v. 4, lit.) is a confirmatory phrase. The second pattern is formed by the contrast already mentioned between God's presence and help for Jehoshaphat (vv. 3, 5) and the latter's commitment to God (vv. 4, 6). These literary forms confirm that God's help and Jehoshaphat's obedient faith are the basis of his success.

Several refinements are worth noticing. Jehoshaphat's *father* could be either Asa or David (v. 3). Only NIV among EVV retains *David* (MT), with the rest following LXX because of the unusual reference to David's 'former years' (though it is not entirely without analogy, *cf.* 1 Ch. 29:29).[1] In fact, Asa is probably meant, since his reign is divided into two parts (chs. 14–15 and 16), and because a king is often compared in nearby chapters with his own father (20:32; 21:12; 22:9). The *Baals*, mentioned for the first time in Chronicles (v. 3), probably allude to Elijah's conflict with Ahab and Jezebel. God's

---

[1] NIV has also erroneously transferred the 'early years' from Jehoshaphat's father to Jehoshaphat himself. MT is, however, supported in D. Barthélemy, *CTAT*, p. 493.

establishing of *the kingdom* (v. 5), which ties in with Chronicles' emphasis on God's gift of a kingdom to Israel (*cf. e.g.* 1 Ch. 10:14; 14:2; 22:10), fulfils part of the promises of the Davidic covenant (1 Ch. 17:11; 28:7). It is a firm hint of God's continuing authority over his people. The expression 'took pride in' (v. 6, GNB, REB, NEB; *devoted to*, NIV; 'courageous', NRSV, RSV) is unique in this positive sense, but it conveys well Jehoshaphat's determination to follow the Lord. Mention of the *high places* is doubly problematical, since Asa was supposed to have removed them in Judah (14:3, 5), but a later statement indicates that they were not all removed (20:33; *cf.* also 15:17). Though these conflicting statements might be partly explained by the Chronicler's quoting of different sources, they may also witness to the deep hold of Canaanite and syncretistic forms of religion on ordinary Israelites. Popular views and practices are often quite different from pronouncements by religious authorities. On the *Asherah poles* (v. 6), see on 14:3.

b. Jehoshaphat's blessings (17:7–11). This paragraph continues to look forward to chapters 18–20, summarizing three of Jehoshaphat's achievements. The first is the commission of *officials* (v. 7), *Levites* (v. 8), and *priests* (v. 8) to *teach* (vv. 7, 9) the people from the *Book of the Law of the* LORD (v. 9). This event is associated with, if not identical to, a similar campaign by some judges in 19:4–11, since both involved the same range of leaders and were based on the law, which was presumably some form of the Pentateuch (*cf.* 19:8, 10).

A teaching ministry by the priests is known in various parts of the Old Testament (*cf. e.g.* Lv. 10:11; Dt. 33:10; Ho. 4:1–6; Mal. 2:7), but evidence for teaching by the Levites is otherwise restricted to the post-exilic period (especially Ne. 8:7–9). This is not to undermine the historical likelihood of such activity in the ninth century BC, but to stress its importance for post-exilic Israel, where reformation arose from the conviction that God's word should be the foundation of national life. Jehoshaphat's campaign in fact may have been rooted in Asa's covenant (15:12–15), which was equally concerned to apply the demands of God's word to the people's current situation. Though the people were fully involved in both events, now God's word was brought to where the people lived. Jehoshaphat may also have been attempting to wean the people away from their attachment to the local high places (*cf.* v. 6). If so, it represents a move from a sacramental form of religion to one where worship according to God's revealed pattern (*cf.* chs. 5–7) was combined with the authority of his written word. It also invited ordinary people and the civil leaders to take the word of God seriously (*cf.* also v. 16). The date in the king's *third year* (v. 7) implies a co-regency with Asa which would make this the first year in which he reigned alone (*cf.* 16:12 and comment on 20:31).

The second and third of Jehoshaphat's achievements are peace (v. 10) and wealth (v. 11). These are attributed to *the fear of the LORD* (v. 10), *i.e.* a recognition by outsiders of some special protection on Judah. The fact that they are mentioned straight after the 'Back to the Bible' campaign suggests that they are the result of faithfulness to God's word. As in verses 1–6, several phrases anticipate later elements of Jehoshaphat's reign. For example, *the fear of the LORD* recurs in 19:7, 9; 20:29; the appointing of *priests* and *Levites* in 19:8 (*cf.* also the role of a Levite and the singers in 20:14, 21); *the kingdoms of the lands* in 20:29, *cf.* 20:6; and the absence of war in 20:29. Since these themes and phrases are indicative of divine blessings throughout Chronicles, Jehoshaphat is presented as one who is specially favoured (for the *fear of the LORD*, *cf.* 1 Ch. 14:17; 2 Ch. 14:14; the *kingdoms of the lands*, *cf.* 1 Ch. 29:30; and the lack of war, *cf.* 1 Ch. 22:9; 2 Ch. 14:1; 15:19).

The word for *tribute* (v. 11) would have this meaning only here, and may be better translated as 'a great quantity' (REB, NEB, *cf.* GNB). The *Arabs* (v. 11) are mentioned several times in Chronicles alongside the Philistines as tribes living in south-west Palestine (*cf.* 2 Ch. 21:16–17; 26:6–8). The earliest texts mentioning the Arabs date from the ninth century BC, and this description matches those in Assyrian inscriptions of only a century later.[1]

c. Jehoshaphat's military resources (17:12–19). Details of Jehoshaphat's fortification and supplies (vv. 12–13a) and troops (vv. 13b–19) are given in anticipation of Jehoshaphat's battles in chapters 18 and 20 (*cf.* also vv. 1–2). He apparently increased the number of *forts* (v. 12) beyond those built by

---

[1] *Cf.* I. Epha'al, *The Ancient Arabs* (Jerusalem: Magnes Press, 1982), pp. 75–78.

Rehoboam (11:5–12) and Asa (14:6–7). This was a sign of God-given strength, though it had its dangers (2 Ch. 26:15–16). In these towns, he probably kept *supplies* (NIV, *etc.*) rather than being engaged on 'much work' (v. 13, REB, NEB).

Troop numbers are based on a 'muster' (v. 14, NRSV, RSV) or *enrolment* (NIV, *cf.* REB, NEB). They are counted by *families* (v. 14, NIV, JB; 'fathers' houses,' RSV; either is better than 'clans', GNB, REB, NEB) of the tribal levies, though a standing army is mentioned in verse 19 and probably verse 13b. The list's style suggests it originated from some kind of military census list (Williamson). As elsewhere, *thousand* is probably best understood as a military unit, though these figures are still unusually high (*cf.* 14:8; 25:5–6; 26:12–13). The note that one of the commanders 'volunteered for the service of the LORD' (v. 16, REB, NEB) is unfortunately not explained, though it shows that the sacrificial spirit of David's time was still evident (1 Ch. 29:5; *cf.* 2 Ch. 29:31). The phrase, which means literally 'offered himself freely', finds an echo in the New Testament (Rom. 12:1; 2 Tim. 4:6; Heb. 10:7).

ii. Jehoshaphat, Ahab and the prophets (18:1 – 19:3)

'Jehu . . . said to the king, "Should you help the wicked and love those who hate the LORD?"' (19:2).

18:2–34 – cf. 1 Kings 22:2–35

The attempt by Jehoshaphat and Ahab to recapture Ramoth Gilead from the Syrians is a highly intriguing narrative involving the weaving together of two different strands. Although overtly about the war, it shows primarily that God fulfils his prophetic word despite all human efforts to the contrary. In this case, that word led to contrasting results, bringing death for Ahab (vv. 33–34) but a miraculous deliverance for Jehoshaphat, though the latter also received a warning (18:31–32; 19:1–3).

The text follows 1 Kings 22 very closely, except for additions at the beginning and the end (18:1–2; 19:1–3), with other minor changes in verse 31 and in some verbs which move from singular to plural (*e.g.* vv. 5, 14, 29). The alterations are not extensive, but, in the light of a different context for the chapter, they are sufficiently important to change the interpretation of the whole story. Whereas 1 Kings 22 is really about Ahab's confrontation with Elijah and the prophets in the context of his war with Syria, here Ahab plays only a supporting role to Jehoshaphat.

In its new setting, the story reflects two of the Chronicler's prime interests, of which the first is the importance of prophecy. Although the dialogue form is rather different from the more usual pronouncement style of prophecies in Chronicles (*e.g.* 1 Ch. 17:4–14; 2 Ch. 15:17; 24:20), the importance of Micaiah's message (vv. 7–27) is underscored by the addition of a second prophecy (19:1–3). The result is that prophecy is applied to both kingdoms instead of primarily to Israel. This links in with the Chronicler's second interest, namely, Jehoshaphat's relationship with the northern kingdom (18:1–2; 19:1–3). Despite Jehoshaphat's well-intentioned motives (vv. 3–4), he provides a further example of an unacceptable unity between the two kingdoms (*cf.* 10:18–19; 11:1–4; 13:3–19; 16:1–9). As before, though, Chronicles shows that failure is not final, and a preferred alternative route to reunification is still available (19:4; *cf.* 11:13–17; 13:12; 15:8).

These issues were very relevant to the Chronicler's time, when Ezra and Nehemiah ensured that God's word was restored to its proper role as the primary source of authority in Israel. Fulfilment of the prophets' word was a key element in that reformation (*e.g.* Ezr. 1:1; 5:1; 9:11; Ne. 1:8–9; 9:30), as was Judah's relationship with the northern kingdom's successors. Specific examples of the latter include the debate over mixed marriages (Ezr. 9–10; Ne. 13:1–3, 23–29) and the rebuilding of Jerusalem (Ezr. 4:1–23; Ne. 2:19–20; 4:1–15; 6:1–9; 13:4–9). Conflicts of a similar kind affected the New Testament church. Challenges were made to the authority of God's word, including the word of the prophets, even to the extent of some going back on the foundations of their faith (*e.g.* Gal. 3:1–5; 2 Pet. 2:1–3; 1 Jn. 4:1–3). Others such as Jehoshaphat were censured for entering into formal partnerships with those who denied the very basis of the gospel. As here, this could include those who participated in idolatry (2 Cor. 6:14 – 7:1; *cf.* 1 Ki. 16:30–33; 18:18–19; 21:25–26) as well as people who denied Christ's incarnation (2 Jn. 7–11).

a. An alliance for war (18:1–3). A proper link with 1 Kings 22 begins only in verse 3, following a quite different introduction (vv. 1–2) which sets out the theme that Jehoshaphat's relationship with Ahab was a deviation from God's purposes (*cf.* 19:1–3). It also makes clear that their association was the result not of Ahab's opportunism but of a formal 'alliance' (v. 1, NRSV, RSV). This alliance had been sealed several years before the battle (*cf.* v. 2) by a marriage between Jehoshaphat's son Jehoram and Ahab's daughter Athaliah (*cf.* 2 Ki. 8:18; 2 Ch. 21:6). Such marriage alliances were typical in the ancient world, often serving as an expression of peace between those who had previously been opposed (*cf.* 1 Ki. 22:44). Since, on this occasion, peace had come after fifty years of hostilities, to many it must have been welcome at any price. For the Chronicler, however, even the two kings' uniting against a common enemy was not sufficient to give the alliance divine approval (*cf.* 10:18–19; 11:1–4; 13:3–19; 16:1–9). The reasons for God's displeasure are hinted at in verse 1, which could be translated, 'Though he had great wealth and honour, he allied himself . . .'. Jehoshaphat's *great wealth and honour*, though a divine blessing (17:5), blinded him to the reality that Ahab was a man implacably opposed to the ways of God (19:2; *cf.* 1 Ki. 16:30–33; 18:18; 21:20, 25–26).

Ahab probably expected that it would be quite easy to recapture *Ramoth Gilead*, a walled city southeast of the Sea of Galilee (probably Tell Ramith), since with prophetic encouragement his forces had twice repulsed Syrian attacks (1 Ki. 20:1–21, 22–34). The vagueness of the Chronicler's date (*Some years later*, v. 2) is due to his omitting the previous course of the war (*cf.* 1 Ki. 22:1–2). Ahab may have been motivated by Ben-Hadad's failure to observe the terms of his treaty with Israel (1 Ki. 20:34), but, whatever the reason, Jehoshaphat was ready to join in fully. His words, *I am as you are . . .* (v. 4), imply commitment to a contract or treaty (*cf.* Ru. 1:16; 2 Ki. 3:7), as is also implied in the prophet's criticism (19:2).

b. The prophets and the war (18:4–27). The major part of the chapter is a dialogue between the two kings and the prophets. It moves through several distinct stages.

i. Misleading prophecies (18:4–14). The first group of prophecies arise in response to Jehoshaphat's (but not Ahab's) repeated attempt to 'consult' the Lord (vv. 4, 6, 7, GNB). The Hebrew verb is often translated 'seek' (*cf.* 15:2; 19:3), and is used here in its more familiar Old Testament sense of seeking guidance from the prophets (*cf.* 1 Ki. 14:5; Je. 21:2; Ezk. 14:7,

10). Ahab at first seemed quite willing to listen, though not apparently with any intention of complying with what he heard. He therefore gathered *four hundred prophets* (v. 5), who probably belonged to the group of Baal and Asherah prophets that formed a kind of government department in Israel (1 Ki. 18:19). Jehoshaphat does not recognize them as belonging with the Yahweh prophets who had recently been persecuted (v. 6; *cf.* 1 Ki. 18:4), though it would have been quite acceptable in those syncretistic times to speak in the name of more than one deity (*cf.* v. 11).

These prophets unequivocally promise victory: *God will give it into the king's hand* (v. 5). The promise is reaffirmed twice in slightly different words (vv. 11, 14), including once by *Micaiah* (!), and is also supported by *Zedekiah's* symbolic action (v. 10). Dramas of this kind were a typical method of prophetic revelation (*cf.* Je. 27–28), based on this occasion on the *horns* as a symbol of strength (*cf.* Dt. 33:17; Dn. 7:19 – 8:12; Zc. 1:18–21). But though the promise is so dominant, several hints suggest that it is not God's will. Neither Jehoshaphat (v. 6) nor Ahab (v. 7) accept that the prophets really speak in Yahweh's name, while Micaiah's contribution is clearly made under duress (v. 12). Also, the picture of the two kings in full regalia in a public 'open space', *i.e. threshing-floor* (v. 9, NIV, NRSV, RSV), reveals a greater concern for their public image than for discovering God's truth.

To some extent one can understand why this particular prophecy was given. It was, for example, merely a repeat of earlier prophecies ('given into your hand' is identical to 1 Ki. 20:13, 28), though the prophets failed to realize that borrowed religion always goes stale. The sense of the kings acting together is stronger here than in 1 Kings 22, strengthening the prophets' reason for wanting to conform to their masters' wishes (*shall we go to war . . .?*, v. 5, and *Attack and be victorious*, v. 14, are plural here and singular in 1 Ki. 22:6, 15; also the final verb in v. 29). There was a long-established tradition going back at least to the eighteenth-century BC kingdom of Mari that prophets should comply with royal policy, *i.e.* to speak what the king regarded as *good* (vv. 7, 17; the same Heb. word also underlies *success* and *favourably* in v. 12).

It is still perplexing, however, why Micaiah should have conformed with the other prophets, when his allegiance to Yahweh was universally acknowledged (vv. 7, 12, 13). Possibly

Micaiah was simply being ironic or Yahweh's prophets too were affected by the contemporary malaise. It is more likely, however, that this was a deliberate ploy, giving Ahab a taste of his own medicine as a sign of God's judgment on him. It can hardly have been an accident to omit God's name, for example, as a hint that this was not Yahweh's real guidance. This, however, is to anticipate the next section of the dialogue.

ii. Micaiah's prophecy (18:15–22). Ahab's reaction (v. 15) suggests that he was not deceived by Micaiah, and would like to hear God's real opinion, in the hope that it might support his own views. This is granted through two visions (both begin with *I saw*), the first giving God's direction about the intended battle (v. 16) and the other explaining why the prophets spoke as they did (vv. 18–22).

Far from encouraging Ahab, however, the first prophecy or vision commands everyone to *go home in peace* (NIV, REB, NEB, GNB). Its message is conveyed through a traditional picture of Israel as God's flock being shepherded by its leaders. In this case, however, Israel was without a *master*. Though this is usually regarded as a prediction of Ahab's defeat and death (*cf.* v. 34), it is more probably a depiction of his current total ineffectiveness in God's sight. Tragedy of this kind was neither new nor unrepeatable (*cf.* Nu. 27:16–17; Ezk. 34:5–6; Zc. 10:2), but it was a situation for which God was deeply concerned and led ultimately to the coming of the Good Shepherd (*cf.* Mt. 9:36; Mk. 6:34).

Ahab's view, however, was that God's word is *bad* (Heb. *ra'*, v. 17; NIV, GNB; 'evil', RSV, REB, NEB). Unfortunately for Ahab, God was of the same opinion about him, and corresponding *disaster* (Heb. *rā'â*, v. 22; NIV, REB, NEB, NRSV; 'evil', RSV) was decreed for him. To reinforce his message, Micaiah goes on to describe Israel's true master in his heavenly court (v. 18). Heavenly court scenes are usually mentioned during major national crises (*cf.* Is. 6:1–8; Ezk. 1; Dn. 7:9–10, 13–14; for an individual setting, *cf.* Jb. 1–2), with the function of under-lining God's sovereign control over his people. In this instance there is also an ironic contrast with the two kings in their finery (vv. 9–11). The *host of heaven* (v. 18) are the heavenly armies, including the angels and servant spirits, who carry out God's will (*cf.* Pss. 103:21; 148:2; Lk. 2:13). They are to be sharply distinguished from two quite different senses of the same phrase, namely, the physical heavens (*e.g.* Is. 40:26; Dn. 8:10) or the astral deities of pagan religions (2 Ch. 33:3, 5; Zp. 1:5).

The heavenly court provides the setting for an explanation of God's purposes for the false prophets. God is portrayed as inviting the spirits in his court to *entice* Ahab to his death (v. 19), and one of them is eventually sent as a *lying spirit in the mouths of all his prophets* (v. 21). This strange incident can only be understood against the background of other Old Testament passages, especially Deuteronomy 13:11 and Ezekiel 14:1–11. Both these passages speak of people being enticed by false prophets, in each case as a result of a link with idolatry. Ezekiel 14:1–11 is particularly appropriate, since it describes God enticing a prophet to prophesy as a judgment against idolatry and in order to purify Israel.[1] It seems therefore that the words of the false prophets here are God's response to Ahab's trust in false gods and a condemnation of his idolatry (*cf.* Ps. 40:5; Am. 2:4 for the deceptiveness of idols). Ahab was in fact renowned for idol worship (1 Ki. 16:30–33; 21:22, 26) and also for his commitment to evil (1 Ki. 21:20, 25; vv. 7, 17 here). In consequence, the Lord had already decreed *death* (v. 19) and *disaster* (v. 22; 'evil', RSV) through Elijah (1 Ki. 21:21), which the false prophets were unwittingly putting into effect (for New Testament examples of the same principle, *cf.* 2 Thes. 2:9–12; Rev. 13:13–14).

Three comments are worth noting. Firstly, the concept of a punishment fitting the crime is a typical biblical principle (*cf.* Ob. 15). Secondly, Ahab was not actually deceived, even by Micaiah, and recognized his need to know the *truth* (v. 15). The difficulty was not that he could not understand what God wanted, but that he did not want to understand (v. 26). Thirdly, God's inciting or luring a person in this way is never to be understood as his final word. God's aim was to purify his people (*cf.* Dt. 13:11; Ezk. 14:11) and to give them an opportunity to repent. This is well illustrated by David, who had also been enticed as a punishment, but eventually realized that he must turn to God for mercy (2 Sa. 24:1, 14; 1 Ch. 21:1, 13; *cf.* 1 Sa. 26:19). Ahab, however, set his course firmly in the opposite direction (v. 25).

---

[1] Since Ezk. 14 is later than the original version of this incident in 1 Ki. 22, it is likely that the prophet's formulation of this principle has been influenced by the incident concerning Micaiah.

iii. Rejection of Micaiah's prophecy (18:23–27). Zedekiah (vv. 23–24) and Ahab (vv. 25–27) reacted by rejecting God's message, so confirming the rightness of his judgment. Zedekiah's words show his prime motive to have been jealousy, which sadly led on to violence. His treatment of Micaiah is strikingly similar to that meted out to Jesus the Suffering Servant (*cf.* Is. 50:6; Mt. 26:67; 27:30; Jn. 18:22). He probably referred to a *spirit from the* LORD (v. 23) rather than the 'Spirit of the LORD' (RSV; *cf.* REB, NEB). The Hebrew expression (lit. 'the spirit', also v. 20) refers to one particular spirit, and nothing in the context requires this to be God's own Spirit.[1] On the other hand, it is not an evil spirit or an elementary form of Satan but one of God's servants who has been sent to carry out a special task. For the concept of prophetic words being uttered in God's court and conveyed to the prophet through angelic intermediaries, *cf. e.g.* Isaiah 40:1–6; Jeremiah 22:18, 22; Zechariah 1:9, 14.

Ahab's treatment of Micaiah is also paralleled in the treatment of other prophets, particularly Jeremiah (Je. 37:15–16). Though the persecution of prophets had already begun under Asa (2 Ch. 16:10), the same tradition of suffering continued in the experience of Jesus and his disciples (Mt. 5:12; 23:30–35). Micaiah is given a 'prison diet' (v. 26, REB, NEB) of bread and water (lit. 'bread/water of oppression'; *cf.* Is. 30:20). Ahab hoped that his incarceration would be merely temporary, but for Micaiah that would be a denial of God's word (v. 27). The phrase *return safely* (vv. 26, 27) is identical in Hebrew to 'go home in peace' (v. 16) – if Ahab will not go home in peace now, he will never do so.[2]

c. Fulfilment of Micaiah's prophecy (18:28–34). By entering into battle, Ahab therefore fulfils the original prophecies (*cf.* v. 20) and brings God's judgment on himself. His ploy to use *disguise* (v. 29) may well be a superstitious attempt to prevent God's word coming to pass, as if Ahab recognized that God had indeed spoken to him. Jehoshaphat's acceptance of

---

[1] *Cf.* GK #126r.

[2] Since 'Hear, all you peoples' (v. 27, NRSV, RSV) is not in some LXX MSS and is also found in Mi. 1:2, it is sometimes omitted here (as REB, NEB). Neither the occurrence of the phrase elsewhere, however, nor the similarity between Micaiah's and Micah's names, is sufficient ground for excising it. It is already present in 1 Ki. 22:28 and makes a fitting conclusion.

the plan (v. 29) is one of several indications that Ahab is the stronger partner (*cf.* vv. 3, 30).

'Many are the plans in a man's heart, but it is the LORD's purpose that prevails' (Pr. 19:21) is an apt summary of the outcome at Ramoth Gilead, for Jehoshaphat's deliverance and Ahab's death represented a totally unexpected turn of events. Presumably the Syrian charioteers recognized at the last moment who Jehoshaphat was (or was not!), but Chronicles has made an interesting addition at the end of verse 31 which shows that this was a miraculous intervention of providence (*and the LORD helped him. God drew them away from him* is not in MT of 1 Ki. 22:32).[1] Jehoshaphat's cry of desperation (1 Ki. 22:32) is understood as a prayer, illustrating the principle of 2 Chronicles 6:34–35 that God answers prayer (*cf.* also 2 Ch. 14:10). This understanding is also indicated by *helped*, a typical term used for God's deliverance in the context of battle (*cf.* 1 Ch. 5:20; 2 Ch. 25:8; 26:7; 32:8). *Drew away* is significant, since the same Hebrew verb in verse 2 is translated *urged* ('induced', NRSV, RSV; 'incited', REB, NEB), and both are synonyms of 'lure' or *entice* (v. 19). Whereas Ahab was lured into judgment, Jehoshaphat was led out of it through prayer.

Conversely, there was no escape for Ahab. Even 'chance' (v. 33, GNB; *random*, NIV, JB, REB, NEB) is made to serve God's sovereign purpose, when an archer 'in his simplicity' (lit.; *cf.* Ackroyd) fired his deadly arrow. Ahab was wounded between two sections of his armour (the exact details are not agreed), and died the same day. Though neither Chronicles nor Kings is explicit about it, this seems to have been the signal for Israel's retreat and defeat (*cf.* 1 Ki. 22:36).

d. *Jehu's prophecy (19:1–3).* Chronicles has omitted the details of Ahab's death (1 Ki. 22:35–38), including how it fulfilled a further prophecy (*cf.* 1 Ki. 21:19; 22:38), in favour of the consequences of the battle for Jehoshaphat. This paragraph is an addition to 1 Kings 22, probably taken from one of the prophetic sources quoted by Chronicles. *Jehu the seer* (v. 2) was an aged prophet who had been active some forty years previously in Baasha's reign (1 Ki. 16:1, 7; for Jehu's father Hanani, *cf.* 2 Ch. 16:7, 10). *Seer* (Heb. *ḥōzeh*) is a synonym for

---

[1] The first part does occur, however, in some LXX MSS of 1 Ki. 22:32, and Ch. may have followed a different Heb. text at this point.

prophet (*cf.* 1 Ch. 29:29; Am. 7:12). The fact that Jehoshaphat reached home *safely* (v. 1) is significant. It contrasts his fate with Ahab's (the phrase is identical to 'in peace', 18:16, 26, 27, NRSV, RSV, *etc.*; *cf.* 18:33–34), and testifies to God's grace given to a person who was almost destroyed by undiscerning folly.

Jehu develops a previously implied criticism (18:1–2) that Jehoshaphat had made a serious error in allying himself with a *wicked* person who *hated* the Lord (v. 2). *Love* and *hate* in this context are formal terms for actions within a covenant or treaty relationship rather than emotional feelings, and *help* is a typical Chronicles expression for formal support (*cf.* 1 Ch. 18:5; 22:17; 2 Ch. 28:16). The description of Ahab is severe. From time to time he had shown signs of repentance (*e.g.* 1 Ki., 20:13–14; 21:28–29), but it was always skin-deep and short-lived, and his commitment to Baal fully justifies Jehu's summary (*cf.* Ahab's hatred of Micaiah, 18:7). Nevertheless, the instruction to keep away from Ahab is a rare one in the Bible, and implies that Ahab was really to be treated as a Canaanite.

Jehoshaphat's failure to recognize the gravity of Ahab's behaviour is also regarded as sin, and explains why God's *wrath* (v. 2; 'anger', GNB) was against him. *Wrath* is another formal term in Chronicles, though a distinction is made between wrath which can and which cannot be averted (for the latter, *cf.* 2 Ch. 34:25; 36:16). It could be turned aside through sacrifice (*cf.* 1 Ch. 21:14–18) and repentance (*cf.* 2 Ch. 12:7; 32:25–26), and Jehoshaphat's 'good things' (v. 3; *some good*, EVV) are meant to convey such repentance. These not only included his removal of the *Asherahs* (*cf.* 17:6) and his heartfelt seeking after God (*cf.* 17:4, 6; for the whole phrase, *cf.* 1 Ch. 22:19; 28:9; 2 Ch. 11:16; 15:12), but also looked forward to his campaign to teach God's law (19:4–11, especially v. 10). Chronicles earlier message is again repeated, that the way back to God was always open.

iii. Jehoshaphat's legal reforms (19:4–11)
'He appointed judges in the land' (19:5).
Jehoshaphat responded to Jehu's warning about God's wrath (vv. 2–3, 10) by leading a movement of spiritual renewal (v. 4) whose chief feature was a reform of the judicial system (vv. 5–11). The modern reader used to distinguishing between the

sacred and the secular aspects of life may find this combination of events a little strange, but it is a product of the
comprehensiveness of biblical covenant faith. The Chronicler
in fact has previously associated the covenant with Israel's
armies, buildings, and civil administration, including brief
allusions to the judicial system (1 Ch. 23:4; 26:29; 2 Ch. 1:2),
but now gives fuller consideration to the legal system.

One should beware of false expectations of this chapter,
however, since it is definitely not a fully fledged description of
Judah's legal system. The style is of a 'general, somewhat
homiletic kind' (Ackroyd), indicating that the chapter concentrates on the character of the reform. In terms of structure,
for instance, the chapter is dominated by two exhortatory
speeches (vv. 6–7, 9–11), while the contents of the reform are
limited to various judicial appointments (vv. 5, 8). The main
concerns are to ensure that the appointed officials act faithfully ('to do, act' occurs four times in Heb.: 'Consider what you
do', v. 6, RSV; 'take heed what you do', v. 7, RSV; 'Thus you
shall do', v. 9, RSV; and 'Deal courageously', v. 11, NRSV, RSV),
and are aware of God's presence ('he is with you', v. 6, NRSV,
RSV; *may the LORD be with those who do well*, v. 11, NIV).

Much of the chapter is based on Deuteronomy 16:18–20;
17:8–13 (*cf.* especially vv. 6–7, 9–11), though with some
important administrative differences. There too one finds the
same concern for right attitudes in relation to human law, and
for the purposes and presence of God (Dt. 16:20; 17:12). The
reform therefore attempts to restore the principles of the
Mosaic covenant in people's hearts as well as in their actions.

A concern for social and corporate justice as well as personal justice has been a feature of both Judaism and
Christianity, even though interest in these matters has not
always been consistent. The New Testament has a dual
emphasis on this issue. Though Jesus (*e.g.* Mt. 18:15–17;
23:23; Lk. 18:3–8) and Paul (*cf.* 1 Cor. 6:1–11; 1 Tim. 5:21)
both gave instructions about the principles and practice of
law, it is also clear that no legal system can properly institute
God's justice. That is possible only through absolute obedience to God's law (Rom. 3:25–26; Mt. 12:18, 20), as Jesus
uniquely demonstrated. Though Jesus' obedience ironically
deprived him of human justice (*cf.* Acts 8:33; Is. 53:8; 1 Pet.
3:18), his obedience brings permanent freedom from the
threat of God's wrath for those who cannot meet the standard

of God's justice (*cf.* Rom. 5:9; 8:3–4; 1 Jn. 1:9).

Because the closest analogy to Jehoshaphat's reform occurs in the reformation of the fifth century BC (*e.g.* Ezr. 7:25–26), it is sometimes alleged that it is really the Chronicler's own creation based on Jehoshaphat's name (= 'Yahweh has judged'). However, the lack of a suitable earlier parallel is not sufficient to undermine the historicity of the narrative. Evidence of a separate source in verses 5–11 has been noted (*cf.* Williamson), and there are important differences from the reforms in Ezra and in Deuteronomy (*cf.* 'in every town', Dt. 16:18, as against the fortified cities, v. 5, and also the role of 'the judge', Dt. 17:9). Further, Jehoshaphat's contribution can be seen not only as continuing David and Solomon's work (*cf.* 1 Ki. 3:16ff.; 1 Ch. 26:29), but as 'the culmination of monarchical judicial authority in ancient Israel'.[1] The criticisms of the eighth-century prophets also require the existence of a system of this kind (*cf.* Is. 1:21–26; Mi. 3:1–2, 9–11).

a. Religious renewal (19:4). This verse introduces and sets the tone for what follows. The word *again* shows that this campaign continues the Levites' teaching (17:7–9), and the Levites may well have assisted the king. These itinerant campaigns have no real equivalent in the Old Testament, and the prophets, even though they travelled about, were not involved in systematic teaching of the word of God. The nearest parallel is in the New Testament, in Jesus' own itinerant ministry.

The geographical details are significant. Apart from betraying the Chronicler's style by describing Judah's limits from south to north (*cf.* 1 Ch. 13:5; 21:2), reference to the *hill country of Ephraim* (*cf.* 15:8; 17:2) implies a new opportunity for reunification in contrast to Jehoshaphat's failed alliance with Ahab (18:1 – 19:3). Only by accepting the authority of God's law did an acceptable basis for unity become possible. *Turned them back to the LORD* ('brought back', NRSV, RSV) indicates repentance by both king and people – the verb is the same as 'turn' in 7:14. This turning involved a deep change of heart, a commitment to obey God's word, and abandoning of

---

[1] K. W. Whitelam, *The Just King* (Sheffield: JSOT Press, 1979), p. 206; *cf.* Japhet, *Ideology*, p. 432; Myers, *2 Chronicles*, p. 108.

all forms of idolatry (*cf.* Dt. 30:10; 1 Sa. 7:3; 2 Ki. 23:25; Je. 24:7).

b. Appointment of judges (19:5–7). 5. The details of Jehoshaphat's appointment of *judges* are so minimal that an adequate picture of the nature of this reform is impossible. Much depends on whether the *fortified cities* (*cf.* 11:5–12; 14:6–7; 17:2, 12–13, 19) belonged to the royal administration, in which case the judges were part of a process of centralization which replaced the older tribal system of justice. Recent investigation, however, has concluded that the king's legal authority was limited to Judah's military organization, and had little effect on the parallel system of local courts.[1]

A further complication is that the requirement of Deuteronomy 16:18 to appoint judges 'in every town' is only partially fulfilled. The king therefore could have extended, restricted, or more probably left intact the existing system.

6–7. Jehoshaphat's speech affirms that Israel's legal system was *not for man but for the LORD* (*cf.* Dt. 1:17; Pr. 17:23; Eph. 6:6; Col. 3:23). It must reflect the reality of God's presence (he is *with you*), and of his character (he is without *injustice or partiality or bribery*). These emphases suggest that the appointments were more of a reform than an innovation, perhaps responding to difficulties in current legal practice. They also illustrate the need to apply covenant law to new situations (*cf.* Dt. 16:19; also Dt. 10:17).

c. Appointment of other officials (19:8–11). The pattern of the previous paragraph is repeated, that is, a brief statement about new appointments in *Jerusalem* (v. 8) is followed by a speech concerning the values by which they should be guided (vv. 9–10).

The list of newly appointed officials confirms the traditional nature of the reform. The *priests'* role alongside the judges is mentioned in Deuteronomy 17:9, 12 (*cf.* 1 Sa. 2:25; Je. 18:18), the *Levites* were appointed by David as their assistants (1 Ch. 26:29), and tribal leaders (*heads of families*) had been the backbone of Israel's legal system for centuries (*cf.* Dt. 19:12; Ezr. 10:14; Mt. 26:57). This traditional emphasis is confirmed by

---

[1] See *e.g.* H. J. Boecker, *Law and the Administration of Justice* (Minneapolis: Augsburg, 1980), pp. 47–48; K. W. Whitelam, *op. cit.*, pp. 192–197.

the king's absence. *Amariah the chief priest* (v. 11) occurs in the list of high priests in 1 Chronicles 6:11, though Judah's tribal head *Zebadiah* (v. 11) is unknown elsewhere.

The chief difficulty is to decide on the function of these courts. There are two problems: whether the Jerusalem court was a higher court, and how the division between sacred and secular cases worked in practice (v. 11). On the first issue, the fact that cases were referred to Jerusalem from 'your brothers living in their towns' (v. 10, JB) has sometimes suggested that it was a higher court of appeal (*e.g.* Williamson, Dillard). This view, however, assumes an underlying centralization policy, whereas evidence has been adduced to show that the basic system was little changed. The Jerusalem court is more likely therefore to have been an auxiliary to the local courts, probably a court of reference in difficult cases (Boecker, Whitelam).[1] As such, it would have extended the king's existing judicial authority over problematic cases (*cf.* 2 Sa. 14; 1 Ki. 3:16–28). The matter is complicated by a textual difficulty at the end of verse 8, where MT's 'they returned to Jerusalem' (so RV) makes little sense in the context. Of the two possible alternatives, it is much simpler to read 'they had their seat at Jerusalem' (RSV).[2] This strengthens the idea of a national role (*cf.* v. 10), which may also find support by translating 'for Israel' in verse 8 (rather than 'of Israel', NRSV, RSV; or *Israelite*, NIV, REB, NEB). The second alternative is that the court was both a national court and a local court for Jerusalem, but this seems unnecessarily confusing (*cf.* NEB, 'to arbitrate in lawsuits among the inhabitants of the city').[3]

The second issue concerns the division between sacred (*any matter concerning the LORD*) and secular (*any matter concerning the king*) cases mentioned in verse 11. Though this distinction was well known in post-exilic Israel, as exemplified by Zerubbabel's and Joshua's joint leadership (*cf.* Hg. 1:1, 12, 14), it was already established in David's time (1 Ch. 26:30, 32). No further details can be deduced from verses 8, 10, since the phrases *to administer the law of the LORD and to settle disputes* (v. 8)

---

[1] H. J. Boecker, *op. cit.*, pp. 48–49; K. W. Whitelam, *op. cit.*, pp. 197–201.
[2] This reading merely involves repointing the Heb. text. 'They lived at Jerusalem', NIV, *etc.*, though based on the same revocalized text, adds nothing to the sense.
[3] This is based on LXX, Vulg., and is also followed by *e.g.* GNB, Rudolph, Williamson, Barthélemy (*CTAT*, pp. 494–495).

and the subjects of the court's jurisdiction (v. 10) are too general to be divided up under these headings. The *law, command, decrees or ordinances* (v. 10) are simply synonyms for the Torah, and would have included civil and religious matters. It is less clear why matters of *bloodshed* were included, perhaps because all capital cases were to be referred to a central court (Macholz), or because a more specific issue was causing debate.[1]

The speech in verses 9–10 parallels that in verses 6–7 in both form and content, and, as before, a Deuteronomic law is applied to a new situation (*cf.* Dt. 17:8–13). The elliptical nature of some phrases in verse 10 is due to their being quoted from the earlier text.[2] The main aim of setting up a court to handle difficult cases was that 'guilt' might not be incurred (v. 10, NRSV, RSV, *etc.*; *sin*, NIV) and to avoid God's *wrath* (*cf.* Dt. 17:12–13). These terms are frequently linked in Chronicles (*e.g.* 1 Ch. 21:3; 2 Ch. 24:18; 28:10, 13), but their potentially disastrous effects could always be removed through repentance (*cf.* v. 2).

Act with courage (v. 11) is reminiscent of the familiar phrase, 'Be strong and courageous' (Jos. 1:6–7; 1 Ch. 22:13; 28:20; 2 Ch. 32:7; *etc.*). Since it is usually linked with major events, it shows the importance of the reform. The final phrase is certainly a promise of God's presence, but 'good' (REB, NEB) could refer either to the work of reform (*cf.* NIV) or to those who will carry it out (*cf.* NRSV, RSV, REB, NEB, *etc.*).

iv. Jehoshaphat's faith (20:1–30)
'The battle is not yours, but God's' (20:15).

Chapter 20 contains one of the outstanding stories not only in Chronicles but in the whole Bible. It describes first of all a unique Israelite victory. Though on other occasions God enables Israelite forces to be victorious, here the credit is due entirely to God while the army is reduced to the level of spectators. Secondly, it is the showpiece of Chronicles' account of the Divided Monarchy (chs. 10–36). Israel's faith and trust and God's actions on Israel's behalf are presented in particularly glowing terms. Even the triumphs of other kings (*e.g.*

---

[1] G. C. Macholz, 'Zur Geschichte der Justizorganisation in Juda', *ZAW* 84, 1972, pp. 314–340.
[2] Japhet, *Ideology*, pp. 245–246.

13:3–19; 14:9–15; 26:6–15) pale into insignificance in comparison with what is achieved here. Thirdly, the chapter creates the impression of a luxuriant literary and theological tapestry in the way its themes are interwoven. Although it focuses on God's victorious action (vv. 15, 17, 29), this is closely linked with other themes such as prayer and worship, prophecy, the temple and its officials, the assembly of the people, the nature of God, and God's relationship with the nations. Fourthly, the central themes of Chronicles as a whole seem to come together in a climactic fashion. Here the Davidic line, as represented by Jehoshaphat (*cf.* 1 Ch. 17), and the various elements of temple worship (*cf.* 2 Ch. 6–7) combine to show God's people responding to him through his gifts. Finally, the chapter quotes extensively from other parts of the Old Testament, either directly or through frequent allusions. Although this is most explicit in prayer (vv. 6–12), prophecy (vv. 15–17) and praise (v. 21), almost every verse reflects some element of Old Testament vocabulary, style, or theology. It is as though God's work through Moses and David, in the psalms and the prophets, were all rolled together in this one incident.

It is not immediately easy to see how this chapter fits into the Bible's over-all portrayal of Jehoshaphat. Though in verses 1–30 his faith is exemplary, in verses 33, 35–37 Chronicles has also sharpened the examples given in Kings of Jehoshaphat's willingness to compromise (*cf.* 18:1–2; 19:1–3). In other words, the positive results of verses 1–30 have not been achieved at the expense of losing touch with serious weaknesses in Jehoshaphat's life. This remains true even though much of Chronicles' version of Jehoshaphat is written in a rather stylized form characterized by typical elements and supernatural aspects of the events described. A second problem is to sort out how the two battles in the Old Testament involving Jehoshaphat and the Moabites are connected. In 2 Kings 3, Jehoshaphat is involved with Israel and Edom against Mesha of Moab as Mesha attempted to throw off the Israelite yoke on his kingdom.[1] Though similarities certainly exist between the two incidents, particularly in the crucial encouragement given by the prophets and in the miraculous victories, the differences are too great for this account to be

---

[1] An important supplement to the biblical information is Mesha's inscription known as the Moabite stone (translation in *ANET*, pp. 320–321).

based on 2 Kings 3. However, the fact that Mesha rebelled against Israel in the reign of Jehoram of Israel (2 Kings 3:5) may give a clue as to what lay behind this attack. The fact that the Moabites are listed first (v. 1; though *cf.* vv. 10, 22) suggests that here too they led the invasion, especially as the invading army seems to have entered Judah from Moabite territory. As to the order of events, it is possible that this invasion is a renewed attempt at revenge against Israel and her allies. Whereas the Moabites remained bloodied but unbowed after their battle with Jehoram (2 Ki. 3:27), their defeat here has a strong element of finality about it (vv. 22–25). They may have chosen to attack Judah as the weaker partner in an alliance which Jehoshaphat had made first with Ahab (2 Ch. 18:1–3) and also with Ahaziah (2 Ch. 20:35–37) and then Jehoram (2 Ki. 3:7–24). Even though that would mean that the two sections of this chapter were not in chronological order, such a practice is familiar in Chronicles (*cf. e.g.* 1 Ch. 14; 18–19). The present order probably shows that Jehoshaphat's victory results from his faithfulness (ch. 19), just as David's victories are portrayed as a result of his concern for the ark (notice the prominence of 'seeking' God in both cases, 1 Ch. 13:3; 14:10, 14; 2 Ch. 20:3–4).

The historical significance of this incident is hard to evaluate, since, although many agree it has a historical nucleus,[1] much of the geographical data cannot be verified. It may have been a local conflict (*e.g.* Williamson), though the frequent mention of all Judah, including women and children (*e.g.* vv. 4, 13, 18), suggests that it was of wider importance. The problem was made more serious because Jehoshaphat was probably now an old man, ruling alongside his son Jehoram who had a very different approach to life (*cf.* 2 Ki. 1:17; 3:1).[2] Jehoshaphat therefore must have felt internal as well as external pressure.

The abiding value of the account, however, is its concern for faith and worship. Rather than encouraging his contemporaries to revolt against their Persian masters, the Chronicler's aim is to show how faith in God is always productive even in the most oppressive circumstances. Such faith has

[1] *E.g.* Rudolph, Myers, Williamson. For a more negative view, *cf.* P. Welten, *Geschichte und Geschichtsdarstellung* (Neukirchen-Vluyn: Neukirchener, 1973), pp. 140–153.
[2] *Cf.* Thiele, pp. 98–101.

benefits to be gained here and now, as many could testify in the post-exilic community (*cf. e.g.* Ezr. 8:21–32; Ne. 4:7–23; 6:15–16), where the power of God's Spirit was clearly at work (*cf.* v. 14; Hg. 2:5; Zc. 4:6). Similarly, the New Testament writers were confident that God would deliver his persecuted people through prayer in their present circumstances, though the church also had a new assurance about the life to come (2 Cor. 1:10–11; Heb. 12:2–3).

a. Judah invaded (20:1–2). The reader is probably intended to see the ultimate blessings of this chapter (vv. 24–30) as a consequence of Jehoshaphat's faithfulness in the matter of God's law (*cf. After this*, v. 1, with ch. 19; *cf.* also 2 Ch. 32:1), though there may well have been a gap of some years (see above for the possible chronological aspects). Jehoshaphat's first task, however, is to deal with the invading coalition's army. They were possibly led by the *Moabites* (see above), with their northern neighbours the *Ammonites* and also the *Meunites*. The latter are sometimes linked with the Arabs (*cf.* 17:11; 26:7), and lived in the southwestern area of Judah. They are replaced later in this chapter by 'Mount Seir' (vv. 10, 22, 23), a vague term associated with the general area of Edom and Judah's southern border (*cf.* Dt. 2:1–8; Jos. 11:17; 12:7; 2 Ch. 26:7). The invaders came from across the *Sea* (v. 2), *i.e.* the Dead Sea, probably by a shallow ford across the Lisan at the Sea's southern end. *En Gedi* is approximately in the centre of the western shore, though *Hazazon Tamar* (*cf.* Gn. 14:7) cannot be more precisely located. This route was probably chosen because Judah was better defended further west (*cf.* 11:5–10).[1]

The *vast army* (v. 2; 'great multitude', NRSV, RSV; also vv. 12, 15, 24) is one of a number of terms in the chapter from the tradition of 'Yahweh's war' (also in 2 Ch. 13:8, 14:10; 32:7). In view of Jehoshaphat's own military statistics (*cf.* 17:12–19), the description is a little surprising, but comparison is impossible since no figures are provided for the coalition forces. The Judeans clearly believed they were outnumbered, however, and the king was *alarmed* (v. 3).

[1] Though neither 'Meunites' (v. 1) nor 'Edom' (v. 2) are in MT or well attested in the ancient vss, they are almost universally adopted. Both involve only minor changes to MT, of which the reading for the former is impossible and very unlikely for the latter.

b. Jehoshaphat prays (20:3–13). In his fear, Jehoshaphat turns to prayer rather than despair (vv. 6–12) and to fasting (v. 3). His attitude is summed up by the word 'seek', which occurs twice in Hebrew though it is variously translated in EVV. This is a key word in Jehoshaphat's reign (*cf.* 17:3–4; 18:4; 19:3), where it has the basic sense of 'worship' (*cf.* 2 Ch. 1:5; 15:12), but also means to discover God's will (*cf.* 2 Ch. 15:4). It shows that Jehoshaphat has a higher trust in God than in his military resources, and that he rightly sees the *temple* as the place to seek God's face (v. 5; *cf.* 2 Ch. 7:14).

The people gathered in an *assembly* (v. 5, 14, 26; *cf.* 'assembled', v. 4, NRSV, RSV, JB). The repetition of *all Judah* (vv. 3, 13, 15, 18; *cf.* vv. 20, 27), and reference to *every town in Judah* (v. 4) and the women and children (v. 13) shows how strong was this idea of a gathered community (*cf.* also *e.g.* Ezr. 10:7–15; Ne. 8:2–12; 13:1–3). Special fasts were sometimes held as well as the regular ones (Lv. 16:29, 31; Zc. 8:19) to seek God's help in special circumstances (*e.g.* Jdg. 20:26; Ezr. 8:21–23; Joel 1:14; 2:15–16). The *new courtyard* (v. 5) was for the people, and was separate from the priests' court (*cf.* 2 Ch. 4:9).

Jehoshaphat's prayer employs the recognized form of a national lament (*cf. e.g.* Pss. 44, 74, 79), though it is closer in structure, content, and language to the prose prayers in Chronicles than to the psalms (*cf.* 1 Ch. 17:16–27; 29:10–19; 2 Ch. 6:14–42; 14:11; 30:18–19). Like the prayers of David and Solomon (1 Ch. 17:16–27; 2 Ch. 6:14–42), it occurs at a key point in the Chronicler's narrative, and is intended as an 'effective means of carrying the community through difficult and trying times'.[1] It falls into four sections.

i. Praise for God's sovereign power (20:6). This theme is especially appropriate here in view of the fact that the prime problem is Israel's powerlessness (v. 12). It is also one of Chronicles' regular themes. For example, *you rule over all . . . Power and might are in your hand* is repeated from David's prayer (1 Ch. 29:12), with Chronicles' typical phrase *kingdoms of the nations* relevantly inserted (*cf.* 1 Ch. 29:30; 2 Ch. 17:10, 20:29). Chronicles regularly emphasizes too that God is *in*

---

[1] P. H. Eveson, 'Prayer Forms in the Writings of the Chronicler', unpubl. M.Th. diss., University of London, 1979, p. 94.

heaven (*cf.* 2 Ch, 2:5; 6:18), because that is where he hears prayer (2 Ch. 6:21, *etc.*; *cf.* Pss. 11:4; 103:19; 115:3).

ii. Praise for the gift of land and temple (20:7–9). The rhetorical questions (vv. 6, 7) are a form of praise indicating absolute certainty.[1] Jehoshaphat concentrates on God's gifts of the *land* (vv. 7–8a) and the *sanctuary* (vv. 8b–9), which were promised in the covenants given to Abraham, Moses, and David/ Solomon. *Abraham your friend* (*cf.* Is. 41:8) recalls Genesis 18:17–19, God's driving out of the land's former inhabitants is based on the Mosaic covenant (*e.g.* Ex. 33:2; Dt. 4:38), and verse 9 is an excellent summary of the promises associated with the Davidic covenant (*cf.* 2 Ch. 6:14–42). This pattern of recalling earlier covenant promises, which is found in other prayers in Chronicles (*e.g.* 1 Ch. 17:21–22; 29:15, 18; 2 Ch. 6:15–17), gives fresh assurance of God's commitment to *hear* prayer and *save* his people from their *distress* (v. 9).[2]

iii. Complaint against invaders (20:10–11). The complaint is a typical lament, describing Jehoshaphat's problem in very plain terms. His sense of injustice is surprisingly directed not so much at the invading army as at God. Though he did not *allow* (v. 10) Israel under Moses to attack these nations, he now permits them to deprive Israel of *the possession you gave us as an inheritance* (v. 11; *cf.* Nu. 20:14–21; Dt. 2:1–19; Jdg. 11:14– 18). The ironic use of 'repay/reward' (v. 11) shows how history can give contradictory signals (*cf.* vv. 7–8). Though Jehoshaphat's language is strong, however, it is going too far to speak of 'Yahweh's sin of omission'.[3] Rather, God had showed grace to Moab and Ammon, and will show yet greater grace to Judah.

iv. Plea for help (20:12). Only at the end does Jehoshaphat make a specific request. As in other prayers in Chronicles, the plea is not for one particular answer but for God to show his power, in this case to *judge* those who have challenged his

---

[1] It effectively means, 'Surely . . .'. *Cf.* Throntveit, *Kings*, pp. 67–68.
[2] MT's 'sword of judgment' (NIV, *cf.* GNB) is often replaced by 'flood', which is read in LXX(L) (so REB, NEB, *etc.*). Textual support for the latter is not strong, however, and MT makes good sense.
[3] D. L. Petersen, *Late Israelite Prophecy* (Missoula: Scholars Press, 1977), p. 73; Throntveit, *Kings*, p. 71.

purposes (*cf.* 1 Ch. 16:35; 2 Ch. 14:11). The final phrase, *We do not know what to do, but our eyes are upon you*, is one of the most touching expressions of trust in God to be found anywhere in the Bible. To recognize one's weakness is a position of much strength (*cf.* Jn. 15:5; 2 Cor. 12:9), for 'it is at Wits' End Corner that you meet the miracles'.[1]

   c. Jahaziel prophesies (20:14–19). God's answer to Jehoshaphat comes from an unexpected source, through a prophecy given by the *Spirit of the LORD* to a *Levite* (v. 14). Prophetic gifts originating from God's Spirit are given to prophets (*e.g.* 2 Ch. 15:1; 18:23; 24:20) and to non-prophets (*e.g.* Nu. 11:25, 29; Jdg. 6:34; 1 Ch. 12:18). The New Testament expects these gifts to continue and even expand among ordinary people (*cf.* Acts 2:18–19; 1 Cor. 14:1, 5). The Levites are something of a special case, however, since their musical ministry is also regarded as prophesying (1 Ch. 25:1–3). Jahaziel's prophecy therefore may well have been accompanied by music, as in the case of his contemporary Elisha (2 Ki. 3:15; *cf.* Ex. 15:10; 1 Sa. 10:5, 10). However, this prophecy in which direct guidance is given is to be distinguished from the more typical form of Levitical musical prophecy, which probably consisted in leading Israel's praise to God (*cf.* vv. 19, 21–22). Jahaziel's genealogy of five generations would go back to David's day (for *Asaph, cf.* 1 Ch. 16:4, 37; 25:1–6).
   Jahaziel's remarkable prophecy centres on the double pronouncement that it is God and not Israel who will have to fight, literally, 'it is not for you the battle / to fight' (vv. 15, 17). In all there are four main elements: (a) a repeated command *not* to *be afraid* (vv. 15, 17); (b) repeated statements that *the battle is not yours, but God's* (v. 15, *cf.* v. 17); (c) a repeated promise that God will be *with you* (v. 17; the repetition is visible only in Heb.); and (d) instructions for *tomorrow* about where to go and *see* their *deliverance* (NIV, REB, NEB), 'victory' (NRSV, RSV, GNB), or 'salvation' (JB; vv. 16–17). The basic promise in fact combines several earlier Old Testament passages which affirm that the Lord fights for Israel (*cf.* Ex. 14:13–14; Dt. 20:4; 1 Sa. 17:37). What is distinctive here is that Israel has only to take her place in the spectators' gallery (*cf.* v. 24), though the use of military language instructing Judah to *take up your positions* and

----

[1] Wilcock, p. 196.

stand firm (v. 17; NIV, *cf.* JB) is a nice ironic touch. Exodus 14:13–14 offers a particularly close analogy, which suggests that the Chronicler saw this incident as a unique parallel to the exodus itself. Only in these two passages are the following phrases combined: 'do not be afraid', 'take your stand', 'see the LORD's deliverance', while the two statements in verses 15, 17 that Judah does not have to fight are but a negative version of 'the LORD will fight for you' (Ex. 14:14).

Judah is instructed not to fear, because of God's promise to be with them. *Do not be afraid* is a regular biblical command (*e.g.* Nu. 14:9; Dt. 20:3; Is. 41:9), and God's presence is a well-known form of encouragement, especially in Chronicles (*cf.* 2 Ch. 13:12; 17:3; 32:7). Both are applicable to Christians, who can be assured of God's constant presence through Christ's resurrection and the gift of the Spirit (*cf.* Mt. 28:20; Jn. 14:16–18). These words of support are backed up by specific commands about the time, the place, and the actions required. Unfortunately, the places mentioned in verse 16 cannot be decided with precision, though there is a route which led from Engedi to *Tekoa* (v. 20), about 6 miles south of Bethlehem, which was in use during the Judean monarchy.

The people responded with adoration (v. 18) and *very loud* praise (v. 19), illustrating the confidence of their faith (*cf.* v. 20). Dependence on God was of greater importance than merely winning the battle. Again the Levites play a key role, especially the *Korahites* who were one of the subdivisions of the *Kohathites* (it is probably best to translate 'that is, even' before Korahites). It is not clear whether they represent the Levites in general, among whom they provided the gatekeepers (*cf.* 1 Ch. 9:19; 26:19), or the musicians in particular (Heman, Asaph's contemporary, was a Kohathite, 1 Ch. 6:33–38).

d. Judah believes (20:20–26). As the army complies with God's instructions (v. 20), two significant events take place. Firstly, Jehoshaphat makes a call to faith (v. 20), apparently in fulfilment of the priest's role in Deuteronomy 20:2–4. It is also a positive version of Isaiah's words to Ahaz (Is. 7:9), with 'believe' and *be upheld* (NIV, REB, NEB; 'stand firm', GNB; 'be established', NRSV, RSV) central to both passages. Both verbs are actually based on the same Hebrew word, being connected in a cause-and-effect relationship. 'To believe' really means 'to exercise firm trust', so that the person who believes is made

427

firm or secure. The *prophets* who are to be believed would
seem to include Jahaziel, the Korahites, and possibly Isaiah,
through whom the king has moved from fear (v. 3) to faith
(v. 20).

The second pre-battle event is Judah's praise (vv. 21–22a).
The idea of an army going into battle singing the praises of
God is unique in Scripture, though it is related to the earlier
practice in Yahweh's wars of sounding the trumpet call and
battle cry (*cf.* 2 Ch. 13:12; Jos. 6:4–20; Jdg. 7:18–20; Ps. 47:5).
Both the form and content of this song of praise are based on
the use of psalms in temple worship. The appointed 'musi-
cians' (GNB; *cf.* 1 Ch. 15:16ff.; *to sing*, NIV, *etc.*) were Levites (*cf.*
1 Ch. 6:31–32; 25:1–31), their song was taken from Chron-
icles' favourite psalm (Ps. 136:1; *cf.* 1 Ch. 16:34; 2 Ch. 5:13;
7:3), and the phrase *the splendour of his holiness* (REB, NEB; 'in
holy array', RSV) is found elsewhere only in the Psalms (Ps.
29:2; 96:9; 1 Ch. 16:29). The outstanding feature, however, is
that as they *began to sing and praise* (v. 22), the Lord started the
battle. There can be no clearer indication that this was neither
an ordinary battle nor a traditional holy war, but Yahweh's
war in which he acted on his own. In that sense, it anticipates
Jesus' victory on the cross, though that was accompanied by
silence rather than singing.

The form of the word for *ambushes* (v. 22) is slightly unusual
and really means 'ambushers', and, since it is said that God
sent them, some have thought they must be supernatural
agents. However, the fact that all other ambushers in the Old
Testament are human suggests the same is true here, presumably meaning that the coalition members attacked each
other. The men of Mount Seir were *annihilated* first, perhaps
suspected of some kind of treachery, before the rest *destroyed
one another* (v. 23; *cf.* also Jdg. 7:22; 1 Sa. 14:20).

As the Judean soldiers arrived at the 'watchtower' (v. 24,
NRSV, RSV, *etc.*; *place that overlooks the desert*, NIV), there were *only
dead bodies . . . no-one had escaped* (*cf.* 2 Ki. 19:35). This scene of
total devastation was regarded as evidence of God's work, as
also was the amount of *plunder* (v. 25).[1] Another link between
this event and the exodus (*cf.* also v. 17) is that the Hebrew for

---

[1] Though the plunder almost certainly included 'clothing' (EVV, following
Vulg. and seven Heb. MSS) rather than 'corpses' (MT), whether 'many cattle'
(REB, NEB, *etc.*, with LXX) are meant is less clear. The Heb. in the latter case is
unusual but intelligible, lit., 'great quantities among them' (*cf.* NIV).

'took for themselves' (v. 25, NRSV, RSV; 'plundered', REB, NEB) is used elsewhere only of despoiling the Egyptians (*cf.* Ex. 3:22; 12:26). The only possible response was to *praise* God (v. 26), though whether the valley was renamed as a result is impossible to say (*Beracah* means 'praise, blessing').

e. Jerusalem rejoices (20:27–30). The final paragraph of the war is a reversal of the first two sections of the chapter. The *joyful* assembly (vv. 27–28) forms a happy contrast with the earlier assembly for prayer (vv. 6–12), with both taking place in the *temple*. The note of joy in worship (*cf.* 1 Ch. 12:40; 29:9, 17; 2 Ch. 29:30) and the fact that it was accompanied by musical instruments are typical emphases in Chronicles (*cf.* 1 Ch. 15:16, 25; 2 Ch. 30:21).

So too is the summary of the *peace* that followed the war (vv. 29–30), which is in contrast with the account of the initial invasion (vv. 1–2). This peace is linked with Jehoshaphat's reign as a whole (*cf.* 17:10), and with wider blessings of *peace* and *rest* resulting from victories elsewhere (*cf.* 1 Ch. 22:9; 2 Ch. 14:1, 5, 6; 23:21), and all because *the LORD had fought* (*cf.* vv. 15, 17) for Israel.

v. Concluding formula (20:31 – 21:1).
    20:31–34 – *cf.* 1 Kings 22:41–45 (EVV) / 41–46 (MT)
    20:36 – 21:1 – *cf.* 1 Kings 22:48–50 (EVV) / 49–51 (MT)
This is an extended version of the concluding formula, which includes an additional paragraph (vv. 35–37) inserted into the usual pattern (vv. 31–34; 21:1). Jehoshaphat's *twenty-five* year reign (v. 31) included a three-year co-regency during his father Asa's final illness (*cf.* 2 Ch. 16:12–13; 17:7), so that his twenty-two years (*cf.* 2 Ki. 3:1; 8:16) as sole king would be approximately 869–848 BC (Thiele) or 876–852 BC (Hughes). The favourable comparison with *Asa* (v. 32) and mention of the *high places* (v. 33) hark back to the introduction (17:3, 6). Although the statements about the high places seem contradictory (*cf.* 14:3, 5; 15:17), the hint about the superficial standards of popular religion (v. 33) may give a clue as to why they persisted in some areas. It is also a salutary reminder about the limited success of Jehoshaphat's campaigns for religious and legal reform (17:7–9; 19:4–11). Though the king had set his heart on God (19:3; *cf.* 1 Ch. 29:18; 2 Ch. 30:19), his example was not widely followed (*cf.* 2 Ch. 12:14).

Further information is typically to be found in a prophetic source (v. 34; *cf.* 19:2), which is included in a larger work. *Kings of Israel* really means kings of Judah, indicating as usual that this small kingdom remained the true Israel (*cf.* 16:11; 27:7).

The final paragraph shows a number of changes from Kings, with the aim of concentrating on Jehoshaphat's relationship with Ahab's son *Ahaziah*. Out go statements about his wars (presumably because of fuller details in chs. 18, 20), the male cult prostitutes (all four references in Ki. are omitted in Ch.), and arrangements in Edom (1 Ki. 22:45–47). Also, the brief details of his *alliance* with Ahaziah are quite different, the description of his building a fleet of ships as a result of an alliance contrasting with 1 Kings 22:48–49 where Ahaziah's offer of assistance follows the wrecking of the ships. In fact, the chronological differences may not be so great, especially if the beginning of Ahaziah's offer in 1 Kings 22:48 is translated, 'At that time, Ahaziah had said . . .'.[1] Chronicles' point, however, is to underline through two particular Hebrew words the implications of the link between Jehoshaphat and Ahaziah. The first is *made an alliance with* (NIV, GNB), which occurs once each in verses 35–37 but not at all in 1 Kings 22. This same word also described Jehoshaphat's alliance with Ahab (18:1), indicating that Jehoshaphat is repeating his error (this is brought out clearly in REB, NEB, 'he did wrong in joining with him', vv. 35–36). The second important word is *destroy* (v. 37, NIV, *etc.*; 'bring to nothing', REB, NEB), which has previously occurred in 1 Chronicles 13:11; 15:13 as 'break out' (Heb. *pāras*), also with God as the subject. It speaks of God's wrath bringing human plans to a sudden end on both occasions. Eliezer's prophecy (he is unknown elsewhere) is to be compared with Jehu's (19:2–3), showing that Jehoshaphat was blessed in spite of his actions rather than because of them (*cf. e.g.* 21:7).

The ships are probably to be understood as *trading ships* (NIV), rather than those that literally went to 'Tarshish' (NRSV, RSV, *etc.*). Tarshish was simply a distant place, but Jehoshaphat was unable to emulate Solomon in establishing a successful

---

[1] Willi, *CA*, p. 219; Williamson, p. 303. There is no reason why this could not have been the original sense in Ki., making it unnecessary to regard Eliezer's prophecy as the Chronicler's own creation (though the style of the prophecy is another matter).

maritime trade (*cf.* 2 Ch. 9:21). *Ezion Geber* (v. 36), which was at the northern end of the Gulf of Aqaba, had been rebuilt by Solomon (2 Ki. 8:17) but was soon lost again by Jehoshaphat's son (*cf.* 2 Ki. 8:21–22; 2 Ch. 21:8–10). These changes of fortune are intended to show that as faith and unbelief followed each other in quick succession, only God's grace ensured Judah's preservation.

D. Judah and the house of Ahab (21:2 – 22:12)

i. Jehoram (21:2–20)

'The LORD was not willing to destroy the house of David' (21:7).

21:5–10b – *cf.* 2 Kings 8:17–22
21:20a – *cf.* 2 Kings 8:17
21:20b – *cf.* 2 Kings 8:24

The kingdom of Judah suddenly enters a very dark phase (chs. 21–23). The reigns of Jehoram and Ahaziah (chs. 21–22) and their sequel in Athaliah's overthrow and death (ch. 23), brought the nation to the brink of internal destruction. The chief cause was the insidious influence of *the house of Ahab* (21:6; 22:3, 4, 7, 8), which was known in contemporary non-Israelite documents as 'the house of Omri' (*cf.* 22:2). Ironically, that dynasty had been introduced into Judah's affairs by the godly Jehoshaphat (*cf.* 22:9), but the latter's faith and courage were unfortunately no guarantee of his wisdom. The disastrous nature of his alliance with Ahab has been mentioned already (*cf.* 18:1–2; 19:1–3; *cf.* 20:35–37), but now its consequences begin to unfold. The wider story of the house of Ahab's commitment to Baal worship and conflict with the prophets Elijah and Elisha is assumed to be known to the reader (1 Ki. 17 – 2 Ki. 11), leaving Chronicles to concentrate on their relationship with Judah.

Chapters 21–22 belong together, as evidenced by a number of common expressions. In addition to *the house of Ahab* (21:6; 22:3), these include the death of the royal princes (21:17; 22:8; *cf.* 21:4), the *youngest son's* preservation (21:17; 22:1; *cf.* 22:11–12), invasions by *Arab* raiders (21:17; 22:1), and the fact that both kings *did evil in the eyes of the LORD* (21:6; 22:4). The legacy of *Jehoshaphat* also continues (21:12; 22:9), though in contrasting ways. Though both kings failed to follow his example of seeking God (22:9; *cf.* 17:34; 18:4, 7; 20:3), they did maintain his dangerous liaison with Ahab's house in their policies concerning marriage (21:6; *cf.* 18:1) and war (22:5–6; *cf.* 18:2–3).

Chronicles' account of *Jehoram* is marked by several additions to Kings' version (2 Ki. 8:16–24). The key changes, however, are to be found in references to the Davidic covenant (v. 7) and the prophetic judgment against Jehoram (vv. 10b–19). What emerges is a more explicit emphasis on God's involvement with his people as they pass through troubled times. They can be assured that he remains totally committed to his promises, and deals severely with individual rulers who deny the very covenant that brought them to power.

The wider perspective of Jehoram, therefore, is that evil is ultimately a passing phenomenon because God stands unconditionally by his word. For post-exilic Israel, the chapter amounts to a call to perseverance, supporting the faithfulness under pressure which official leaders and prophets had shown (*cf.* Ezr. 8:22; Ne. 9:31–37; Zc. 6:9–15; Mal. 3:6–12). For the New Testament, the experience of the cross shows that relief from evil is now absolutely certain, though it does not necessarily happen quickly. The cross is the sign of God's ultimate commitment, so that whether persecution leads to life or death, his people cannot be separated from the promises of his eternal covenant (Rom. 8:39; Heb. 12:24; 13:20).

a. God preserves the house of David (21:2–7). The account of Jehoram opens with an extended version of the regular introductory formula. The familiar chronological information and theological evaluation (vv. 5–6; *cf.* 24:1–2; 26:3–5) are accompanied by a favourite phrase in Chronicles that Jehoram *established himself firmly* (v. 4; lit. 'made himself strong'). This material is preceded, however, by unusually full details concerning Jehoram's family (vv. 2–3). The family shows regular signs of God's blessing, including many sons (*cf.* 1 Ch. 14:3–7; 2 Ch. 13:21), wealth in *silver* and *gold* (*cf.* 2 Ch. 9:13–28; 32:27), and *fortified cities* (*cf.* 2 Ch. 11:5–12; 17:12). Jehoram's response to God's goodness, however, was to put not only *all his brothers to the sword* (v. 4), but some of his leading 'officials' as well (v. 4, NRSV, GNB, JB; not *princes*, RSV, NIV, NEB). 'Made himself strong' (v. 4), therefore, clearly means the violent removal of all other possible claimants to the throne (*cf.* also 12:1; 25:3; contrast 17:1; 23:1).

Verses 2–4, which have no parallel in Kings, are widely thought to have come from an official record, since they show little sign of the Chronicler's influence apart from the verb 'to strengthen oneself'. That two of Jehoram's brothers had almost identical names (*Azariah, Azariahu*, v. 2) is a surprise. However, the full list is well supported textually (LXX specifically has 'six' brothers), and, since the names are spelled differently, it is possible that they had different mothers. Jehoram is called *king of Israel* (v. 1, NIV, *etc.*; 'Judah', REB, NEB, RSV, GNB), because the Chronicler regarded the kingdom of Judah as the true Israel. Though Jehoram was the *firstborn son* (v. 3), it seems that his kingship was not an automatic right. Not only was he *given* the kingdom, but sons apart from the eldest were sometimes appointed as king, either by the preceding king (1 Ki. 1:13, 30; 2 Ch. 11:20–22) or by the people of the land (2 Ki. 23:31; *cf.* 2 Ki. 23:36; 1 Ch. 3:15, where Shallum is another name for Jehoahaz).

The chronological details refer to Jehoram's reign of *eight years* as sole ruler, approximately 848–841 BC (*cf.* 2 Ki. 1:17). However, as is frequently the case, the dominant element in the introductory formula is the theological evaluation, which mentions two contrasting covenants. The first is Jehoram's marriage to Athaliah, *a daughter of Ahab* (v. 6; *cf.* 22:2; 22:10 – 23:21).[1] Marriage contracts in the ancient Near East were known as covenants (*cf.* Ho. 2:14–20; Je. 31:32), and often sealed political alliances (*cf.* 2 Ch. 18:1). However, the agreement between Jehoshaphat and Ahab resulted in Jehoram (and Ahaziah, 22:4) doing *evil in the eyes of the LORD* (v. 6). God's response was to invoke the greater *covenant he had made with David* (v. 7). The importance of this statement is indicated by its expansion from 2 Kings 8:19. *House of David*, which was previously 'house of Judah', is now directly opposed to the 'house of Ahab' (v. 6), while 'David my servant' has become *the covenant the LORD had made with David*. The only other specific mention of the Davidic covenant in Chronicles is in 2 Chronicles 13:5, where the Davidic house was again under threat. Both passages refer back to 1 Chronicles 17:4–14, though the language here may well reflect the influence of the Psalms (*e.g.* Pss. 89:3, 35–36; 132:11–12) and the prophets (*e.g.* Is. 55:3;

---

[1] Though P, Ar, read 'sister of Ahab' (*cf.* Begrich, Rudolph), this is probably a harmonization based on 2 Ki. 8:26 = 2 Ch. 22:2.

Je. 33:21), which speak of the Davidic covenant in terms of God's unchanging and unconditional commitment to his people. The *lamp* is also best understood in the same light (v. 7; *cf.* 1 Ki. 11:36)! While this unusual metaphor has been explained as symbolizing either 'life' (Curtis and Madsen, Ackroyd) or 'dominion' (Hanson),[1] the context here and elsewhere in the Old Testament shows that it is about permanence. Though 'the lamp of the wicked is snuffed out' (Jb. 18:5; Pr. 13:9; 24:20), God's people shine on in the surrounding darkness. The Chronicler's special interest in the lampstand shining every night in the temple may well express similar confidence (*cf.* 2 Ch. 4:7; 13:11, both unparalleled in Ki.). It was not God's will (lit. 'not willing') *to destroy* Jehoram's whole family (v. 7; *cf.* v. 17; 22:10–11), and the Chronicler seems to have underlined the promise for his readers by adding 'and' before 'to his sons for ever' (v. 7, RSV).

b. God punishes Jehoram (21:8–20).

In addition to promising security for David's dynasty, the Davidic covenant also specifies that individual kings are to be punished for their waywardness (*cf.* 1 Ch. 28:9; 2 Ch. 7:19–22). The implications of this for Jehoram are pointed out in two ways, firstly in a short passage from Kings (vv. 8–10b) and then in material unique to Chronicles (vv. 10c–19).

The first evidence is a rebellion by *Edom* (vv. 8–10a) and an internal revolt by the Judean city of *Libnah* (v. 10b). Edom had probably been regained for Judah under Jehoshaphat (*cf.* 2 Ki. 3:9; 2 Ch. 30:36), but had now *set up its own king* (v. 8). The most likely understanding of Jehoram's attempt to restore control is that he just about managed to escape by night from an Edomite stranglehold (v. 9). Less probably, Judah was 'defeated' by the Edomites (NEB, also Šanda, Williamson).[2] Nothing else is known of trouble in Libnah, a town of uncertain location on Judah's western border not far

---

[1] *Cf.* P. D. Hanson, 'The Song of Heshbon and David's Nir', *HTR* 61, 1968, pp. 297–320.

[2] A further problem is that 'with his officers/commanders' has replaced 'to Zair' (2 Ki. 8:21) possibly because the original place name may well have disappeared by the Chronicler's time, though perhaps also as a result of his interest in democratization (Japhet, *Ideology*, p. 418).

from Lachish.[1] What is more important for the Chronicler is that these military reverses symptomized the fact that Jehoram had *forsaken the LORD* (v. 10c). This final phrase of verse 10 is an explanatory addition to Kings, reflecting the idea that to forsake God is the opposite of seeking him (1 Ch. 28:9; 2 Ch. 7:19, 22; 15:2). The basic principle is that God forsakes those who forsake him (*cf.* Mt. 10:33; 1 Tim. 2:12), not in an impersonal deterministic way but as a matter of deliberate choice (*cf.* v. 14). However, an element of choice also extends to those under judgment, as may be seen in the contrast between Jeroboam's persistence in rejecting God (2 Ch. 13:11–20) and Rehoboam's humble repentance (2 Ch. 12:1–12).

The Chronicler then develops his theme (vv. 10c–19) by identifying more of Jehoram's sins. He is the first Judean king who actually constructed *high places* (v. 11; *cf.* 2 Ch. 15:17; 20:33), among which is probably to be counted a Baal temple in Jerusalem (*cf.* 2 Ch. 23:17). The two expressions *caused to prostitute* (NIV, JB) and *led astray* (lit. 'thrust aside') belong to the Old Testament traditional vocabulary of idolatry, the former being particularly common in the prophets (*e.g.* Je. 3:1; Ezk. 16:16; Ho. 4:18) and the latter in the Deuteronomic law (*e.g.* Dt. 4:19; 13:10, 13; *cf.* 2 Ki. 17:21). The former term has also been used to explain why the northern kingdom went into exile (1 Ch. 5:25), and shows that Judah is under the same condemnation.

It is no surprise that God responds to this apostasy through prophecy, though the presence of a *letter* from *Elijah* is unexpected (vv. 12–15). Elijah makes no other appearance in Chronicles, is only known to have prophesied in Israel (though *cf.* 1 Ki. 19:3, 8), wrote no other letters, and is thought by many to have been dead by this time! Since the letter's style is also consistent with the Chronicler's, it is understandable that many commentators view it as the Chronicler's own creation. However, Elijah was certainly alive for part of Jehoram's reign (2 Ki. 1:17), and it is quite possible that he and Elisha functioned alongside each other for a while before his translation (2 Ki. 2:1–12). Letters (*cf.* 1 Ki. 21:8–10; 2 Ki.

---

[1] For the identification of Libnah, which is almost certainly not the traditional site of Tell es-Safi, *cf.* Z. Kallai, *Historical Geography* (Jerusalem: Magnes Press, 1986), pp. 379–382; D. Baly, *Geography of the Bible* (Guildford: Lutterworth, ²1974), pp. 139, 142.

5:5–7; 10:1–7) and written prophecies were also well known (*cf.* 1 Ch. 28:9; 29:29; 2 Ch. 20:34) at this time, and, if Elijah was now unable to travel because of age, he could well have found it easier to communicate in written form. The letter's contents also reflect Elijah's conflicts with Ahab's house, and its present style may indicate the Chronicler's redrafting rather than his composition.

The letter has the typical form of a prophetic judgment, with a messenger formula (v. 12b) introducing an indictment (vv. 12c–13) and an announcement of judgment (vv. 14–15). The indictment summarizes verses 2–11, drawing together a number of phrases from the early part of the chapter. It begins by contrasting the ways of *Asa* and *Jehoshaphat* with those of the *house of Ahab*, to illustrate how Jehoram has betrayed God's purposes for Judah (vv. 12c–13a). The sins of idolatry and fratricide are then mentioned, which are directly linked with what precedes by the words 'kill' (Heb. *hāraḡ*, *cf.* v. 4) and 'prostitute' (Heb. *zānâ*, *cf.* v. 11). *Better than you* (v. 13) has been variously interpreted. The most likely meanings are either that Jehoram's brothers were not idolaters or that they were legally innocent and were put to death without cause.

The judgment (vv. 14–15) is in two parts, whose fulfilment is separately described in verses 16–19. The first part is directed against the people, with Jehoram's *sons* and *wives* singled out for special treatment (vv. 14, 16–17). They will suffer a 'great calamity' (JB; *heavy blow*, NIV, REB, NEB), a phrase which is invariably associated with divine punishment. This could take the form of military defeat (*cf.* 1 Sa. 4:17; 2 Sa. 18:7) though it was more often a plague, especially in the exodus and wilderness periods (*cf.* Ex. 9:14; Nu. 16:48–50; 2 Ch. 21:14, 22; Ps. 106:29–30). The actual punishment is an invasion by *Philistines* and *Arabs* (v. 16). The former may have been associated with the rebellion in Libnah (v. 10), and the latter are probably from northern Arabia, though they may have come from southern Arabia if the *Cushites* (NIV, REB, NEB) are really 'Ethiopians' (RSV; 'Sudanese', GNB; *cf.* also 14:9–15; 17:11; 26:7). The style is reminiscent of the 'Yahweh war' theme, for God had *aroused the hostility of* (v. 16, NIV) or 'stirred up the anger of' (RSV) the invaders, and ensured the punishment was carried out (v. 17). Elijah's word is fulfilled, and Jehoram's murders avenged (*cf.* v. 4). The *king's* 'house' (v. 17; *palace*, REB, NEB) is almost certainly in one of the fortified cities (*cf.* v. 3), not Jerusalem. 'Jehoahaz' (RSV, REB, NEB) is another name for *Ahaziah* (NIV, JB, GNB; *cf.* 22:1; the two parts of the name are simply in reverse order).

The second part of the judgment falls directly on Jehoram (vv. 15, 18–19), who suffers an *incurable disease*. Unfortunately, it cannot be described any more specifically than as a very unpleasant *disease of the bowels* (despite REB, NEB). Translation problems have increased the difficulty, and the end may have come suddenly, 'in two days' (*cf.* Keil, Dillard), rather than at the end of the *second year* (EVV).

The factual details of Jehoram's passing also indicate God's judgment. There are three negatives, that he was not honoured with the customary funeral *fire* (v. 19; *cf.* 2 Ch. 16:14; Je. 34:5), that there was no regret at his passing, and that he was not buried in the royal cemetery (v. 20). Three items are also unusually omitted, *viz.* any source of further information, the direct succession, and that he rested with his fathers (*cf. e.g.* 2 Ch. 12:15–16; 13:22 – 14:1; 16:13–14). In this matter-of-fact way, the author shows that he regarded Jehoram's reign, as also those of his successors Ahaziah and Athaliah, as an aberration.

ii. Ahaziah (22:1–9)

'The house of Ahaziah had no one able to rule the kingdom' (22:9, RSV).

22:1–6 – *cf.* 2 Kings 8:24b–29
22:7 – *cf.* 2 Kings 9:21
22:8 – *cf.* 2 Kings 10:13–14
22:9 – *cf.* 2 Kings 9:28

The real subject of chapter 22 is the *house of Ahab* (vv. 3, 7, 8) rather than the two rulers of Judah, *Ahaziah* (vv. 1–9) and *Athaliah* (vv. 10–12). The influence of Ahab's house was felt during Ahaziah's brief reign through *Athaliah*'s role as queen mother (v. 2) and through various *advisers* (vv. 4–5). External pressure was brought to bear by *Jehoram* king of Israel (also called *Joram*), who in one case is given the full title of *son of Ahab king of Israel* (v. 5; *cf.* vv. 6, 7, 8). Ahaziah was little more than a puppet, and, after his death, Athaliah ruled Judah while there was no effective male claimant (v. 12). During both reigns, therefore, Ahab's dynasty was in effective control of Judah. The unity of Judah and Israel is eloquently symbolized by the names of their kings. No other Israelite king was called

Jehoram or Ahaziah, yet both names are used of successive contemporary rulers in Judah and Israel.

Ahaziah and Athaliah represent two further stages in the subversion of Judah by Ahab's dynasty before the denouement in chapter 23. While Jehoram of Judah is merely open to its influence (ch. 21), Ahaziah is fully co-operative. When Ahaziah dies, however, the situation becomes even more desperate. No male in David's house can assume kingship (v. 9), and any remnants of hope are dashed by Athaliah's violent purge of what was left of the royal family (vv. 10–12). The overwhelming threat is no more evident than in the repeated group murders which affect the Davidic house four times within two generations (21:4; 22:1, 8, 10). It is true that one baby escapes Athaliah's cruelty (vv. 11–12), but what could one baby do against such a tyrant? In all this, God's own integrity is increasingly under question, for he seems to have failed to keep his promises, and to have left his people utterly defenceless.

Significant changes have been made to the account in Kings, and some awareness of that background is assumed. Individual words and phrases in verses 1–6 have been adjusted so as to strengthen the link with chapter 21 (*e.g. youngest son*, v. 1 and 21:17; *He too / also walked in the ways of the house of Ahab*, v. 3, *cf.* 21:6), and to underline Ahaziah's subjection to the house of Ahab (*cf.* the threefold addition of 'counsel, advice' in vv. 3–5). The Chronicler has also rewritten the much longer story of Jehu's revolution (vv. 7–9) by skilfully incorporating scattered phrases from 2 Kings 9–10. Whereas in Kings interest is focused on Jehu's actions in Israel, here God's plan to *destroy the house of Ahab* (v. 7; *cf.* v. 8) centres on Ahaziah, though God still refuses 'to destroy the house of David' (21:7). Through all the disasters, God's providence is at work to remove evil and restore his rightful rule. It is God who has really anointed Jehu, and who has brought about Ahaziah's downfall (v. 7).

Assurance of God's sovereign control was just as appropriate in the troubles of the post-exilic period when the Davidic house had become no more than a memory (*cf.* Ezr. 9:6–7; Ne. 9:36–37). It is equally applicable to suffering believers of every generation who feel that God seems to have relinquished effective control over their situation. Such an assurance brought comfort too to the apostles (*cf.* 2 Cor. 1:3–11; 6:3–10; 1 Pet. 2:20–25), and the biblical witness as a whole encourages believers to look to the unseen hand of God even when the darkness is at its thickest.

a. Ahaziah and the house of Ahab (22:1–4). By means of the standard introductory formula, Ahaziah is linked in every verse of this paragraph with the *house of Ahab*. Even his accession is a reminder of God's judgment on the partnership (v. 1), though Ahaziah will still continue his father's policy. Responsibility for the death of Ahaziah's older brothers is attributed to *the raiders who came with the Arabs*, presumably the Philistines (v. 1; *cf.* 21:16–17). The role of *the people of Jerusalem* in appointing the next king suggests a similarity between them and 'the people of the land' (*cf.* 26:1; 33:25; 36:1). Both responded in crises when the regular arrangements for the succession, usually involving a co-regency, had broken down. They had also carried on the tradition of the people who came to Shechem to appoint Solomon's successor (*cf.* 2 Ch. 10:1).

The date of Ahaziah's reign of *one year* (v. 2) is variously reckoned as being somewhere between 845 BC (Begrich) and 841 BC (Thiele). His age is problematical, however. Where MT has 'forty-two' years (NEB, NRSV, RSV), 2 Kings 8:26 and one Greek text have *twenty-two* (NIV, REB, GNB), and the major Greek MSS have 'twenty'. Though one of the Greek readings is to be preferred since Ahaziah would otherwise have been older than his father (*cf.* 2 Ch. 21:5, 20), it is not easy to explain how at that age his brothers' sons (v. 8, lit.) were old enough to be his attendants.

The chief characteristic of Ahaziah's reign was his dependence on counsellors from Ahab's house (vv. 3–5). Responsibility for this rested with *Athaliah*, who was probably the *granddaughter of Omri* (v. 2, NIV, *etc.*) and daughter of Ahab rather than the 'daughter of Omri' (JB). Though her contribution to Ahaziah's reign is mentioned only in general terms (v. 3), her cruelty to her own family (vv. 10–12) and her idolatry (23:17) showed what she was capable of. The position of royal counsellors was an important one (*cf.* 2 Sa. 15:24; 1 Ch. 27:32; Ezr. 4:5; 7:28), and could be filled by the queen mother apart from her own official status (*cf.* 1 Ki. 2:13–21; 15:13; 2 Ki. 24:15).[1] Good advice was essential to good kingship (*e.g.* 1 Ch.

---

[1] *Cf.* N. Andreasen, 'The role of the queen mother in Israelite society', *CBQ* 45, 1983, pp. 179–193; L. Ruppert, in *TDOT* 6, 1990, pp. 161–163.

13:1; 2 Ch. 20:21), but Athaliah was a 'counsellor in wickedness' (REB, NEB), and Ahaziah's advisers led *to his undoing*, literally, destruction (*cf.* 2 Ch. 10:8–9; 25:17). By adding *he too*/also (v. 3) as well as the phrases beginning with *for/since* in verses 3 and 4, the Chronicler indicates that *after his father's* (*i.e.* Jehoram's) *death*, the ways of the house of David had become indistinguishable from those of the house of Ahab.

b. Ahaziah's downfall and death (22:5–9). Judah and
Israel's joint hostilities against the 'Syrians' (v. 5, RSV; *Arameans*, NIV, *etc.*) exemplify their unity, though Ahaziah's acceptance of Israelite *counsel* (v. 5) and his journey to Jezreel (v. 6) show who was the dominant partner.[1] *Went with* (v. 5) probably indicates Ahaziah's general support for *Jehoram/ Joram* (Heb. has both spellings), which in practice is limited to visiting the wounded king in *Jezreel* (v. 6) rather than assisting in the battle at *Ramoth Gilead* (v. 5).

Ahaziah is probably not condemned for participating in the war as such. Rather, by failing to separate himself from Jehoram, he made himself liable to suffer the same punishment that God had previously announced against Ahab's house and which he had chosen *Hazael* and Jehu to carry out (*cf.* 1 Ki. 19:15–17; 2 Ki. 8:11–13). This lack of discernment shows itself in several attendant ironies. Firstly, though Israel and Judah had been reunited, it was on the basis of self-interest and idolatry rather than the covenant. Secondly, joint action against the Syrians at Ramoth Gilead had already led to one disaster (ch. 18). Thirdly, Jehoram's attempt to *recover* (v. 6, NIV, REB, NEB, etc.), literally 'be healed' (NRSV, RSV) at Jezreel is probably a tacit rejection of the Lord's offer of healing through repentance (*cf.* 2 Ch. 7:14; 30:20). His action may also have been compounded by further idolatry if family tradition is an adequate guide (*cf.* 2 Ki. 1:2–6, 15–17).

The text of verse 6 has several difficulties. 'Ramah' (NRSV, RSV) is to be understood as an alternative name for *Ramoth Gilead* (NIV, *etc.*), and MT's 'Azariah' has been correctly changed to *Ahaziah* in EVV. However, 'from the wounds' (EVV) is a smoothing over of an unfinished explanatory clause, following 2 Kings 8:29. MT has 'because the wounds . . .', and, while

---

[1] 'Syrians/Arameans', which is the reading of 2 Ki. 8:28, Tg., Vulg., and two Heb. MSS, represents the addition of one letter to MT, which is incomprehensible as it stands.

EVV's harmonization may be correct, Vulg.'s addition of '. . . were many' is worth consideration (Rudolph).

Jehu has a role parallel to Hazael's as an agent of God's judgment on Ahab's house (vv. 7–9). He had been *anointed* with oil as a symbol of God's choice and empowering to carry out a particular task (1 Ki. 19:15–17; 2 Ki. 9:1–13). The word for Ahaziah's *downfall* (v. 7) is unique in Hebrew, but it is not to be changed to the rare expression 'turn of affairs' (2 Ch. 10:15; *cf.* the related verb in 1 Ch. 10:14), since the phrase 'downfall of Ahaziah' cannot be easily adapted.[1] In verse 8, Jehu was either *executing judgment* (NIV, NRSV, RSV, *cf.* JB) on Ahab's house or he was 'at variance with' (REB, NEB) them, *i.e.* had accused them of failing to keep God's covenant standards.

The details differ somewhat from 2 Kings 9:16–29; 10:12–14, such as in the order of the deaths of the king and his relatives, and the place of Ahaziah's burial. However, some EVV have added an unnecessary *then* in verse 9 (*e.g.* NIV, REB, NEB), while 2 Kings 9:27 says nothing about the time lag between Ahaziah's being wounded and his death. Also verse 9's silence about the place of his burial probably indicates that he displeased God (*cf.* 2 Ch. 21:20). A more difficult problem is to reconstruct Ahaziah's movements after he was wounded, but, since the places mentioned in verse 9 and 2 Kings 8:18 do not coincide, it is probably unwise to be emphatic about any conclusions. Further problems concern Ahaziah's attendants (v. 8). The Hebrew calls them 'sons of the brothers of Ahaziah', but, since his actual brothers were dead (21:17; 22:1) and their sons were probably no more than children, they are best regarded as 'kinsmen' (REB, NEB).

Ahaziah is contrasted with his grandfather *Jehoshaphat* (v. 9), in whose memory he is given a decent burial (2 Ki. 9:28). Though criticisms had been levelled against Jehoshaphat (18:1–2; 19:1–3; 20:35–37), his general outlook of whole-heartedly seeking to follow God's will contrasts sharply with Ahaziah (17:3–4; 19:3). On the debit side, though, there is now no effective challenger to Athaliah and the latter state of David's line seems worse than the former ('no one able to rule', v. 9, RSV). Though this situation is sometimes compared with the end of Saul's dynasty (1 Ch. 10:13–14; *cf.* Mosis, Williamson, Dillard), a better analogy is the childless Davidic

---

[1] *Cf.* Rudolph, Ackroyd, Williamson.

line at the exile (Je. 22:29–30). The real problem is the conflict between the lack of an heir and God's eternal promise to David, which has no equivalent in Saul's case.

ii. Athaliah (22:10–12)

'Athaliah . . . proceeded to destroy the whole royal family of
the house of Judah' (v. 10).
22:10–12 – cf. 2 Kings 11:1–3

Athaliah now attempts what God had not been willing to do, that is, to destroy finally *the house of Judah* (v. 10; *cf.* 21:7), but even in this she is thwarted by divine providence. *Destroy* (NIV, RSV, *etc.*) is a rare word, and if it is not a corruption of the corresponding word in 2 Kings 11:1, means 'remove' or even 'exterminate'.[1] God's protection of baby *Joash* (v. 11; *cf.* 21:17) is but one example of several vulnerable children through whom God fulfils his purposes (*cf.* Ex. 2:1–10; 1 Sa. 17; Is. 7:14; 9:6; Je. 1:4–8), of whom Jesus is of course the most notable (*cf.* Mt. 1:13–23; Lk. 1:26–33; 2:1–40). His people's destiny is always safe in his hands, no matter how intense their suffering.

This incident is really a tale of two women. One *ruled the land* for *six years* (v. 12), though the lack of the usual formulaic framework shows that the author regarded her reign as illegitimate. She had taken the throne by violence, and was the only non-Davidic ruler in Judah (Begrich gives her dates as 845–840, Thiele as 841–835). The other woman was 'Jehoshebeath' (or *Jehosheba*, as in 1 Ki. 11:2; so NIV, REB, NEB, JB here), who was Athaliah's daughter or stepdaughter and the wife of *the priest Jehoiada* (the usual pre-exilic term for the high priest).[2] The Chronicler has inserted a phrase into verse 11 (*cf.* 2 Ki. 11:2), explaining how as *Ahaziah's sister* she had access to the baby and that her courageous faith was just as vital as her husband's in restoring the legitimate kingship (*cf.* ch. 11).

This paragraph is usually seen as the beginning of Athaliah's end and taken with what follows (*cf.* the headings in NIV, NRSV). It may be equally regarded, however, as the final effort of Ahab's house in Judah. Though the process that began with Jehoram of Judah's fratricide (21:4) had done its

---

[1] *Cf.* W. G. E. Watson, 'Archaic elements in the language of Chronicles', *Bib.* 53, 1972, p. 193; KB, p. 201; *CAD*, D, pp. 186–188.
[2] The form of her name in Ch. is clearly feminine and does not contain a dittograph of *bat*, 'daughter' (Willi, *CA*, pp. 86–87).

worst, the lamp had not been extinguished (*cf.* 21:7). Now, the dark age was about to be replaced by a new era.

E. Three declining kings (23:1 – 26:23)

i. Joash (23:1 – 24:27)

'Jehoiada and his sons anointed him; and they shouted, "Long live the king!"' (23:11, NRSV).

'He [Joash] did what was right in the eyes of the LORD as long as Jehoiada the priest was alive' (24:2, REB, NEB).

23:1–18a – *cf.* 2 Kings 11:4–18
23:20–21 – *cf.* 2 Kings 11:19–20
24:1–2 – *cf* 2 Kings 11:21 – 12:2
24:5–6 – *cf.* 2 Kings 12:4–7
24:8 – *cf.* 2 Kings 12:9
24:11–12 – *cf.* 2 Kings 12:10–12
24:14 – *cf.* 2 Kings 12:13
24:23 – *cf.* 2 Kings 12:17
24:25 – *cf.* 2 Kings 21, 22b
24:26 – *cf.* 2 Kings 12:22a
24:27 – *cf.* 2 Kings 12:20, 22c

Superficially, chapter 23 describes a *coup d'état* in which queen Athaliah is removed by the high priest Jehoiada, who then installs seven-year-old Joash on the throne as the rightful king (vv. 1–15). The underlying significance, however, is about restoring God's covenant principles to their proper place in the fabric of national life (vv. 16–21). Joash's accession therefore was really an attempt to retain Judah's distinctive *raison d'être* in the face of the onslaught of Canaanite values, and was not just about the re-establishing of the legitimate king. This aim was undoubtedly successful in the short term, because of the courage and commitment to God's promises shown by Jehoiada and the people. In the medium and long term, though, the results were not so straightforward. Things began to go wrong again even during Joash's reign (24:17–27), and the apostasy illustrated by Ahab's house ultimately prevailed. That led of course not to the removal of a single ruler but to the nation's removal from their land (2 Ch. 36:15–16). On the other hand, God's protective hand never left his people, and ultimately it is this to which the author directs the reader's attention. Though the benefits of Joash's accession are short-lived, in the end it is the kind of faith and trust shown by

Jehoiada and the people that see God's kingdom truly established in the hearts of his people.

This account basically follows 2 Kings 11:4–20, though with a large number of changes, such as the additions to verses 1–2a, 6, 18b–19. By means of the changes three themes already present in the earlier text have become central. The most obvious is the concern for the temple, its sanctity and its personnel. The temple is to be kept holy and clean (vv. 6, 19), while the role of the Levites (vv. 6–8, 18; *cf.* 2 Ki. 11:7–9, 18), musicians and gatekeepers (vv. 4, 13, 18–19) is made explicit and clarified. A second theme is the way in which Joash's accession fulfils God's promises about David's house. Though it is striking that both Kings and Chronicles refer to Joash as 'the king' or 'the king's son' (apparently pretending that Athaliah does not even exist!), Chronicles goes further by speaking explicitly of the reinstitution of the Davidic dynasty and Davidic patterns of worship (vv. 3, 18; *cf.* v. 9). By also omitting the parallel story of how Jehu restored Yahwistic kingship to the northern kingdom (2 Ki. 9–10), Chronicles has focused the issue of the survival of covenant kingship entirely on the conflict involving David's family. The third theme is the contribution made by the people. Although they feature strongly in 2 Kings 11:13–20, references to the heads of fathers' houses (v. 2), the assembly (v. 3), and all Judah (v. 8) give them additional prominence as a covenant people (*cf.* vv. 1, 3, 16). Over all, the Chronicler's version underlines God's faithfulness to his covenant, and the part played in the *coup* by the people and their religious leaders rather than by military officials.

These are all typical themes in Chronicles, and their application to the writer's contemporaries would have been fairly obvious. A clear incentive was being offered for the people, especially the priests and Levites, to stand up and be counted for their commitment to God's promises. If God had preserved the Davidic house once when it had come within a whisker of being wiped out, he could do so again. As before, therefore, the Chronicler creates an expectation in the minds of post-exilic readers that another king descended from David could again rule in Israel. It is striking that in so doing he does not appeal to the prophetic pictures of a future messianic figure, but refers to a human representative. This is quite consistent with the way the New Testament refers to the final

Son of David who exercises kingship in Israel. It is an important part of Jesus' humanity that he was descended from the line of kings in which Joash and even Athaliah had a place, a factor which receives due recognition in a variety of New Testament writings (Mt. 1:6–16; Rom. 1:3; 2 Tim. 2:8; Rev. 22:16). Jehoiada's courage therefore plays a necessary part in enabling David's line to be preserved until Jesus revealed his kingdom.

a. Joash's accession under Jehoiada's leadership (23:1–21).

i. The rightful king restored (23:1–11). The high priest Jehoiada (*cf.* 24:6) acts in *the seventh year* (v. 1), that is, when Joash was seven years old (24:1), though the precise significance of this time is not explained. The priest *showed his strength* (*cf.* JB, REB, NEB), which may simply mean that he acted decisively. The phrase is used of several kings at the beginning of their reigns, usually in a positive sense, though in this case Jehoiada was acting on someone else's behalf rather than his own (*cf. e.g.* 2 Ch. 15:8; 17:1; 27:6).

The first aim of the *coup* to see Joash anointed as king (v. 11) took place in three stages. The first stage (vv. 1–3) is an *assembly* of *Levites* and *heads of families* in Judah (vv. 2–3), convened with the help of some military officers (v. 1). The ease with which the 'rebels' gather suggests Athaliah had little popular support. The 'assembly' is a favoured term in Chronicles because of its crucial role in post-exilic Israel (*cf.* Ezr. 10:1; Ne. 8:2). In Chronicles it was usually a representative body, and, though its decisions were often of a political nature, they tended to have religious overtones (*cf.* 1 Ch. 13:2; 29:10, 2 Ch. 30:2). It was regarded as a virtue that leaders should respect the assembly, and it is noticeable that no assembly is mentioned while Judah was under the house of Ahab (the previous reference is 20:5, 14). A *covenant* is agreed (v. 3) which probably contained the terms of Joash's kingship, including those of Jehoiada's regency. The *covenant* with the military officers (v. 1) is most likely to have been a preliminary version.

Most EVV suggest the boy was actually produced in the assembly, 'Here is the king's son!' (v. 3, NRSV). Some feel the crucial element of surprise is thereby lost, and as an alternative, have either proposed that Jehoiada merely established

445

the boy's identity (de Vries) or have combined this phrase with the next, *the king's son shall reign* (NIV). Even if his appearance was only brief, however, *with the king* (not in Ki.) does presume the boy's physical presence, as does the statement (2 Ki. 11:4) that the priest 'showed' them the child. The final sentence of verse 3 about God's promise to *the descendants of David* is an addition, but clearly shows why the author believed the *coup* took place (*cf.* 1 Ch. 17:10b–14; 2 Ch. 6:10; 21:7).

Jehoiada's specific instructions constitute the second stage (vv. 4–7), though the details are hard to unravel. There are two main difficulties, of which the first is the relationship between the various groups. While Chronicles has three groups of guards officiating at the temple and the palace with the rest of the people gathered in the temple courts, 2 Kings 11:5–7 speaks of three rather different groups accompanied by two companies of temple guards. The second problem is that Chronicles (but not Ki.) identifies some of these men as *priests and Levites* (vv. 6, 8) whereas Kings speaks only of 'the Carites and the guards', *i.e.* the royal bodyguard (2 Ki. 11:4). Although the Chronicler has not simply substituted the former for the latter (*cf.* vv. 1, 5, 10, 20 with 2 Ki. 11:4, 6, 11, 19), he does seem to have interpreted those who guarded the king in the temple precincts as Levites (*cf.* v. 6; 2 Ki. 11:7). Since the Levites were not exempt from military service, they would have been armed just like everyone else (*cf.* 1 Ch. 11:22–24; 12:26–28; 27:5–6). Further, Chronicles' inclusion of laymen (vv. 2–3) and of *all Judah* (v. 8), together with Kings' mention of temple guards who were presumably Levites (2 Ki. 11:7), suggests that both Kings and Chronicles refer to laymen and Levites, with the latter as usual emphasizing the Levites' contribution.

The *people* (vv. 5–6) remain outside in the temple *courts*. They are required to *observe the LORD's command not to enter* (v. 6, NIV mg., *cf.* GNB), whereas the Levites must guard the king who had been hidden in the temple (22:12). The gates cannot be identified, though the *Foundation Gate* (v. 5) is probably the same as the Sur Gate (2 Ki. 11:6). Those appointed as *gate-keepers* (v. 4) may be the same as the group who guarded an unnamed temple gate (2 Ki. 11:6).

The plan depended on two crucial elements. One was that the timing would not create suspicion, since the changing of temple and palace guards on the Sabbath involved the natural movement of the maximum number of armed men. The only irregularity was that all leave was cancelled (v. 8). The second was that Athaliah probably knew very little of what went on in the Lord's temple, since she worshipped Baal (v. 17). The element of surprise is therefore realistic.

The third stage culminated in Joash's anointing and acclamation (vv. 8–11). The weapons used by the guards (v. 9) were readily available in the temple, and were probably a mixture of trophies captured from *David*'s defeated enemies (1 Ch. 18:7–11) and decorated weapons specially made for Solomon (2 Ch. 9:15–16). The word translated *small shields* (NIV, NRSV, RSV, JB; 'buckler', REB, NEB) is probably 'quivers' (*cf.* also 1 Ch. 18:7).[1]

As the boy king came out of the front of the temple, he seems to have been fully protected by armed men standing between *the temple* and *the altar* and flanking him to left and right (*north* and *south*, v. 10). Ironically, this was the same general area where Joash would later order Jehoiada's son to be murdered for speaking out of turn (2 Ch. 24:21). The word for *side* (NIV, RSV; 'corner', REB, NEB, JB) may well refer to part of the entrance between the main opening and the next corner.[2]

The ceremony was a coronation and an anointing (v. 11). This is the fullest reference in Chronicles to such an event, and two of its three key features occur only here in Chronicles. One of these is the *crown*, really a 'diadem', which was worn by high priests as well as kings (Ex. 29:6; Lv. 8:9). The other is the 'testimony' (REB, RSV; *copy of the covenant*, NIV). This has been understood either as some form of jewellery or insignia, parallel to the diadem, or as a document.[3] The latter is more likely, but could be a copy of the terms of kingship (*cf.* NEB), a copy of the covenant law as a whole (*cf.* JB) or of the laws concerning kingship (Dt. 17:14–20; *cf.* GNB), or a dedicatory inscription.[4] The context favours the idea that it

[1] R. Borger, 'Die Waffenträger des Königs Darius', *VT* 22, 1972, pp. 385–398. Note also the uncertainty in NIV, JB in translating Heb. *māḡēn* as 'small shield' in 2 Ch. 9:16 and 'large shield' here.

[2] R. D. Haak, 'The "shoulder" of the temple', *VT* 33, 1983, pp. 271–278.

[3] An emendation to 'bracelet' (*cf.* 2 Sa. 1:10; Is. 3:30), originally proposed by Wellhausen, has now been generally discounted, partly because the rarity of the suggested form gives little confidence about its restoration here.

[4] For the latter, *cf.* T. N. D. Mettinger, *King and Messiah* (Lund: Gleerup, 1977), p. 287; Hobbs, p. 141.

contained the assembly's decisions (v. 3), but, if the meaning 'testimony' is preferred, that would support a wider reference to the covenant. Irrespective of the document's precise identity, it was a symbol that Joash was to rule according to God's covenant promises and not on his own terms (*cf.* v. 3). His being *anointed* also speaks of him as a person chosen for God's purposes. Apart from Joash, Chronicles records the anointing only of David (1 Ch. 11:3; 14:8), Solomon (1 Ch. 23:1; 29:22), and Jehu (2 Ch. 22:7).

ii. The usurper removed (23:12–15). Athaliah was taken completely by surprise, but, attracted by the unusual sound of popular enthusiasm, made a hurried but rare visit to the Lord's temple (v. 12). She saw Joash *the king*, standing either *by a pillar*, presumably one of the pillars Jakin or Boaz at the temple entrance (2 Ch. 3:17), or on a 'dais' (NEB), though the latter involves a slight emendation. Among the happy crowd were also 'singers' (*cf.* REB, NEB, 'outbursts of song'; the reading of a few MSS against MT's *officers*, NIV, or 'captains', RSV) and 'musicians' (GNB; usually translated 'singers'). These clearly refer to the Levites (*cf.* 1 Ch. 23:5; 25:1–6), with the priests blowing the *trumpets* (*cf.* 1 Ch. 15:24; 2 Ch. 5:12–14).

Athaliah's cry of *Treason!* is ironic in the extreme, given the violent circumstances in which she had seized the throne (22:3, 10–11). Her reaction is a classic example of Jesus' teaching about the mote and the beam (Mt. 7:3–5; Lk. 6:41–42). The lack of any concluding formula reveals the writer's view of the illegitimacy of her reign, which was due not to her crimes, for others were equally guilty (*cf.* 21:4; 28:22–24; 33:2–9), but because she had no right to the throne in the first place.

Death was the due reward for her murders (v. 15; *cf.* 22:10–11), though she was killed at the palace gates so as not to defile the temple any further (*cf.* vv. 6–7, 19). She was taken from the *precincts* (v. 14, NIV mg.; *cf.* 1 Ki. 6:9), a word which is uncertain but is preferable to *ranks* (NIV, NRSV, RSV), since the context is all about temple geography. They 'laid hands on her' (RSV) is a unique expression in Hebrew, and, though it has been translated since medieval times as 'they made room for her' (Ackroyd; *cf.* vss), the few occasions where Hebrew 'hand' might mean 'room, space' occur in quite different contexts (*cf.* Gn. 34:21; Jos. 8:20; Ps. 104:25). Though *she reached* (v. 15,

NIV, JB; 'went', RSV) might imply that Athaliah came to the palace of her own volition, the whole paragraph strongly suggests otherwise.[1]

iii. The covenant renewed (23:16–21). The climax is not Joash's coronation but a covenant renewing the nation's relationship with God. The participants (v. 16) are described differently from 2 Kings 11:17, especially in replacing 'between the LORD' with 'between him', *i.e.* Jehoiada (*cf.* RSV)! The Chronicler has probably interpreted *that* they *would be the* LORD's *people* as implying God's participation, though he may have regarded the word for 'him' (*he*, NIV) as an abbreviation for Yahweh. The Chronicler has also omitted the covenant between the king and the people, but that has already been mentioned in verses 3, 11. This covenant is different from that in verse 11, since this one is made between the people and God rather than the people and the king. The follow-up confirms this distinction, since verses 17–21 are concerned more with religious matters in general than with the specific issue in verses 4–15 of who should be the rightful king. The aim of this covenant was to put current wrongs to right. As often in Chronicles, it resulted in a purge of pagan worship (v. 17; *cf.* 2 Ch. 15:12–16; 34:31–33) in obedience to the Deuteronomic law (*cf.* Dt. 4:23; 7:6). It also led to the reinstitution of the twin pillars of the Davidic covenant, reorganized temple worship according to God's laws (vv. 17–19) and setting the Davidic king on his rightful throne (vv. 20–21).

The *Baal temple* (v. 17), which had presumably been constructed under the auspices of Ahab's house (*cf.* especially 21:11, 13), was demolished in an action that is remarkably similar to Jehu's handiwork in Samaria. The latter may have inspired Jehoiada, except that this occasion was less bloody (*cf.* 2 Ki. 10:18–28). On the positive side, temple worship was revised according to the instructions given to *David* and *Moses* (v. 18; *cf.* also 24:9–10), a typical example of the Chronicler's concern that any changes in worship required proper authority (for Moses, *cf. e.g.* 1 Ch. 16:40; 2 Ch. 31:3; 34:14). David had given particular instructions about music and temple personnel. The special responsibilities of *priests, Levites*

---

[1] This would be even clearer if 2 Ki. 11:15's 'gave orders' (v. 14, REB, NEB) were read instead of 'brought out' (RSV; 'called out', JB, GNB). MT could easily have been influenced by the following verb.

(v. 18, note the mention of *singing*), and 'gatekeepers' (v. 19, NRSV, RSV) are all mentioned.[1] In that verses 18b–19 are unique to the Chronicler, they doubtless reflect the special concerns of his own day.

Those who brought the young king from the temple to the palace (v. 20) are now the *nobles* and *rulers of the people* rather than the royal bodyguard as such, emphasizing the leaders' commitment to the new king. With the king properly installed, joy and peace flourished (v. 21). The people's *rejoicing* augmented the joy of temple worship (v. 18), and sounded a note unheard since the days of Jehoshaphat (20:27). That the city was *quiet* was a sign of God's blessing, which often followed special acts of faith and obedience (*cf.* 1 Ch. 4:40; 22:9; 2 Ch. 13:23; 14:4–5; 20:30).

b. Joash's faithfulness while Jehoiada lives (24:1–16).
Joash's story is one of the saddest in Chronicles. It describes a king who deliberately turned his back on God after he had received personal experience of God's mercy and had initiated a religious reformation. What is more, the pattern of early success followed by a sharp decline becomes established for the reigns of his two successors Amaziah (ch. 25) and Uzziah (ch. 26). The pattern is not new, having applied to Rehoboam (2 Ch. 11–12) and Asa (2 Ch. 14–16), but it plumbs new depths in chapters 24–26. Positive balancing factors at the end of these reigns are no longer to be found (*cf.* 12:12; 16:14), and each concludes in disaster.

Although the Chronicler has made use of the essential elements of 2 Kings 12, he has divided Joash's reign into three different periods:

23:1–21   Accession under Jehoiada's leadership
24:1–16   Faithfulness during the rest of Jehoiada's life
24:17–27   Apostasy after Jehoiada's death

The reason for this arrangement is not to impose a simplistic scheme on Joash's personal history, but to illustrate certain basic theological principles. Key words set the tone in each of the two main sections of chapter 24. First, Joash *restores* ('renovates', REB, NEB) the temple (vv. 1–16). The thematic

---

[1] 'And Levites' (v. 18, REB, NEB, GNB) should probably be read (with most vss) rather than 'levitical priests' (NRSV, JB).

significance of this word is indicated by its appearance in the introduction (v. 4) and conclusion (v. 12) to the main section dealing with the temple. Once again, a king's attitude to the temple is the litmus test of his faith, reflecting the biblical conviction that the worship of God is the highest priority for any human being. The second section, however, is a total contrast. Its central term is *forsake* or *abandon* (vv. 18, 20, 24, 25), and Joash becomes the exact opposite of what a king of David's line ought to be (*cf.* 1 Ch. 28:9). The effects are as devastating as the legacy of Athaliah and her family.

Even though 2 Kings 12 supplies the raw material for this chapter, considerable variation if not apparent contradiction exists between the two versions (*cf.* vv. 5, 8, 14, 23–25). Though some of the changes, such as the inclusion of the Levites (vv. 5–6, 11) and links with the period of the Tent in the wilderness (vv. 9–10) can be attributed to the Chronicler's special interests, others do not have any particular point to make (*e.g.* vv. 11b–12 and the omission of 2 Ki 12:8, 14–16). Since the details of a Syrian invasion (vv. 23–25) seem to be taken from a separate written record, the same is probably true of other parts of the chapter, though it may well be that more than one source has been consulted (*cf.* v. 27 and Rudolph, Myers; against Curtis and Madsen, Williamson).

No doubt the changes reflect the Chronicler's circumstances, but it would be unwise to limit their purpose. Certainly, financial support for the temple and its staff was an ongoing challenge (*e.g.* Ne. 10:32–39; Hg. 1:1–11; Mal. 1:6–14; 3:6–12), and the need to keep the temple in good working order was a constant concern (2 Ch. 29:3 – 31:21; 34:1 – 35:19). But these matters may also be applied more generally, not just as an encouragement to look after church buildings, but above all to ensure that God receives the worship that is due to him (*cf.* v. 14; Lk. 24:53; Acts 2:46; 5:42). To neglect God or turn to other forms of worship is not a neutral choice, even for those who have previously worshipped faithfully. Joash is fully responsible for all his actions, according to the doctrine of individual responsibility outlined in Ezekiel 18:24–32, which fits Joash's situation perfectly. His sin is too serious to be atoned for by previous good deeds, even though it seems harsh for him to be judged on the basis of his failures. The response provided in both Ezekiel and Chronicles, however, is that God takes no pleasure in a sinner's death, and repeatedly sends the prophets with offers of mercy. But though others responded in humility (12:6, 12; 33:12–13), what happened to Joash is a serious warning to all who turn their backs on God's grace (*cf.* Heb. 6:4–12; 10:26–31).

i. Introduction to Joash's reign (24:1–3). These verses set the scene for Joash's reign. The statement that the king did what was *right* (v. 2) in the earlier part of his reign because of *Jehoiada the priest* interprets 2 Kings 12:2, which should be translated, '. . . all the years Jehoiada instructed him' (NIV), not '. . . all his days, because Jehoiada instructed him' (RSV, *etc.*). His influence is felt even in Joash's family (v. 3), which is a typical focus of God's blessing (*cf.* 1 Ch. 26:4–5; 2 Ch. 11:21; 13:21). The number of wives and children shows God restoring the years the locusts had eaten (21:4, 17; 22:1, 8, 10). Joash's *forty years* (v. 1) are dated between 840–801 (Begrich) and 835–796 (Thiele).

ii. Repairing the temple (24:4–16). The basic restoration work (vv. 4–12) is treated separately from its results (vv. 13–16). The term *restore* ('renovate', REB, NEB) marks the beginning and end of the first part (vv. 4, 12). This word really means 'renewal', and is most often used of personal renewal (Pss. 51:10; 103:5; La. 5:21), being applied to buildings only in 2 Chronicles 15:8 (the temple altar) and Isaiah 61:4. The idea of 'giving new life' to buildings also occurs in 1 Chronicles 11:8, and verse 14 implies that this includes the use to which they are put as much as the physical task of reconstruction.

Athaliah and her family (v. 7; lit., *sons*, but *cf.* 22:10; 'adherents', REB, NEB) are the chief cause of the temple's troubles, though it had probably suffered from general neglect for some time before that (the most recently mentioned work is in 15:8). The first stage of the work was clearly unsuccessful, however, because of insufficient annual contributions (v. 5). Four significant alterations from 2 Kings 12 require comment. Firstly, Chronicles has simplified the different types of temple income (2 Ki 12:4), perhaps distinguishing between regular support and a special restoration fund. Secondly, 2 Kings 12:6 implies that the first phase took several years, since Joash did not call the priests to account until his twenty-third year. Thirdly, the *Levites* (vv. 5–6) are blamed for the failure as well as the priests. Such criticism is unusual in Chronicles but not unique (*cf.* 30:15), and is not necessarily part of a later addition (contrast Williamson, de Vries; *cf.* also Ezk. 44:10; Mal. 3:3). Fourthly, Athaliah, who is not mentioned in 2 Kings 12, is really described as the embodiment of 'wickedness' (v. 7). Since this description is remarkably similar to that found in one of Zechariah's visions, this may well be another example of the Chronicler's use of prophetic imagery (Zc. 4:7–8).

Joash now takes responsibility himself for the proper funding of the temple (*cf.* 1 Ch. 29:1–5). He sets up a separate fund by royal *proclamation* (v. 9), requiring the people to put their 'tax' (v. 10, RSV; *contributions*, NIV) in a 'box' (GNB; *chest*, other EVV) specially made for the purpose (vv. 8–10). His actions are another example of faithfulness to the ways of *Moses* (v. 9) and David (*cf.* also 23:18). The word for 'proclamation' links a practice from the Chronicler's time (*cf.* 2 Ch. 30:5; 36:22 = Ezr. 1:1; Ezr. 10:7; Ne. 8:15) with the wilderness period (Ex. 36:6). The tax itself was based on the half-shekel tax for the *Tent* (vv. 6, 9; *cf.* Ex. 30:12–16; 38:25–26), though it was also renewed by Nehemiah (Ne. 10:32; *cf.* Mt. 17:24). In fact, the people responded as they had done in the case of the Tent by bringing too much (v. 14; *cf.* Ex. 36:4–7; *until it was full*, NIV, NRSV, *etc.*, in v. 10 is better than 'until they had finished', RSV), as though this were a freewill offering rather than a tax. The blessings of David's temple preparations are recalled as the people 'rejoiced' (RSV) in making their contributions (v. 10; *cf.* 1 Ch. 29:1–9), and hired *masons and carpenters* and *workers in iron and bronze* (v. 12; *cf.* 1 Ch. 21:15–16). Popular enthusiasm for the Lord's work is a favourite theme in Chronicles (*cf.* 2 Ch. 11:16–17; 15:15; 20:4).

Administration of the fund was taken away from the priests and placed in the hands of two officials, one appointed by the king and the other by the high priest, who allocated resources to the workmen (vv. 11–12a).[1] The box's location *outside the gate* (v. 8) varies from 2 Kings 12:9 where it is 'beside the altar . . . as one entered the house of the LORD'. The latter phrase, however, could have influenced the Chronicler, who was possibly thinking of his own day when the inner court was reserved for priests (*cf.* 2 Ch. 4:9; 6:13; Ezk. 40:44–47). One

[1] MT has 'master of works' (v. 12, JB), but the plural is generally found in EVV, with the vss and 2 Ki. 12:11 (EVV) = 12:12 (MT).

interesting harmonization is that a layman might have paid a Levite gatekeeper who then put the money in the box![1]

Finally, the temple was restored to its 'proper condition' (v. 13, NRSV, RSV; 'former state', JB; *original design*, NIV, REB, NEB). The Hebrew word contains the notion of a 'standard' (*cf.* Ex. 30:32, 27; Ezk. 45:11), which harks back to the plans for the temple revealed by God (1 Ch. 28:12, 19). Once the building was *finished* (v. 14), two further things were required to complete the restoration. Various *articles* ('utensils', RSV; 'vessels', NEB) were manufactured, and daily worship, especially the *burnt offerings*, reorganized (v. 14). An apparent contradiction with 2 Kings 12:13–14 over the temple vessels seems to be explained by reference to different funds. Kings alludes to the main fund for the actual temple, but these temple vessels were paid for out of surplus contributions.

The brief death notice for Jehoiada describes the restored temple as the chief *good* he had done (v. 16). This word recalls Nehemiah's prayers (Ne. 5:19; 13:31), and his similar work of renewal in *the service of God* (*cf.* v. 16). Jehoiada's age at death, *a hundred and thirty*, is unparalleled since patriarchal times (v. 15), though that does not make it unhistorical.[2] Burial in the royal cemetery is unique for a high priest. Though these details mark him out as a special character, his desire to see the legitimate king installed distinguished him from the trend in the later post-exilic period where the high priests gradually assumed greater civil powers.

c. Joash's apostasy after Jehoiada's death (24:17–27). After Jehoiada died, Joash's policy turned full circle under the influence of *the officials of Judah* (v. 17; 'leading men', REB, NEB). The apparent swiftness of the change may owe more to the Chronicler's editorial technique than to what actually happened, though two factors help to explain the transition. Joash was always more of a follower than a leader, and the priests and Levites had already anticipated the officials' lack of enthusiasm for what seemed like new ways (*cf.* vv. 5–6). A sizeable number in Judah undoubtedly preferred the easier ways of Ahab's house, and, as soon as the awkward Jehoiada

[1] Cogan and Tadmor, p. 138.
[2] See further A. Malamat, 'Longevity: biblical concepts and some ancient Near Eastern parallels', *Archiv für Orientforschung*, Beiheft 19, 1982, pp. 215–224.

was out of the way, they saw their opportunity to return to the worship of *Asherah poles and idols* (v. 18; 'sacred poles and idols', REB, NEB, NRSV, RSV). Asherah was a Canaanite fertility goddess whose symbol was some kind of wooden object, possibly a pole (*cf. e.g.* 14:3; 15:16; 33:3; 34:3). She was closely associated in the Old Testament with Baal worship (*cf.* 21:11; 23:17), though in the Ugaritic texts she was the consort of El, the head of the pantheon.

To worship idols was to *abandon* (v. 18) the temple (or possibly 'the covenant', with two Heb. MSS, *cf.* Rudolph, Ackroyd). As a result, guilt came upon them followed by God's *anger*.[1] But instead of punishing them at once, God sent *prophets* to *bring them back* to him (vv. 18–19). This may or may not refer to renewed prophetic activity under Joash, but in any case it underlines the wider principle that God offers a second chance to those who have offended him (*cf.* Zc. 1:4). This message of reconciliation is a regular feature of prophetic ministry in Chronicles (*cf.* 2 Ch. 36:15), but, it also could involve godly kings (2 Ch. 19:4) and the temple personnel (2 Ch. 7:14; 'bring back' is from the same Heb. verb as 'turn' in 7:14).

The people listened to the officials (v. 17) but they did not *listen* to the prophets (v. 19). Therefore, God pronounced judgment through a prophesying priest, Jehoiada's son *Zechariah* (v. 20), whom the *Spirit of God* 'clothed' ('took possession of', REB, NEB, NRSV, RSV). Two of the three Old Testament examples of this distinctive expression occur in Chronicles (*cf.* Jdg. 6:34; 1 Ch. 12:18), though it continues in the New Testament (Lk. 24:49; *cf.* Gal. 3:27). It refers to the exercise of a prophetic gift, and is parallel to a similar phrase in 2 Chronicles 15:1; 20:14. Zechariah's message is typical of the prophecies in Chronicles in expounding earlier Scripture as well as one of Chronicles' central themes. The scripture is Numbers 14:41, '*Why do you disobey the LORD's commands? You will not prosper.*' The familiar theme is that *because you have forsaken the LORD, he has forsaken you* (1 Ch. 28:9; 2 Ch. 15:2; *cf.* 2 Ch. 7:19; 15:13). The biblical principle that the form of punishment is appropriate to the sinner's offence is confirmed by two

---

[1] 'Judah and Jerusalem suffered' (REB, NEB) is an inadequate translation, since although *qeṣep*, 'anger', is not explicitly linked here with God, it is only ever used in Ch. of divine anger (*cf.* 1 Ch. 27:24; 2 Ch. 19:2, 10; 29:8; 32:25, 26).

further occurrences of the Hebrew verb '*āzaḇ* in verses 24–25 (EVV 'abandon', 'forsake' or 'left').

This idea that the punishment fits the crime is illustrated further by a whole string of ironies concerning Zechariah's murder (vv. 21–22) and Joash's death (vv. 23–26). As for Zechariah, the people firstly prefer the 'command of the king' (v. 21; NRSV, RSV) to that of the Lord (v. 20, the Heb. word is the same). Secondly, Zechariah's father's *kindness* in saving Joash's life when he was a baby (22:10–12) is cruelly reversed. Thirdly, he was killed in the very place where Jehoiada had anointed Joash king (23:10–11). Fourthly, though Joash had abandoned God, Zechariah prayed that God would still 'seek' him (v. 22). This is the literal meaning of *call to account* (NIV), 'avenge' (JB, NRSV, RSV) or 'exact the penalty' (REB, NEB; *cf.* the meaning 'hold accountable' in Dt. 23:21, EVV; Jb. 10:6; Ps. 139:1, 23; Ezk. 34:10). It is significant because 'seeking' and 'forsaking' are antithetical terms in Chronicles, though they are not simple opposites. This is illustrated in 1 Chronicles 28:9, the only other verse in Chronicles where God is the seeker. The phrase 'God searches (or seeks) every heart' could mean either being found by God or being found out by him and forsaken, depending on one's response. It is the latter for which Zechariah now asks.

This prayer should not be compared unfavourably with those of Jesus and Stephen (Lk. 23:34; Acts 7:60). For one thing, Jesus actually quotes this incident in pronouncing the same judgment on his contemporaries (*cf.* Mt. 23:33–36; Lk. 11:47–51). For another, Zecharaiah is not looking for personal revenge but asking God to act in keeping with his declared principles of justice. If God were inactive, the result would be anarchy and God's claims to sovereignty would be seriously jeopardized.

God's response takes the form of an invasion by Hazael of Syria (vv. 23–26; 2 Ki. 12:17–18). This description of the incident is taken from in 2 Kings 12, though some of Chronicles' variations are probably explicable through use of an alternative source. In fact, the only additional factual details are the date *at the turn of the year* (NIV, REB, NEB; *i.e.* the spring, *cf.* 2 Sa. 11:1) and a confirmatory note about the *plunder*. Chronicles concentrates on the irony and appropriateness of God's *judgment* (v. 24, NIV, RSV; 'punishment', REB, NEB, GNB). For example, the same word is used for the *leaders* (v. 23;

'officials', NRSV, RSV) who suffer as in verse 17. Joash's officials *conspired* (vv. 25, 26) against him as he and they had 'conspired' (v. 21, NRSV, RSV; *plotted*, NIV; 'made common cause', REB, NEB) against Zechariah. The Hebrew verb *killed* is the same for Joash (v. 25) as for Zechariah (v. 22). The Syrian army *left* Joash wounded (v. 25, NIV, JB; 'leaving', RSV, REB, NEB) as he had abandoned God, using the same Hebrew word as 'abandoned/forsaken' in verses 18, 20, 24. Even the 'Yahweh war' theme is reversed. Whereas in earlier generations, God had helped Israel's armies against stronger opposition (*cf.* references to a 'vast army' in 2 Ch. 13:8; 14:11; 20:2), now he delivered *a much larger army* into the hands of *a few men* (v. 24).

25b–27. The concluding formula confirms God's judgment on Joash. The fact that he was not honoured by a place in the royal cemetery (in contrast to Jehoiada, v. 16) is important in Chronicles. Also, that his conspirators were sons of foreign women adds to the ignominy.[1] Further information can be found in a 'commentary' (GNB, NRSV, RSV) or *annotations* (literally, 'midrash' (JB), but neither here nor in 13:22 does this word carry the connotations which it had in later Jewish literature. It seems to include prophetic or historical material or both. The intriguing comment that it contained many prophecies *about* (REB, NEB, NIV) or 'against' (GNB, NRSV, RSV) Joash presumably refers to verse 19, and reflects Chronicles' continuing emphasis on prophetic interpretations of history.[2]

ii. Amaziah (25:1 – 26:2)
'God has the power to help or to overthrow' (25:8).

> 25:1–2 – *cf*. 2 Kings 14:2–3
> 25:3–4 – *cf*. 2 Kings 14:5–6
> 25:11 – *cf*. 2 Kings 14:7
> 25:17–24 – *cf*. 2 Kings 14:8–14
> 25:25–28 – *cf*. 2 Kings 14:17–20
> 26:1–2 – *cf*. 2 Kings 14:21–22

That *Amaziah* did *what was right . . . but not wholeheartedly* (v. 2) aptly summarizes a reign vitiated by compromise. Though he could respect the Mosaic law (v. 4) and respond to prophecy (vv. 9–10), it is all tinged with mixed motives, and it is no

---

[1] Certainty about the exact form of these names is impossible, especially as inner confusion exists in the text of Ki.

[2] JB's 'heavy tribute imposed on him' for 'many prophecies about him' owes more to LXX(L) and 2 Ki. 12:18 than to this context.

surprise that in the end he *turned away from following the* LORD (v. 27). His reign is difficult to classify, and commentators have disagreed as to whether it should be divided into favourable and unfavourable parts (Williamson, Allen, Becker, *etc.*) or whether he is fundamentally half-hearted and double-minded (*e.g.* Coggins, McConville). In favour of the former, Amaziah's emphatic if violent victory against the Edomites (v. 12) is an apparent turning-point, since any good features that do exist are limited to verses 1–12. On the other hand, Amaziah's weaknesses are distributed throughout the chapter, even though they gather momentum from verse 14 onwards. Over all, while his reign does fit the periodization scheme of chapters 24–26, he declines from bad to worse rather than from good to bad!

Chronicles has kept fairly closely to the structure of Kings, except for the expansion of the Edomite war from a single verse (2 Ki. 14:7) into a whole section (vv. 5–16). By omitting brief items such as the synchronisms with the kings of Israel (2 Ki. 14:1, 4, 15–16, 20), the focus is now on Amaziah's wars against Edom (vv. 5–16) and Israel (vv. 17–24). In particular, two additional prophecies (vv. 7–9, 15–16) and an extra phrase in verse 20 clarify God's view of Amaziah, *viz.* that *God has determined to destroy you* (v. 16; *cf.* v. 20) through the war with Israel. One can only guess at the available sources, though the factual description of the conscript army indicates an independent military source (vv. 5–6) and the extra prophetic material (vv. 7–9, 15–16) is probably connected with Chronicles' frequent references to other prophetic sources.

Though it is a little depressing to read about yet another wayward king, the possible value of a story such as this is worth considering before turning quickly to the next chapter (which is equally depressing though perhaps more colourful!). Firstly, repeated stories about sinful rulers testify to God's patience. Secondly, people who turn away from God after receiving his grace are also found in the Christian church (*e.g.* 1 Cor. 5:1–13; 2 Tim. 2:16–18; Rev. 2:4–6, 20–25). Thirdly, such incidents are exemplary warnings to others not to fall into the same temptations (1 Cor. 10:11–13; *cf.* Rom. 15:4). Fourthly, merely to belong to God's people or being part of their traditions is insufficient before God. No-one is immune from pride and complacency (1 Cor.

10:12; 1 Jn. 1:8, 10), but God's forgiveness to anyone who falls is always close at hand (*cf.* Ps. 51:7–15; 2 Ch. 7:13–16; 1 Jn. 1:9; 2:1–2).

a. Amaziah's strength (25:1–4). The date of Amaziah's reign is a seemingly intractable problem, and his *twenty-nine years* (v. 1) has been reduced to varying lengths such as thirteen, sixteen, or nineteen years.[1] One solution regards Amaziah as sole ruler for only five years before being taken hostage by Jehoash of Israel (vv. 23–24), with his son Uzziah being co-regent for the remaining twenty-four years. This rather surprising conclusion has found support in the unique comment that Amaziah *lived* for *fifteen years* after Jehoash's death (v. 25) and in the participation of the people at Uzziah's accession, perhaps indicating some kind of crisis (26:1; *cf.* 22:1).[2] If this is correct, the two wars belong to Amaziah's first five years, though the whole reign has been dated between 801–773 (Begrich) and 796–767 (Thiele).

The one occasion where no criticism of Amaziah may be intended is when he put to death his father's murderers (v. 3). Even here, however, he followed the letter of the law at best (v. 4), and his later behaviour suggests that this is an act of revenge rather than keeping the kingdom *firmly in his control*. For example, 'killed' (RSV, JB; 'put to death', REB, NEB; *executed*, NIV) translates the same word as in 21:4, 13; 22:1, 8; 23:17; 24:22, 25, and is really a thematic term in chapters 21–28 for violence (*cf.* also 28:6, 7, 9), even though it sometimes involved retributive justice (23:17; 24:25). Behind the Mosaic law that individuals should be responsible in capital offences for their own sins (*cf.* Dt. 24:16; Je. 31:29–31; Ezk. 18:1–20) was the principle that justice should always be limited (even in visiting the fathers' sins on their descendants, God's mercy to thousands far exceeds his judgment to the third and fourth generations; *cf.* Ex. 20:5–6). As in chapter 24, the influence of the teaching of individual responsibility in Ezekiel 18 is again evident.

b. War against Edom (25:5–16). Several stages may be discerned in this battle, which illustrates Amaziah's strengths and weaknesses.

---

[1] *Cf.* Jones, II, p. 507.   [2] See further Thiele, pp. 113–116.

i. Muster of Judean troops (25:5). This description of the tribal levies follows a familiar format (11:1; 14:8; 17:14–19; 26:11–15). The minimum age of *twenty years* is in line with ancient practice (Nu. 1:3, 18; 1 Ch. 27:23), though the numbers are significantly lower than the most recent comparable figures given in 17:14–19.

ii. Muster of Israelite troops (25:6–10). Amaziah may have been pressured to *hire* Israelite mercenaries (v. 6) because of the reduced number of conscripts. According to an unnamed prophet (*man of God*), however, this is not the way to fight in the Lord's name (vv. 7–9), for two reasons. Firstly, *the LORD is not with Israel* (v. 7), who were still committed to idolatry (2 Ki. 13:11). Secondly, Amaziah's chief weapon must be trust in God (*cf.* 14:11; 20:20–23; 32:6–8, 20–21), for God has *the power to help or to overthrow.* God's power and help, which are a central theme in the 'Yahweh war' passages (2 Ch. 14:11; 20:6; 32:7), are especially given to weak and powerless people who have faith in God (14:11; 20:12; 32:8). Indeed, as the cross shows supremely, God's power shows up particularly well in human weakness (*cf.* 1 Cor. 1:25; 2 Cor. 12:9–10; 13:4). The exact meaning of verse 8a is unclear. Most EVV assume a hypothetical attack by making slight changes to MT (*if you go and fight,* NIV; 'if you make these people your allies', REB, NEB), but the actual Hebrew is ironic, 'go by yourself and act; be strong in battle' (NRSV).

In addition to his lack of trust, Amaziah shows he is committed to materialism by trying to have Mammon as well as God on his side (v. 9; *cf.* Mt. 6:24; Lk. 16:13). The prophet, however, gives him an assurance, not of a trouble-free campaign if he sent the mercenaries home (Dillard, Williamson, *etc.*), but that God could supply *much more* than he expected (*cf.* Gn. 22:14; Mk. 10:28–31; Eph. 3:20). To his credit, Amaziah responds positively (v. 10a). Conversely, the Israelites' *great rage* (v. 10b, NIV, JB; 'fierce anger', RSV), repeated in Hebrew for emphasis, shows further why the Lord is not with them.

iii. The battle against Edom (25:11–13). Intent on obtaining their reward of *plunder* (or 'spoil' or 'booty') by fair means or foul, the Israelite soldiers turn their anger to theft and murder (*cf.* Mt. 5:21–22; Jas. 4:1–2) by wreaking vengeance on various *Judean towns* (v. 13). The statement that they came from *Samaria to Beth Horon* suggests that they made a special raid from their homes in Ephraim (v. 10).[1] Beth Horon was about ten miles from Jerusalem on the borders of Judah and Israel in the Aijalon valley, an important route leading from the coastal plain to Bethel and Jerusalem.

Amaziah's first concern, however, is with *the men of Seir, i.e.* the Edomites (v. 11; *cf.* 2 Ki. 14:7). The purpose and location of the battle depend on where the *Valley of Salt* was (also 1 Ch. 18:12). If it was the Wadi el-Milh, east of Beersheba,[2] then Amaziah was defending himself against invasion, but many prefer to think of a Judean offensive in the Arabah south of the Dead Sea. Unless the Edomites were exacerbating the problems at Amaziah's accession (24:25–26), the context supplies no real clue about Amaziah's intentions (Edom had previously revolted in 21:10). His victory is definite enough, though it is achieved without any acknowledgment of God's help and with excessive violence (v. 12). The *cliff* (NIV, REB, NEB) is the place name *Sela* in Kings (and NRSV, RSV, GNB), but the tradition that this verse refers to the Edomite capital Petra is almost certainly wrong. The word means 'rock', and could refer to several possible locations.

iv. The aftermath of victory (25:14–16). Amaziah's achievement seems to bring out the worst in him. Whereas he had previously made some response to God, now he turns to idolatry (vv. 14–15), persecution (v. 16), revenge (v. 17), intransigence (vv. 16, 20), pride (v. 19), and apostasy (v. 27). The decisive factor is Amaziah's worship of Edomite gods (v. 14). This is the only explicit reference to Edomite worship in the Bible, even though there was a persistent sense of brotherhood between Israel and Edom (*cf.* Dt. 23:7; Am. 1:11). The Edomites did worship a deity by the name of Qos, though the earliest evidence comes from a few decades later than Amaziah.[3] Sacrifice to a defeated enemy's gods is unique

---

[1] It is therefore unnecessary to read a Judean place name such as Migron instead of Samaria (Rudolph, Myers, Williamson), especially as there is no textual support for such a change.

[2] F. M. Abel, *Géographie de la Palestine*, I (Paris: Gabalda, 1933), p. 407; J. Simons, *The Geographical and Topographical Texts of the Old Testament* (Leiden: Brill, 1959), p. 221.

[3] *Cf.* J. Bartlett, *Edom and the Edomites*, JSOTS 77 (Sheffield: JSOT Press, 1989), pp. 187–207.

in the Old Testament, but several features are readily under-standable in the light of ancient Near Eastern custom. In the first place, it was a well-known practice to take captive the divine images of defeated enemies. The purpose of this has been variously understood, but one of the effects was to reduce the likelihood of future conflict by leaving opponents defenceless. Secondly, defeat in war was often thought to be due to divine displeasure, and Amaziah's action may be intended to placate the presumed anger of the Edomites' gods.[1] Thirdly, worship of the deities of defeated foes is not without analogy. The seventh-century Assyrian conqueror Ashurbanipal made a dedicatory offering to the deity of a defeated Arab foe in return for help received.[2] Also, the Chronicler would have been familiar with the practice of Persian kings who endowed gifts in their own name to the deities of subject peoples (*cf. e.g.* Ezr. 6:9–10; 7:21–23). Amaz-iah was certainly not the only ruler who recognized his debt to the gods of another nation.

Though Amaziah was simply following contemporary cus-tom, his blatant idolatry made God *angry* (v. 15; *cf.* Jas. 4:4) and invoked the sanctions of the Davidic covenant (*cf.* 2 Ch. 7:19–22). By God's grace, however, a second anonymous prophet invites Amaziah to think again (vv. 15–16; *cf.* vv. 7–8). His message was that the Edomite deities had manifestly failed the basic test of any god, to *save* ('deliver', NRSV, RSV) *their own people*, in contrast to Amaziah's own experience of Yahweh (vv. 8–10). The prophet's logic as well as his courage is a regular biblical answer to attempts to reduce him to the level of other deities (*cf.* 1 Ki. 18:20–39; Is. 41:21–29; Acts 4:12). Two plays on words show how serious was Amaziah's refusal to listen. Though the prophet *stopped* because the king said *Stop!* (the Heb. verb is repeated), the word of God continued to speak: *God has determined to destroy you.* Further, *determined* is related to the words 'counsellor', *counsel* (v. 16), and *consulted* (v. 17). Amaziah might reject the prophet's counsel (v. 16) in favour of his own advisers (v. 17), but he could not avoid God's counsel, as the following incident demonstrates.

---

[1] *Cf.* B. Meissner, *Babylonien und Assyrien*, 2 (Heidelberg: Winters Universitätsbuchhandlung, 1925), p. 128.

[2] *Cf.* M. Cogan, *Imperialism and Religion* (Missoula: Scholars Press, 1974), pp. 9–41, especially pp. 15–21.

c. War against Israel (25:17–24). Amaziah's invitation to Jehoash of Israel has been interpreted as a neutral act (*e.g.* NEB, Coggins, Jones) which may even have been intended to bring about an alliance by marriage (Curtis and Madsen; *cf.* v. 18). But Jehoash suspects a thinly veiled threat (*cf.* REB, GNB), as Amaziah reacts to the prophet's criticism by seeking revenge against the Israelite mercenaries (vv. 6–10, 13).

Jehoash responds with a colourful but insulting fable (vv. 18–19). He accuses Amaziah of being *arrogant and proud* (v. 19, NIV, *cf.* NRSV, RSV) and predicts that he will cause his own *downfall* (v. 19) as well as Judah's. Some of the detail of verse 19 is obscured by uncertainty about the extent to which the text diverges from Kings, but the over-all meaning is clear.[1] Again, however, *Amaziah would not listen* (*cf.* v. 16; *cf.* 24:19). This time, however, Chronicles adds (*cf.* 2 Ki. 14:11) that his deliberate deafness is (lit.) 'from God' ('God's doing', v. 20, NRSV, REB, NEB, JB; *cf.* the identical phrase in 2 Ch. 10:15; 22:7), though that does not mean it was contrary to Amaziah's intentions. God would therefore 'hand them over' (v. 20, NRSV). The Hebrew is abrupt, and most EVV add either *to Jehoash* (NIV, REB, NEB; with LXX(L)) or 'to their enemies' (JB, *cf.* RSV). This all happened because Amaziah *sought* (v. 20) Edomite gods (*cf.* v. 15), *i.e.* he had 'worshipped' them (GNB; *cf.* 1 Ch. 22:19; 2 Ch. 15:2, 12; 17:4). Saul is the only other king in Chronicles who seeks foreign deities (1 Ch. 10:13), though others were equally guilty by failing to seek Yahweh (*cf.* 1 Ch. 13:3; 2 Ch. 12:14; 16:12).

The result is as both the prophet and Jehoash predict (vv. 21–24). This time 'Yahweh war' language shows that God is no longer for Amaziah (*cf.* vv. 7–8) but against him. He is *routed* (v. 22, NIV, REB, NEB; 'defeated', JB, NRSV, RSV; also in *e.g.* 13:15; 14:12; EVV; 20:22) and everyone *fled* (also in *e.g.* 1 Ch. 19:14, 15, 18; 2 Ch. 13:16; 14:12; EVV). *Beth-Shemesh* (vv. 21, 23), about fifteen miles south-west of Jerusalem (*cf.* Jos. 15:10; 1 Ki. 4:9), implies a westerly attack on Jerusalem and Jehoash's desire to control trade routes. Jehoash captures Amaziah and other *hostages* (v. 24b), breaks down part of Jerusalem's wall, probably in the north-western corner (v. 23),

---

[1] Artificial harmonizing with Ki. is to be avoided at two key points. It is therefore preferable to read, 'You say, "See, I have defeated ..."' (NRSV, *cf.* JB; with VSS), and later in the verse, 'in boastfulness' (NRSV, *cf.* NIV; with MT) against 'enjoy your triumph' (REB; *cf.* NEB, JB).

and plunders the temple and palace treasures (v. 24a). Such is his respect for Yahweh's house! In fact, the raid on the temple must be seen as a punishment against idolaters in line with the principles of 2 Chronicles 7:19–22. The additional reference to *Obed-Edom* (*cf.* 2 Ki. 14:14) looks back to a specially favoured family of gatekeepers (1 Ch. 13:13–14; 26:4–8, 15). Mention of hostages contrasts with a similar incident in 2 Chronicles 28:8–15 when the northerners had second thoughts about the validity of taking fellow Israelites hostage.

d. Amaziah's end (25:25 – 26:2). If the chronology mentioned earlier is correct, this final paragraph covers Amaziah's last twenty-four years when his son *Uzziah* acted as co-regent (26:1), for nine years of which he may have been Jehoash's captive (*cf.* v. 1). At what point he *turned away from following the LORD* (v. 27) is not clear. It may refer to worshipping the Edomite gods (vv. 14, 20), in which case the conspiracy which led to his death took place many years afterwards. Alternatively, the whole of verse 27 refers to some otherwise unknown incident at the end of his life. However, divine judgment in Chronicles can often take place at a later date (*cf.* chs. 21–23), so that dogmatism over the timing of events is unwise. Amaziah may, for example, have sought protection for much of his last fifteen years in *Lachish*, a fortified city in south-western Judah. The significance of his body being returned *by horse* is unknown. *City of Judah* (v. 28) is unique in the Old Testament, but, though it occurs in Assyrian and Babylonian sources, most EVV have the more usual '*City of David*' (with 2 Ki. 14:20 and the vss).[1]

Some difficulty is usually implied when the people (26:1) are involved in putting a new king on the throne (*cf.* 22:11; 33:25; 36:1), perhaps connected here with Amaziah's defeat (*cf.* 25:21–24). However, the idea that the king could be chosen by the will of the people was never entirely lost in Judah. 'Eloth' (REB, NEB, NRSV, RSV) or *Elath* (NIV, GNB, JB) was an important port at the northern end of the Gulf of Aqaba, very close to Ezion-Geber where Solomon and Jehoshaphat had kept ships (2 Ch. 8:17–18; 20:35–37). Uzziah's reclaiming

---

[1] *Cf. e.g.* A. K. Grayson, *Assyrian and Babylonian Chronicles* (Locust Valley: Augustin, 1975), p. 102 (= D. J. Wiseman, *Chronicles of Chaldean Kings*, London: British Museum, 1956, p. 73); G. A. Smith, *Jerusalem from the Earliest Times*, 1 (London: Hodder & Stoughton, 1907), p. 268.

it for Judah signified two things. It brought Amaziah's un-finished Edomite business to an end (2 Ch. 21:8–10; 25:11–12), and symbolized the beginning of a prosperity un-paralleled in Judah since the days of Solomon.

iii. Uzziah (26:3–23)

'But after Uzziah became powerful, his pride led to his downfall' (26:16).

26:3–4 – *cf*. 2 Kings 15:2–3
26:20b–23 – *cf*. 2 Kings 15:5–7

Apart from the introductory and concluding sections (vv. 3–5, 22–23), Uzziah's reign is divided clearly into two, each of which is loosely based on the brief account in Kings. Uzziah's extensive achievements (vv. 6–15) incorporate various scattered comments in 2 Kings 14:22; 15:3, 6, while the story about his divinely sent skin disease (vv. 16–21) is developed from 2 Kings 15:5. This is the last of three successive reigns which concludes with a period of disobedience and disaster (chs. 24–26), and it seems that nothing is able to prevent Judah and their kings sliding into sin and judgment. Idolatry, rejection of the prophets, violence, and pride repeat themselves with devastating regularity. The picture is made worse by the fact that each of these kings did what was right before God (24:2; 25:2; 26:4), but no-one, it seems, can escape the fatal flaw (*cf*. Rom. 3:23). Even with the Lord's help (vv. 7, 15; *cf*. 25:8), Judah had as yet no visible guarantee of a secure future.

In addition to the periodization scheme, this chapter exhibits many typical features of the Chronicler's style. Each section, for example, is characterized by well-known topics. Uzziah's prosperity is symbolized by combining the three themes of Uzziah's *fame* and *power* and God's *help*, especially in verse 15 (also vv. 7–8). That strength also marks the turning-point at verse 16, where it develops its darker characteristic of pride. From then on, the key word is that Uzziah is *unfaithful* (vv. 16, 18). The significant features of his offence are that it took place in the *temple* (vv. 16, 19, 21) before the *incense altar* (vv. 16, 19) and that God afflicted him as a result with a skin disease (EVV, *leprosy*; vv. 19, 20, 21, 23).

Most of these features, though not all, occur in Chronicles' additional verses (vv. 5–20a). Where this new material came from is unknown, apart from what the Chronicler himself states (v. 22). Most commentators are confident of the historical value of much of verses 6–15, but this does not apply to verses 15–21, a passage which is often regarded as the Chronicler's own interpretation of 2 Kings 15:5. Such inconsistency is hard to justify, even though supporting evidence is available only for the former section from the prophets and archaeology. Nevertheless, our knowledge of Uzziah is heavily dependent on Chronicles, and this chapter contains important historical information about eighth-century BC Judah.

The main thrust of the chapter is Uzziah's *pride*, which is the result of his success and the cause of his failure (v. 16; *cf.* 2 Ch. 25:19; 32:25). Of course this is not just an Old Testament problem, since Christians are just as vulnerable as anyone else to its seductions, which, as Uzziah discovered, are all the more potent in a time of success and in matters to do with faith (*cf.* Dt. 8:10–20; 1 Cor. 8:1; 10:12; 13:4; Col. 2:18; 1 Tim. 3:6). Uzziah's problem was that he was not content with the authority God had given him and wanted to add more priestly functions to his royal power. Absolute power, however, has no place in God's kingdom, for at least two reasons. Effective biblical leadership is always aware that it is a gift rather than a possession, and it always involves some kind of partnership or team dimension. For these and other reasons, Jesus' own leadership was chiefly characterized by obedient servanthood. Unfortunately, Uzziah's prosperity made him blind as to how generous God had been, and, when he tried to take a leadership gift that was not his, even what he had was taken away (*cf.* Lk. 19:25).

a. Uzziah seeks God and is successful (26:3–15).

Though Uzziah reigned for *fifty-two years* (v. 3), his reign included co-regencies with his father Amaziah (probably for twenty-four years) and his son Jotham (for ten years). His over-all dates vary between 792–740 (Thiele) and 787–736 (Begrich), though the chronology of this period is particularly difficult.[1] He is consistently called *Uzziah* in Chronicles (*cf.* Is. 1:1; 6:1; *etc.*) but Kings has Azariah (2 Ki. 14:21; 15:1ff.) as well as Uzziah (2 Ki. 15:13, 32, 34). The two names are best understood as variants arising from the interchangeability of two

[1] Another proposal is to reduce his reign to approximately 26 years, *viz.* 772–?747, *cf.* Hughes, pp. 219–222.

closely related Hebrew roots. Uzziah may be preferred here to distinguish him from the high priest Azariah (vv. 17, 20), who does not appear in Kings. As Azariah he may appear in the annals of the contemporary Assyrian ruler Tiglath-Pileser III, as a leader of a group of rebels against the Assyrians in about 739–738 BC, but both the location and the date cause problems.[1]

The apparent double introduction to Uzziah arises because verses 1–2 really conclude Amaziah's reign (*cf.* 2 Ki. 14:21–22). Uzziah's account begins with verses 3–4, to which the Chronicler has added his own material in an extra verse (v. 5). That Uzziah did *what was right . . . as his father Amaziah* (v. 4) is not meant to be a blanket commendation of either king, as both Kings and Chronicles recognize. Though the phrase originally occurred in 2 Kings 15:3, the Chronicler in fact provides much more positive evidence about Uzziah, in spite of his later criticism (vv. 16–21).

The supplementary verse 5 continues this positive outlook, but uses the Chronicler's typical language: God *gave* Uzziah *success* because he *sought* God (the latter verb occurs twice). Uzziah's attitude was directly opposed to that which had brought down his father (25:15, 20), but, more importantly, it showed that he lived in obedience to Yahweh (*cf. e.g.* 2 Ch. 15:2, 4, 12; 17:4; 30:19), at least while he was under the tutelage of the otherwise unknown *Zechariah*. The latter was a kind of 'religious adviser' (GNB), as Jehoiada had been to Joash (2 Ch. 24:2), though his exact status is not clear. Nor is it certain in what Uzziah was instructed. Though EVV mention the *fear of God* (with the VSS), this phrase is unique in Chronicles (even 'fear of the LORD' occurs only in 2 Ch. 19:9). The reading of most Hebrew MSS, 'seeing God' or *vision* (NIV mg.), cannot simply be dismissed. 'Vision' is another word for prophecy (*e.g.* Is. 1:1; Na. 1:1; 2 Ch. 32:32), which is of course central to Chronicles. Also, the Chronicler's dependence on Isaiah as a source for Uzziah (v. 22) could have resulted in his interest in Isaiah's theme of spiritual sight (*e.g.* Is. 6:10; 29:18; 35:2; *cf.* Je. 23:18) and in the influence of expressions for 'seeing God' in Isaiah 6:1, 5 on the wording here. 'Seeing God' therefore could mean obedience to God's prophetic word and an awareness of God's presence in the temple.

[1] *Cf.* Cogan and Tadmor, pp. 165–166.

Zechariah's guidance clearly brought *success*, a typical expression in Chronicles. The practical side of this is detailed in verses 7–15, but it resulted first of all from seeking God. Elsewhere obedience to the law (1 Ch. 22:13; 2 Ch. 31:21) and the prophets (2 Ch. 20:20) brings prosperity, while disobeying the prophets or resisting God in other ways leads to disaster (2 Ch. 13:12; 24:20). The underlying theology is not so much materialistic as expecting to see the results of obedience in this life. Even so, visible success was certainly not automatic. Obedient kings often experienced undeserved trouble (2 Ch. 13:8, 13–14; 14:9–11; 32:1), though trust in God on these occasions usually resulted in a successful conclusion.

6–15. Uzziah achieved success in three areas, war (vv. 6–8), building and agriculture (vv. 9–10), and the army (vv. 11–15). He fought against three opponents to the south and south-west, where he may have had an eye on controlling trade-routes as already implied by the capture of Eloth (v. 2). First, the *Philistines* lost two of their major cities, *Gath* and *Ashdod* as well as *Jabneh*. The latter was formerly Jabneel of Judah (Jos. 15:11) and later became Jamnia where the Sanhedrin was re-formed after Jerusalem's destruction in AD 70. The last phrase of verse 6 is sometimes omitted (Ackroyd, Williamson), but good sense can be made of it as in REB, NEB, 'built towns in the territory of Ashdod and among the Philistines' (*cf.* NRSV, RSV). Second, *the Arabs* is a general term for nomadic groups such as the *Meunites* (v. 7). Their proximity to the Philistines and the *border of Egypt* (v. 8) as well as a reference in an inscription of Tiglath-Pileser III of Assyria indicates that they are to be located in south-western Judah.[1] *Gur Baal* (v. 7) is otherwise unknown, and indeed is often emended to either Gur (= Gari of the Amarna letters) or Gerar (*cf.* Tg.). The third group is the *Meunites* (v. 7), whose name is probably to be restored in place of *Ammonites* (v. 8), since the latter have no connection with the border of Egypt (though *cf.* 27:5).[2] The chief reason for Uzziah's success is God's *help* (v. 7; *cf.* v. 15). This is a special word in Chronicles (*cf. e.g.* 1 Ch. 12:19; 2 Ch. 14:10; 25:8) whose meaning is equivalent in the New Testament to the enabling work of the Holy Spirit (*cf.* Rom. 8:26; 2

[1] *Cf.* I. Epha'al, *The Ancient Arabs* (Jerusalem: Magnes Press, 1982), pp. 75–81, 91.

[2] The change involves inverting two letters. Also, the usual expression is 'the sons of Ammon'. 'Ammonite', as here, is very rare.

Tim. 1:14; *cf*. Acts 26:22; 1 Thes. 2:2). Two benefits accrue to Uzziah. The first is *fame* (vv. 8, 15), which associates him especially with David (*cf*. 1 Ch. 14:17; 17:8), and the second is that he became *very powerful* (vv. 8, 15). The latter often characterized the first part of a reign (*cf*. 2 Ch. 12:1; 17:1; 27:6), and may be a play here on Uzziah's name (it means, 'Yahweh is strong').

Uzziah's building work in Jerusalem (v. 9) and in Judah (v. 10) is a second sign of God-given success, and is well supported by archaeological data (*cf*. Myers, Williamson). Repairs in Jerusalem were necessitated by the damage incurred during the previous reign (note the specific mention of the *Corner Gate* in 25:23) and possibly by an earthquake (Am. 1:1; Zc. 14:5). The country is divided into three areas, the *desert*, *i.e.* the Negev, the *foothills* (*cf*. GNB) or *Shephelah*, and the *plain*, *i.e.* the Judean parts of the Philistine plain. The latter was recaptured and rebuilt by Uzziah (v. 6), and cannot in this context be the Transjordanian 'tableland' (JB). The *fertile lands* are actually Carmel, a Judean town seven miles south of Hebron in an area where large flocks could graze (1 Sa. 25; *cf*. Jos. 15:55). 'Farmers and vinedressers' (REB, NEB, NRSV, RSV) would have worked on royal estates (*cf*. 1 Ch. 27:25–31). Evidence for some of the officials in charge of such workers has come from seals bearing the name of Uzziah/Azariah, one of which was actually found in a *cistern* at Tell Beit Mirsim.[1] The rather touching description *he loved the soil* is unique in the Bible.

The description of the army (vv. 11–15) is the last of several in Chronicles, all but one of which (25:5) represent a mark of God's blessing (*cf*. 14:8; 17:14–19). Though the army includes as usual the tribal levies led by the 'heads of families' (v. 12, REB, NEB), it is now supervised by the king's commanders and organized into *divisions* (v. 11). The numbers (v. 13) have been explained as 300 units comprising 7,500 men. The expression 'to help the king' (v. 13, NRSV, RSV) is a deliberate echo of God's help (vv. 7, 15), and is paralleled by similar assistance for David (1 Ch. 12:1, 18, 21–22), Solomon (1 Ch. 22:17), and Hezekiah (2 Ch. 32:3).

In addition to his many other skills, Uzziah seems to have been something of an inventor (v. 15). His (lit.) 'inventions'

[1] *AASOR* 21–22, 1943, pp. 63f., 73.

were probably protective shields or screens on city walls enabling archers and others to operate in comparative safety.[1] This is more probable than 'engines' (RSV, JB) or *machines* (NIV, NRSV, REB, NEB), which implies some kind of catapult, but the latter is not known before the fifth century BC (*cf.* Williamson). Verse 15 forms an inclusion with verses 7–8 by repeating the three key terms, *fame*, *helped*, and *powerful*/strong (v. 15), which characterize the section. The adverb 'marvellously' (NRSV, RSV) or 'wonderfully' (REB, NEB) always implies that God is the subject, *cf.* GNB, 'the help he received from God' (*cf.* Is. 28:29; 29:14; Joel 2:26; Ps. 31:21).

b. Uzziah's pride and downfall (26:16–23). Uzziah's strength is also his weakness, however, for 'when he had become strong he grew proud, to his destruction' (v. 16, NRSV). *Pride* and *destruction* are important words, both having been used of Amaziah (25:16, 19). Another form of the latter lies behind the 'corrupt practices' of Jotham's reign (27:2). Uzziah's earlier faithfulness is unable to prevent Judah's gradual destruction, though the full consequences are not felt till Ahaz' reign (ch. 28). The seriousness of the problem is indicated by two phrases. Firstly, pride here and in 25:19 is a matter of the 'heart' being 'lifted up'. It is a deep-seated disease which might be described as heart trouble. Secondly, Uzziah is *unfaithful* (vv. 16, 18). This is the most important expression for sin in Chronicles, and it can bring down a dynasty (1 Ch. 10:13) or take a nation into exile (1 Ch. 5:25; 9:1; 2 Ch. 33:19; 36:14). The term has not appeared since Rehoboam's time (2 Ch. 12:2), but will now become a regular theme to the end of the book (28:19, 22; 29:6, 19; 30:7; 33:19; 36:14). Though Uzziah's pride did not cause the exile, it is an excellent illustration of why the exile eventually came about. From now on, Judah's end is definitely in sight.

Uzziah's offence was not that he fell foul of important cultic regulations but that like Uzzah before him (1 Ch. 13), he was unaware of the true nature of God's holiness. In practice, he encroached on two aspects of worship which God had reserved to the Aaronic priests and the Levites – he *entered the temple* (v. 16) and attempted to make an offering at the *incense*

[1] *Cf.* Y. Yadin, *The Art of Warfare in Biblical Lands* (London: Weidenfeld & Nicolson, 1963), pp. 325–328; A. Mazar, *Archaeology of the Land of the Bible* (New York: Doubleday, 1990), pp. 430–433.

altar (vv. 16b–19). The temple was for the priests and Levites. It is true that Solomon and Ahaz offered sacrifice at the temple, but they did so on altars outside in the courtyard (2 Ch. 6:12–13; 7:7; 2 Ki. 16:12–15), while young Joash was either kept in the living quarters in the surrounding rooms or was treated as an exception in view of the threat to his life (22:12; 23:11). *To burn incense to the LORD* on the inner altar was *not right* for Uzziah, only for the *consecrated* priests (v. 18; *cf*. Ex. 30:1–10; Nu. 16:40; 18:1–7).

Uzziah's action reflects three earlier Old Testament incidents, involving Aaron's sons (Lv. 10:1–3), Korah (Nu. 16:1–40) and Jeroboam I (1 Ki. 12:33 – 13:1). Aaron's sons had offered incense in an unholy manner, while Korah and Jeroboam were laymen who attempted to act as priests by offering incense. *Azariah*'s opposition and that of the *eighty courageous priests* (v. 17) has analogies with the role played by Moses (Nu. 16:4ff.) and the unnamed man of God in 1 Kings 13:1–3, especially as Azariah's words are a kind of prophetic warning (v. 18; *cf*. 12:5; 24:20; 25:15–16). The link with Numbers 16 is especially close, however, and shows not only that Uzziah should have known better, but also that God does not stand idly by when his holiness is tampered with. Specific connections include Uzziah's *leprosy* (vv. 19–23) with the plague on the people (Nu. 16:46–50), the fact that the punishments broke out suddenly from the Lord (vv. 19–20; *cf*. Nu. 16:35, 46), the need for hurry to prevent a greater spread of disease (v. 20; *cf*. Nu. 16:46), and that God's 'glory' (JB) had departed from the offenders (v. 18; *cf*. Nu. 16:19, 42). In view of the latter parallel, the final phrase of verse 18 should be 'God will not reveal his glory to you' (Ackroyd, *cf*. JB, GNB) rather than 'bring you no honour . . .' (RSV, *etc*.).

Despite the seriousness of what Uzziah had done, God still does not act until Uzziah becomes 'enraged' (REB), an emphatic word occuring twice in verse 19. God's righteous anger only breaks out against human rebellious anger. Uzziah's punishment is described in terms of yet another earlier Scripture: compare (lit.) 'And Azariah ... turned to him and behold he was leprous' with Numbers 12:10: 'And Aaron turned towards Miriam, and behold, she was leprous' (RSV, *cf*. also 2 Ki. 5:27). The disease is not leprosy as it is known today, but a general term for all kinds of skin diseases.

The account in Kings is resumed with a note that the king

had to be confined permanently in a *separate house* (v. 21). This probably means a 'house of freedom', *i.e.* free from the responsibilities of ruling (*cf.* REB, NEB, GNB), though it could mean 'house of corruption, pollution', on the basis of a cognate phrase in Ugaritic referring to the underworld. Uzziah's exclusion *from the temple* (v. 21) was required by the law (Lv. 13:46; Nu. 5:1–3), though, since other kings who were afflicted with serious disease may have carried on some functions of government, it is possible that Uzziah did so too (*cf.* 2 Ch. 16:11–13; 21:18–19). Meanwhile, responsibility for royal administration (*charge of the palace*, v. 21; *cf.* Is. 22:15) was given for several years to his son and regent *Jotham*, until Uzziah died (*cf.* on v. 3). The fact that the king's son occupied this post testifies to its increased importance in the later monarchy.[1] The special nature of Jotham's role is conveyed by the verb 'governed' (*cf.* NRSV, RSV), which is more often used of rulers in the book of Judges.

The Chronicler's source mentions a canonical prophet for the first time (v. 22). Since *Isaiah's* call came in the year of Uzziah's death (Is. 6:1), Isaiah probably collected earlier material (also 2 Ch. 32:32). This work may be reflected in several allusions to Isaiah noted above (vv. 5, 15, 21). The burial notice (v. 23) qualifies 2 Kings 15:7 by noting that Uzziah's disease in life affected his place of rest in death. Reference to a separate burial place may be confirmed by an ossuary inscription of the Hasmonean period: 'Here were brought the bones of Uzziah, king of Judah, and not to be moved.'[2] However, one cannot be absolutely certain that the inscription is independent of this verse.

F. Three alternating kings (27:1 – 32:33)

i. Jotham's obedience (27:1–9)

'Jotham became strong because he ordered his ways before the LORD his God' (v. 27:6, NRSV).

> 27:1–3a – *cf.* 2 Kings 15:33–35
> 27:7 – *cf.* 2 Kings 15:36

---

[1] *Cf.* S. C. Layton, 'The steward in ancient Israel', *JBL* 109, 1990, pp. 633–649.
[2] Translation in J. M. Miller and J. H. Hayes, *A History of Ancient Israel and Judah* (London: SCM Press, 1986), p. 310.

27:8 – *cf.* 2 Kings 15:33
27:9 – *cf.* 2 Kings 15:38

Jotham's reign introduces a new phase of the Chronicler's history. Where each of the last three reigns have been divided into contrasting periods (chs. 24–26), each of the next three is presented through a single theme which then contrasts with what precedes or follows. While therefore Jotham is a model of obedience and blessing, Ahaz (ch. 28) is 'most unfaithful', and Hezekiah (chs. 29–32) is a major reformer. This three-generation sequence of a faithful man followed by a wicked son and a faithful grandson corresponds exactly to the situation described in Ezekiel 18:1–20, on which Chronicles' pattern is probably based. As in 2 Chronicles 24–25, the basic principle is that each person is responsible to God for their own behaviour, with its corollary that no-one is bound by their upbringing or their environment. This was potentially of great significance for the Chronicler's generation, some of whom believed they were still under God's judgment (*cf.* Ne. 9:32–37). On the contrary, Jotham's example shows they had every opportunity to obey God faithfully and every hope of seeing signs of his blessing.

The turn-round from the latter part of Uzziah's reign is all the more remarkable when one remembers that part of Jotham's rule, perhaps the majority, took place while his father was still alive (*cf.* comment on 26:3, 21). Perhaps his father's experience in the temple was a salutary warning of the value of living according to God's word (v. 6). Jotham's obedience led to renewed prosperity, and enabled him to resume several of Uzziah's earlier achievements (*cf.* vv. 3–5; 26:6–10). However, what stands out in comparing Jotham and Uzziah is their contrasting attitudes to their power or strength. While Uzziah's success had gone to his head, Jotham showed it was still possible to be submissive to God's word and yet be successful (*cf.* the uses of *power*/strength (in 26:16; 27:6). A notable feature of Jotham's achievement was that it meant turning away from the unhelpful ways of his predecessor. Though the New Testament contains no exact parallel, a similar problem existed in some of the first-century AD churches which had settled down into ways from which they needed to repent (*e.g.* Rev. 2:4–5, 14–16; 3:1–3). A fresh generation, however, can always break away from the ungodly practices and attitudes they inherit.

a. Jotham's contrast with his father (27:1–2). Though *Jotham* is said to have reigned for *sixteen years* (v. 1), his chronology raises difficulties to which no convincing solution exists. In contrast to this datum, Hoshea of Israel became king in Jotham's twentieth year (2 Ki. 15:30) as well as in Ahaz' twelfth year (2 Ki. 17:1). Most solutions involve Jotham in co-regencies with either Uzziah or Ahaz or both, usually with some adjustment of the numbers. Begrich gives his dates as 756–741, and Thiele as 750–732, though others prefer a much shorter reign. Jotham's name has been thought to occur on a seal found near Eloth (*cf.* 26:2), but it is now widely interpreted as Edomite.[1]

Jotham continued to do what was right before God (v. 2), since he did *not enter the temple of the LORD*, in contrast to his father. Though the latter phrase is sometimes regarded as a criticism of Jotham (Myers; *unlike him*, NIV, REB, NEB, is not in Heb.), this phrase is the exact opposite of Uzziah's offence (26:16). In any case, entering the temple was forbidden to any except priests and Levites. The *people*, on the other hand, persisted in their *corrupt practices*, which refers to worship at the high places (2 Ki. 15:35). However, the Hebrew word comes from the same root as 'destruction, downfall' (26:16), and its main purpose may be to show how Uzziah's errors spread throughout the country, despite the example of the new king/regent.

b. Jotham's continuity with his father (27:3–6). Three aspects of Jotham's achievements are mentioned, all of them developing Uzziah's earlier work. The first is his building, which is very obviously the theme of verses 3–4 in Hebrew where *he (re)built* occurs four times. The *Upper Gate* of the temple was on the northern side (Ezk. 9:2; *cf.* Je. 20:2), and was perhaps part of the rebuilding required after the attack by Jehoash of Israel (*cf.* 25:24), since Uzziah is not known to have worked on the temple. On the other hand, Uzziah had done *extensive work* on the city wall (26:9; *cf.* 25:23), which Jotham continued at the southern end of the city on the *Ophel* hill. The latter is usually thought to be the part of the south-eastern hill between the temple and the City of David. Both

---

[1] Cogan and Tadmor, p. 181; J. C. L. Gibson, *Textbook of Syrian Semitic Inscriptions* (Oxford: Clarendon Press, ²1973), p. 63.

Uzziah and Jotham also did some building in the hill country of Judah, and both constructed *towers* (v. 4; *cf.* 26:10). The *wooded areas* were presumably in the hills, and their being turned into *towns*/cities may be intended as a reversal of a general judgment theme (Is. 17:9). The fortifications may be a defensive move against a possible threat by a coalition between Syria and Israel (2 Ki. 15:37).

Secondly, Jotham's victory over the *Ammonites* continues Uzziah's military successes, though in the east rather than the south-west (v. 5; *cf.* 26:6–8). Though the mention of Ammonites in 26:8 has been questioned (that verse may have been influenced by this one), the word for Ammonites here is the familiar 'sons of Ammon', and the details here are specific and likely to be authentic. The tribute was substantial, something over three tons of *silver* and approximately *ten thousand* donkey loads of *barley* (the *kor* was equivalent to a homer or donkey load). The Ammonite war may also reflect real or potential danger from the Syro-Ephraimite coalition, either in a defensive ploy by Jotham or as a reason why tribute ceased after three years.

Thirdly, Jotham became strong/*powerful* as Uzziah had done, but without falling for his father's temptations (v. 6; *cf.* 26:8, 15, 16). The reason for Jotham's success was that he 'ordered his ways' as God required (v. 6, NRSV, RSV; *walked steadfastly*, NIV). This particular expression is unique in Hebrew (lit., 'he established his ways'), but it seems to be synonymous with a similar phrase, 'to set the heart (on God)' (*cf.* 1 Ch. 29:18; 20:33; 30:19).

c. Jotham rests with his fathers (27:7–9). The concluding formula contains the expected information, except that verse 8 repeats the details of verse 1a. This technique of reprise, however, has already been used by the Chronicler in 2 Chronicles 21:5, 20. *All his wars* (v. 7) presumably refers to the initial stages of conflict with the Syro-Ephraimite coalition which turned into a major crisis under Ahaz (*cf.* 2 Ch. 28:5–8; Is. 7:1–9). This has been alluded to in verses 3–5, which is the most likely reason why the reference in 2 Kings 15:37 is not repeated here. The statements about his burial (v. 9) are unusually normal! It has been rare in recent reigns for a king to *rest with his fathers* in the main section of the royal cemetery (*cf.* 2 Ch. 25:28 with 21:20; 22:9; 23:21; 24:25; 26:23).

ii. Ahaz' unfaithfulness (28:1–27)
'For the LORD had humbled Judah because of Ahaz king
of Israel' (28:19).
28:1–2a – *cf*. 2 Kings 16:2–3a
28:3b–4 – *cf*. 2 Kings 3b–4
28:16 – *cf*. 2 Kings 16:7a
28:21 – *cf*. 2 Kings 16:8
28:26–27 – *cf*. 2 Kings 16:19–20

The Chronicler's history reaches another low point with the reign of *Ahaz*. To start with, Ahaz *did not do what was right* before God (v. 1), in contrast to his immediate predecessor Jotham (27:2). Secondly, the totally negative assessment of Ahaz puts him on a par with the rulers of Ahab's house (2 Ch. 21–23) and with the kings whose reigns led directly to the exile (2 Ch. 36; *cf*. also 2 Ch. 33:21–25). Thirdly, Chronicles has made Kings' descriptions of Ahaz' failings much more explicit. Additional interpretative comments explain that Judah was being punished because they had *forsaken* God (v. 6) and because Ahaz had been *most unfaithful* (v. 19), in sharp contrast with the merciful attitudes shown by the inhabitants of Israel (vv. 12–15).

This distinctive presentation has been put together from three separate components. The first is 2 Kings 16, with which this chapter shares the same basic structure, even though the details overlap very little. Apart from similar introductions and conclusions, both accounts deal with the same three topics and in the same order, *viz*. a war against Syria and Israel (vv. 5–15; *cf*. 2 Ki. 16:5–6), an appeal to the king of Assyria (vv. 16–21; *cf*. 2 Ki. 16:7–9), and Ahaz' apostasy (vv. 22–25; *cf*. 2 Ki. 16:10–18). Secondly, some of the military and administrative details (*e.g.* vv. 5–8, 12, 16–18) as well as Oded's prophecy (vv. 9–11) probably derive from various unknown sources. Though the separate existence of this material cannot be directly substantiated, enough independent evidence of events in Edom and Philistia (vv. 17–18) exists to indicate that the Chronicler has painted an accurate picture of eighth-century Judah. The third component is the model of three successive generations in Ezekiel 18:1–20. Ahaz represents the second of the three, the wicked son of a righteous father, who must accept responsibility for his own actions rather than rely on his father's obedience as a way of escaping the consequences of his behaviour (see also comment on ch. 27).

The Chronicler's own contribution is seen in the use of special vocabulary and of distinctive patterns. The first main section (vv. 5–15), for instance, refers repeatedly to the taking of Judean captives/*prisoners* (vv. 5, 8, 11, 13, 14, 15; *cf.* v. 17). This theme anticipates the exile itself, indicating that Ahaz' actions jeopardized the very existence of God's covenant people. The reasons for this are developed in the second section (vv. 16–21), where the key word is *help* (vv. 16, 21; also v. 23; NIV, GNB in v. 20 translate a different word). The occurrences in verses 16, 21 are especially significant, since they mark the beginning and end of the paragraph, in both cases as part of phrases that are additional to Kings (*cf.* 2 Ki. 16:7, 8). Judah went into captivity because Ahaz sought false help from the king of Assyria and also from the gods of Damascus (v. 23). No single word stands out in the third section (vv. 22–25) but the phrase *even more unfaithful* (NIV, *cf.* REB, NEB) is probably intended as a heading (v. 22). It translates a Hebrew word (*mā'al*) which is central to the Chronicler's thought, and which is especially frequent from chapter 26 onwards as an explanation for Judah's final exile.

Ahaz' reign is also patterned on those of other rulers. Saul (1 Ch. 10) and Athaliah (2 Ch. 22:10 – 23:2) provide some analogies, though few specific connections exist between Saul and Ahaz (against Mosis). As Judah's last king under the Divided Monarchy, Ahaz has also been compared with its first king Rehoboam. In each case, the inhabitants of one kingdom recognized those of the other as brothers (*kinsmen* or *fellow countrymen*, vv. 8, 11, 15; *cf.* 11:4), and, while both kings forsook God (v. 6; *cf.* 12:6, 7, 12), Rehoboam repented and Ahaz did not. Two other analogies are more important than either of these, however. Firstly, Judah under Ahaz is like Israel under Jeroboam I (*cf.* 2 Ch. 13:8–18). Both forsook God (v. 6; *cf.* 13:11) by committing themselves to idolatry (vv. 2–4, 23, 25; *cf.* 13:8–9) and abandoning the temple in Jerusalem (v. 24; *cf.* 2 Ch. 13:9–11), and both suffered 'a severe defeat' by the army of their kinsmen because God handed them over (v. 5; *cf.* 2 Ch. 13:16–17). Secondly, Judah's experience of captivity under Ahaz is a direct forerunner of the Babylonian exile. That too was the result of unfaithfulness (vv. 19, 21; *cf.* 2 Ch. 36:14) which ended proper worship in the temple (v. 24; *cf.* 2 Ch. 36:14). Because God was angry with his people (vv. 9, 13; *cf.* 2 Ch. 36:16), he handed them over (vv. 5,

9; *cf.* 2 Ch. 36:17) to foreign invaders (vv. 5, 17–18; *cf.* 2 Ch. 36:17), and as a result the temple and palace were despoiled and the temple vessels damaged (vv. 21, 24; *cf.* 2 Ch. 36:18–19).

The one ray of hope is provided by some good Samaritans. In repenting of the northern army's excessive violence, they tend to their captives' needs and send them home again (vv. 14–15) in an attempt to avert at least some of God's anger (v. 13). The Chronicler's message, which must have been clear to his contemporaries, is that God's mercy was freely available even to captives. The story is in fact so striking that Jesus used it twice in his teaching. Anointing of the prisoners' wounds, the mention of donkeys and of Jericho make this an important source of the parable of the Good Samaritan (Lk. 10:25–37), while the provision of food and clothing to brothers who are naked and hungry prisoners clearly lies behind Matthew 25:34–46.[1] No-one's situation is too hopeless for God to redeem, and he reserves the right to show mercy through the most unexpected people, even one's traditional enemies (*cf.* Jon. 1–4; Acts 10:1 – 11:18).

a. Ahaz' apostasy (28:1–4). As in the case of several preceding reigns, the chronology is difficult. The age at which Ahaz died (v. 1) and that at which Hezekiah became king (29:1) seem to indicate that Ahaz became a father at eleven! The most probable explanation is that a co-regency with his father Jotham should be added to his reign of *sixteen years*, though some LXX MSS suggest he may have been twenty-five when he ascended the throne.[2] The dates of his reign vary between 741–725 (Begrich) and 735–715 (Thiele, Albright).

The most serious criticism of any king of Judah was that *he walked in the ways of the kings of Israel* (v. 2). This explicit reference to idolatry has been used only of Jehoram (2 Ch. 21:6; though *cf.* 22:4), though even the latter could not offer the variety mentioned in verses 2–4, 25. The most noteworthy features are the elements added to Kings (vv. 2b–3a). Ahaz' worship of the *Baals* puts him in the tradition of the house of Ahab (1 Ki. 18:18; 2 Ch. 24:7). Also, the reference to the

---

[1] See F. S. Spencer, '2 Chronicles 28:5–15 and the parable of the Good Samaritan', *WTJ* 46, 1984, pp. 317–349.
[2] *Cf. e.g.* Cogan and Tadmor, p. 186. This might be an assimilation to the 25 years of 27:8, however.

hideous practice of child sacrifice (v. 3) is clearer than in 2 Kings 16:3, where 'caused his son to pass through' has become 'burnt his sons' (REB, NEB). The Hebrew name of the *Valley of Ben Hinnom* (*cf.* 2 Ch. 33:6; 2 Ki. 23:10; Je. 7:31–32; Ezk. 16:20–21), where the fires of Jerusalem's rubbish dump burned, has become popularized as Gehenna, 'hell'.

b. Massacre and mercy (28:5–15). This paragraph divides clearly into the war against Syria and Israel (vv. 5–8) and its unexpected aftermath (vv. 9–15). Though the war is described several times in the Old Testament (2 Ki. 15:37; 16:5–6; Is. 7:1 – 9:6; Ho. 5:8 – 7:16), the Chronicler has presented it in such a way as to give the impression that this version contradicts the earlier ones.[1] Syria and Israel, for example, seem to be treated separately here but as a coalition elsewhere (2 Ki. 16:5; Is. 7:1–2), while Chronicles' concentration on Judah's defeat contrasts with the coalition's failure to achieve complete victory. The differences are more apparent than real, however. The actions of the two invaders are so similar as to imply some kind of partnership (v. 5), while verses 6ff. concentrate on Israel's role. Also, 2 Kings 16 and Isaiah 7 make quite clear that the coalition armies must have overrun most of northern Judah, failing only to capture Jerusalem.

It is therefore consistent to say that Judah suffered a (lit.) 'great captivity' and a 'great defeat' at the hands of the Syrians and Israelites respectively (v. 5), and it is no surprise that the victors *took captive* a large number of Judeans (vv. 5, 8). The large numbers (vv. 6, 8) are probably not to be taken at face value, though the problem of casualty statistics is somewhat different from calculating the size of an army (*cf. e.g.* 13:3; 14:8). It may still be possible, however, to think in terms of fatalities from 120 military units and the women and children from 200 families or clans being carried off. Whatever the precise figures, the fact that the dead included a member of the royal family and the two most senior administrative officials (v. 7) indicates how serious the crisis was.

The reason for the disaster was just as important as the extent of it. Chronicles states in typical style that because

---

[1] See especially M. E. W. Thompson, *Situation and Theology* (Sheffield: Almond, 1982), for the various ways this war is interpreted in the OT.

Judah *had forsaken God* (v. 6), God had become *angry* (v. 9) and *handed* them *over* (v. 5) to their enemies. Judah had broken the covenant by forsaking God (1 Ch. 28:9; 2 Ch. 7:19–22; 15:2), which made them liable to military defeat and captivity as a sign of divine anger (2 Ch. 6:36). Isaiah had earlier made the same point (*cf.* Is. 7:1–12). The same divine sovereignty that had protected Jerusalem against the armies of Syria and Israel now used them as agents of divine punishment.

For the moment, however, Chronicles shows how God's anger can be unexpectedly turned aside. A prophet from Samaria called *Oded* intervenes to greet the returning victorious Israelite army with the apparently unwelcome message that the prisoners must be sent back (vv. 9–11). He gives three reasons, that the Israelites had reacted with excessive *rage* (v. 9), that their plan to subject the Judean prisoners of war to the usual fate of slavery was unacceptable (v. 10a), and that they had 'committed sins' (v. 10b, JB; 'are guilty', REB, NEB) before God. As with many previous prophecies in Chronicles, Oded uses earlier Scripture. Excessive violence in war regularly met with God's disapproval (*cf.* Is. 10:15–16; Ho. 1:4; Hab. 2:2–20; Zc. 1:15), even though the Israelites might claim that they were simply getting their own back on Amaziah (*cf.* 25:11–12). Slavery of fellow Israelites was against the law of Leviticus 25:42–43, 46, because they were (lit.) 'brothers' (vv. 8, 11, 15; 'kinsmen', REB, NEB; 'kinsfolk', RSV), a significant theme throughout Chronicles (*cf.* 1 Ch. 12:39; 13:2; 2 Ch. 11:4). Also, 'to force into slavery' (v. 10, REB, NEB) is a phrase always associated with God's disapproval, and occurs only in Jeremiah 34:11, 16 and Nehemiah 5:5, in the latter case perhaps not too distant from the Chronicler's own experience. Finally, the prophecy is an appeal for repentance (v. 11). The only hope against God's anger for both Israelites and Judeans (vv. 9, 11) is in God's mercy, which according to 2 Chronicles 6:36–39 was available even in captivity. Though they had sinned against the law and the prophets, Scripture also pointed the way to forgiveness.

To their credit and in contrast to the Judeans, the Israelite leaders responded to God's word (vv. 12–13). Indeed, they are aware that the actions of their army have increased their *guilt* and God's *fierce anger* (v. 12–13). The original reference is probably not so much to the division of the kingdoms but to the northerners' rejection of the Davidic covenant and the worship of the Jerusalem temple (*cf.* 2 Ch. 11:14; 13:8). The absence of any reference to a king in Israel (v. 12) is significant (though *cf.* v. 6). This and the mention of the northern *assembly* (v. 14; *cf.* 10:1, 12, 15) is one of several indications in Chronicles where the people of the north respond favourably to God (*e.g.* 11:13–17; 15:9; 30:11). The *men designated by name* were a specially appointed committee, a procedure of the assembly familiar in Ezra's time (Ezr. 10:16; *cf.* 1 Ch. 12:31; 16:41; 2 Ch. 31:19). On the mercy shown to the prisoners as a background to Jesus' teaching on showing love to others, see above. The question, 'Who is my neighbour?' is just as relevant here (*cf.* Lk. 11:29).

c. False help (28:16–21). The origins as well as the outcome of Ahaz' appeal to *Tiglath-Pileser* III, *king of Assyria* (745–727), vary from the brief account in 2 Kings 16:7–9,[1] Whereas Kings makes the Syro-Israelite invasion the reason for Ahaz' desperate request, here the *Edomites* (v. 17) and *Philistines* (v. 18) are the cause of the trouble. Both these nations, however, fought against the Assyrians as the Syrians and Israelites had done, and 2 Kings 16:6 suggests that the Syrian and Edomite attacks may even have been coordinated.[2] The yoke imposed by Uzziah also gave them further reason to be hostile (2 Ch. 26:2, 6–7). The Philistines attacked the strategic valleys in the Shephelah, though *Gimzo* was probably further north in Israel.

Any relief brought by Ahaz' 'bribe' (2 Ki. 16:8, NEB), however, was short-lived, since ultimately the Assyrians *gave* him *trouble* (v. 20; 'afflicted', RSV; 'oppressed', NRSV). Isaiah's prediction (Is. 7:17) that God would send the king of Assyria in judgment was soon fulfilled, with Judah becoming Assyria's vassal for some thirty years, and most of Israel immediately being turned into three Assyrian provinces (*cf.* Is. 9:1). The considerable cost of sending temple and palace treasures was all to no avail (v. 21).[3]

Ahaz' real failure, however, was to seek human rather than

[1] The unexpected 'kings [plural] of Assyria' (v. 16, JB) also occurs in 30:6; 32:4, which may if taken together refer generally to the Assyrian empire.
[2] *Cf.* J. Gray, 'The period and office of the prophet Isaiah in the light of a New Assyrian tablet', *Exp.T.* 63, 1952, pp. 263–265; H. W. F. Saggs, 'The Nimrud letters – II', *Iraq* 17, 1955, pp. 126–160, especially pp. 131–132, 149–153.
[3] This is mentioned in Tiglath-Pileser's annals, where Ahaz appears under his fuller name Jehoahaz (*cf. ANET*, p. 282).

divine *help*. One of the Chronicler's principles is that 'God has the power to help or to overthrow' (2 Ch. 25:8; *cf.* 32:8), and that he helps those who put their trust in him (*cf.* 1 Ch. 5:20; 14:10; 18:31). Ahaz' turning to Assyria was therefore a sign of his unbelief (*cf.* Is. 7:9–12). Ahaz also 'behaved without restraint' (v. 19, NRSV) and was *most unfaithful*. The former expression really means to favour licence rather than true liberty, while the latter is a typical term in Chronicles for failing to give God his due. Therefore God *humbled* Judah as he had Israel under Jeroboam (2 Ch. 13:18), but with even more disastrous results.

d. Ahaz' further apostasy (28:22–25). Though this paragraph seems brief and repetitive, it represents an important development. Ahaz' *trouble* (v. 22; *cf.* also v. 20) is to be understood in the light of further occurences of the word in 2 Chronicles 6:28 ('attacked by their enemies', GNB) and 33:12 ('in his distress') as an opportunity for prayer for God to restore his people. Ahaz, however, is quite unaware of this possibility, and instead becomes *even more unfaithful* (v. 22; *cf.* v. 19). He worships the gods of his conquerors (v. 23), destroys ('broke', REB, NEB, GNB) the temple equipment, shuts the temple doors, and establishes shrines on every *street corner* in Jerusalem (v. 24). These are all new developments in Judah, though his seeking *help* from Syrian deities is particularly futile. Just as Amaziah's downfall had come about because he worshipped the gods of defeated enemies who could not save (25:14–15, 19), so Ahaz suffers the same fate for worshipping his victors' gods. Because Ahaz consistently failed to recognize that his defeat was due to the LORD *his God* (v. 5) rather than the Syrians' gods, God overthrew him and his people. *Downfall* (NIV, JB, REB, NEB; 'ruin' NRSV, RSV) is the same word as 'overthrow' in 25:8, illustrating again that those who will not rely on God for help will ultimately be brought down.

In place of the altar from Damascus which is the main criticism of Ahaz in 2 Kings 16:10–18, Chronicles prefers to include wider evidence of Ahaz' increasing apostasy. Shutting the temple doors (*cf.* 29:7) does not contradict Ahaz' worship on the new altar, since the latter was outside the temple. All these activities *provoked . . . God . . . to anger* (v. 25). This phrase is very reminiscent of Kings (*cf. e.g.* 1 Ki. 16:33;

2 Ki. 17:11; 23:19), suggesting that though this material is unique to Chronicles, it may derive from a source also available to Kings.

e. Ahaz' burial (28:26–27). The concluding formula twice associates Ahaz with the *kings of Israel* (v. 27; *cf.* v. 26), which must be noted alongside his title 'king of Israel' (v. 19) and Judah's description as 'all Israel' (v. 23). These may all allude to the fact of the northern kingdom's assimilation by Assyria in 722, representing a fresh opportunity for southerners and northerners to consider their religious unity as Israel as more important than the new political divisions. Previous failures did not augur well, however (*cf.* 11:1–4; 13:3–18; 16:1–9; 19:2–3; 20:35–37; 21:2 – 23:21; 25:7–10, 17–24), even though the repentant Israelites showed that God's mercy was never far away. Further opportunities for unity based on worship at the Jerusalem temple came under Hezekiah and Josiah, but only a later king still could truly bring Jews and Samaritans to worship together (Jn. 4:19–24).

Meanwhile, Ahaz' reign came to its sad end, though his burial apart from the royal cemetery is hardly to be interpreted as part of the theme of exile (v. 27).[1] As with several other kings (*cf.* 21:20; 24:25; 26:23), it is rather a mark of God's judgment.

iii. Hezekiah's reforms (29:1 – 31:21)

'So the service of the temple of the LORD was re-established' (29:35).

'The king, his officials, and the whole assembly decided to celebrate the Passover in the second month' (30:2).

'The LORD has blessed his people, and this great amount is left over' (31:10).

29:1–2 – *cf.* 2 Kings 18: 1b–3
31:1a – *cf.* 2 Kings 18:4a
31:20–21 – *cf.* 18:5–7a

Hezekiah's accession heralds the dawn of a new reformation after the nadir of Ahaz' reign. In fact, Hezekiah is so important to the Chronicler that four chapters are devoted to him, more than for any other king apart from David and Solomon (chs. 29–32). This presentation is quite different from that in

---

[1] *Cf.* M. E. W. Thompson, *op. cit.*, p. 97.

2 Kings from which only the introduction (2 Ki. 18:1–7; *cf.*
2 Ch. 29:1–2; 31:1, 20–21) and conclusion (2 Ki. 20:20–21; *cf.*
2 Ch. 32:32–33) reappear, together with the events of the
main part of 2 Chronicles 32. Though the Chronicler certainly agrees with Kings' positive view, he has selected very
different examples of Hezekiah's faith. Hezekiah here is primarily a reformer of worship (chs. 29–31), with his military
successes and international reputation (ch. 32) as a consequence of the nation's new relationship with God.

Nothing is more central to the Chronicler's message than
worshipping God. The temple as God's earthly residence must
therefore be cleansed from all impurity and rededicated (ch.
29) so that both the Passover (ch. 30) and regular worship can
be re-established (ch. 31). Only on this basis could Israel look
forward with any confidence to God's blessing.

This is in fact consistent with the wider message of the
Bible, which is that every human being's first priority should
be to acknowledge God's worth. That, for example, is how the
ten commandments begin (Ex. 20:3–6), it is the reason for
Jesus' obedient death on the cross, and it is the chief characteristic of the community in heaven (Rev. 4:1 – 5:14; 22:1–9).
When Hezekiah, therefore, made it the first act of his reign to
prepare properly for worship, he was observing a basic biblical
principle, and not just indulging in antiquated ceremonial.
His action also reminds believers today that their pattern of
worship should always express their wholehearted commitment to God (*cf.* 1 Cor. 12–14; Rev. 2:14–16, 20–23). Indeed,
for the New Testament, sacrificial worship makes a claim on
the whole of one's life (Rom. 12:1).

Purifying the temple was no casual matter, and involved
Hezekiah in three separate activities: (a) an invitation to consecration (29:3–11); (b) purifying the temple buildings
(29:12–19); (c) worshipping in sacrifice and song (29:20–35).

These really constitute distinct elements in an act of repentance, which often brings movements of spiritual renewal. This
repentance illustrates the principles of 2 Chronicles 7:14, with
three particular features standing out. Firstly, repentance
often involves corporate action as well as an individual change
of heart. Secondly, corporate repentance depends on wise,
godly leadership (*cf.* the king's role in vv. 3–5, 20, 31).
Hezekiah was obedient to what God wanted, while remaining
aware that any success was due to God (v. 36). Thirdly,

repentance removed God's anger (*cf.* 28:25) and led to joy throughout the nation (v. 36).

Chapter 29's special emphases are expressed in three different patterns. In the first, Hezekiah's reign revives the combined era of David and Solomon. David's reign is recalled by two specific references (vv. 25–27, 30) as well as by the parallels between the Levites' role in verses 3–19 and 1 Chronicles 15. Solomon is reflected in the parallel between his dedication of the temple (2 Ch. 7) and Hezekiah's worship at the rededicated altar (vv. 20–35) and in the Passover (ch. 30). The link with David, which is especially strong in this chapter, shows that Hezekiah is much more than a second Solomon (against Williamson), a view which is based too much on 30:1–12. The second pattern contrasts Hezekiah with two other kings, namely Jeroboam I (as described by Abijah in 2 Ch. 13:8–12) and Ahaz (2 Ch. 28:22–24; 2 Ki. 16:10–18). Not only does this make Hezekiah's reign the start of a new era, it confirms the message of Ezekiel 18 that Israel was not inevitably bound by its past (*cf.* chs. 27–28). The third pattern has been called a 'festival schema', and is based on the dedication of the temple (2 Ch. 7:8–10). This includes four components, a date (*cf.* vv. 1, 17), identification (and purification) of the participants (*cf.* vv. 4–20), details of the ceremonies (*cf.* vv. 21–35), and a joyful celebration (*cf.* v. 36).[1] It is repeated in the reigns of Asa (2 Ch. 15:9–15) and Josiah (2 Ch. 35:1–19) as well as occurring twice in Hezekiah's (*cf.* also 30:13–27), all of which confirms Hezekiah's desire to participate in a living tradition of temple worship.

a. Invitation to consecrate the temple (29:1–11).

i. Introduction (29:1–2). This is the only paragraph in the chapter which is dependent on Kings (2 Kings 18:1b–3) and, apart from the usual omission of the synchronism (2 Ki. 18:1), it keeps closely to its source. It should not be treated as merely routine, however. Hezekiah is the first king to be fully compared with *David* (*cf.* 17:3) and verse 2 also contrasts him with his predecessor (*cf.* 28:1). Indeed, verse 2 really sets the theme by anticipating several direct analogies with David in the chapter. Hezekiah's dates, as with most eighth-century kings,

---

[1] De Vries, p. 373.

remain uncertain, and are given by Begrich as 725–697 and by Thiele as 715–686.

ii. An invitation to consecration (29:3–11). Hezekiah began to repair the damage he inherited from Ahaz on the very first day (vv. 3, 17; *cf.* 28:22–24). Though the *first month of the first year* probably indicates his official year rather than the first month of his actual reign, his speed throughout the whole enterprise shows the depth of his commitment (*cf.* vv. 17, 20, 36). This first month of the calendar year was the proper time for the Passover (*cf.* 30:2), and also the most probable beginning of each regnal year. The first act of the reformation was to *open* the temple *doors* (v. 3) which Ahaz had closed (28:24). They belonged to the main building rather than the temple court (*cf.* v. 7), since Ahaz had continued to require access to his new altar in the courtyard (2 Ki. 16:10–18).

As was the custom with wise kings, Hezekiah first *assembled* the people who would carry out the intended task (v. 4; *cf.* vv. 20, 23, 28, 31, 32; 2 Ch. 5:2–3; 28:14; 34:29). They were the *priests and Levites*, whose predecessors David had employed for transporting the ark (*cf.* 1 Ch. 15:4; *cf.* 23:2). The Chronicler's approved model of leadership was always corporate and never autocratic. The *square on the east* (v. 4) was probably in front of the temple (*cf.* Ezr. 10:9), where the assembled Levites could see the temple's uncleanness for themselves, though another square existed near the city gate outside the temple precincts (Ne. 8:1, 3).

The chapter's main theme is set out in a royal speech (vv. 5–11). It is apparently addressed only to the *Levites*, but mention of incense (v. 11) shows that the priests were included too. Such speeches usually occur at key points in Chronicles. Here the theme is the need for faithfulness to the temple, as a new opportunity to worship God after the fall of the kingdom of Israel in 722 (*cf.* 30:6–9). It has several parallels with Abijah's speech (13:4–12), which was equally strategic in confirming the pattern of worship for the new southern kingdom of Judah.

Hezekiah makes three points, of which the first calls the priests and Levites to *consecrate* both themselves and the *temple* (v. 5; *cf.* vv. 10–11). This was the first step in restoring fellowship with God (vv. 15, 34; 30:15, 24; 31:18; see also comment on 1 Ch. 15:11–15), since only a true priesthood could offer acceptable worship (contrast 2 Ch. 13:9–10). 'Consecrate' means 'to make holy, hallow', that is, to set apart someone or something for God's service (*cf.* 1 Pet. 1:15–16). Though it included positive commitment to God, it also required removing every kind of *defilement* (v. 5, NIV, REB; 'what is impure', JB). This latter term (Heb. *niddâ*) was used in the exile and later to describe the general state of God's people (*e.g.* Ezr. 9:11; La. 1:8, 17; Ezk. 36:17), though it referred elsewhere to ritual uncleanness (*e.g.* Lv. 15:19–33). The Chronicler's audience was doubtless intended to understand both meanings, though they would also have known God's promise of a fountain to cleanse away all impurity (Zc. 13:1).

Secondly, the people had been *unfaithful*, turning their *backs* instead of their *faces* to God (v. 6). Worship was meant to be a face to face meeting with God (Ex. 33:11; Ps. 27:4–9), but they had personally rejected him by failing to recognize his presence (*cf.* Je. 18:17). That is why they had closed the temple (v. 7; *cf.* 13:11; 28:24), and established pagan patterns of worship (28:2–4, 22–25; 2 Ki. 16:12–16). The problem went back not just to one generation, however, but to *our fathers* (v. 6) in general. The use of terms such as *unfaithful* (*cf.* 2 Ch. 26:16, 18; 28:19, 22; 36:14) and *forsook* (*cf.* 2 Ch. 15:2; 24:18, 20; 28:6) typify the attitudes towards God that ultimately led to the punishment of exile.

Thirdly, Hezekiah underlines that to reject God arouses his *anger* (vv. 8, 10). This theme provides another connection with the exile (*cf.* 2 Ch. 36:16), as does the description of Jerusalem as an object of 'horror, astonishment and hissing' (v. 8, *cf.* NRSV, RSV), a phrase which is paralleled only in Jeremiah 29:18 (*cf.* also the individual terms in Je. 15:4; 19:8; 24:9; 25:9). Seeing the *captivity* (v. 9) *with your own eyes* (v. 8) could also refer to the exile, but its primary reference is to Ahaz' reign in chapter 28 where the notion of captivity is repeated eight times (vv. 5, 8, 11, 13, 14, 15, 17). It was also under Ahaz that their fathers died by the *sword* and their *sons and daughters and wives* were taken captive (v. 9; *cf.* 28:6, 8). The key to Hezekiah's speech, however, is that punishment does not have to follow automatically from God's anger (v. 10). The New Testament principle that 'God did not appoint us to suffer wrath but to receive salvation' applies equally here (1 Thes. 5:9; *cf.* Rom. 5:9; 1 Thes. 1:10), so long as there was real repentance (2 Ch. 12:7; 19:10; 32:26).

Hezekiah's commitment to repentance is signified by his intention to make a *covenant* with God (v. 10). No details of this covenant are given, and there is not even any formal acknowledgment that it actually took place, though the calling of an assembly (v. 15) and the action that followed it (vv. 16–35) provide strong testimony of its being put into action. The use of the Hebrew preposition l^e ('with') has suggested that this is more in the nature of a one-sided oath before God, but since covenants were in any case generally confirmed by an oath, the argument is unconvincing.[1] The preposition in this case seems to be synonymous with 'before the LORD' (2 Ch. 34:31). Hezekiah's act came from his 'heart' (v. 10, NRSV; *intend*, REB, NEB, NIV), that is, his will. The expression has a direct analogy with David's inner desires for the temple (*cf.* 1 Ch. 22:7; 28:2; 2 Ch. 6:7). The fact that God has *chosen* the priests and Levites (v. 11) is a further link with David, for the Levites' election occurs elsewhere only in 1 Chronicles 15:2. The final exhortation may be stronger than not to *be negligent* (v. 11). It could mean that either they were not to err (*cf.* 2 Sa. 6:7, AV, RV) or that they must not commit blasphemy (*cf.* Dn. 3:29, REB, NEB).[2]

b. Renewing temple worship (29:12–36).

Purifying the temple (29:12–19). Before describing a particular activity, Chronicles typically lists the names of those involved. The Levites in verses 12–14 are the leaders in the work of purification (vv. 15–19), a format that is closely paralleled by the Levites of David's day (1 Ch. 15:4–10). In both instances, the first four groups in the lists are identical, and the only real difference is that the three musical families in verses 13b–14 replace the two groups in 1 Chronicles 15:9–10. Both sets of leaders must consecrate themselves for their task (vv. 15, 17, 19; *cf.* 1 Ch. 15:12, 14), which these Levites did by removing *everything unclean* (v. 16).

The work itself took two consecutive weeks, first clearing the courtyard up to the 'porch' (v. 17, REB, NEB; 'vestibule', NRSV, RSV) and then the temple (v. 16). The time taken overran the proper date for Passover, for which special arrangements had to be made (ch. 30). The whole enterprise is

---

[1] *E.g.* Gn. 31:44–53; Dt. 29:12, 14; 2 Ch. 15:12–15; Ezr. 10:3–5. Against Japhet, *Ideology*, pp. 112–115.
[2] On the various possible meanings of the root *šlh*, *cf. e.g.* Anderson, p. 103; J. Goldingay, *Daniel*, WBC (Waco: Word Books, 1989), p. 67.

characterized by a concern to do everything as God required, especially as the king's command was regarded as 'the words of the LORD' (v. 15, NRSV, RSV). This latter phrase may refer to God's original revelation to David about the temple (1 Ch. 28:12, 19) rather than portray Hezekiah as a prophet, since Chronicles sometimes speaks in a general way about 'the word of the LORD' (cf. 1 Ch. 10:13; 11:2–3). One example of this carefulness is that the priests alone purified the 'inner part' of the temple (v. 16, NRSV, RSV), that is, the Holy of Holies, since this was the only part from which Levites were excluded (cf. 2 Ch. 5:7; 23:6). Special care was also taken with the temple vessels (vv. 18–19), which in post-exilic times came to symbolize active temple worship (cf. Ezr. 1:7–11; Dn. 5:2–3, 23). When the pagan symbols had finally been removed in the traditional way to the *Kidron Valley* and destroyed (v. 16; cf. 2 Ch. 15:15; 30:14; 2 Ki. 23:12), the temple could be properly *purified* (v. 18) and *consecrated* (v. 19) for God's service.

ii. Restored worship (29:20–36). Hezekiah immediately 'rose early' (v. 20, NRSV, RSV) to gather the civil and religious leaders to reinaugurate worship.[1] As on previous occasions, the temple was only fully restored when it became operational (cf. 2 Ch. 5:2 – 7:10; 15:8–15; 24:13–14). Each section of the reopening service is characterized by its own individual themes of atonement (vv. 21–24), dedication and praise (vv. 25–30), and thanksgiving (vv. 31–35).

First the leaders brought offerings *to atone for all Israel* (v. 24), or more specifically *for the kingdom, for the sanctuary and for Judah* (v. 21). Though the kingdom may be a reference to the royal house, such a meaning would be unique in the Old Testament, and it is not impossible that Chronicles' important theme of the kingdom of God is intended. 'The kingdom' is used in precisely this sense in 1 Chronicles 29:11, and it would provide yet another analogy with Abijah's speech (2 Ch. 13:8).

The *burnt offering* and the *sin offering* (v. 24) provided the atoning sacrifices. The burnt offering seems to have comprised the *bulls, rams,* and *lambs* (vv. 21–22), and its atoning function is paralleled in *e.g.* Leviticus 1:3–4 and Job 1:5. The *sin offering* (NIV, RSV) is singled out. Actually, it is better described as a 'purification offering' (NEB), since by it were

---

[1] Though Heb. does not specify 'next morning' (against NIV, REB).

removed all forms of evil and impurity, personal and impersonal. Even the sanctuary was cleansed, an idea found also in the rituals for the Day of Atonement (Lv. 16:16, 20) and for Ezekiel's visionary temple (Ezk. 45:18–20; *cf.* 43:18–27). Hezekiah's ceremony comprehensively removes every stain (*cf.* v. 5), as well as all God's anger (*cf.* vv. 8, 10). It is for all *Israel* (v. 24), the people of north and south,[1] and the larger number of animals in comparison with the Day of Atonement also underlines the sense of completeness (v. 21; *cf.* Lv. 16:3, 5, 24). Hezekiah in fact, seems to have partly modelled the occasion on the Day of Atonement, for that was the only day each year when every sin was sacrificially atoned for (Lv. 16:16, 21). Another link with the Day of Atonement is that they *laid their hands* on the goats of the purification offering (v. 23). This recalls the scapegoat ritual, in which Israel's sins were confessed over the animal before it was banished as a further symbol that all their sins were gone (Lv. 16:21). Both this incident and the Day of Atonement also anticipate Jesus' own sin offering at the cross, which not only removes all sin but does so once and for all (*cf.* Is. 53:10– 11; Rom. 8:3; 2 Cor. 5:21; Heb. 10:11–12).

The second set of sacrifices were the burnt offerings (vv. 27–28) accompanied by *praise* and *singing* (vv. 25–30). Because burnt offerings occur more than once in the rituals, it has sometimes been concluded that the ones in verses 27–28 must be the same as those in verse 24, and that verses 21–24 and verses 25–30 are contemporary with each other. In fact, burnt offerings accompanied each stage of the ritual, including the various types of fellowship offering (vv. 31–35) and the sin offering (v. 24), as well as the songs of praise. In any case, burnt offerings are associated with a variety of attitudes in worship. Here they accompany an act in which the worshippers *dedicated* themselves (v. 31; 'consecrated', NRSV, RSV), an expression normally used of ordination to the priesthood, and which offers further parallels with both David (1 Ch. 29:5) and Abijah (2 Ch. 13:9). As in David's day, the whole people set themselves apart for God as his priests to offer worship (*cf.* Ex. 19:6; 1 Pet. 2:4, 9–10). Their self-offering is dramatized in the animal sacrifice and verbalized in the sacrifice of praise. A

[1] The term normally includes the old northern kingdom as well as the south in 2 Ch. 29–36 (Williamson, *IBC*, pp. 126–130).

special point is made of the fact that the singing began (v. 27) and ended (v. 29) at the same time as the burnt offering. It symbolizes not only the harmony that ought to exist between the physical and spiritual aspects of worship, but also the restoration of the true pattern of worship, especially in the relationship between atonement and praise. The praise of God is made possible only by the previous removal of sin (*cf.* vv. 21–24), and only a forgiven person can truly sing God's praises (*cf.* Ps. 51:14–15; Rev. 7:9–17). Chronicles also implies that atonement is not to be seen as an end in itself but as a preparation for praise and thanksgiving (*cf.* vv. 25–35; *cf.* 30:27). It is these latter which the Chronicler regards as the normal activities of regular worship, expressed through music and sacrificial offering together (*cf.* 1 Ch. 16:40–41; 23:30–31; 2 Ch. 8:12–14).

The musical praise returned to the standards set by David (vv. 25–26, 30). David's *instruments* (v. 26) and *words* (v. 30) were revived, as were the words of *prophets* who were contemporary with him (v. 25). If the words of *David* and *Asaph* (v. 30) are the same as those psalms whose titles bear their names, the prophets and psalms became the basis of Hezekiah's praise. It is also a good illustration of the use of Scripture in worship.

The third group of offerings was the *sacrifices and thank-offerings* (vv. 31–35). Though associated with burnt offerings, they were actually two separate offerings linked by the general term 'fellowship' or 'peace offerings' (*cf.* v. 35; *cf.* Lv. 7:11–21). They were communion offerings where the worshippers enjoyed fellowship together, and were often used on occasions of special thankgsgiving rather than at regular times. They differed from those previously offered (vv. 21–30) in that they were individual rather than public sacrifices, brought by *all whose hearts were willing* (v. 31). This precise phrase is paralleled only in the gifts made for Moses' Tent (Ex. 35:5, 22), though a very strong connection again exists with David. The word 'willing' (v. 31) is from the same root as 'to offer freely' which appears seven times in 1 Chronicles 29, again in association with the building of the temple.

A special note reports that the priests were slower than the Levites and the rest of the people in consecrating themselves for their role (v. 34). Why the priests rather than the offerer skinned the animal is unknown, since this is a change from Leviticus 1:6, but the more important emphasis is that the

491

Levites *helped* the priests (v. 34). David had assigned the Levites a new role as priestly assistants (1 Ch. 23:28, 32). The incident also highlights the over-all *abundance* of sacrificial animals (vv. 32–35) and the depth of the *assembly*'s sincerity.

So the life of the temple was fully *re-established* (vv. 35b–36). The chapter in fact includes all the major types and functions of sacrificial offerings in its pattern of worship: that is, for sin, for praise, and for communion. It also combines the external and internal aspects of worship as well as its Godward and manward dimensions. Since all these elements are found in the New Testament, all the basic features of biblical worship are therefore included. Sacrifice for sin in both the Old Testament and the New is the springboard for the sacrifice of praise (Col. 3:15–16; Heb. 13:15–16) and for the fellowship or communion meal (1 Cor. 11:23–26). Two consequences followed from these offerings. The first was to acknowledge that only God has made it all possible (v. 36; *cf.* 1 Cor. 12:3; Eph. 2:18). The second was that everyone *rejoiced* (v. 36), in complete contrast with the situation with which they had begun.

c. Invitation to the Passover (30:1–12). Chapter 30 describes Hezekiah's arrangements for a special celebration of *Passover* and *Unleavened Bread* in the newly reopened temple. Why this particular festival was singled out is uncertain, though three possible reasons may be offered. The first is a purely practical one that because the cleaning-up operation had continued beyond the regular date for Passover, Hezekiah was indicating his commitment by rearranging the date rather than letting it slip by altogether (vv. 2–3). The second is that Passover may have been appropriate at the inauguration of a new reign because it commemorated Israel's beginning as a nation (*cf.* Ex. 12:27; Dt. 16:1; the second month is that of Hezekiah's first full year, *cf.* 29:3). The third is that because Passover had originally been instituted to avoid the consequences of God's wrath (*cf.* Ex. 12:13 and v. 8 here), this was a way for Israel to put the past behind and look to new opportunities with God (*cf.* Phil. 3:13–14; Heb. 10:19–25).

This Passover is part of the opening ceremonies of Hezekiah's reign, since chapters 29 and 30 really belong together. Both have a similar structure, with an invitation to worship (vv. 1–12; *cf.* 29:3–11) being followed by an act of purification (v. 14; *cf.* 29:12–19), before the main ceremonies take place (vv. 15–27; *cf.* 29:20–35). The content of Hezekiah's letter (vv. 6–9) is also remarkably similar to his earlier speech to the Levites (29:5–11). A further factor is the number of common themes, such as consecration for worship (*e.g.* vv. 15, 24; 29:15–19, 34), the role of the assembly (*e.g.* vv. 2, 4, 23–25; *cf.* 29:23, 31–32), the people's faithfulness to the past (vv. 16, 26; *cf.* 29:25–26, 30), and the joy of worshipping God (vv. 21, 23, 25–26; *cf.* 29:30, 36). All this clearly links the Passover with the *temple*'s rededication.

Chapter 30 does, however, contribute two emphases of its own. The first is that of a new potential for unity between south and north. The congregation included people from the northern tribes (vv. 5–6, 10–11, 18, 25; 31:1) who responded to Hezekiah's invitation to come to the temple (v. 11). In comparison with previous failures, this incident shows that the only really effective approach to unity has to be based on the principle of faithful worship. Where force (2 Ch. 11:1–4; 13:13) and formal agreements (2 Ch. 18:1; 19:2; 25:6–8) had failed, submitting together before God brings a new attitude. The way forward had previously been shown by incidents in the reigns of Rehoboam and Asa (2 Ch. 11:13–17; 15:9), but this event was much more significant. Far more northerners participated than previously, and the recent fall of the northern kingdom in 722 BC meant that Jerusalem now offered the only alternative for corporate worship of the Lord. Also, in comparison with the previous acts of united worship, only the Passover linked Israel's present with its origins. The importance of this unity should not be exaggerated, however, since it was certainly not the case, even in theory, that 'the whole population was reunited in worship at that time at the Jerusalem temple'.[1] Hezekiah was not a second Solomon, for his reign in no way witnessed a return to the conditions of the United Monarchy. Though the principle by which reunification could take place was established, in reality comparatively few responded, and Israel as a whole was further divided by the northern kingdom having been turned into Assyrian provinces.

The second emphasis is the nature of the *Passover*, an issue which is complicated by the question whether it took place at

---

[1] H. G. M. Williamson in R. E. Clements (ed.), *The World of Ancient Israel* (Cambridge: Cambridge University Press, 1989), p. 157.

all, and, if so, whether or not it was an innovation. The main difficulty is that 2 Kings mentions no Passover in Hezekiah's reign and further asserts that Josiah's Passover was unparalleled throughout the monarchy period (2 Ch. 35:18; *cf.* 2 Ki. 23:22–23). When these factors are combined with the theory that Passover and Unleavened Bread did not become a single festival until Josiah's centralized Passover, it is easy to see how Hezekiah's Passover could be regarded as an idealized version of Josiah's. This theory of the origins of the centralized Passover remain unproven, however, and other interpretations of the biblical data are possible. Firstly, it is to be noted that Hezekiah's festival is marked by various irregularities, such as a date in the second rather than the first month (v. 2), a duration of two weeks rather than one (v. 23), and the impurity of some of the participants (vv. 17–20). These were issues of considerable importance, and are not likely to have been invented by a writer such as the Chronicler who was meticulous about cultic matters.[1] Secondly, the two Passovers vary in several important details. Several elements are included in Josiah's but not Hezekiah's Passover, such as transporting the ark (35:3), roasting the lamb after the exodus pattern (35:13), offering sacrifices until nightfall (35:14), and observing the Book of the Covenant (2 Ki. 23:21). Perhaps the most significant difference, however, concerns the Levites, about whom the Chronicler is very particular. While Josiah's Levites were expected to slaughter the animals (35:5–6), here they did so only for people who were unclean (v 17). These variations show that Hezekiah's Passover cannot have been written up on the basis of Josiah's. Further, 2 Chronicles 35:18 does not claim that the Passover was unknown between the eleventh and the late seventh centuries BC, but that it had not been celebrated in Josiah's manner during that time. Though the evidence is sparse, Hezekiah's initiative is best explained by his inheriting some tradition of Passover observance. In the light of the irregularities present on this occasion, that tradition is likely to have owed more to precedent than to scriptural authority, but it was strong enough to convince Hezekiah of the potential spiritual and political impact of Passover.

---

[1] The Chronicler might even have been aware that these kinds of issues, including the date of Passover, were a matter of dispute perhaps not long before his own time (*cf.* the so-called 'Passover papyrus' from the Jewish community at Elephantine, *ANET*, p. 491).

Three brief comments may be made about the character of this Passover. Firstly, it is consistently combined with Unleavened Bread, which is described twice as a 'pilgrimage festival' (vv. 13, 21). The term 'passover' has a double meaning, being the name of a festival (vv. 1, 2, 5), and the chief item on the menu (vv. 15, 17, 18). The two festivals are combined as is usual in the Bible (*cf.* Ex. 12:8; Dt. 16:1–8; 2 Ch. 35:17; Mk. 14:1; Lk. 22:1), against the theory (Williamson) that the main account here concerns Unleavened Bread with later supplementary references to Passover. Secondly, the extension of the festival to a fortnight echoes the temple dedication (*cf.* 2 Ch. 7:8–9), as indicated by the special sense of unrestrained joy on each occasion (vv. 23, 25, 26; 7:10). Thirdly, Hezekiah's actions recall the Davidic-Solomonic period (also ch. 29), of which the link with the temple dedication is but one example. Both kings are mentioned directly in verse 26, and are closely allied with the *all Israel* theme (vv. 1, 5; 31:1). David is associated with the phrase *Beersheba to Dan* (v. 5; *cf.* 1 Ch. 21:2) and the musical *instruments* (v. 21; *cf.* 1 Ch. 23:5; 2 Ch. 7:6; 29:26–27), and Solomon with God's hearing prayer (vv. 18–20, 27; *cf.* 2 Ch. 6:18–42) and the repeated vocabulary of 2 Chronicles 7:14. The following words are all based on that verse, *viz. humble* (v. 11), *pray* (vv. 18, 27), *seek* (v. 19), *turn* (vv. 6, 9), *hear* (vv. 18, 27), and *heal* (v. 20). These references to the past reveal much more than an interest in historical analogy or literary artistry. The God of the exodus and of David and Solomon was a living God, always ready to hear and answer the prayers of those who worshipped him in spirit and in truth.

In terms of the New Testament, two aspects of the Passover stand out. Firstly, Jesus is the ultimate Passover lamb, who by his own body and blood established a new covenant (*cf.* Lk. 22:14–20). Just as Hezekiah's congregation were cleansed and healed, Christians are made clean by their Passover sacrifice, except that Jesus' sacrifice is the ultimate and unrepeatable Passover. Secondly, the benefits of Passover must be received separately by those on whose behalf the sacrifice is offered. One way of doing this is by eating the sacrificial lamb, which is why Christians 'feed on him by faith' at their communion services (*cf.* Jn. 6:53–56). Another is by living in sincerity and truth, based on the analogy of unleavened, that is undefiled, bread (1 Cor. 5:7–8). By these means, the effects of Jesus' final Passover are continually available to all believers.

i. The assembly's decision (30:1–5). A heading (v. 1) introduces the three central themes, that *all Israel* should celebrate a *Passover* in the *temple*. All Israel is represented by *Ephraim and Manasseh*, the two major tribes of the former kingdom of Israel. Though the names of the northern tribes vary throughout the chapter, the emphasis on unity is consistent (*cf.* vv. 10, 11, 18). As this is a heading, the *letters* (v. 1) are the same as those mentioned in verse 6.

The first move towards the Passover is an invitation issued by the *king* and the *assembly* (vv. 2, 4). The assembly is especially important in Chronicles' version of Hezekiah (it occurs nine times in this ch.: vv. 2, 4, 13, 17, 23, 24, 24, 25, 25; *cf.* 29:4, 20, 23, 28, 31, 32; 31:18), and is one symbol of the people's unity. The assembly comprised ordinary people as well as leaders (*cf.* 1 Ch. 13:1–2; Ne. 8:2), though its most significant feature is that the king took 'counsel' (v. 2, NRSV, RSV; 'agreed', REB, NEB, GNB) with the assembly. Kings who consulted in making decisions are invariably approved in Chronicles, in contrast to those with an autocratic style of leadership. This feature is a further link with David and Solomon (*cf.* 1 Ch. 13:1–5; 29:1, 10, 20, for David; 2 Ch. 1:3–5; 6:3, 12, 13 for Solomon; also especially Jehoshaphat, 2 Ch. 20:5, 14, 21).

The decision to hold a Passover in the *second month* (v. 2) is based on Numbers 9:9–13, which provides for anyone who was ceremonially unclean or absent in the first month not to be left out. These reasons are essentially the same as those in verse 3, except that the original individual reference is now extended to the community and the concept of defilement has been widened from physical contact by lay people to cultic impurity by priests. This is a notable development in the interpretation of earlier Scripture, involving an extension of the original application and lay people taking decisions on cultic matters.[1] The *proclamation* (Heb. *qôl*, v. 5) is also based on the Pentateuch, though it was also a feature of Ezra's assembly (Ex. 36:6; Ezr. 10:7; *cf.* 2 Ch. 24:9; 36:22; Ezr. 1:1).

---

[1] See further M. Fishbane, *Biblical Interpretation in Ancient Israel* (Oxford: Clarendon Press, 1985), pp. 154–159.

Even the *large numbers* (v. 5) are evidence of a desire to do *what was written* in Scripture (NIV; 'as prescribed', NRSV, RSV; *cf.* REB, NEB). The context of verse 5 suggests that these numbers reflect participation by people from all over Israel, though it could refer to the centralized nature of the occasion (*cf.* Dt. 16:1–8). However, the description of Yahweh as *God of Israel* and of the land as stretching *from Beersheba to Dan* (*cf.* 1 Ch. 21:22) supports the former view.

ii. Letters of invitation (30:6–12). The proclamation was written down (vv. 6–9) and sent by *couriers* (v. 6a) to 'all Israel and Judah' (REB, NEB, NRSV, RSV), that is, to the remnant of the northern tribes as well as to Hezekiah's kingdom. It was addressed to the *people of Israel* (v. 6b), emphasizing Israel's religious rather than political character. Their current political circumstances were less important than their status as God's people.

Surprisingly, the letters do not mention the Passover, despite an invitation to *come to his sanctuary* (v. 8). Merely 'coming to church', even for a special festival, was not the real issue. Rather, an appeal was made for the people to *return to the LORD* (vv. 6, 9), that is, to enter into a fresh spiritual relationship with God through the Passover. The whole message is a play on the word 'turn' (Heb. *šûḇ*), which also sounds very like the word for 'captors' (Heb. *šôḇîm*). 'Turn' is used with several different nuances. When Israel returns to God in repentance (vv. 6, 9), their exiles will physically return (*come back*) to the Promised Land (v. 9). God will then *turn his face* from them no longer (v. 9) but *turn away* instead his *fierce anger* (v. 8), as he *returns* to them in compassion (v. 6; *cf.* v. 8).

Three further characteristics stand out from the letters. The first is that the present troubles have happened because their *fathers and brothers* have been *unfaithful* (vv. 7, 9, NIV, REB, NEB) to God and *stiff-necked* (v. 8, NIV, NRSV, RSV). Exactly the same was said to the priests and Levites in the previous chapter (29:6), and the language of both passages is typically given as a reason why Israel went into exile (*cf.* 1 Ch. 5:25; 9:1; 2 Ch. 28:19; 36:14). This leads on to the second point, that some of Hezekiah's addressees are assumed to be in exile (v. 9) and others are a 'remnant' in the land (v. 6, NRSV). The latter have become *an object of horror* (v. 7, NIV, REB, NEB; Heb. *šammâ*), a well-known prophetic term associated with the judgment of exile (*e.g.* Je. 25:9, 11, 18; Mi. 6:16; *cf.* 2 Ch. 29:8). Although these descriptions assume the loss of the northern kingdom (*cf.* 2 Ki. 18:7–8), they are also well suited to the conditions of Chronicles' readers. They too were a remnant who needed to turn to God and trust his compassion. Thirdly, frequent quotations from other scriptures are evident, especially in relation to God's character. God's turning towards those who repent, for example, is found in Solomon's dedicatory prayer (*e.g.* 1 Ki. 8:33–34; 2 Ch. 6:24–25; 7:14) and in Jeremiah (Je. 3:22; 15:19; 31:18–19) and Zechariah (Zc. 1:2–6). That he is *gracious and compassionate* (v. 9, NIV, REB, NEB) is one of the most frequent Old Testament confessions of faith (*e.g.* Ex. 34:6; Ps. 103:8; Ne. 9:17, 31), and that he is the *God of Abraham, Isaac, and Israel* (v. 6) recalls his answer to Elijah's prayers (1 Ki. 18:36).

The heart of the message, therefore, is an appeal to *submit to the LORD* (v. 8, REB, NEB, NIV; 'yield', JB, NRSV, RSV) and 'worship' him (v. 8, REB, NEB, GNB; *serve*, NIV, NRSV, RSV). The beginning and end call for Israel's return, stressing that God prefers to see his people face to face rather than turn his back on them (*cf.* vv. 8–9; 29:6). The response was predictably mixed, and many in the pagan north 'laughed and scoffed' (v. 10, JB), but others were receptive (vv. 11–12). More northerners than usual responded in the spirit of 2 Chronicles 7:14 and *humbled themselves* (v. 11), while in the south the *hand of God* gave unexpected *unity* (v. 12).

d. Celebrating the Passover (30:13 – 31:1).
i. Celebrating the festival (30:13–22). The week-long festival of *Unleavened Bread* (vv. 13, 21) is one of the three traditional 'pilgrim-feasts' (REB, NEB; *cf.* Ex. 23:14–17; Dt. 16:16–17; 2 Ch. 8:13). In the Bible it is always associated with Passover, since the latter was held on the first day and unleavened bread was always on the menu at the passover meal. As usual, the *Passover* is the dominant feature (vv. 15–21). The festival as a whole has the following characteristics.

(a) Unusually large numbers, especially the *many people* from the north (v. 18; *cf.* vv. 13, 17). The people as a whole had clearly complied with the requirements of the law (v. 5), and reflected Hezekiah's desire that representatives of all Israel were present (*cf.* v. 1).

(b) Removing sin and impurity. This took place in three

stages. The first is the removal of the *altars* which Ahaz had set up in Jerusalem, with the debris being discarded in the *Kidron Valley* (v. 14; *cf.* 29:16). The second is when the people, especially the priests and Levites, purified themselves (v. 15; *cf.* v. 17). *Consecrated* ('sanctified', NRSV, RSV, JB) really means 'made themselves holy', *i.e.* set themselves apart for God, and involved separation from all forms of uncleanness (*cf.* 1 Ch. 15:12, 14; 2 Ch. 29:5, 15; 31:18). The third stage is the offering of sacrificial *blood*, which was a distinctive feature of Passover. The original smearing of doorposts and lintels (Ex. 12:7, 22–23) is replaced by sprinkling on the altar (v. 16), but the underlying atoning function of this action remains unchanged (*cf.* Ex. 12:13, 23; Nu. 28:22; Ezr. 6:21). A special problem arose with some of the northerners who were ceremonially unclean. As a result, their animals had to be killed by the Levites (v. 17) and Hezekiah prayed for their forgiveness (vv. 18–20). Both actions have special significance. The former brought about a permanent change in the Levites' role, since by Josiah's time it was expected that Levites would kill all the lambs (2 Ch. 35:5–6; *cf.* Ezr. 6:20), whereas previously this was the community leaders' responsibility (*cf.* Ex. 12:6, 21; Dt. 16:5–6). Hezekiah's intercession is one of many significant prayers in Chronicles (*cf. e.g.* 1 Ch. 4:9–10; 5:20; 2 Ch. 14:11; 33:13). This one illustrates two important principles: that God honours prayer requests offered in the spirit of Solomon's dedicatory prayer (6:18–42; 7:12–16) and that prayer can overcome any formal deficiency in religious practice. Hezekiah prays for *pardon* (v. 18), literally, that God would 'make atonement' alongside the people's sacrifice. God's acceptance is indicated by the fact that he *heard* and *healed* the people, fulfilling his promise in 2 Chronicles 7:14. Healing is mentioned specially in Chronicles only in these two verses (though *cf.* 2 Ch. 36:16). Though this verse may assume some physical affliction, more probably it is God's direct answer to the request for forgiveness. This healing is therefore primarily of a spiritual nature, as frequently in the Old Testament (Ps. 41:4; Is. 53:5; Je. 30:17).

(c) Joyful praise. With their sin and uncleanness removed, the people were released into 'great joy' (v. 21, GNB) and *praise* (vv. 21–22). This is a regular feature of worship in Chronicles, and the joy frequently follows special signs of God's forgiving grace (*cf.* 1 Ch. 12:40; 15:25; 29:22; 2 Ch. 29:30). Again, the

Levites have a central role (*cf.* vv. 15–17), this time with their music (v. 21; *cf.* 29:25–27) and in making voluntary *fellowship offerings* (v. 22, NIV; *cf.* 29:31–35; according to NRSV, RSV, GNB, these sacrifices were made by the people). They participated either with 'loud instruments' (NRSV; *cf.* NIV mg., GNB mg.) or, by a slight change in the text, 'with all their might' (JB; *cf.* REB, NEB). Either way, their enthusiasm was not in doubt, nor was their 'good skill' (v. 22, NRSV, RSV, *cf.* GNB; *good understanding*, NIV, *cf.* NEB).

ii. Continuing the blessing (30:23 – 31:1). The ceremony was so successful that it was extended for a second week, as at the temple dedication (v. 23; *cf.* 2 Ch. 7:9–10). The second week continues in the same vein as the first, though with two variations. The large numbers are applied to the amount of offerings rather than to the size of the crowd (v. 24; *cf.* 29:32–25), and the note of *joy* is accentuated (vv. 23, 25, 26). The reason for this deeper joy is that the people had become more aware of their togetherness (v. 25) and of being part of God's long-term purposes (v. 26). To be in God's will always ends in joy, as Jesus himself confirmed (Jn. 15:9–11; Heb. 12:2).

The sense of common purpose is particularly striking, with the *whole assembly* deciding to continue (v. 23). A unique insight into the make-up of the assembly is given in verse 25, which mentions four constituent parts, *viz.* separate assemblies for Judah and for Israel (for the latter, *cf.* 28:14), for priests and Levites and for 'resident aliens' (REB, NEB). The latter could be either the foreigners resettled in Israel by the Assyrians (*cf.* GNB) or an early version of proselytes (Ackroyd). The former is a particularly attractive interpretation, adding an interesting evangelistic dimension to the Passover, but in any case, the presence of foreigners is another example of a return to the spirit of the Mosaic law (*cf.* Nu. 9:14). This is also one of the most comprehensive examples in the Old Testament of the inclusion of non-worshippers of Yahweh among God's people, for neither the northerners nor the resident aliens would have had much accurate knowledge of the ways of the Lord. It is noteworthy too that they seem to be included in Israel's worship before becoming incorporated into its political structures.

The end of the festival saw two further consequences. First,

the people were blessed by the 'Levitical priests' (v. 27, JB).[1]
The blessing was a *prayer* which God heard (*cf.* v. 20), confirming the temple as a genuine house of prayer. It also
illustrates again Israel's return to the principles of the Pentateuch (*cf.* Nu. 6:22–27) and of Solomon (*cf.* 2 Ch. 6:21, 30, 33).
Secondly, the people spontaneously destroyed centres of
pagan worship in the former northern kingdom (*Ephraim and
Manasseh*) as well as Judah (*Judah and Benjamin*). Hezekiah's
previous emphasis on removing the paraphernalia of idol
worship (*cf.* 29:15–19; 30:14; also 2 Ki. 18:22) now became a
popular movement. While 31:1 is loosely based on 2 Kings
18:4, the *Israelites* rather than Hezekiah have become the
subject of the verbs. The same democratic interest was noted
in Chronicles' version of David (*cf.* 1 Ch. 13:1–4; 15:25–28),
and is probably intended in both cases to encourage the
people of the Chronicler's day to restore faithful patterns of
worship for themselves.

e. Reorganizing tithes and offerings (31:2–21).
Hezekiah's
cleansing of the temple (ch. 29) and celebration of the Passover (ch. 30) enabled him to re-establish regular worship. This
involved two further tasks, reorganizing the priests and
Levites (v. 2) and establishing proper financial support for
temple personnel and the system of offerings (vv. 4–19). The
dominant emphasis of chapter 31 falls on the practical giving
of the people, however. Though the king's leadership provided an important stimulus, an effective system of worship
was not possible without full popular involvement.

The apparently routine character of this chapter is decep-
tive, for it deals with two principles of first importance. The
first is that worship cannot be left to the 'professionals'. The
latter must certainly fulfil their God-given roles, but direct
participation by the people is equally crucial (*cf.* 1 Cor. 14:26).
For that reason, it was not only the inhabitants of the towns of
Judah (v. 6) as well as of *Jerusalem* (v. 4) who made their
contributions, but possibly also migrants from the north (vv. 5,
6). However, the most distinctive feature of the people's support is not the fact of it but its generosity. They gave 'in
abundance' (v. 5, NRSV, RSV) and brought *a great amount, a tithe*

---

[1] EVV generally follow the vss in reading 'priests and Levites', though the
Deuteronomic style of MT (*cf.* Dt. 17:9; 18:1; 27:9) is continued in the sections
dealing with the high places (31:1) and the tithes (31:4–8).

of everything (v. 5), with their gifts standing in piles or *heaps* (vv. 6, 8, 9). As a result, Judah enjoyed a double blessing: recognizing that the Lord had *blessed his people* (v. 10), the leaders blessed *the LORD and his people Israel* (v. 8).

The second principle is the care needed to ensure that Israel's worship is carried out 'decently and in order' (*cf.* 1 Cor. 14:40). Good planning and the implementation of adequate supporting structures provide a framework in which wholehearted and meaningful worship can take place. Hezekiah therefore prepared storerooms to receive the gifts, and various officials were appointed to collect and distribute them (vv. 11–19). The key characteristic of this administrative work is that it was done *faithfully* (vv. 12, 15; *cf.* v. 18). The Hebrew word (*'emûnâ*) which this translates is always used in Chronicles of the Levites' carefulness over financial matters (1 Ch. 9:22, 26, 31; 2 Ch. 19:9; 34:12) and illustrates that right attitudes are essential to make any structure function effectively. In this case, the Levites' faithful observance of their duties enabled the maximum number of people to benefit from God's blessing (*cf.* Pr. 28:20; Mt. 25:21, 23).

The divine blessing which forms the climax in this chapter has several distinguishing marks. Firstly, it is the result of Hezekiah's faithfulness to the principles established by David and Solomon. It was they who had originally organized the divisions of priests and Levites (v. 2; *cf.* 1 Ch. 28:13, 21; 2 Ch. 8:14), established the pattern of regular sacrificial worship (vv. 2–3; 1 Ch. 23:31; 2 Ch. 2:4; 8:13), led the way in generosity (v. 3; 1 Ch. 29:2–5; 2 Ch. 7:5), and blessed the people (v. 8; 1 Ch. 16:2; 2 Ch. 6:3). Secondly, it is associated with Hezekiah's wholehearted commitment to God's law (vv. 3, 4, 21). Thirdly, God blesses his people through their own generosity (*cf.* 1 Ch. 29:14–16). Fourthly, God blesses beyond his people's normal expectation (*cf.* 1 Ch. 13:14; 17:27). The sense of unlooked-for bonus is repeated elsewhere in the Bible (*e.g.* Mt. 14:20; 19:29; 2 Cor. 9:8), as one would expect from God's own promise (Mal. 3:8–10). God's blessing is never granted on a *quid pro quo* basis, as a reward or a right, for God can never be bound by any human action. The real guarantee of God's overflowing love is his own character.

i. Heaps of gifts (31:2–10). The first stage in restoring regular worship was to appoint the *priests* and *Levites* to their *divisions*

(v. 2). This represented a return to the system originally set up by David (1 Ch. 28:13, 21; *cf.* 1 Ch. 24:3; 26:1) and Solomon (2 Ch. 8:14), but which had obviously been allowed to lapse. Supervision of the priests and Levites was ultimately the responsibility of the Davidic house. It was all part of the continuing task of building God's house, which was a mere empty shell if the physical building was not filled daily with the sound of praise.

It was the priests' *duty* to offer *burnt offerings* and 'peace offerings' (v. 2, RSV). The former basically represented worship offered completely to God. The latter was character-ized chiefly by a fellowship or communion meal, though it is particularly difficult to translate. It is variously rendered as *fellowship offerings* (NIV, GNB), 'shared-offerings' (REB, NEB), 'offerings of well-being' (NRSV), or 'communion sacrifice' (JB). The combination of these two types of sacrifice symbolized restoration with God and with fellow human beings.

The Levites' task was to *minister* in *thanks and praise* (v. 2; *cf.* 1 Ch. 16:4; 23:30–31; 2 Ch. 8:14). The actual Hebrew expres-sion is unusual, for two reasons. Firstly, the literal meaning is that they gave praise *at the gates* (NIV, REB). More probably it means 'within' the gates (JB), rather than 'minister' in the gates (NEB, NRSV, RSV), which involves a change of word order. The second feature is the final phrase, literally, 'the camp of the LORD' (NRSV, RSV, *cf.* JB, generally paraphrased in EVV, as in *the LORD's dwelling* (NIV) or 'the various parts of the Temple' (GNB; *cf.* REB, NEB). This expression belongs to the period of the Tent (*cf.* Nu. 2:17; 1 Ch. 9:18), and, as elsewhere in Chron-icles, illustrates faithfulness to Mosaic principles (*cf. e.g.* 2 Ch. 4–5).

The theme of verses 3–19 is that adequate support was vital to regular worship. This support was provided first by the king (v. 3) and then the people (vv. 4–7). Hezekiah's gener-osity closely mirrors David's (1 Ch. 29:2–5), though the basic pattern of royal patronage also appears in Ezekiel's vision of the restored temple (Ezk. 45:17, 22; 46:2).

The pattern of daily, weekly, monthly, and annual offerings is often repeated in Chronicles (v. 3; *cf.* 1 Ch. 23:31; 2 Ch. 2:4; 8:13; 13:11), and was clearly of great importance. It indicates that God must be worshipped at all times, and that worship was not to be subject to the whims of human circumstances and emotions. The underlying authority for this was *written in the Law of the* LORD (v. 3; *cf.* Nu. 28–29), a phrase which was often quoted in the context of reforming sacrificial worship (1 Ch. 6:49; 16:40; 2 Ch. 8:13; 12:18).

Though various groups of people brought their own contributions (vv. 4–6), the exact identity of those who contributed is disputed. The inhabitants of *Jerusalem* (v. 4) were certainly included, as were those who lived in the *towns of Judah* (v. 6), but who the 'Israelites' (vv. 5, 6, REB, NEB; 'people of Israel', NRSV, RSV) were is less certain.[1] The term is used most often of anyone who belonged to the covenant people. If the same is so here, those in verse 5 are presumably the same as the Jerusalemites (as v. 4) and those in verse 6 are some or all of the inhabitants of the Judean towns. Alternatively, verse 5 could refer to representatives from both sides of the old north–south divide, and verse 6 to people who had moved south from the old northern kingdom.

The speed and size of the giving are highlighted. As soon as the order went out, contributions flowed 'in abundance' (v. 5, NRSV, RSV). They brought the *firstfruits* of 'all the produce of the land' (v. 5, *cf.* REB, NEB) and *a tithe of everything* (v. 5), piling their gifts into 'countless heaps' (v. 6).[2] The *firstfruits* were the priests' prerogative (Nu. 18:12–13) but the *tithe*, whether of crops and fruit (v. 5) or the herds (v. 6), was presented to the Levites (Nu. 18:21; *cf.* Lv. 27:30–33). The *tithe of the holy* or *dedicated things* (v. 6) probably refers to gifts made by the Levites to the priests from what they themselves had received. 'Holy things', which can refer to various kinds of offerings, are tithed in this way in Numbers 18:32.[3] If this view is correct, some Levites in their settlements are included among the inhabitants of Judean towns (v. 6; *cf.* 1 Ch. 6:55–60, 65; 9:14–16).

All the gifts were ultimately regarded as *dedicated* or consecrated *to the* LORD rather than to fellow human beings (v. 6). This spiritual commitment is the real explanation of the people's generosity, in addition to the fact that the priests

---

[1] Heb. has *bᵉnê yiśrā'ēl* in both vv., though NIV translates them differently and GNB paraphrases v. 6. The proposal to omit 'and Judah' (v. 6; Williamson, Curtis and Madsen, *etc.*) is without textual support and assumes that 'Israelite' must mean the same as in v. 5.

[2] The repetition in Heb. of 'heaps' intensifies the expression to the highest degree (*cf.* GK #123e; also Ex. 8:10 [MT] = 8:14 [EVV], though that verse has a different word for 'heaps').

[3] This interpretation also avoids the need to omit 'tithe', as RSV, Rudolph, *etc.*

devoted themselves to God's *Law* (v. 4). This latter expression is unique, and really means to hold firmly to God's word, which in this context applies particularly to the subject of worship (*cf.* vv. 2–3). Such devotion would have been a helpful model for Chronicles' readers, who tended to neglect the needs of temple worship, especially the tithes for the Levites (Ne. 10:32–39; 13:10–13; Mal. 3:8–9; *cf.* Dt. 12:19; 14:27).

The people's commitment surprised even Hezekiah (v. 9), who discovered from the *chief priest* that the priests and Levites had been blessed with more than enough. The chief priest, however, saw this as evidence of God at work. God typically provides beyond human expectation (*cf.* Ps. 23:6; 1 Ch. 13:14), for undeserved bounty is at the heart of the gospel (Jn. 10:10; 2 Cor. 9:15). The fact that *a great amount was left over* (v. 10) is an interesting anticipation of Jesus' feeding of the five and four thousand (Mt. 14:20; 15:37; *etc.*).

The chief priest's testimony (v. 10) sums up the whole chapter, resonating as it does so with other parts of Scripture. Acts of sacrificial giving towards the Tent (Ex. 36:2–7) and the temple (1 Ch. 29:6–9; 2 Ch. 24:8–12) are recalled, as is David's explanation that all human giving is merely a response to God's greater gift (1 Ch. 29:16). Underlying all these examples is the most basic principle of worship, that men and women can give to God only because he has first given far more to them (*cf.* 1 Jn. 4:19). This applies to the physical gifts and to praise and blessing, for the Israelites *praised* and *blessed* the Lord (v. 8) only because he had first *blessed his people* (v. 10).

This *Azariah* the chief priest is otherwise unknown apart from in verse 13, though the name was common in his family (*cf.* 1 Ch. 6:9–14), which went back to *Zadok* in the time of David and Solomon. For the king's priestly act of blessing the people, compare the examples of David (1 Ch. 16:2) and Solomon (2 Ch. 6:3).

ii. Faithful distribution (31:11–19). The gifts are distributed to the priestly and Levitical families in various stages.

(a) They were placed first in the temple *storerooms* (vv. 11–13). These were located either around the main building (*cf.* 1 Ch. 28:11) or near the gates (*cf.* 1 Ch. 9:26; 26:15, 17; Ne. 12:25), where they were most naturally supervised by gatekeepers (1 Ch. 9:26). A distinction seems to be made between the various types of gifts, the *tithes* for the Levites and the *contributions* and *dedicated* or consecrated things for the priests (v. 12). The *contributions* seem to be the same as the firstfruits (v. 5). In over-all charge is the priest, here called *the official in charge of the temple of God* (v. 13; *cf.* v. 10; also 1 Ch. 9:11; 2 Ch. 35:8; Ne. 11:11).

(b) Gifts were then distributed, first to those *priests* living in outlying *towns* whose names were not apparently recorded in genealogical lists (vv. 14–15). The *keeper of the East Gate* seems to have been the senior gatekeeper (*cf.* 1 Ch. 9:18; 26:14). The people's gifts are *freewill offerings* (v. 14), that is, given over and above what was actually required in the law.

(c) Three further groups of people whose names were listed in *genealogical records* then received gifts (vv. 16–19). First the *males* who performed regular duties in the temple (v. 16), then the priestly and Levitical families living in Jerusalem (vv. 17–18), and finally the priestly families outside Jerusalem (v. 19). The latter were the registered counterparts of those mentioned in verses 14–15. Fuller details are unfortunately unavailable, but two emphases stand out. One is the completeness of the work. Nobody was omitted, not even the youngest (vv. 16, 18), those who lived at a distance (vv. 15, 19), or those who were unregistered (v. 15). The other emphasis is the faithfulness of those who gave and received (vv. 15, 18). This even included faithful consecration by the priests (v. 18), in sharp contrast with their previous casual attitude (*cf.* 29:5, 34).

One may only guess at what lies behind the actual ages of those involved. Perhaps children began to be set apart for priesthood as early as the age of *three* (v. 16), while the Levites took on full responsibilities at the age of twenty (v. 17). The latter figure varies throughout Old Testament times (*cf.* Nu. 4:3; 8:24; 1 Ch. 23:3, 24), presumably because of the realities of the labour supply.

How long these activities took is not recorded. The collection was completed in five months (v. 7), and, though it may be assumed that the initial distribution was carried out quickly, the Chronicler probably intends in the light of verse 2 to give the impression of a regular rather than a unique practice. Certainly, in Israel as well as the church, adequate ministerial leadership cannot be sustained without regular structured support by the people, with the tithe as a minimum requirement (*cf.* Mt. 23:23).

iii. Hezekiah's prosperity (31:20–21). This summary of chapters 29–31 is loosely based on 2 Kings 18:5–7a. The whole account of Hezekiah's restoration of temple worship has followed the basic structure of 2 Kings 18:1b–7a, into which the Chronicler has integrated extensive additions. Even parallel passages such as this, however, reveal the Chronicler's distinctive style and vocabulary. One characteristic emphasis is that at various stages a note is made that work on the temple was properly completed and its services restored (*cf.* 2 Ch. 7:11; 8:16; 24:13–14; 29:35). No doubt the author had in mind the almost fatal delay in the construction of the second temple (Ezr. 3:1 – 6:22).

Hezekiah finished his task because he *sought* God *wholeheartedly* (v. 21). In this, he complied with David's advice (*cf.* 1 Ch. 22:19; 28:9) and followed the pattern of other kings (*cf.* 2 Ch. 15:17; 22:9; *cf.* 2 Ch. 11:16; 19:3). To seek God in this way inevitably meant giving temple worship first priority, but it also affected his whole life. As a result, Hezekiah *prospered*, as had several of his predecessors.[1] Though the path to prosperity involved Hezekiah in disappointment (2 Ch. 30:10), severe crisis (32:1–23), and coming to terms with the reality of his sin (32:25–26), God never fails to bless those who look to him (*cf.* Ps. 1:1–3; 32:1–2; Mt. 5:3–12; 19:29).

iv. God saves Judah through Hezekiah's faith (32:1–33)
'So the LORD saved Hezekiah' (32:22).
32:1 – *cf.* 2 Kings 18:13; Isaiah 36:1
32:9–10 – *cf.* 2 Kings 18:17–19; Isaiah 36:2–4
32:12 – *cf.* 2 Kings 18:22; Isaiah 36:7
32:13–14 – *cf.* 2 Kings 18:35; Isaiah 36:20
32:15 – *cf.* 2 Kings 18:29; Isaiah 36:14
32:16 – *cf.* 2 Kings 18:27–28a; Isaiah 36:12–13a
32:17 – *cf.* 2 Kings 18:33, 35; Isaiah 36:18, 20
32:18 – *cf.* 2 Kings 18:28a; Isaiah 36:13a
32:19 – *cf.* 2 Kings 19:18; Isaiah 37:19
32:20 – *cf.* 2 Kings 19:15a; Isaiah 37:15
32:21 – *cf.* 2 Kings 19:35–37; Isaiah 37:36–38
32:24 – *cf.* 2 Kings 20:1–2; Isaiah 38:1–2
32:32–33 – *cf.* 2 Kings 20:20–21

---

[1] *Cf.* 1 Ch. 22:11, 13; 29:23; 2 Ch. 7:11; 13:12; 14:7; 18:11, 14; 20:20; 24:20; 32:30.

Hezekiah's efforts to restore faithful worship (chs. 29–31) forms the background to Chronicles' version of Hezekiah's confrontation with *Sennacherib* of Assyria (vv. 1–23). Though this was one of the most important events in the history of the monarchy (*cf.* 2 Ki. 18:13 – 19:37), what Chronicles describes is no ordinary military battle. Neither the Assyrian nor the Israelite army plays any part in what is effectively a war of words. A speech by Hezekiah (vv. 6b–8) is followed by spoken and written threats by Assyrian officials (vv. 9–19). Hezekiah and the prophet Isaiah then turn to prayer (v. 20), and only after that does any action take place (v. 21).

The format is the result of the unusual way the Chronicler treats his source material. He clearly expects the reader to be familiar with 2 Kings 18–20, but, whereas the Chronicler normally adapts sections of earlier Scripture, here everything has been simplified and summarized in order to concentrate on the theme of Yahweh's supremacy. The number of speeches has been drastically reduced, an important prophecy is omitted (2 King 19:20–34), and the intricate progress of negotiations has been cast aside. Even the historical events are of secondary importance, and the well-known problem in 2 Kings 18–19 of trying to harmonize two contrasting versions of Sennacherib's invasion do not recur. The Chronicler simply envisages a single Assyrian campaign, which is to be dated to 701 BC.

The key question is whether Yahweh can *save* or *deliver* his people. The underlying Hebrew word (*haṣṣîl*) is mentioned eight times (vv. 10–17), with the Assyrians constantly challenging any deity to counteract the apparently superior power of the Assyrian army. Yahweh is assumed to be a god just like any other, and the Assyrians attempt to undermine the Israelites' *confidence* (v. 10) by casting doubt on his effectiveness. The turning-point comes when Judah's leaders pray (v. 20). Yahweh listens to their desperate plea and saves his people (v. 22), with Hezekiah as no more than a spectator. It is therefore Yahweh who really rules in Israel, and the chapter aims to stimulate faith in Israel's God rather than admiration for Israel's king.

This message is not new in Chronicles, and clearly needed repetition as far as the Chronicler's readers were concerned (*cf.* 2 Ch. 14:9–15; 20:1–30). Though not under military threat, they desperately needed reminding that God could deliver them from foreign domination. It was one thing to accept in general terms that God was in control and quite another to believe that he could actually intervene in their lives as their Saviour. The writers of the New Testament were equally convinced that God was Lord and Saviour, and that it was essential to be committed to both aspects of God's character. To lose sight of one is to become blind to both. Faith in God meant trusting him to preserve them in the kingdom as well as bring them into it. Paul, for example, believed that, through prayer, God would go on delivering him because he had already done so in the past (2 Cor. 1:8–11). Though being a Christian often means suffering and persecution, God still works for good in every experience of life, and the New Testament has many testimonies to God's saving power (Acts 12:6–19; 16:16–40; 27:9 – 28:10; Rom. 8:28, 35–39).

a. Hezekiah defends (32:1–8). 'These things' (v. 1, NRSV, RSV) refers to Hezekiah's temple reforms (chs. 29–31), which are characterized as 'acts of faithfulness' (v. 1, NRSV, RSV; *cf.* 'faithfully', 31:12, 15, 18). The fact that these are followed by the plan of Sennacherib (705–689 BC) to *conquer* Judah (v. 1) brings out the contrast between the two episodes. Where Hezekiah had acted faithfully, the Assyrian king had no regard at all for Yahweh, and conflict was inevitable. These events are also a reminder that even for leaders who trust God, things do not always go smoothly, and it is surely significant that Asa and Jehoshaphat as well as Hezekiah suffered acts of foreign aggression after carrying out acts of piety (*cf.* 2 Ch. 14:9–11; 20:1–13; notice the repetition of *after this* or *these things* from 20:1). The genuineness of faith often emerges only in one's reaction to trouble.

Sennacherib's invasion is reported in detail in extant Assyrian records, where he claimed to have captured forty-six Judean towns, overrunning practically the whole of Judah outside Jerusalem (*cf.* 2 Ki. 18:13). His *thinking* about conquest (v. 1) refers not to unfulfilled intentions, but rather to the fact that this was what he had determined to do. The phrase (lit.) 'set his face for war against Jerusalem' (v. 2) marks the climax of his campaign, though it also forms a fascinating contrast with Jesus' determination to 'set his face to go to Jerusalem' (Lk. 9:51, NRSV, RSV) for a totally different purpose.

Hezekiah's reaction, like that of wise kings before him, was to *consult* with others (*cf. e.g.* 1 Ch. 13:1; 2 Ch. 20:21). As a result, they decided on a two-pronged response. The first involved three practical steps, to prevent the Assyrians gaining access to Jerusalem's water supply (vv. 3b–4; *cf.* v. 30), to repair the city walls (v. 5a), and to reorganize and re-equip the army (vv. 5b–6a). Jerusalem's water supply was vulnerable to any attack, since it was totally dependent on two springs, Gihon in the Kidron valley (v. 30) and En-Rogel two miles to the south. The *stream that flowed through the land* (v. 4) is probably a local watercourse (*cf.* JB) supplying parts of the city. Mention of the stream and the springs may well be a double allusion, to God's special provision for Jerusalem (*cf.* Ps. 46:4) and to Sennacherib's boast to have personally dried up Egypt's streams (2 Ki. 19:24; Is. 37:25). Reference to the *king*s (plural) *of Assyria* (v. 4) also suggests that Sennacherib was seen as a typical foreign invader and an enemy of God. Part of a *wall* (v. 5) which could well be Hezekiah's has been uncovered on the western hill. At seven metres thick, it is the thickest Iron Age wall known in Palestine, and was presumably designed to withstand powerful Assyrian battering rams. It was constructed from demolished houses and seems to have enclosed a reservoir of water (*cf.* Is. 22:8–11), possibly brought from Gihon via Hezekiah's famous tunnel.[1] The 'Millo' (v. 5, REB, NEB, *etc.*; *supporting terraces*, NIV) was part of the old city of David, and the mention of repairs in this area provides a further link with David and Solomon (1 Ch. 11:8; 1 Ki. 11:27).

Hezekiah's second response is to encourage the *military commanders* (v. 6) *not* to *be afraid* of the invaders but to trust in God (vv. 7–8). He clearly shared Isaiah's view that the danger of trusting in military defences alone was very real (Is. 22:8–11). The quality of faith is marked by the extent to which a person's attitude is focused on God. Physical resources can be of real assistance where they are available, but they are no substitute for relying on God. Hezekiah's message concentrates on rejecting fear and accepting the difference between human and divine strength. His answer to the power of fear is to repeat a series of four imperatives previously issued by Moses, Joshua (Dt. 31:7–8, 23; Jos. 1:6–9), and David (1 Ch. 22:13,

---

[1] *Cf.* N. Avigad, 'Excavations in the Jewish Quarter of the Old City of Jerusalem, 1970', *IEJ* 20, 1970, pp. 129–140; A. Mazar, *Archaeology of the Land of the Bible* (New York: Doubleday, 1990), p. 420.

28:20), *viz. Be strong and courageous. Do not be afraid or discouraged* (v. 7). The reason for his confidence is that he is utterly convinced about the supremacy of his God in every situation. He again appeals to Scripture to support his point, especially the prophets, though the key phrase, 'there is one greater with us than with him' (v. 7, NRSV), is based on 2 Kings 6:16. As verse 8 makes clear, the question is not simply who has the greater *power* (NIV, GNB) or numbers (REB, NEB), but which God is intrinsically greater. In fact, Sennacherib has no divine support, for he relies entirely on an *arm of flesh* (v. 8; *cf.* Je. 17:5), that is, mere human strength. Israel on the other hand, can count on God's being *with us* (*cf.* Is. 7:14; 31:1, 3) and being ready to *help us* (*cf.* 1 Ch. 12:18; 15:26; 2 Ch. 14:10; contrast 2 Ch. 28:23).

It is not surprising that the people 'were encouraged by' (NRSV), literally, 'leaned on', Hezekiah's words (*cf.* 2 Ki. 18:13, where the same word reappears). Many were clearly afraid and tempted to rely on the defences they had constructed. The fact that they met the Assyrians by an aqueduct (2 Ki. 18:17–18) suggests they had to endure fresh threats even while working on the water supply (2 Ki. 18:19–37; 2 Ch. 32:9–15). However, under Hezekiah's leadership unity and faith both increased. They joined together as a 'great many people' (v. 4, NRSV, RSV) to *help* the king (v. 3) before assembling for their encouragement in one of the city's squares (v. 5; *cf.* 29:4).

b. Sennacherib attacks (32:9–19). The speech by Assyrian officers (vv. 10–15) is in reality a masterly combination of several addresses (2 Ki. 18:10–25, 27–35; 19:9–13). The variety of arguments in the original speeches has been reduced to a single theme, whose significance is further underlined by the Chronicler's own editorial summaries (vv. 16, 18–19). Also, Chronicles has supplied a résumé of several *letters* sent to Hezekiah by Sennacherib (v. 17), even though in Kings only one is mentioned without any precise indication as to its contents (2 Ki. 19:14–19).

It is not entirely clear from Chronicles alone where the Assyrian army was located. The 'large army' (2 Ki. 18:17) which accompanied the officers to Jerusalem has been omitted, creating the possible impression that the Assyrian forces remained at *Lachish* (v. 9) and that no siege took place at

Jerusalem (Childs, Williamson; though *cf.* v. 10).[1] However, since it is clear elsewhere in the chapter that the Chronicler assumes his readers are aware of the detailed version of events in Kings, it would be odd if the same were not true here.

The central question is whether Yahweh can rescue his people in their hour of need or whether he is as ineffective as the gods of Assyria's previous defeated opponents. The key phrase, *deliver you from my hand*, based on 2 Kings 18:30, 32, 35, is constantly repeated as a direct challenge to the people's *confidence* (v. 10) in the Lord. Sennacherib's aim was to undermine the object of Israel's trust, which is all the more interesting in that trust is also a common theme in Assyrian historical inscriptions. The Assyrians employ two main arguments. The first is that Hezekiah must have displeased Yahweh by destroying so many of his altars (vv. 11–12). Detailed knowledge of the internal affairs of other countries is often paralleled in contemporary Assyrian letters. The Assyrians are clearly aware of Hezekiah's policy to centralize worship long before Josiah (2 Ch. 34–36), though their neutral stance indicates it was not seen as an anti-Assyrian move. More importantly from the Chronicler's point of view was that this amounted to opposition to Hezekiah's faithfulness to God (chs. 29–31).

The Assyrians' second strategy is to appeal to history (vv. 13–15). The victories by Sennacherib's predecessors (*my fathers*, vv. 13, 14, 15) showed how impotent were the gods of their defeated foes. Sennacherib in contrast boasts that his achievements have been won not by Assyria's deities but by *my hand* (vv. 13, 14, 15, 17). The Chronicler has summarized his source extensively at this point, omitting not only the names of foreign gods (2 Ki. 18:34; 19:12), but also an offer of peace and plenty in Assyria for anyone who wished to surrender (2 Ki. 18:31–32; *cf.* the mention of *hunger and thirst* in v. 11). All this, however, merely supports his accusation that Hezekiah is deceiving and misleading the people by ignoring reality (vv. 11, 15).

Chronicles' editorial summaries confirm that these accusations were repeated (v. 16) and delivered in plain *Hebrew* (v. 18; lit. 'Judean'). This is the only direct reference in the Old

---

[1] The translation 'fortress of Jerusalem' (v. 10, Myers) instead of the usual 'under siege' (EVV) is most unlikely, since Heb. *māṣôr* is never applied to Jerusalem in this way.

Testament to the Hebrew language (though *cf.* Is. 19:18), which is used rather than the international language of Aramaic (2 Ki. 18:26) in order to *terrify* (v. 18) the people. The ultimate ignominy, however, is that Yahweh should be placed on a par with all other deities. Religious pluralism is simply inconsistent with biblical faith, since other gods are merely 'the work of human hands' (v. 19, NRSV). The Assyrians had dealt Yahweh the final *insult* (v. 17), the Hebrew term for which is central to the story of David and Goliath (1 Sa. 17:10, 25, 26, 36, 45) as well as to the Kings account (2 Ki. 19:4, 16, 22, 23). Ironically, the fate of Sennacherib's army was just as sudden and complete as that of the former Philistine hero (v. 21).

c. The LORD saves (32:20–23).

The *prayer* of Hezekiah and Isaiah (v. 20) and God's answer (v. 21) are much shorter than in 2 Kings 19, which includes the content of Hezekiah's praying and Isaiah's prediction of Sennacherib's downfall (2 Ki. 19:15–34; Isaiah's prayer is only implied in 2 Ki. 19:4). The Chronicler's emphasis is on the faithfulness of God in answering prayer, as being yet another example of the effectiveness of the principles of 2 Chronicles 6–7 (*cf.* v. 24 and *e.g.* 2 Ch. 20:4–12; 30:18–20; 33:13). The word *heaven* particularly recalls the language of Solomon's prayer, and the circumstances of 2 Chronicles 6:24–25.

God's immediate answer is to send an *angel* (v. 21). Though earlier in Chronicles an angel acted as God's agent of judgment (1 Ch. 21:12–30), this one undertakes the equally important role of being sent by God as a rescuer (*cf.* Pss. 34:7; 91:11; Mt. 4:6, *etc.*). Some of the details of Assyria's calamity are omitted from Kings, especially the casualty figures which have caused modern (and ancient?) readers so much difficulty (2 Ki. 19:35–37). Instead, Chronicles concentrates on the link between prayer and answer. The latter is in two parts, since, though Sennacherib's army returned home almost immediately, Sennacherib's death twenty years later in 681 BC is also part of God's response. To look for answers to prayer only in the short term is often to miss what God is doing. The murder of Sennacherib is confirmed in Babylonian and Assyrian inscriptions, though only one son is mentioned there by name.[1]

---

[1] See especially *ANET*, p. 289; A. K. Grayson, *Assyrian and Babylonian Chronicles* (Locust Valley: Augustin, 1975), p. 81:34–35; S. Parpola, in B. Alster (ed.), *Death in Mesopotamia* (Copenhagen: Akademisk Forlag, 1980), pp. 171–182.

God's part in the king's death is also indicated by the use of several phrases from the Psalms. There God's enemies are repulsed by angels and put to 'shame' (v. 21, RSV; *disgrace*, NIV, NRSV, *etc.*; *cf.* especially Pss. 34:4–6; 35:4–6), and God scoffs at rulers who oppose him and his *servant* (v. 16; *cf.* Ps. 2:2).

Chronicles confirms that God had *saved* his people (v. 22). Salvation in Chronicles usually has the sense of military victory, and is very often employed in a summarizing fashion (1 Ch. 11:14; 18:6, 13; 2 Ch. 20:9). It is also used more widely in the Bible as an umbrella word for God's intervention in a variety of circumstances (*e.g.* Acts 27:20; 2 Cor. 1:10–11). Such experiences are also often corporate, in the New Testament as well as the Old (*e.g.* Acts 2:47; 1 Cor. 1:18; 2 Cor. 2:15). God's salvation is also specific: *from the hand of Sennacherib* (v. 22) contrasts directly with *from my hand* (vv. 13, 14, 15). 'His enemies' (v. 22) has been added in most EVV, but, though this is a reasonable suggestion, MT simply has 'all (others)' (*cf.* NIV). Mention of *rest* (NIV mg.) on every side follows LXX (v. 22, NRSV, RSV; 'peace', GNB, JB), and is consistent with 1 Chronicles 22:9; 2 Chronicles 14:5–7, *etc.*, though MT actually has 'guided, led'. Foreign recognition of Hezekiah is the Chronicler's typical way of expressing God's follow-up to victory (*cf.* 1 Ch. 14:17; 2 Ch. 9:23–24; 17:10–11; 20:29; 26:8).

d. Hezekiah's successes and failures (32:24–33). This comparatively long concluding section of Hezekiah's reign lists several other achievements, and does not spare his blushes. It really comprises four brief paragraphs.

i. Hezekiah's prayers answered (32:24–26). After the success of Hezekiah's praying in verse 20, two further examples combine to illustrate different ways in which God answers prayer. They are taken from two separate incidents in 2 Kings 20:1–19, both of them probably dating from 705–701 BC, that is, before the events of verses 1–23. The first concerns an unidentified life-threatening illness from which Hezekiah was miraculously and suddenly healed (v. 24; *cf.* 2 Ki. 20:1–11; Is. 38:1–22). This is a comparatively rare case in the Old Testament of a healing miracle, though as here such events often involve prophets (*cf. e.g.* Ex. 15:22–26; Nu. 21:7–9; 1 Ki. 17:17–24; 2 Ki. 4:8–41). The *sign* refers to the movement of a shadow contrary to the laws of physics (2 Ki. 20:8–11; Is. 38:7–8, 22). The second incident concerns a prayer of repentance rather than one for healing (vv. 25–26; *cf.* 2 Ki. 20:12–19; Is. 39:1–8). Hezekiah had incurred God's *wrath* by issuing a foolish invitation to Babylonian *envoys* (vv. 25, 26; *cf.* v. 31). *Pride* was at the root of his problem, but though the Hebrew expression, literally, 'his heart was lifted up', was also used of Uzziah (*cf.* 2 Ch. 26:16), Hezekiah's reaction was exactly the opposite. He and the people 'humbled themselves' (GNB; *cf.* NRSV, RSV; *repented*, NIV), a term that is almost the central theme of 2 Chronicles 29–36.[1] This was sufficient to avert God's anger, even though Hezekiah's motives were not entirely pure (2 Ki. 20:19; Is. 38:8). The punishment was delayed until more than a century later (2 Ki. 20:16–18; Is. 38:5–7).

Both incidents illustrate God's faithfulness to his promise about prayer (2 Ch. 7:14; *cf.* vv. 20–21). What is more, Chronicles seems to emphasize God's gift of healing to Hezekiah as well as that of forgiveness. Hezekiah had already had one prayer answered in this area (2 Ch. 30:18–20), and the Chronicler's inclusion of verse 24 may well have been motivated by a further promise to heal in 2 Kings 20:5.

ii. Hezekiah's wealth (32:27–30a). Riches and honour (Heb. *'ōšer wᵉḵāḇôḏ*; 'wealth and fame', REB, NEB) are regularly combined in Chronicles, almost invariably as visible signs of divine blessing, as with David (1 Ch. 29:28), Solomon (2 Ch. 1:11, 12; 9:22; *cf.* 1 Ki. 3:13), and Jehoshaphat (2 Ch. 17:5; 18:1). However, because they are properly divine qualities (1 Ch. 29:12), they are to be regarded not as rights but as what God has *given* (v. 29; *cf.* Ec. 6:2; Pr. 22:4). Such gifts are often elsewhere linked with the gift of wisdom (Pr. 3:16; 8:18). Hezekiah's wealth comprised various kinds of *valuables* (v. 27; 'costly objects', NRSV), *buildings* (v. 28), large *flocks and herds* (v. 29), and water engineering projects (v. 30a). The last clearly includes the Siloam tunnel, especially as *outlet* (Heb. *môṣā'*) is also found in the tunnel inscription.[2] This work is certainly connected with that in verses 3–4, and probably also with the building of a new wall (v. 5), and all of it was associated with an

[1] See 2 Ch. 30:11; 33:12, 23; 34:27; 36:12; *cf.* also 2 Ch. 7:14; 12:6, 7, 12.
[2] J. C. L. Gibson, *Textbook of Syrian Semitic Inscriptions,* I (Oxford: Clarendon Press, 1971), pp. 21–23.

increase in Jerusalem's population under Hezekiah and a westward expansion of the city.

iii. Hezekiah's successes and failures (32:30b–31). *Succeeded* is the same word in Hebrew as that which EVV usually translate 'prospered' in 31:21 (see comment there for further references). Here, however, it both summarizes verses 27–30a, and forms a contrast with the incident of the Babylonian *envoys* (v. 31; 'ambassadors', GNB). Though the latter issue has been mentioned in verses 25–26, its interpretation is now taken further. *God left him* implies divine judgment, as is normal when God is the subject of the Hebrew verb *'āzaḇ* (*cf.* 2 Ch. 12:5; 15:2; 24:20, where it is often translated 'abandon, forsake'). This is confirmed by the mention of God's wrath in verse 25, though the cases of David (1 Ch. 21:7) and Rehoboam (2 Ch. 12:5) show that God's judgment was neither irrevocable nor permanent. The reference to God's testing (v. 31) also implies a degree of openness about this judgment. When God wants to *know everything that was in his heart*, this does not mean that God is ignorant, for he knows every heart (1 Ch. 29:17; 2 Ch. 6:30; Ps. 94:11). Rather, he wishes to 'make [something] known' (*cf.* Gn. 18:21; Dt. 8:2), that is, to provide an opportunity for people to show heartfelt repentance. God tests in order to refine, to stimulate repentance and to deepen faith (*cf.* Gn. 22:1; Ex. 20:20; Dt. 8:16). This positive aim separates God's testing from Satan's temptations, for the devil merely incites (1 Ch. 21:1; Jb. 2:3) in order to devour and destroy (Mt. 4:1–10; 1 Pet. 5:8). God's purpose is also to be distinguished from the curiosity of the Babylonians, who were only attracted by what seemed to them to be the latest astrological novelty.

iv. Sources for Hezekiah (32:32–33). *Acts of devotion* (v. 32; 'works of piety', REB, NEB) is apparently a post-exilic expression (*cf.* 2 Ch. 35:26; Ne. 13:14) which covers not only Hezekiah's religious reformation (de Vries) but everything associated with his 'devotion to the LORD' (GNB). As frequently in Chronicles, further information is available from a prophetic source included in a historical work (v. 32; *cf.* 2 Ch. 16:11; 20:34). The *vision of the prophet Isaiah* is very similar to the title of the biblical book of Isaiah (1:1), and it is possible that the compilers of both Isaiah and Chronicles were dependent on the same source. As with other kings approved in Chronicles, Hezekiah's burial was accorded special *honour* (v. 33; *cf.* 2 Ch. 16:14; 35:25). This was possibly marked by a prominent location in the royal cemetery (Rudolph), on the 'ascent' (NRSV, RSV) or *hill* (NIV).

G. Three kings and repentance (33:1 – 36:1)

i. Manasseh (33:1–20)

'In his distress he sought the favour of the LORD his God and humbled himself greatly before the God of his fathers' (33:12).

33:1–10a – *cf.* 2 Kings 21:1–10a
33:18–20 *cf.* 2 Kings 21:17–18

The events of chapter 33 are surprising, for two main reasons. The first is that this account appears to contradict 2 Kings 21, which portrays Manasseh as the worst ruler to sit on David's throne. Here, however, he becomes a reformed character after experiencing conversion in exile (vv. 11–16), though neither his deportation to Babylon nor his religious encounter is even hinted at in the earlier passage. Secondly, nothing in the context leads the reader to expect either the fact or the extent of Manasseh's conversion. Having been more committed to idolatry than any of his predecessors (v. 9), and having rejected severe warnings from the Lord (v. 10), change seems out of the question.

Manasseh's conversion is clearly crucial to this chapter, given its central position and its use of typical Chronicles expressions. However, it has to be appreciated that both Chronicles and Kings have been extremely selective in summarizing Manasseh's fifty-five-year reign, and that their aims are rather different from each other. Manasseh illustrates one of central themes of Chronicles, that God can fulfil his promise of restoration in 7:12–16 to the repentant even in the most extreme circumstances. 2 Kings 21 on the other hand, focuses on the relationship between the depth of Manasseh's sins and the certainty of exile. In other words, where Chronicles concentrates on Manasseh's personal reactions and the implications for his own reign, Kings takes a long-term view.

Careful examination reveals that these contrasting approaches are not contradictory. The Chronicler is fully aware of the judgment prophecy in 2 Kings 21:10–15, which he summarizes in verse 10: *the LORD spoke* is repeated from 2 Kings 21:10 and *they paid no attention* is based on 'the people did not listen' (2 Ki. 21:9). He also agrees with the view that Manasseh's sins ultimately contributed to the exile (*cf.* vv. 8–9 with 7:19–20; 36:15–16). The Chronicler has therefore supplemented the account in Kings, not replaced it. What is more, the additional material develops a point already present in Kings, that the exile could be delayed by the repentance and faith of successive kings. This was already clear in the case of Hezekiah (2 Ki. 20:16–19; 2 Ch. 32:25–26) and Josiah (2 Ki. 22:11–20; 2 Ch. 34:19–28), and Manasseh simply furnishes a further, if distinctive, example. In fact, Manasseh's conversion helps to explain a longstanding problem in Kings, namely, why the exile did not fall in Manasseh's reign if his sins were really so serious. God's judgment had clearly been at least delayed, though if God's basic decision could not be overturned by Josiah's extensive reformation, Manasseh's more limited changes (*cf.* v. 17) were not likely to be any more successful.[1]

The link between Manasseh and Josiah is probably not accidental, for along with Manasseh's son Amon they appear to form a distinct trio (chs. 33–35). The connecting thread is the theme *humbled himself* (Heb. *hikkāna'*), though all respond differently. Manasseh and Josiah humbly repent (33:12, 19; 34:27), but Amon sadly does not (33:23). The significance of this becomes apparent when it is realized that none of this information appears in Kings, not even in Amon's brief reign where in Chronicles the Hebrew verb (not usually reflected in EVV) appears twice. This pattern also contrasts with those of two preceding trios, first Joash, Amaziah, and Uzziah (chs. 24–26), whose reigns are all bipartite, and then Jotham, Ahaz, and Hezekiah (chs. 27–32), who are presented in terms of a single alternating theme.

Elements of both these patterns reappear in chapters 33–35. As with the first trio, Manasseh's reign falls into two parts, while Amon and Josiah provide contrasting portrayals of the theme of humility. In each case, however, Manasseh's reign breaks with previous expectations. In comparison with Joash, Amaziah, and Uzziah, his life changes direction not for

---

[1] For further discussion of the view that Chronicles' account of Manasseh is based on historical tradition, *cf.* W. M. Schniedewind, 'The source citations of Manasseh: King Manasseh in history and homily', *VT* 41, 1991, pp. 450–461.

the worse but for the better. Only Manasseh turns *from* sin. He also seems to continue the alternating pattern of unfaithfulness and obedience represented by Jotham, Ahaz, and Hezekiah, by following Ahaz' attachment to wickedness (*cf*. vv. 3, 23, and 28:3, 13), but then breaks the mould through his repentance. Neither wayward behaviour nor God's judgment must follow automatically. In this context, Manasseh's exile (in Babylon! v. 11) is crucial, since the theme of exile overshadows chapters 28–36 (*cf*. 28:5–8; 29:8–9; 30:8–9; 34:23–25). Manasseh's change of heart represents an opportunity for a premature ending or even reversal of God's judgment, if only Judah's final generation could have humbled itself (36:12–16).

The Bible consistently affirms that God's door remains open to anyone, even after what should have been closing time. If such an invitation could be extended to Manasseh, as it was to a guilt-ridden tax-collector, a thief on a cross, or the chief of sinners, no-one is excluded (Lk. 18:9–14; 23:40–43; 1 Tim. 1:15). The condition of humble repentance remains unchanged, for 'everyone ... who humbles himself will be exalted' (Lk. 14:11; 18:14). Even Jesus walked the same road as Manasseh, for he 'humbled himself and became obedient to death – even death on a cross' (Phil. 2:8).

a. Manasseh's unparalleled evil (33:1–9).

a. Manasseh's unparalleled evil (33:1–9). This paragraph, which is closely based on 2 Kings 21:1–10a, is dominated by Manasseh's *evil* actions (vv. 1, 6, 9) and the contrast between them and God's declared purposes (vv. 4, 7–8).

According to the opening formula (vv. 1–2a), Manasseh reigned for *fifty-five years* (v. 1). This is usually dated to 696–642 BC (694–640, Hughes), though a co-regency with Hezekiah might be included for the first decade. Curiously, the names of royal mothers are omitted from now on, though since the same also applies to two phrases normally occurring in the death formulae, *viz.* 'with his fathers' and 'in the city of David', the changes are probably due to textual reasons.[1]

The rest of this section seems to fall into two parts (vv. 3–6, 7–9), each perhaps originating from a separate source. The *carved image* in the temple (vv. 7–9) is dealt with separately

---

[1] *Cf.* McKenzie, *Use*, pp. 174–176. For the suggestion that the women's Edomite or Arabian origin may have encouraged pagan religious practices, *cf.* J. McKay, *Religion in Judah* (London: SCM Press, 1973), pp. 23–25.

from other pagan symbols, and God's promise about the temple (vv. 4, 7–8) and the extent of Manasseh's evil (vv. 6, 9) are both mentioned twice. The paragraph summarizes the religious aspects of Manasseh's evil, including idolatry (vv. 3–5, 7) and the occult (v. 7), though Manasseh was also responsible for widespread murder and oppression (2 Ki. 21:16). The familiar *high places* were *rebuilt* again (v. 3; *cf.* 2 Ch. 14:3, 5; 15:17; 17:6; 20:33; 21:11; 28:4, 25; 31:1), though such extensive interest in *witchcraft* and *divination* (v. 6) was unparalleled since the time of Saul (1 Ch. 10:13). A particularly sad comment is that he made his sons pass through the fire (v. 6, NIV mg., REB), that is, almost certainly practised child sacrifice.

Chronicles has made several minor adjustments throughout this paragraph, in which two characteristics stand out. The first is that at several points, Manasseh follows the direct example of Ahaz (*cf.* vv. 2–6 with 28:2–4, 25). The latter has replaced Ahab as Manasseh's model (*cf.* 2 Ki. 21:3), which is quite appropriate since Ahaz figures directly in Chronicles (2 Ch. 28) but Ahab only indirectly (*e.g.* 18:1–34; 21:6). Secondly, a certain intensification is evident in comparison with Kings, highlighting even further Manasseh's preoccupation with pagan religion. For example, the *Baals*, the *Asherah poles* (v. 3), and the *sons* (v. 6) are singular in 2 Kings 21, God's name is now in Jerusalem *for ever* (v. 4), *Judah and the people of Jerusalem* (v. 9) are specifically mentioned, and verse 6 really begins with an extra Hebrew word, 'It was he who . . .'. Judah's evil also increases, first to *much evil* (v. 6) and then to *more than* that of the *nations* whom the Lord had *driven out* (v. 2) and *destroyed* (v. 9). They had even desecrated the temple with pagan *altars* (vv. 4, 5) and a *carved image* (v. 7) of the goddess Asherah (*cf.* 2 Ki. 21:7). They had denied in the process their very distinctiveness as God's people, as well as any right to occupy their land and temple.

The paragraph is marked by various scriptural quotations and allusions. Verse 6, for example, is based on Deuteronomy 18:9–13, where these activities and those who engage in them are an abomination before God. Most of the remaining quotations (vv. 4, 7–8) are based on other passages in Chronicles. God's *name* is most closely associated with the temple in 2 Chronicles 7:16 (*cf.* also 1 Ki. 8:16; 9:3), the election of the *temple* and of *Jerusalem* follows 2 Chronicles 6:5–6, and the need for obedience is based on 1 Chronicles 28:8. The most influential source however, is 2 Chronicles 7:19–22. It contains the clearest statement in Chronicles about the consequences for the temple and the land when Israel abandons God's laws, and it ties in with the use of 2 Chronicles 7:14–16 in verses 4, 12–13, 18–19. The whole chapter therefore is best understood as a kind of commentary on God's speech in 2 Chronicles 7:12–22, both in its promises and its threats. If the *temple* which bears his *Name* (vv. 4, 7; *cf.* 2 Ch. 7:16, 20) is not to be used properly, then Israel must expect to see the relevant penalties brought into play.

b. Manasseh's repentance and God's favour (33:10–20).

Sadly, neither Manasseh nor the people seemed initially aware of any danger (v. 10), and so Manasseh was taken captive to Babylon. It is notable that this happened because *the LORD brought* the Assyrians against him, as he did ultimately with the Babylonians (v. 11; *cf.* 2 Ch. 36:17). Manasseh's fate was not in Assyria's hands (*cf.* 32:7–8) but in God's.

No mention is made of Manasseh's exile in Assyrian sources, even though Manasseh appears in the annals of Esarhaddon (680–669 BC) and Ashurbanipal (668–626 BC) as a rather unwilling vassal forced to provide supplies for Assyria's building and military enterprises.[1] It is quite possible that he rebelled against these impositions at some point, though other specific events known from Mesopotamian sources have also been suggested as the occasion for his exile.[2] The most probable of these is that he was associated with the rebellion in 652–648 BC of Shamash-shum-ukin king of Babylon. He was the brother of Ashurbanipal, the Assyrian king, and there was discontent in various parts of the Assyrian empire, especially the west, during this period. Once Shamash-shum-ukin had been dealt with, the Assyrians could well have brought Manasseh to account. At any rate, Manasseh's being captured with 'hooks' and 'fetters' (v. 11, RSV) suggests some misdemeanour rather than that he had been invited with Esarhaddon's other

---

[1] *Cf. ANET*, pp. 291, 294.
[2] For these various proposals, *cf. e.g.* B. Oded in J. H. Hayes and J. M. Miller (eds.), *Israelite and Judean History* (London: SCM Press, 1977), pp. 454–456; J. M. Miller and J. H. Hayes, *A History of Ancient Israel and Judah* (London: SCM Press, 1986), pp. 374–376.

vassals in 672 BC to ensure support for Ashurbanipal's succession to the throne. Manasseh's presence in *Babylon* is not surprising, since Assyria had had a long interest in Babylon, which was under their direct control for the whole of Esarhaddon's reign and after Shamash-shum-ukin's demise.

Since the effect of Manasseh's conversion seems to have been limited (*cf.* v. 17 and 2 Ki. 21:10–16), it most likely belongs to his last few years, between the end of the Babylonian rebellion in 648 BC and his death in 642 BC. The translation of 'hooks' (v. 11, RSV, GNB, JB, *cf.* NIV) is uncertain, and, on the basis of its usual meaning ('brier, thorn'), 'spiked weapons' (REB, NEB), is also possible.[1] However, the use of a very similar word to describe Sennacherib's humiliation (2 Ki. 19:28 = Is. 37:29; *cf.* also Ezk. 19:4, 9) and the known Assyrian custom of putting rings or hooks in their captives' noses are in favour of the usual view.

The Chronicler's interest, however, is less to do with Manasseh's just deserts than with the restoration he certainly did not deserve (vv. 12–13). His conversion is a remarkable one, not only for its lack of any parallel in 2 Kings 21 (see above), but because of its apparent suddenness and extent. In dramatic impact, it ranks in the Bible only with the experience of Saul of Tarsus (Acts 9:1–19, *etc.*), though Christian history has furnished many examples such as that of John Newton the slave-trader.

This account is characterized by Chronicles' distinctive vocabulary and by further Scripture quotations. *In his distress* (v. 12) is a deliberate contrast with Ahaz' response in a similar situation (2 Ch. 28:22; *cf.* vv. 3, 6). Manasseh was restored through prayer and humble repentance (vv. 12b–13a), though it was God's listening to his prayer rather than Manasseh's act of praying that brought about effective change. It was also the Lord who *brought him back* ('restored him', NRSV) to *Jerusalem* and to his *kingdom* (v. 13a), as Manasseh himself recognized (v. 13b). The influence of other parts of Chronicles is very evident, especially 2 Chronicles 7:14 which comes through as Manasseh *sought the favour of* God (*cf.* 'seek my face', 7:14), *humbled himself* (v. 12), and *prayed* (v. 13), and as God heard (v. 13). The theology of answered prayer is also derived from 2 Chronicles 6, as in the word *plea* (v. 13, NIV,

---

[1] *Cf.* KB I, p. 284.

NRSV; 'supplication', RSV, REB, NEB) which occurs in Chronicles only here and in 2 Chronicles 6:19, 29, 35, 39. God *brought him back* from exile is based on 2 Ch. 6:25, and Manasseh's repenting in exile on 2 Chronicles 6:24–25, 36–39. Finally, the phrase *knew that the LORD is God* occurs in Ezekiel over seventy times. Both Manasseh and Ezekiel's hearers found God unexpectedly in exile.

Verses 14–16 describe God's healing of the land (*cf.* the language of 2 Ch. 7:14). Three separate reforms are mentioned, each of them typical of the Chronicler's understanding of practical faith. Manasseh repaired and extended Jerusalem's city *wall* (v. 14a), reorganized the army outside Jerusalem (v. 14b), and restored temple worship in line with his turning from idols to serve the living God (vv. 15–16; *cf.* 1 Thes. 1:9). Building and repairing Jerusalem's walls is mentioned repeatedly in Chronicles (*e.g.* 1 Ch. 11:8; 2 Ch. 26:9; 27:3–4). Manasseh's work is probably connected with the westward and northward expansion of the city which began under Hezekiah (2 Ch. 32:5; Is. 22:10–11), though *afterwards* (v. 14) may indicate co-operation with Ashurbanipal's need to strengthen his defences against possible trouble from Egypt following the defeat of Shamash-shum-ukin. If verse 14 were translated '. . . extended the outer wall of the city of David westwards, from Gihon in the valley to the entrance at the Fish Gate . . .', it would clearly suggest a westward movement, since the *city of David, Gihon,* and *Ophel* were all located in the south-east. The Fish Gate is thought to have been in the north-west of the city (*cf.* Zp. 1:10; Ne. 3:3; 12:39).[1] Reorganization of the army (v. 14b) is another common feature of faithful kings in Chronicles (*cf.* 2 Ch. 11:5–12; 14:6; 17:12–19).

Manasseh's religious reforms represented a direct reversal of earlier policies (vv. 2–9), since each of the items removed in verse 15 is mentioned in verses 3, 7. Some form of regular worship was recommenced (v. 16), though its range seems rather limited (*cf.* 1 Ch. 23:31; 2 Ch. 2:4; 8:13; 31:3). This view seems borne out by the sequel. Although Manasseh 'commanded' (v. 16, REB, NEB, NRSV, RSV) Judah to 'worship' (*serve*, EVV) the Lord, pagan worship continued throughout the country during the next two reigns (v. 17; 2 Ch. 33:22;

---

[1] See further A. Mazar, *Archaeology of the Land of the Bible* (New York: Doubleday, 1990), pp. 420–424.

34:3–7, 33). As with all previous attempts to eradicate the signs and symbols of Canaanite religion, in practice its undemanding morality and sensuous practices proved irresistible to the majority of the people (*cf.* 2 Ch. 14:3; 15:17; 17:6; 20:33). Despite the formal changes, the people as a whole saw no need for a change of heart (*cf.* Is. 29:13; Je. 3:10; 2 Tim. 3:5).

The concluding formula (vv. 18–20) differs significantly in at least three ways from 2 Kings 21:17–18. Firstly, it underlines the centrality of Manasseh's conversion for the Chronicler's understanding of his reign, especially his *prayer* and that he *humbled himself* (v. 19; *cf.* vv. 12–13). Secondly, whereas the prophets or *seers* (vv. 18, 19) were persecuted under Manasseh (2 Ki. 21:10–16), Chronicles reports their courage in speaking to him and writing about him. On the basis of previous passages, the *records of the seers* (v. 19) are probably the same as, or at least incorporated in, *the annals of the kings of Israel* (v. 18; *cf.* 2 Ch. 20:34; 24:27; 32:32).[1] Thirdly, Chronicles has summarized the details of Manasseh's burial (*cf.* 2 Ki. 21:18). Since the same thing happens with Amon (*cf.* 2 Ki. 21:26), the most likely reason for the change is a textual one, unless, as with the Millo, 'the garden of Uzza' (2 Ki. 21:26) was no longer identifiable in the Chronicler's time.

ii. Amon is unrepentant (33:21–25)

'He did not humble himself before the LORD' (v. 23).

33:21–25 – *cf.* 2 Kings 21:19–24

Amon's reign lasted a mere *two years* (642–640 BC), but he plays a significant role in Chronicles. This emerges particularly from two typical expressions of Chronicles which do not occur in Kings, *viz.* he *did not humble himself* and he *increased his guilt* (v. 23). The former contrasts Amon with his father (*unlike his father Manasseh, he did not humble himself; cf.* vv. 12, 19), and is regarded as one of the causes of the exile in its only other occurence in Chronicles (2 Ch. 36:12). The distinction between father and son was not that they *did evil*, for Amon did *as his father Manasseh* (v. 22; *cf.* v. 2), but that Amon did not repent, even though Manasseh's example must have

---

[1] EVV are surely correct to adopt the reading 'seers' at the end of v. 19 in place of MT's personal name 'Hozai' (JB; = 'my seers'), though the latter interpretation is still favoured in Barthélemy, *CTAT*, pp. 513–514.

been well known to him. The Bible is realistic in acknowledging that 'there is no-one who does not sin' (2 Ch. 6:36; *cf.* Is. 53:6; Rom. 3:23), but it does condemn those who fail to take whatever opportunity they have to repent (*cf.* Jn. 3:18–20; Rom. 2:12–16).

Because he did not repent, Amon *increased his guilt* (v. 23). Though in all its other occurences in Chronicles, guilt is directly associated with God's wrath (1 Ch. 21:3; 27:24; 2 Ch. 19:10; 24:18; 28:9–10, 13, 25), the consequences were not inevitable. Guilt could be expunged through the temple sacrifices, as exemplified by David's forgiveness at the site of the future temple (1 Ch. 21:3; 22:1). Alternatively, Amon could follow the ways of Ahaz (2 Ch. 28:9–10) and of the final pre-exilic generation, both of whom suffered God's wrath through the judgment of exile (2 Ch. 28:5–8; 36:16). Although the cloud of exile hangs over chapters 28–36 (*e.g.* 29:8–9; 33:10–11; 34:23–25; 36:15–20), Manasseh and Amon in their contrasting ways show that a fatalistic attitude in the face of God's judgment is quite unjustified.

The details of Amon's death are unknown, and though most commentators assume that it was his policy towards Assyria that had caused offence, this remains unproven. It is more important to recognize that all other examples of conspiracies in Chronicles are interpreted as God's judgment (2 Kings 24:25–26; 25:27), and presumably the same applies here. The *people of the land* (v. 25) play a consistent role in Chronicles, appointing a new king when the unexpected death of his predecessor had led to a crisis (2 Ch. 22:1; 26:1; 36:1). This group clearly had a position of some authority, and previous examples suggest they included more than just family heads or elders (*cf.* 1 Ch. 11:1–3; 2 Ch. 10:1–17).[1] Though the final paragraph in 2 Kings 21:25–26 is omitted, a statement about *Josiah's* succession is already found in 2 Kings 21:24 and makes a perfectly adequate introduction to chapter 34.

iii. Josiah (34:1 – 36:1)

'Because you humbled yourself before me ... Your eyes will
not see all the disaster I am going to bring on this place'
(34:27–28).

---

[1] The basic alternatives are summarized in Dillard, p. 270.

'At that time the entire service of the LORD was carried out for
the celebration of the Passover' (35:16).

34:1–2 – *cf.* 2 Kings 22:1–2
34:8–12a – *cf.* 2 Kings 22:3–7
34:15–32 – *cf.* 2 Kings 22:8 – 23:3
35:1 – *cf.* 2 Kings 23:21
35:18–19 – *cf.* 2 Kings 23:22–23
35:20 – *cf.* 2 Kings 23:29
35:24 – *cf.* 2 Kings 23:30a
36:1 – *cf.* 2 Kings 23:30b

Along with David, Solomon, Asa, Jehoshaphat, and Hezekiah,
the extensive treatment accorded to *Josiah* (chs. 34–35) is a
sign that he has qualities to be commended to Chronicles'
readers. Though, like the others, Josiah is not without failure
(35:22), his reformation is the last opportunity for Judah to
return to their God-given foundations in an otherwise inexor-
able slide towards exile.

Apart from the introductory and concluding paragraphs
(34:1–2; 35:25 – 36:1), Josiah's reign is divided into three
sections: (a) his faithfulness in seeking God (34:3–33); (b) his
Passover (35:1–19); (c) his death (35:20–24).

Within this structure, the theme of humility continues from
chapter 33. In 2 Kings 22, *humbled himself* occurs once (2 Ki.
22:19), but here it is repeated and given fresh prominence (v.
27) as the basis on which the threat of judgment can be lifted,
even though the respite is only temporary (*cf.* 32:26; 33:12,
19). Josiah's humility is supplemented by another of Chronicles' favourite themes, namely, seeking God. *Seek* or *enquire*
occurs three times, each unparalleled in Kings, confirming
Josiah as a person who makes God's kingdom his first priority
(vv. 3, 21, 26; *cf.* Mt. 6:33). This combination of humble
seeking after God gives his reign a consistency which contrasts
with both his father's persistence in evil (2 Ch. 33:23) and with
Manasseh's need for cataclysmic change (2 Ch. 33:12–13).

The chapter is based on 2 Kings 22:1 – 23:3, with additional
paragraphs (vv. 3–7, 12b–13), summaries (vv. 14, 33), and
words such as *Levites* (vv. 9, 12b–13, 30), *remnant* (vv. 9, 21), or
curses (v. 24) being included at several points. These individual
changes, however, are less significant than two major alterations to the chapter's structure. Firstly, whereas in Kings
Josiah's reformation centres on the discovery of an old biblical
scroll, that event is now merely the third and last stage (v. 8) in

a process that goes back another ten years to Josiah's first spiritual awakening (v. 3). Chronicles concentrates on Josiah's over-all attitude rather than on any single event. The second change concerns Josiah's reaction to the scroll. Despite Josiah's vigorous campaign against the paraphernalia of idolatry in Kings (2 Ki. 23:4–20, 24–25), God's decision to remove his people from the Promised Land is strongly affirmed (2 Ki. 23:26–27). Chronicles, on the other hand, highlights the possibility that those who are guilty might receive God's forgiveness even though judgment is certain to fall on the community as a whole. Despite the inevitability of the disaster (vv. 24–25, 28), God's covenant can still be renewed by people who take his word seriously.

The biblical accounts of Josiah's reign raise several important background questions on which only the briefest assessment is possible here. It is now generally agreed, for example, that the main factors in the reform were religious rather than political. Although the reform coincided with a significant decline in Assyrian influence, attempts to compare stages of the reform with Josiah's increasing independence of Assyria are uncertain and possibly largely irrelevant.[1] Secondly, though a close connection between Josiah's scroll and Deuteronomy has been accepted for a long time, the implications of this for the origins of Deuteronomy are much more uncertain, since neither Kings or Chronicles provides direct evidence for the thesis, advocated repeatedly since 1805, that the scroll was composed as part of a Deuteronomic reform movement. The date of Deuteronomy and of the scroll and the reasons for the latter being hidden are issues which go far beyond the immediate concerns of this passage. Thirdly, though the varying accounts of the reform in Kings and Chronicles cannot be entirely harmonized, it is acceptable to follow the recent scholarly trend of distinguishing the separate emphases in each work. Each presentation is clearly very selective, and it is unwise to be unduly influenced by one at the expense of the other. This means one must take seriously Chronicles' various stages leading to the discovery of the scroll, and that the finding of the scroll may be seen as a result of the reform rather than its primary cause.

---

[1] *E.g.* F. M. Cross and D. N. Freedman, 'Josiah's revolt against Assyria', *Journal of Near Eastern Studies* 12, 1953, pp. 56–58.

Though these historical and literary issues are important, the most vital thing about the scroll, according to both Josiah and Huldah the prophetess, is that it is his [*i.e.* God's] *words* (v. 26; 'what I have spoken', 2 Ki. 22:19). What is more, Josiah takes whatever action is necessary on the basis of his understanding of God's message. It is especially interesting that he regards the written orm of God's word as superior to inherited tradition and is willing to pay the cost of correcting his priorities. This is one of the clearer examples in the Old Testament of the underlying concept of an authoritative Scripture, which is equally at one with the spoken word of prophecy. Whatever form it takes, God's word is never entirely comfortable for those whose lives it confronts. The issue is just as clear in the New Testament, where the word of God is incarnate as well as written. Jesus' word is no less authoritative than that of Scripture, for he too challenges all human traditions and authorities, ultimately making all things subject to himself (*e.g.* Jn. 1:1–14; Mk. 7:13; Eph. 2:20–23; 2 Tim. 2:9; Heb. 4:12–13).

a. Josiah seeks God faithfully (34:1–7). The opening formula (vv. 1–2) introduces an ongoing link between Josiah and both David and Joash. As well as mentioning *David* explicitly in verse 2, Josiah follows him in seeking God (vv. 3, 21, 26), taking responsibility for the temple (v. 8), organizing the Levitical musicians (vv. 12–13), and obeying God (v. 31). Joash and Josiah both became king as minors (v. 1; *cf.* 2 Ch. 24:1), and both undertook a major repair of the temple (vv. 8–12a). Not turning to *the right or to the left* (v. 2) usually means obedience to God's law (*cf.* Dt. 5:32; 17:20; 28:14; Jos. 1:7; 23:6), and sets the tone for Josiah's response to the temple scroll (vv. 19–33).

Josiah reigned for *thirty-one years* (v. 1; *i.e.* 640–609 BC), but not for the first time Chronicles has used chronological markers to divide a reign (vv. 3, 8; *cf.* 2 Ch. 14–16). The first stage starts while Josiah was a 'youth' (v. 3a, REB, JB) of fifteen (*the eighth year of his reign*, v. 3a) when he *began to seek* God. Though Solomon had once been debarred from building the temple because he was only a youth (Heb. *na'ar*, 1 Ch. 22:5; 29:1), no such age restriction applies to seeking God (*cf.* Mt. 18:3–4; 1 Tim. 4:12). 'Seeking' in Chronicles describes the habit of looking to God in every situation, and also the attitude which God looks for in those who pray (2 Ch. 7:14; 30:19). *Began* implies the start of a spiritual pilgrimage for young Josiah (*cf.* the same Heb. verb *dāraš* in vv. 21, 26). Other kings who sought God include David (1 Ch. 28:19; 28:8–9), Solomon (2 Ch. 1:5), and Hezekiah (2 Ch. 31:21).

The next stage of Josiah's reign is a reformation which results directly from his seeking God. It is described as a purging, first of *Judah and Jerusalem* (vv. 3b–5) and then in 'all the land of Israel' (vv. 6–7, NRSV, RSV). The two areas are clearly set apart, the first by an inclusion around verses 3b–5 formed by the word *purge*, the second by the phrase *he went back to Jerusalem* at the end of verse 7. Josiah's actions in the south are effectively repeated in the north. Even the same expressions are used: for example, he *tore down* (Heb. *nittēṣ*) *the altars* (vv. 4, 7) and *cut to pieces* (Heb. *giddēaʿ*) *the incense altars* (vv. 4, 7) before he 'ground them to powder' (Heb. *hēḏaq*, vv. 4, 7, REB).[1]

Some similarity also clearly exists between this reformation in Josiah's twelfth year and what seems to be the main stage of reform in his eighteenth year as described in 2 Kings 23:4–20. Most commentators therefore assume that verses 3b–7 summarize 2 Kings 23:4–20. This view could be correct if 2 Kings 23:4–20 is regarded as summarizing a longer process of reformation, for the latter passage does not actually mention the discovery of the temple scroll. However, if 2 Kings 23:4–20 does belong to Josiah's eighteenth year, this conflicts with Chronicles' dating, and a comparison of the details indicates that different events may be intended. 2 Kings 23:4–14, for example, is confined mainly to the temple and the area around Jerusalem rather than Judah and Jerusalem as a whole (vv. 3b–5). Differences also exist over the various acts of desecration. Burning the bones of Judean priests (v. 5) is not clearly referred to in 2 Kings 23, even in verse 14. By contrast, while Chronicles mentions no such defamatory action in Israel, 2 Kings 23:19–20 even describes Josiah slaughtering priests in the northern sanctuaries. In reality, it would not be surprising if some events in the reformation were repeated,

---

[1] 'In their ruins' (v. 6, NIV, NRSV, RSV; *cf.* JB, GNB) is a conventional attempt to make sense of an uncertain MT, but the most convincing solution is to read 'destroyed their temples' (I. Seeligmann, 'Indications of editorial alteration and adaptation in the Massoretic Text and the Septuagint', *VT* 11, 1961, p. 202, n. 1; *cf.* Williamson, Dillard and 2 Ch. 19:3).

since no previous attempt to eradicate Canaanite religion had ever proved entirely successful (*cf.* 2 Ch. 14:5; 15:17; 17:6; 20:33; 33:15–17).

b. Josiah repents over God's word (34:8–33). By Josiah's *eighteenth year* (622 BC), the reform reached the *temple* (v. 8). A specific policy *to repair the temple of the LORD* was put in place, though the over-all aim to *purify* or purge (*cf.* vv. 3, 6) *the land* was still in operation. Unfortunately, the sense of continuing action is obscured in NRSV, RSV, REB, NEB, GNB, *etc.*, by the translation, 'when he had purged', but the Hebrew clearly means, '*to* purge'.

The temple reforms are the centre rather than the climax of Josiah's actions, and four stages are clearly discernible.

i. The plan to repair the temple (34:9–13). This evokes memories of David (1 Ch. 26:27) and especially of Joash who also collected *money* for a special rebuilding fund (v. 9; 2 Ch. 24:5, 12; see also on vv. 1–2 above). Contributions from the north (*Manasseh, Ephraim and the entire remnant of Israel*, v. 9) had probably been *brought into the temple* (v. 9) as a result of the campaign in verses 6–7. Josiah clearly assumed jurisdiction over religious affairs there (*cf.* vv. 6, 9, 21, 33) even though he may not have enjoyed formal political control. A sense of common feeling with the Chronicler's own audience is implied by describing the northerners as a *remnant* (vv. 9, 21), since 2 Kings 22 has no equivalent term. Indeed, their faithful contributions to temple funds (v. 9) may well have jolted the minds of some readers to do likewise.

Josiah's administrative arrangements largely follow those of Joash. As treasurers ('keepers of the threshold', NRSV, RSV, *i.e.* doorkeepers, NIV; *cf.* 1 Ch. 26), the *Levites* were responsible to the king and his officials (*cf.* 2 Ch. 24:5, 8, 11). The funds then passed from the high priest to the supervisors, the workmen, and the specialist craftsmen (vv. 10–11). Two reasons are given for the success of the operation. One was that the men worked *faithfully* (v. 12), a word often associated in Chronicles with the Levites' attitude to financial matters (*cf.* 1 Ch. 9:26, 31; 2 Ch. 19:9; 31:12, 15, 18). This is in contrast with the *kings of Judah*, that is, Ahaz, Manasseh and Amon, who had allowed things to *fall into ruin* (v. 11). The other was that the Levites provided effective leadership (vv. 12b–13). This is another

Levitical practice emphasized in Chronicles but not in Kings, which may well reflect conditions from the Chronicler's time (*cf.* 1 Ch. 15:21; 23:4; Ezr. 3:8, 9; *cf.* 2 Ch. 2:2, 18). The information about the Levites in verses 12b–13 can be read in two ways. The preferred option is to treat the Levites' musical skill (v. 12) as a passing comment comparable with a similar note about Levitical occupations at the end of verse 13 (*cf.* REB, NEB). Alternatively, one must assume the highly doubtful ploy of putting musicians in charge of construction work! Either way, the Levites were fulfilling a wide range of traditional tasks originally assigned to them by David (*cf.* 1 Ch. 26).

ii. Discovery of the scroll (34:14–18). The central event of the chapter, the discovery of the scroll by Hilkiah the high priest, is actually mentioned quite briefly (*cf.* v. 9). Greater attention is given to what happened afterwards, though the discovery is doubly introduced by an objective report (v. 14) and by personal testimony (v. 15). Since the preceding verses are also in narrative form (vv. 9–12a; they are in direct speech in 2 Ki. 22:4–7), Hilkiah's personal announcement, '*I have found the Book of the Law*', stands out sharply (the directness of his words is lost in REB). Secretary Shaphan confirms that the find took place in the context of the workers' faithfulness (vv. 16–17; *cf.* v. 12).

Hilkiah's discovery is entitled both *the Book of the Law* (vv. 14–15) and *the Book of the Covenant* (v. 30). It is traditionally identified with Deuteronomy, though probably not the whole book, since it was read twice in one day (2 Ki. 22:8, 10). Some commentators have been less pragmatic, however, like a medieval Archbishop of Canterbury who assumed that Josiah listened to the whole book at one sitting: 'What a contrast to our present-day kings and magnates! If once a year they hear the word of God preached, they find it nauseating and leave the church before the end of the sermon'![1]

One of the strongest links with Deuteronomy is its repeated references to a Book of the Law (Dt. 28:61; 29:21; 30:10; 31:26; *cf.* Jos. 1:8; 8:31, 34; 23:6; 24:26). Another is the phrase *all the curses written in* (v. 24; in place of 'everything written in', 2 Ki. 22:16), referring to the contents of the Book

---

[1] See A. Saltman, *Stephen Langton's Commentary on the Book of Chronicles* (Ramat-Gan: Bar-Ilan University, 1978), pp. 42–43.

of the Law in Deuteronomy 29:20, 21, 27; Jos. 8:34. Further connections with Deuteronomy include the centralizing of worship (vv. 3–7, 33; *cf.* Dt. 12), the centralized Passover (35:1–19; *cf.* Dt. 16:1–8), and above all the covenant ceremony (vv. 29–32; *cf.* Dt. 31:10–13). Hilkiah's scroll was also recognized as having *Moses'* authority (v. 14), just like the Book of the Law in Joshua's day (Jos. 8:31, 34; 23:6), and there is little doubt that its antiquity increased its sense of authority.

EVV's translation of the title as Book of the Law is somewhat misleading. For example, it was almost certainly a written scroll (*cf.* Je. 36:2; Ezk. 2:9). Also 'law' (Heb. *tôrâ*) is better understood as 'teaching, instruction', so that a better alternative might be 'Scroll of the Teaching' or even 'Scroll of [God's] Instruction'. God's *tôrâ* and covenant are designed for life and blessing rather than death and curse, enabling his people to trust him with all their heart and soul (*cf.* v. 31 and Dt. 30).

iii. Recognition of God's word (34:19–28). Josiah seems to have quickly realized that what was being read to him was God's own word (vv. 19–21). Acknowledging the word of God for what it is, is always an essential first step towards seeing God at work (*cf.* Acts 8:14; 1 Thes. 2:13). Josiah also recognized that *the LORD's anger* was *great* because his people had *not kept the word of the LORD* (v. 21). God's anger is a recurring theme in chapters 28–36 (*cf.* 2 Ch. 28:9, 11, 13, 25; 29:8, 10; 32:25; 33:6; 36:16), for Israel's disobedience went back for generations (*our fathers*, v. 21; 29:8–9; 36:16). Josiah was therefore right to be worried about the consequences, for the ultimate penalty of exile was no idle threat (2 Ch. 28:9; 30:9; 36:16).

Despite this, Josiah knew that God's anger could still be turned away by humble repentance (*cf.* 2 Ch. 29:10; 30:8; 32:26; 33:13), though an assurance about its permanent removal had to wait until Jesus came and died (Rom. 5:9; 1 Thes. 1:10). In fact, Josiah was deeply convicted about his people's plight, as he showed by two separate responses. First *he tore his clothes* and *wept* (vv. 19, 27), which was a traditional sign of distress (*cf. e.g.* Gn. 37:34; 2 Ki. 19:1; Jb. 1:20). Then he sent his officials to a *prophetess* (v. 22) in order to *enquire of the LORD* (v. 21). Though 'enquire' translates the same word as 'seek' (v. 3), here it has the sense of asking for specific guidance (and in v. 26) rather than describing Josiah's basic orientation towards God. As on this occasion, its meaning can be closely linked with *humbled yourself* (v. 27), especially in connection with Chronicles' favourite promise of God's deliverance (2 Ch. 7:14). Josiah's choice was not easy, and contrasts with the behaviour of two other kings whom the Chronicler probably had in mind. Jehoiakim also had God's word read to him, but he just tore it up and had it burnt (Je. 36). Similarly Joash, who has already been compared with Josiah (*cf.* vv. 8–13), was resistant when challenged about angering God (2 Ch. 24:18–20). On the other hand, Jehoiakim's officials who were descended from *Shaphan* and *Abdon* (Akbor, 2 Ki. 22:12) were attentive to God's word, even protecting Jeremiah from the king (Je. 36:10–19; *cf.* Je. 26:22, 24).[1]

The prophetess *Huldah* lived in Jerusalem's *Second District* or Quarter (v. 22; *cf.* Zp. 1:10), which, though usually thought to be in the north, could just as easily have been part of the recent south-western expansion of the city. Named female prophets in the Bible are rare, though, like Miriam, Deborah, and Anna, Huldah prophesied at a crucial moment in the history of God's people (Ex. 15:20; Jdg. 4:4; Lk. 2:36; *cf.* Is. 8:3; Acts 21:9). On the other hand, the existence of other prophetesses who opposed God is not to be ignored, so that the mere exercise of prophecy is no particular sign of divine favour (Ne. 6:14; Rev. 2:20).

Huldah's prophecy (vv. 23–28) is largely carried over from 2 Kings 22:15–20, which contains several key concepts familiar in Chronicles. Over all, the spoken word of prophecy confirms the written word of the law. The message is in two sections (vv. 23–25, 26–28), of which the first underlines that the exile was certain. God himself will *bring* the *disaster* (v. 24, 28), because the people have *forsaken* him (v. 25). This latter term (Heb. *'āzaḇ*) is widely used in Chronicles as an expression for sin (*cf.* 2 Ch. 12:1, 5; 15:2; 24:18), though the emphasis in this and other passages in chapters 28–36 is on a cumulative turning away from God by successive generations (*cf.* vv. 21, 25 and 29:6; 30:7). The point is further strengthened by the addition of *all the curses* (v. 24; *cf.* 2 Ki. 22:16), a clear allusion to the covenant curses (Dt. 27:9–26; 28:15–68), and implying that the covenant had been broken irretrievably. Where

---

[1] Though some of the names in vv. 20, 22 are different from those in 2 Ki. 22:12, 14, they are best understood as textual variants.

previously God's anger might have been turned away (2 Ch. 29:10; 30:8), it could *be quenched* no longer (v. 25).

Hope was still not totally extinguished, however, for the second section promises *peace* in the midst of *disaster* (v. 28). People like Josiah, whose hearts were (lit.) 'soft' or 'tender' (v. 27; *responsive*, NIV; 'penitent', NRSV, RSV; 'willing', REB, NEB), could still know God's grace for themselves. The Hebrew phrase 'soft heart' elsewhere speaks of fear and timidity (*cf.* Dt. 20:3, 8; 2 Ch. 13:7), but its meaning here is confirmed by the repeated *humbled yourself* (v. 27). Since, in Chronicles, self-humbling is always the antidote to forsaking God (*cf.* 1 Ch. 28:9; 2 Ch. 7:14, 19; 15:2), God promises Josiah he would *not see* the disaster himself and would be buried in *peace* (v. 28). Though Josiah died in violent circumstances (2 Ch. 35:20–24), this does not invalidate God's promise which really means that the exile would not take place during Josiah's lifetime. In any case, to be 'gathered to one's fathers' is an expression concerned with burial rather than a euphemism for dying (1 Ki. 14:20; 22:40; 2 Ki. 20:21; *cf.* 2 Ch. 35:24b).

iv. Covenant renewal (34:29–32). Though the people had been judged by the covenant, *covenant* renewal became the foundation of a new hope. The facts that the scroll is entitled here 'The Covenant Scroll' (v. 30) and that they acted according to the *covenant of God* (v. 32) show how important the covenant was in determining the shape of Israel's future. Biblical covenants always contain both grace and law, promise and judgment, and Josiah could point to both Asa and Hezekiah for covenant ceremonies which reaffirmed God's grace to a previously disobedient people (*cf.* 2 Ch. 15:1–15; 29:10). Josiah's covenant was characterized by the 'obedience of faith (*cf.* Rom. 1:5). The people agreed to *keep* God's commands and to 'put into practice' (GNB) the 'terms of the covenant' (v. 31, REB, NEB). They had in mind primarily a renewal of the Sinai covenant, as indicated by the phrases *commands, regulations, and decrees* (v. 31; *cf. e.g.* Dt. 6:1; 11:1) and *with all his heart and all his soul* (v. 31; *cf. e.g.* Dt. 6:5; 11:13; 30:2). Elements of the Davidic covenant were also incorporated, since the ceremony was led by the *king* (vv. 29, 31, 32) and took place in the *temple* (v. 30; *cf.* 2 Ch. 7:13–14, 17–18). Even if it was only temporary, Judah had returned to their foundations, for they had acted *in accordance with the covenant of God, the God of their fathers* (v. 32).

While verses 29–32 follow 2 Kings 23:1–3 fairly closely, three changes stand out. The first is that the 'prophets' are now called *Levites* (v. 30; *cf.* 2 Ki. 23:2). This change is most likely allied with the repeated exercise of a prophetic ministry by the Levites (*cf.* 1 Ch. 25:1, 3; 2 Ch. 20:14; 29:30) and the prophetic qualifications of their founders (*cf.* 1 Ch. 25:5; 2 Ch. 29:25; 35:15), though it is unnecessary to assume that the Levites had taken over all the work of the prophets by the Chronicler's time.[1] Secondly, the king now stands 'in his place' (v. 31, NRSV, RSV) rather than 'by the pillar' (2 Ki. 23:3). Though the Hebrew word for 'place' occurs only in post-exilic parts of the Old Testament, this change may also reflect the absence of pillars such as Jakin and Boaz in the second temple (*cf.* 2 Ch. 3:17). Thirdly, verse 32 is a free paraphrase of 'all the people pledged themselves to the covenant' (2 Ki. 23:3). The Chronicler has emphasized that 'all who were present in Jerusalem and in Benjamin' (NRSV, RSV) assented to the new arrangements, and that they did so by reviving an older covenant rather than making a new one.[2] He also stresses that it was the king who made the people *pledge themselves* (NIV, NRSV; 'swear an oath', NEB; 'made' them 'stand to it', RSV) to the covenant. This suggests that Josiah's personal faith was not necessarily copied by the people, an observation that is confirmed by both Jeremiah and subsequent events (*cf.* Je. 3:10; 2 Ch. 36:14–16).

Finally, the people's obedience to the terms of their covenant is summarized along the lines of 2 Ki. 23:4–25 (v. 33). The earlier details are not repeated, presumably because some of the same kind of things had already taken place (vv. 3b–7). Again, however, there are hints that the people needed some coercion. Josiah made them *serve* [*i.e.* 'worship'] the Lord, which they did, but only *as long as he lived.* Nevertheless *all who were in Israel* complied, as exemplified above all by the ensuing

---

[1] *E.g.* D. L. Petersen, *Late Israelite Prophecy*, SBLMS 23 (Missoula: Scholars Press, 1980), p. 85.

[2] REB, NEB have unnecessarily followed Curtis and Madsen, Rudolph, *etc.* in assuming that 'and Benjamin' is an error for 'in the covenant' (2 Ki. 23:3), since not only are the Heb. words 'Benjamin' and 'covenant' quite dissimilar, but 'covenant' occurs later on in v. 32.

Passover (35:1–19) in which representatives from north and south were presumably present (*cf.* 35:3).

c. Josiah celebrates the Passover (35:1–19).

Chapter 35 is largely taken up with a Passover (vv. 1–19) which is reported only briefly in Kings (2 Ki. 23:21–23). Whether the additional material (vv. 2–17) comes from some official temple source or from elsewhere can only be surmised. Since this account follows immediately on the renewing of the covenant, it appears to be part of Josiah's movement of covenant renewal (34:29–32). The Passover in fact gives the reform a much more positive image than in Kings, which concentrates on a crusade against idolatry (2 Ki. 23:4–27). The Chronicler's concern is rather to encourage the right use of the *temple* (vv. 2, 3, 8, 20), its *service* (vv. 2, 10, 15, 16), and its *offerings* (vv. 7, 8, 9, 12–14, 16).

The Passover represents the zenith of temple worship in Chronicles (*cf.* 2 Ch. 30). This prominence is due partly to historical associations with the exodus (Ex. 12:1–13) and Israel's entry into the Promised Land (Jos. 5:10–11), and partly to its place in the worship of the second temple (Ezr. 6:19–22; *cf.* also Ezk. 45:21). The Passover in post-exilic times particularly expressed many of the Chronicler's own emphases, such as the priority of temple worship, the reunification of the exiles, Israel's separation from the impurities of their neighbours, and a desire to seek the Lord (*cf.* Ezr. 6:19–22).

Josiah's Passover represents a return to orthodoxy without parallel since the days of Samuel (v. 18). Although in practice it can be compared only with the irregularities of Hezekiah's festival (2 Ch. 30:2–3, 17–20, 23), it is possible to detect four characteristics which the author may have had in mind: (a) the date (v. 1), (b) the respect for Mosaic (vv. 6, 12) and Davidic (vv. 3–4, 15) authority, (c) the Levites' faithfulness (vv. 4–6, 10–15), and (d) the breadth of attendance (v. 18).

Josiah's respect for God's word particularly stands out, and, despite his last fatal error (vv. 20–24), he is summed up as doing *according to what is written in the Law of the LORD* (v. 27). It is even possible to distinguish the different areas of scriptural authority represented by Moses and David-Solomon. The former was concerned with the sacrifices, and the latter with modifications to Levitical services made necessary by the requirements of temple worship, especially in the area of music. However, Moses' instructions to the Levites are also reflected in their role as representatives of the rest of the nation (v. 5) and ensuring the smooth running of public worship (*cf.* Nu. 3:5–13; 8:15–26).

Josiah's faithfulness to God's word remains extremely relevant. On the one hand, his reformation and Passover show how much younger leaders can achieve when they are fully committed to putting God's word into practice. On the other, he is a good example of the need to receive God's grace, for he was not able to maintain his high standards consistently (v. 22; *cf.* 34:27). It required another descendant of David actually to become a Passover lamb before people could enter into an unbreakable covenant with God (*cf.* Jn. 1:29; 1 Cor. 5:7; Rev. 5:6–14). Just as Josiah acted on what he found written in God's word, so the biblical record of Jesus' Passover sacrifice at Calvary still offers a fresh dynamic for life and worship.

i. Passover preparations (35:1–6). By changing the instruction 'Celebrate the Passover' (2 Ki. 23:21) to the statement *Josiah celebrated the Passover* (v. 1), Josiah is shown to have complied with his own requirements. He was also obedient to Pentateuchal law (Lv. 23:5; Nu. 28:16) and practice (Ex. 12:6), for example, in the matter of the date on the *fourteenth day of the first month* (v. 1), which contrasted with Hezekiah's unorthodox event (30:2). This date in the first month causes a problem, however, for the discovery of the law scroll (34:8; 2 Ki. 22:3) and celebration of the Passover (v. 19; 2 Ki. 23:23) took place in the same year. Since this means that there would have been little or no time to make radical changes of the kind implied by verse 18, this Passover may well have preceded the scroll's public appearance as part of the wider reform movement (34:3b–7). This might explain the existence of features such as the Levites' role (v. 11) or the merging of the Passover with other sacrifices (vv. 12, 14), which are not found in the Pentateuch and were presumably due either to custom or to Josiah's own adaptations (*cf.* vv. 10, 16). Perhaps this might also be why reference to the 'Book of the Covenant' is omitted (2 Ki. 23:21).

Josiah's first task was to allocate the duties of the *priests* and to *encourage* them (v. 2b) and the *Levites* (vv. 3–6). People involved in major events often need the assurance that they are in God's purposes and that he is with them (*cf.* 1 Ch. 22:13; 28:20; 2 Ch. 15:7; 19:11; 32:7). This encouragement is directed mainly at the Levites, who are said to have *instructed all Israel* (v. 3), a role they presumably undertook during the reforms (*cf.* 2 Ch. 17:7–8; Ne. 8:7–9).

The Levites receive a series of instructions (the Heb. has seven imperatives in vv. 3–6) about the preparation of *Passover lambs* (v. 6). The command *Put the sacred ark in the temple ...* (v. 3) is problematical, however, since the ark's removal is never mentioned, either in connection with Manasseh's idolatry (33:4, 7) or Josiah's spring cleaning. Perhaps therefore *Serve the Lord ...* (*i.e.* 'worship ...'; *cf.* 34:33) should be treated as the main clause and the opening words translated as either 'Leave the sacred ark ...' or 'Since the sacred ark ...'. Alternatively, the ceremony by which the ark was deposited in the temple may have been re-enacted to underline Josiah's fresh start.[1] A further difficulty is that in contrast to Hezekiah's practice and the implications of Pentateuchal law (Dt. 16:5–6; 2 Ch. 30:17), the Levites slaughtered all the Passover lambs (v. 6; *cf.* v. 11). Hezekiah's emergency arrangements had presumably become standard practice.

Authority for these instructions is based on *David and Solomon* (vv. 3–4) and on *Moses* (v. 6). The two kings had authorized a change in the Levites' duties (1 Ch. 23–26; 2 Ch. 8:14–15) once the ark had come to rest (v. 3; *cf.* 1 Ch. 23:25–26), while the appeal to Moses is a general reference to the Passover laws (especially Ex. 12:1–13; Dt. 16:1–8).

ii. Passover provision (35:7–9). Gifts by Josiah (v. 7) and other leaders (vv. 8–9) for the sacrifices follows a generous precedent originally set by David (*cf.* 1 Ch. 29:2–5; 2 Ch. 7:5; 30:24). *Administrators* (v. 8; 'chief officers', REB, NEB, NRSV, RSV) is a neutral term used for the senior priests, including the high priest *Hilkiah* (34:9, 14, 18), though it is restricted elsewhere to the high priest (1 Ch. 9:11; 12:28).

As well as being generous, the leaders provided *voluntarily* (v. 8; 'willingly', REB, NEB, NRSV, RSV) for the people. Though this word might be translated 'for the voluntary offerings' (JB; *cf.* 31:14), Chronicles generally emphasizes the willing attitude with which people offered their gifts and themselves to God

[1] McConville, p. 262.

(1 Ch. 29:5–14; 2 Ch. 17:16; 29:31). The same spirit is also evident in the Levites' desire to be fully prepared (vv. 4, 6), including their recognition of the need for self-preparation (v. 4; *cf.* 1 Ch. 29:5; 2 Ch. 17:11). Preparation for worship is especially important in Chronicles, and may be compared with the extensive preparations for the temple (1 Ch. 22) and with Hezekiah's concern for self-purification at the Passover (29:15, 17).

One might include the *cattle* (vv. 7, 8, 9) among the Passover animals, which could come 'from your flock or herd' (Dt. 16:2), except that they are separated from the *Passover offerings*. They are probably provided therefore for the associated burnt offerings (vv. 12, 14). The total number of offerings is more than double that at Hezekiah's Passover (2 Ch. 30:24), a further indication of the greater generosity and significance of this occasion.

iii. Passover offerings (35:10–16). The extent of this paragraph is marked by the repetition of the phrases *the service was arranged* and 'according to the king's command' at its beginning (v. 10) and end (v. 16), though this structure is not recognized in most EVV. Also, the use of different Hebrew words for *at that time* marks verses 16 and 17 as belonging to different paragraphs. *The service was arranged* is a rare but significant phrase occurring additionally in the Old Testament only at 2 Chronicles 8:16; 29:35, meaning that everything had been done as God required. Since it appears elsewhere only in concluding summaries, its appearance in verse 10 underlines the importance of preparing properly for worship, including the the contribution of the king and lay leaders (vv. 2, 7–8).

The Passover ceremony was in two parts, the offering of sacrifice (vv. 11–12) and eating the Passover meal (vv. 13–15). The high point of the sacrifice was when the priests *sprinkled the blood* (v. 11) on the *altar* (v. 16). This was an adaptation to temple ritual of the dramatic action in Egypt when each household had smeared lamb's blood around their doors (Ex. 12:7, 13, 22–23).[1] *Burnt offerings* (vv. 12, 14) are not otherwise

---

[1] Neither the word 'blood' nor the identity of those to whom the hands belong is mentioned in MT. One may either assume the same meaning as in the longer phrase in 30:16 (*cf.* Barthélemy, *CTAT*, 518) or emend the text (as REB, NEB).

part of the Passover, though for several reasons they are not to be regarded as the parts of the Passover sacrifices burnt on the altar (Rudolph, Williamson, Dillard). Firstly, burnt offerings frequently accompanied other sacrifices as at Hezekiah's reopening ceremony (2 Ch. 29:24, 28, 31, 35). Secondly, the partial merging of this Passover with fellowship offerings (see comment on v. 14) makes an association with burnt offerings quite appropriate. Thirdly, burnt offerings could easily have been attached to the Passover as part of the ritual for Unleavened Bread (*cf.* v. 17; Nu. 28:16–25). However, these were probably special burnt offerings for the Passover, since like the Passover they were for 'groups of families' (v. 12, REB, NEB). They were provided to *offer to the LORD* (v. 21), that is, to be consumed on the altar (*cf.* Lv. 1:9) with nothing reserved for a meal, in line with the general regulations for burnt offerings as *written in the Book of Moses* (v. 12).

The second part of the Passover celebrations was the Passover meal, which is described in verse 13a and distributed in verses 13b–15. Attention is focused on the Levites, who are characterized by their obedience to God and a concern for others. The animals, for example, were *roasted as prescribed* (v. 13), that is, as at the Egyptian Passover (Ex. 12:8–9), while *served them quickly* (v. 13; *i.e.* fast food!) alludes to the haste in which that first Passover was eaten (Ex. 12:11).[1] Similarly, the *musicians* (v. 15), NIV, GNB; not 'singers', as REB, NEB, NRSV, RSV; see on 1 Ch. 15:16; 23:28–31; 25:6–7) followed the instructions given by David and his contemporary musical directors (*cf.* 1 Ch. 25:1–8). The *fat portions* (v. 14, NIV, REB, NEB) is a reference to the fellowship or peace offering (*cf.* Lv. 3:9–17), which had been partially assimilated to the Passover since both included a fellowship or communion meal.

The Levites' special concern for their fellow *priests* (v. 14), *musicians* and *gatekeepers* (v. 15), as well as for (lit.) 'your brothers the lay people' (vv. 5, 6; *cf.* v. 13b), offers a better model of how to behave at a communion meal than the

---

[1] 'Roasted' (NIV, NRSV) is lit., 'cooked over the fire' (REB, NEB) rather than 'boiled in the fire' (against *e.g.* Myers, Williamson). The Heb. verb *biššēl* means 'to cook', and the manner of cooking is usually indicated by a qualifying word, as here (*cf.* KB, p. 157; Dillard). 'As prescribed' (*cf.* GNB, NRSV, JB) is preferable to 'according to custom' (REB, NEB), since, although *mišpāṭ* can have either meaning, the direct link with Ex. 12:8–9 (and Dt. 16:7) is decisive.

attitudes shown by the Corinthian Christians (1 Cor. 11:17–22, 27–34)! They distributed the food first to the lay people (v. 13b), but also made sure that those on duty did not lose out (vv. 14–15). *Made (the) preparations* (vv. 14, 15) really means 'made the arrangements for', since the verb is the same as 'arranged' in verses 10, 16 (REB, NEB; *cf.* also 2 Ch. 29:35).

iv. Passover obedience (35:17–19). Josiah's faithfulness is confirmed in this summary. Firstly, the Passover is as elsewhere combined with the *Feast of Unleavened Bread* (v. 17; *cf.* Ex. 12:8; Nu. 28:16–17; Dt. 16:1–8; 2 Ch. 30:13, 21; Mk. 14:1; 1 Cor. 5:7–8). If *Samuel* (v. 18) is understood as representing the period from Moses to the monarchy, his name is an allusion to the Passover in Joshua 5:10–11. In addition to the reasons given above, explaining the uniqueness of this occasion, verse 18 emphasizes the wide range of people involved. Three groups are mentioned, *the priests and Levites, all Judah and Israel,* and *the inhabitants of Jerusalem.* 'All Judah and Israel' includes people from north and south, implying a larger attendance than at Hezekiah's Passover (*cf.* 30:25).

d. Josiah's death (35:20 – 36:1). A sharp change of key marks the transition to the final paragraph on Josiah, though the Chronicler himself supplies the new key signature with the words *After all this* (v. 20). The contrast is between Josiah's 'setting the temple in order' (NRSV) and *Neco's* invasion thirteen years later in 609 BC. Significantly, Hezekiah's sufferings in similar circumstances are introduced in an almost identical way (*cf.* 2 Ch. 32:1).

The Chronicler has interpreted the basic account of Josiah's death in Kings in three distinct ways. Firstly, Josiah's reaction to Neco's invasion is heavily ironic and, indeed, contradicts all that he has previously stood for. On the military level, though the Pharaoh had no quarrel with Josiah, and his threat was far less serious than Sennacherib's (*cf.* 32:1), Josiah was defeated whereas Hezekiah had been delivered (32:20–22). The spiritual contrast is the more damaging, however, for whereas Josiah had formerly listened carefully to God's word (*cf.* 2 Ch. 34:27; 35:6, 12), now he 'did not listen to the words of Neco from the mouth of God' (v. 22, NRSV, RSV). How Josiah was supposed to recognize God's guidance is not specified, though sanctified common sense would have been a perfectly adequate response. Also, like other biblical writers, the Chronicler never limits God's ways of speaking. For example, the expression *by the mouth of God* is used as naturally of Neco as it is of Jeremiah (*cf.* 36:12, 21, 22), and God regularly employs foreigners as his spokespersons (*e.g.* 2 Ch. 2:11–12; 9:8; 36:22–23). Though Neco is surprisingly blunt in claiming that *God has told me to hurry* (v. 21) and that God *is with me* (v. 21; contrast 2 Ch. 13:12; 32:7–8!), his language is no more shocking than that of other non-Israelites (*e.g.* Gn. 20:3–7; Mt. 27:19).[1]

The historical background to this incident is partially clarified through extrabiblical sources. *Neco* was *en route* to Syria to link up with Ashur-uballit, the last king of Assyria, who the previous year (610 BC) had moved to *Carchemish* in a desperate attempt to preserve the tattered remains of his empire.[2] Together they hoped to resist the advance of Babylon, *the house with which I am at war* (v. 21). It is even possible that Egypt and Assyria had both communicated in writing Neco's need to travel via an Egyptian garrison at *Megiddo.*[3] Whether Josiah decided to intercept the Egyptians for internal reasons or as the result of Babylonian pressure remains unknown, but if, as some believe, he was anticipated by the people of Gaza, the consequences were similarly disastrous (*cf.* Je. 47:1).

Secondly, the manner of Josiah's death is also interpreted ironically by being paralleled with Ahab's demise (vv. 22–24; *cf.* 2 Ch. 18:29–34). The links are quite explicit, for each king *disguised himself* (v. 22; *cf.* 2 Ki. 18:29), *archers* delivered the fatal blow (v. 23; *cf.* 2 Ki. 18:33), each king admitted *I am wounded* (v. 23; *cf.* 2 Ki. 18:33), and was propped up in a *chariot* (v. 24; *cf.* 2 Ki. 18:34) before he died. The ultimate irony is that despite Josiah's previous record, he died in the same way

[1] There was a widespread belief in the ancient Near East that the divine will can be communicated to humankind (*cf. e.g.* H. W. F. Saggs, *The Encounter with the Divine in Mesopotamia and Israel* (London: Athlone Press, 1978), pp. 125–152.

[2] *Cf.* D. J. Wiseman, *Chronicles of Chaldean Kings* (London: British Museum, 1956), pp. 18–19, 63; H. W. F. Saggs, *The Might that was Assyria* (London: Sidgwick & Jackson, 1984), p. 120; A. Malamat, 'Josiah's bid for Armageddon', *Journal of the Ancient Near Eastern Society* 5, 1973, pp. 267–278, *cf.* p. 274.

[3] *Cf.* Y. Yadin, 'The historical significance of Inscription 88 from Arad: a suggestion', *IEJ* 26, 1976, pp. 9–14.

as someone who was known to 'hate the LORD' (2 Ch. 19:2).

Thirdly, however, the Chronicler highlighted God's grace and his faithfulness. It is confirmed that Josiah died in Jerusalem (as distinct from being conveyed 'dying' in a chariot), that he was buried in *the tombs of his fathers* rather than just his own tomb (v. 24; *cf.* 2 Ki. 23:30), and that he was extensively *mourned* (vv. 24b–25).[1] Far from being embarrassed by Huldah's prophecy, therefore, the Chronicler is at pains to stress that God kept his promises about Josiah's peaceful burial and the exile's continuing delay despite Josiah's stupidity and violent death (*cf.* 2 Ch. 34:28). Jeremiah's laments for Josiah are not otherwise known, since the written *Laments* (v. 25) have a different title from the Old Testament book of Lamentations.

'Faithful deeds' (v. 26, NRSV; *acts of devotion*, NIV) is a post-exilic expression (*cf.* 2 Ch. 32:32; Ne. 13:14) which illustrates the reality and extent of Josiah's obedience to God's word (*the Law of the LORD*). The unfortunate circumstances of his death therefore did not prevent his achievements from being properly remembered. Nor did the existence of a political vacuum stop *the people of the land* ensuring *Jehoahaz'* succession (36:1), as they had done with Ahaziah (2 Ch. 22:1), Uzziah (26:1), and Josiah himself (33:25), though this was the last opportunity they had to do so. Even so, Josiah's passing removed the last obstacle to the coming catastrophe, and the new king's anointing ceremony no longer seemed worth mentioning (*cf.* 2 Ki. 23:30).

H. Four kings and the end of the kingdom (36:2–20)

This chapter covers the last four kings of Judah, a brief justification of the exile, and an announcement of the possibility of a return. The end comes remarkably swiftly, like a bird of prey suddenly swooping down after circling repeatedly over its victim. The manner of presentation is unparalleled in Chronicles, even though the material bears some resemblance to the account of the same events in 2 Kings. The most noticeable feature is that the last four kings are dealt with not in their own right but as being engulfed by a

---

[1] For the translation of the Heb. participle in 2 Ki. 23:30 as 'dying', *cf.* Gray, p. 680.

common experience of exile. The final collapse under Zedekiah is therefore merely the final stage in a process that has long been inevitable.

This arrangement has its own momentum, since the race to the exilic tape began as far back as Ahaz (2 Ch. 28:5, 8, 11, 13), Hezekiah (2 Ch. 29:9; 30:9), and Manasseh (2 Ch. 33:11). It gathers noticeably in pace through this chapter, as Judah is overwhelmed by an avalanche rushing on quite unchecked. In comparison with the number of verses in Kings, Jehoahaz' reign is reduced by 40%, Jehoiakim's by 55% and Jehoiachin's by 80%, and by Zedekiah's reign whole paragraphs are reduced to a single verse (*cf.* v. 17 with 2 Ki. 25:1–12; v. 18 with 2 Ki. 25:13–17; and v. 19 with 2 Ki. 25:9–10).

The fact that this is the only section of 2 Chronicles 10–36 where Chronicles has dealt more briefly than Kings with the same subject clearly indicates a special purpose.[1] That purpose is revealed in three distinctive emphases. The first is that responsibility for the exile did not belong to any individual or generation, but implicated the whole nation. The sense of corporate guilt is very strong, and is made explicit in verses 15–16. The second is that the exile is remarkably comprehensive, both in its character and its effects. For the land, the monarchy, and the temple *there was no remedy* (v. 16), and only a *remnant* is left (v. 20). The only basis for future hope is that the Lord remains in charge throughout. The third and most surprising emphasis is that despite everything, an alternative still exists. The gathering clouds of judgment have never entirely obscured the brightness of God's grace, though now it shines through the exile rather than instead of it (vv. 22–23; *cf.* 28:14–15; 30:9; 33:12–13). One effect is to put Josiah's reform (chs. 34–35) in a new light, his acceptance of the authority of God's word (*cf.* 34:26–28) standing in stark contrast to those who persistently rejected it (36:15–16). The intended lesson is obvious, especially as God's word is the means by which restoration begins (vv. 21–22).

The book ends, therefore, on a definite note of hope, which neither persistent sin nor the reality of judgment is able to overcome. However, one should not be misled into thinking that this implies that final judgment will never come (*e.g.* Mk. 13:24–31; 1 Thes. 5:1–7; *cf.* Heb. 1:10–12). Though the exile

[1] Japhet, *Ideology*, pp. 364–365.

provides further evidence that God is always gracious and compassionate (*cf.* 2 Ch. 30:9), the opportunity to call on his mercy will not always exist. It is therefore wise to take God's invitation seriously (v. 23).

The reigns of *Jehoahaz* (vv. 2–4), *Jehoiakim* (vv. 5–8), and *Jehoiachin* (vv. 9–10) are presented in standardized form. Whereas the names of the queen mothers and details about their deaths have been omitted, three topics occur repeatedly, that the kings did *evil* (vv. 5, 9), that they went into exile (vv. 4, 6, 10), and that the temple vessels were removed (vv. 7, 10). This patterning is clearly deliberate, especially as some of the material is additional to Kings (*cf.* vv. 6–7). The overriding aim is to provide a corporate interpretation, illustrating that the kings' exiles were not so much separate events but different manifestations of the same phenomenon. Individual actions and even deaths are less important than that the kings experienced exile together because of the attitudes described in verses 12–16.

i. The fall of Jehoahaz (36:2–4)

36:2 – *cf.* 2 Kings 23:31a
36:3–4 – *cf.* 2 Kings 23:33–34

The king who fits the over-all pattern least is *Jehoahaz* (vv. 2–4; 609 BC), whose reign lacks any theological evaluation (*cf.* 2 Ki. 23:32) and is without any reference to the temple. In practice, though, Chronicles assumes what is said about him in Kings and in Jeremiah 22:11–12 (where he is called Shallum), and the pattern should not be pushed into absolute rigidity. No basis exists for assuming that his tribute (v. 3) came from the temple (Williamson), since it is known that he was forced to levy some kind of income tax (2 Ki. 23:35)!

The payment did him no good, however, for he was 'deposed' (v. 3, NEB, NRSV, RSV; *dethroned*, NIV, *cf.* REB), perhaps because his appointment by the people of the land (v. 1) meant he was not sufficiently pro-Egyptian. Neco did not intend to take the same risks with his older brother *Jehoiakim*, changing his name as a symbol of his subservience. A slight textual change confirms that Jehoahaz went to Egypt under duress: 'he came' (2 Ki. 23:34) has become *carried him off* (v. 4).

ii. The fall of Jehoiakim (36:5–8)

36:5 – *cf.* 2 Kings 23:36–37
36:6a – *cf.* 2 Kings 24:1a
36:8 – *cf.* 2 Kings 24:5–6

All that is said of *Jehoiakim* (vv. 5–8; 609–598 BC) is that *Nebuchadnezzar* probably took him into exile and removed some *articles from the temple* (vv. 6–7). Though both events are typical of the exilic pattern of the chapter, Jehoiakim's exile has caused difficulty since it is not mentioned elsewhere. A further problem is that it is not immediately clear whether Jehoiakim actually went to Babylon or was merely threatened with deportation. Since, however, the phrase 'bound him in fetters to take him to Babylon' (RSV) is used elsewhere only of the exile of Manasseh and Zedekiah (note the almost identical expression in Je. 39:7; *cf.* 2 Ki. 25:7 = Je. 52:11; 2 Ch. 33:11), it seems that he did make the journey eastwards. Further, the background to verses 6–7 is greatly enhanced if the Babylonians' theft of the temple vessels is the same as that described in Daniel 1:1–2. The latter took place in the same year (605 BC) as a series of warnings by Jeremiah to Jehoiakim about an impending Babylonian attack (Je. 25:1; 36:1; 45:1; 46:2; especially Je. 25:1–11) after Nebuchadnezzar's decisive victory at Carchemish.[1] The Babylonian Chronicle also states that after Carchemish, 'Nebuchadnezzar conquered the whole area of Hatti', that is, the whole of Syria-Palestine. Jehoiakim would certainly have had to accept Babylonian sovereignty at once, and also in the following year when Nebuchadnezzar captured Ashkelon and 'all the kings of Hatti came before him and he received their heavy tribute'.[2] Jehoiakim could have been taken to Babylon on either occasion, though he obviously found it no easier to accept Babylonian sovereignty than he did God's authority!

Nebuchadnezzar's theft of the temple *articles* (v. 7; 'vessels', REB, NEB, NRSV, RSV; 'furnishings', JB) is a highly symbolic act. To the post-exilic community (*cf.* Ezr. 1:7–11; Dn. 5:2–3, 23), these articles represented continuity with David (1 Ch. 28:14–18) and Solomon (2 Ch. 4:1–22) and living worship in the

---

[1] The third year of Jehoiakim in Dn. 1:1 according to the Babylonian system of calendar reckoning is almost universally recognized to be the same as the fourth year in the Palestinian system used by Jeremiah.

[2] D. J. Wiseman, *Chronicles of Chaldean Kings* (London: British Museum, 1956), pp. 25–27, 66–69.

temple. They were probably deposited in one of Nebu-chadnezzar's *temple*(s) (v. 7; *cf.* Ezr. 1:7), though the Hebrew word can mean 'palace' (REB, NEB, *etc.*).

Only Jehoiakim of the four kings in this chapter receives a concluding formula (v. 8). This may well imply that he died in Judah (*cf.* 2 Ki. 24:6), though the lack of any mention of his burial reflects the prophecies of Jeremiah (22:18–19; 36:30) and is a regular mark of dishonour in Chronicles (*cf.* 2 Ch. 23:21; 33:24). The *detestable things* (v. 8; 'abominations', NRSV, RSV) would include the accusations levelled against him by Jeremiah (*cf.* Je. 22:13–23; 25:1 – 26:24; 35:1 – 36:32). *All that was found against him*, though, is usually a neutral phrase and is perhaps better translated 'what happened to him' (Myers; *cf. hannimṣā'* in 2 Ch. 34:30–33; 35:7, 18), referring to the fulfilment of Jeremiah's words.

iii. The fall of Jehoiachin (36:9–10)
36:9 – *cf.* 2 Kings 24:8–9

Jehoiachin is dealt with so briefly (vv. 9–10) that his reign appears to have no significance except as a further illustration of the themes of exile and temple despoliation. However, his exile is of considerable importance in 2 Kings 24:10–16 and Jeremiah 22:24–30, and is also reported in the Babylonian Chronicle: 'he [Nebuchadnezzar] besieged the city of Judah and ... seized the city and captured the king. He appointed there a king of his own choice, received its heavy tribute and brought it to Babylon.'[1]

The next king is described as Jehoiachin's 'brother' (v. 10, NRSV, RSV), though, since Zedekiah was actually his 'father's brother' (REB, NEB; *cf.* NIV, GNB), 'brother' is best understood as *relative* (NIV mg.; *cf.* JB; as in 2 Ch. 22:8). Most Hebrew MSS of Chronicles give his age on accession as 'eight' (v. 9, REB, NEB, NRSV, RSV, JB), but since it is known from Babylonian sources that five years later he had five children, the reading 'eighteen' (2 Ki. 24:18, with P and some LXX MSS) is definitely preferable. Chronicles adds an extra *ten days* to the length of his reign of *three months* (*cf.* 2 Ki. 24:8; in 597 BC), but this is unlikely to be connected with the previous problem.

---

[1] *Ibid.*, pp. 72–73.

iv. The fall of Zedekiah and of the kingdom (36:11–20)

'The wrath of the Lord became so great that there was
no remedy' (36:16, NRSV).

36:11–13a – cf. 2 Kings 24:18–20; Jeremiah 52:1–3

Zedekiah (597–587 BC) is dealt with quite differently from the
more factual account in 2 Kings 25. His reign is dominated by
a theological explanation of exile which has some general
analogy with 2 Kings 17:1–23, but this account makes frequent use of the Chronicler's distinctive vocabulary and has a
semi-poetic style. In its emotional response to the devastation,
it has been described as having a 'Holocaust-like' quality
(Allen).

12–13. Zedekiah's attitude to events is described first, and
then that of the people (vv. 14–16). The king is condemned
not for any specific actions (events in his reign are dealt with at
length in Je. 27:1 – 28:17; 32:1 – 34:22; 37:1 – 38:28) but for
his over-all rebelliousness towards God and man. This is illustrated by negative versions of two expressions from 2 Chronicles 7:14 (*did not humble himself*; also 2 Ch. 33:23; *would not
turn*, and by other typical phrases which indicate his similarity
with the generation which died in the wilderness (*stiff-necked*;
cf. Ex. 32:9; 33:3, 5; Dt. 9:6; 2 Ch. 30:8) and with the Pharaoh
who opposed Moses (*hardened his heart*; cf. Ex. 8:15, 32). These
same attitudes are identified in the New Testament as the
cause of unbelief towards Jesus and the gospel (Acts 7:51; Mk.
6:52; 8:17; Heb. 3:13).

Though he could be weak-minded (Je. 38:14–28), Zedekiah
basically opposed Jeremiah, who 'spoke from the mouth of
the Lord' (NRSV, RSV; cf. vv. 15–16, 21–22). He was accord-
ingly criticized by both Jeremiah (Je. 37:2) and Ezekiel, the
latter in connection with breaking his *oath* to the king of
Babylon (cf. Ezk. 17:18–20). His pride and hardness of heart
also contrast with Josiah, whose heart was tender and who
humbled himself at God's word (2 Ch. 34:27).

14–16. The people's attitude is, if anything, worse.[1] They
piled their sins one upon another, becoming *more and more*
unfaithful (v. 14) and rejecting the prophets *again and again*
(v. 15). Three complaints are made in particular, that they
were unfaithful (v. 14), defiled the temple (v. 14) and laughed

---

[1] GNB (cf. REB, NEB) reads 'leaders of Judah, the priests' (v. 14) with LXX and 1
Esdras 1:47 as against MT's 'leaders of the priests' (NIV, cf. NRSV, RSV).

at the prophets (vv. 15–16). All three are frequent themes throughout Chronicles, and it is as if the entire message of Chronicles were being summed up.

Being *unfaithful* (Heb. *mā'al*) is about failing to give God what is due to him and taking it for oneself.[1] It is regarded throughout Chronicles (*e.g.* 1 Ch. 2:7; 5:25; 10:13; 2 Ch. 12:2; 28:19; 33:17) as one of the chief underlying causes of exile (*cf.* 1 Ch. 5:25–26; 9:1; 2 Ch. 29:6; 30:7). A particularly close connection exists with 1 Chronicles 5:25–26, since in both passages unfaithfulness is characterized by idolatry and is punished by God's sending an invading army to take his people into exile. Unfaithfulness is also often associated with unholiness. Here it involves defiling the temple which God has *consecrated* (v. 14), of which a good example from Zedekiah's time is found in Ezekiel 8. Such behaviour, however, was an invitation for God to invoke the promised judgment of 2 Chronicles 7:19–22 and destroy the temple.

Rejection of the prophets is an ever-present theme in Chronicles (*e.g.* 1 Ch. 10:13; 2 Ch. 24:19) and elsewhere in the Bible (*cf.* Ne. 9:26; Je. 44:4; Mt. 23:30–31; Acts 7:52). The sense of unending failure is accentuated here by a series of participles, which have no specific time reference in Hebrew (v. 16; *cf.* REB, NEB, 'never ceased to deride ... scorn ... scoff'). The use of several rare words allows the Chronicler's own thought to come through in a distinctive manner. *Deride* ('ridiculed', JB, GNB) and *scorn* ('made fun of', Mason) are unique in the Old Testament, while *messengers* is a rare late term for prophets (*cf.* Is. 42:19; 44:26; Hg. 1:13; Mal. 3:1).

Eventually, however, the end must come when God's *wrath* is finally poured out (v. 16). The cataclysm which has been threatened since Ahaz (2 Ch. 28:9, 13, 25; 29:8, 10; 30:8) has been held back only because of the faith and repentance of individual leaders (*cf.* 2 Ch. 29:10; 30:8–9; 32:25–26; 33:6; 34:21, 25). Now there is *no remedy*, a chilling phrase meaning literally 'no healing'. It implies the cancellation of God's promise to heal his land and that therefore even prayer will be utterly useless (2 Ch. 7:14; *cf.* 30:20). The saddest thing is that all this has happened because they have turned their backs on God's love, neither recognizing nor listening to the messengers of God's 'compassion' (v. 15, NRSV; *pity*, NIV, REB, NEB) In

[1] *Cf.* Johnstone, 'Guilt', p. 118.

549

the end, the exile came about not because Israel sinned, but because they spurned God's offers of reconciliation (*cf.* Dt. 7:7–8; Ho. 11:1–4).

17–20. The final events are passed over very quickly. First of all, the people were *handed over* to the Babylonians, and, because Israel wanted none of God's compassion, 'no compassion' was received from their conquerors (v. 17, NRSV, RSV; *cf.* v. 15). The temple and palace were then looted (v. 18) before the city itself was destroyed (v. 19). The *temple* and the *wall* (v. 19) may have been singled out because they became the focus of the rebuilding projects in the books of Ezra (chs. 1–6) and Nehemiah (chs. 1–6) respectively. The over-all impression is of unrelieved destruction. 'All, every' (Heb. *kōl*) is used fivefold in verses 17–19, which together with *young* and *old* (v. 17), *large and small* (v. 18), and finally (lit.), 'to destruction' (v. 19) confirms that there was no respite, no escape.

I. Beginning to rebuild God's house (36:21–23)

36:22–23 – *cf.* Ezra 1:1–2a

What appears to be the end is not the end, however, for God's word in the law and the prophets must still be fulfilled (vv. 21–23). In other words, the very existence of a future for Israel is due entirely to the fact that God has spoken. Though Israel has reached a dead end, God has certainly not done so.

To start with, the law of Leviticus 26:34–35, 43 must be fulfilled that the *land* will experience its *rest* or *sabbath* as well as *desolation* (v. 21). This is clearly a significant passage for the Chronicler's concept of restoration, since its wording is also reflected in the central promise of 2 Chronicles 7:14.

Then *the word of the LORD spoken by Jeremiah* (vv. 21, 22) finds a double fulfilment. Firstly, the seventy years of exile must be completed (v. 21), and, in accordance with Jeremiah's prophecies, this period is restorative (Je. 29:10) as well as punitive (Je. 25:11–14). This seventy-year period is probably best understood qualitatively rather than quantitatively, as a symbol of a human lifespan (*cf.* Ps. 90:10). An entire generation had to be removed to prevent any human being stealing God's credit by attempting to resurrect a future out of the remains of the past. More mathematical approaches measure the time from the first exile (605 BC) to Cyrus' edict (539 BC) or from the destruction of the first temple (587 BC) to the reopening of the second (516 BC), but this seems less satisfying.

Jeremiah's prophecies are fulfilled, secondly, by God taking action to initiate his rebuilding programme, with God in his own way maintaining the surprise element to the very end. This time he fulfils his word through a foreign emperor's *proclamation* (vv. 22–23)! Williamson has rightly recognized that Cyrus' announcement is quoted in abbreviated form from Ezra. 1:2–4, though he is unnecessarily pessimistic about the possibility of the Chronicler having attached it to the rest of the work.[1] In fact, the extract that is quoted from the edict includes a reinterpretation of God's original promises to David in 1 Chronicles 17:4–14 and 2 Chronicles 7:12–21. 'To build him a house' (v. 23, NRSV, RSV, REB, NEB; *cf.* Ezr. 1:2) is a deliberate echo of the central promise of the Davidic covenant (*cf.* 1 Ch. 17:11–12; 22:10; 28:6; 2 Ch. 6:9–10). Cyrus of course is thinking only of the house in *Jerusalem*, but in the Chronicler's thought this phrase is inevitably connected with both houses of the Davidic covenant, the dynasty as well as the temple. In the end, therefore, the end is also a fresh start. God's promises continue through the exile, on through his own generation and into the future. The actual ending is unexpectedly sudden, but, as with the original conclusion of Mark's gospel (Mk. 16:8), it is apparently deliberate. The final phrase, *let him go up,* which is a single word in Hebrew, breaks off in the middle of Ezra's version of the edict. Its effect is to emphasize that the reader's expected final response to the book is to exercise faith in God's promises.[2] Though for those who first received the words a physical journey was involved (*cf.* 1 Ch. 9:2–34), the invitation is still valid and awaits whatever response is appropriate while God keeps his promise to build his house, that is, his church (*cf.* Mt. 16:18; Eph. 2:19–22). Today, as in the Chronicler's day, only houses that are ultimately founded on the words of God will remain secure when all others will be shaken and fall (*cf.* Mt. 7:24–27; 1 Cor. 3:12–15; Heb. 12:25–29).

---

[1] Williamson, *IBC*, pp. 7–11.

[2] 'Yahweh/the LORD' was probably originally a jussive verb, 'may he be', as in Ezr. 1:3 (*cf.* L. C. Allen, *The Greek Chronicles* – II, *SVT* 27, Leiden: Brill, 1974, p. 121). The alternative suggestion of the indicative 'he is/will be' (de Vries, p. 9) unnecessarily interrupts the sense that God's promise waits to be fulfilled.